Accounting and Finance for Non-specialists

Third Edition

Peter Atrill & Eddie McLaney

FINANCIAL TIMES

Prentice Hall

An imprint of Pearson Education

Harlow, England · London · New York · Reading, Massachusetts · San Francisco · Toronto · Don Mills, Ontario · Sydney
Tokyo · Singapore · Hong Kong · Seoul · Taipei · Cape Town · Madrid · Mexico City · Amsterdam · Munich · Paris · Milan

Pearson Education Limited
Edinburgh Gate
Harlow
Essex CM20 2JE
England

and Associated Companies throughout the world

Visit us on the World Wide Web at:
www.pearsoneduc.com

First published 1995 by Prentice Hall Europe
Second edition 1997 by Prentice Hall Europe
Third edition 2001

© Prentice Hall Europe 1995, 1997
© Pearson Education Limited 2001

The rights of Peter Atrill and Eddie McLaney to be
identified as authors of this work have been asserted
by them in accordance with the Copyright, Designs
and Patents Act 1988

ISBN 0 273 64632 X

British Library Cataloguing-in-Publication Data
A CIP catalogue record for this book can be obtained from the British Library.

Library of Congress Cataloging-in-Publication Data
Atrill, Peter.
   Accounting and finance for non-specialists / Peter Atrill and Eddie McLaney. – 3rd ed.
     1p. cm.
   Includes index.
   ISBN 0-273-64632-X (alk. paper)
     1. Accounting. 2. Financial statements. I. McLaney, E. J. II. Title.

HF5635 .A882 2000
657–dc21   00-039350

10 9 8 7 6 5 4 3 2
05 04 03 02 01

Typeset by 4 in $9\frac{1}{2}/12\frac{1}{2}$ Stone Serif
Printed and bound by Ashford Colour Press Ltd., Gosport

Accounting and Finance
for Non-specialists

We work with leading authors to develop the strongest educational materials in business and finance, bringing cutting-edge thinking and best learning practice to a global market.

Under a range of well-known imprints, including Financial Times Prentice Hall, we craft high-quality print and electronic publications which help readers to understand and apply their content, whether studying or at work.

To find out about the complete range of our publishing please visit us on the World Wide Web at: www.pearsoneduc.com

Contents

Preface

This text provides an introduction to accounting and finance. It is aimed primarily at students who are not majoring in accounting or finance but who are, nevertheless, studying introductory level accounting and finance as part of their course in business, economics, hospitality management, tourism, engineering or some other area. Students who are majoring in either accounting or finance should, however, find the book useful as an introduction to the main principles, which can serve as a foundation for further study. The text does not focus on the technical aspects, but rather examines the basic principles and underlying concepts, and the ways in which accounting statements and financial information can be used to improve the quality of decision making. To reinforce further this practical emphasis, there are, throughout the text, numerous illustrative extracts with commentary from company reports, survey data and other sources.

The text is written in an 'open-learning' style. This means that there are numerous integrated activities, worked examples and questions throughout the text to help you to understand the subject fully. You are expected to interact with the material and to check your progress continuously in a way not typically found in textbooks. Irrespective of whether you are using the book as part of a taught course or for personal study, we have found that this approach is more 'user-friendly' and makes it easier for you to learn.

We recognise that most of you will not have studied accounting or finance before, and we have therefore tried to write in a concise and accessible style, minimising the use of technical jargon. We have also tried to introduce topics gradually, explaining everything as we go. Where technical terminology is unavoidable we try to provide clear explanations. In addition, you will find all the key terms highlighted in the text, and then listed at the end of each chapter with a page reference to help you rapidly revise the main techniques and concepts. All these key terms are also listed alphabetically with a concise definition in the glossary towards the end of the book, so providing a convenient and single point of reference from which to revise.

A further important consideration in helping you to understand and absorb the topics covered is the design of the text itself. The page layout and colour scheme have been carefully considered to allow for the easy navigation and digestion of material. The layout features a large page format, an open design, and clear signposting of the various features and assessment material.

How to use this book

We have organised the chapters to reflect what we consider to be a logical sequence and, for this reason, we suggest that you work through the text in the order in which it is presented. We have tried to ensure that earlier chapters do not refer to concepts or terms that are not explained until a later chapter. If you work through the chapters in the 'wrong' order, you will probably encounter concepts and terms that were explained previously.

Irrespective of whether you are using the book as part of a lecture/tutorial-based course or as the basis for a more independent mode of study, we advocate following broadly the same approach.

Integrated assessment material

Interspersed throughout each chapter are numerous **Activities**. You are strongly advised to attempt all these questions. They are designed to simulate the sort of quick-fire questions that your lecturer might throw at you during a lecture or tutorial. Activities serve two purposes:

- to give you the opportunity to check that you have understood what has been covered so far
- to encourage you to think about the topic just covered, either to see a link between that topic and others with which you are already familiar, or to link the topic just covered to the next.

The answer to each Activity is provided immediately after the question. This answer should be covered up until you have deduced your solution, which can then be compared with the one given.

Towards the middle/end of each chapter, there are one or two **Self-assessment questions**. These are more comprehensive and demanding than any of the activities, and are designed to give you an opportunity to check and apply your understanding of the core coverage of the chapter. The solution to each of these questions is provided at the end of the book. As with the activities, it is important that you attempt each question thoroughly before referring to the solution. If you have difficulty with a self-assessment question you should go over the chapter again.

End-of-chapter assessment material

At the end of each chapter there are four **Review questions**. These are short questions requiring a narrative answer or discussion within a tutorial group. They are intended to help you assess how well you can recall and critically evaluate the core terms and concepts covered in each chapter.

At the end of each chapter, except for Chapter 1, there are five **Examination-style questions** (ESQs). These are mostly computational, and are designed to reinforce your knowledge and understanding. ESQs are graded according to their level of difficulty. The basic-level questions are fairly straightforward; the more advanced ones can be quite demanding, but are capable of being successfully completed if you have worked conscientiously through the chapter and have attempted the basic ESQs. Solutions to two of the ESQs in each chapter are provided at the end of the book; these two are identified by a coloured question number. Here too, a thorough attempt should be made to answer each question before referring to the solution. Solutions to the other three ESQs and to the review questions in each chapter are provided in a separate lecturer's Solutions Manual.

Companion Web Site

A Companion Web Site accompanies
Accounting and Finance for Non-specialists,
3rd edition by Peter Atrill and Eddie McLaney

Visit the *Accounting and Finance for Non-specialists* Companion Web Site at www.booksites.net/atrillmclaney to find valuable teaching and learning material including:

For Students:
- Study material designed to help you improve your results
- Multiple Choice Questions to help test your learning
- Links to relevant sites on the World Wide Web

For Lecturers:
- A secure, password protected site with teaching material
- Complete, downloadable Instructor's Manual
- Extra testbanks with solutions for use with your students
- PowerPoint slides for use with the book

Also: This regularly maintained and updated site will have a syllabus manager, search functions, and email results functions.

Acknowledgements

The publishers are indebted to the following for permission to reproduce copyright material:

Greene King plc for permission to reproduce notes 19 and 20 from their 1999 statutory accounts; Manchester Business School for Exhibit 9.1; Monsoon plc for the 'Statement of directors' responsibilities' and the auditors' report from their 1999 annual report and United Biscuits (Holdings) plc for Exhibit 5.1.

Whilst every effort has been made to trace the owners of copyright material, in a few cases this has proved impossible and we take this opportunity to offer our apologies to any copyright holder whose rights we may have unwittingly infringed.

1

Introduction to accounting and finance

INTRODUCTION

Welcome to the world of accounting and finance! In this first chapter, we provide a broad outline of these subjects. We begin by explaining the role of accounting and finance, and we shall see that both can be valuable tools for decision-making purposes. We recognise that, for many of you, accounting and finance are not the main focus of your studies, and you may well be asking 'Why do I need to study these subjects?' So, after we have provided a broad outline of accounting and finance, we shall go on to discuss why some understanding of these subjects is likely to be relevant to you.

Objectives

Having completed this chapter you should be able to:

- explain the nature and role of accounting
- identify the main users of financial information and discuss their needs
- explain why an understanding of accounting is likely to be relevant to your needs
- distinguish between financial and management accounting.

Nature and role of accounting and finance

✳ A useful starting point for the study of accounting and finance is to understand their respective roles. **Accounting** is concerned with the collection, analysis and communication of economic information. This information can be used as a tool for decision making, planning and control. That is to say, accounting information is useful for those who need to make decisions and plans about businesses, and for those who need to control those businesses. Though managers working within a particular business are likely to be significant users of accounting information, they are by no means the only people who are likely to use accounting information about that particular business.

Accounting exists for a particular purpose, and that is to help people make better decisions. Sometimes the impression is given that the purpose of accounting is simply to prepare financial reports on a regular basis. While it is true that accountants undertake this kind of work, it does not represent an end in itself. The ultimate purpose of the accountant's work is to give people better information on which to base their decisions. This decision-making perspective of accounting fits in with the theme of this book and shapes the way in which we deal with each topic.

✱ **Finance**, like accounting, exists to help decision makers. It is concerned with the way in which funds for a business are raised and invested. A business is basically an organisation that raises funds from investors (owners and lenders) and then uses these funds to make investments (equipment, premises, stocks and so on) in order to make the business, and its owners, more wealthy. Raising and investing funds are important decision-making areas, as they often involve large amounts of money and require relatively long-term commitments. Finance should help decision makers to evaluate the different forms in which

The figure shows that there are several user groups with an interest in the financial information relating to a business organisation. Most of them are outside the business, but nevertheless have a stake in it. This is not meant to be an exhaustive list of potential users, but the user groups identified here are normally the most important.

Figure 1.1 Main users of financial information relating to a business organisation

funds may be raised. It is important that funds are raised in a way that is appropriate to the particular needs of the business. Finance should also help decision makers to ensure that funds are properly managed, and that they are invested in a way that will provide the business with a worthwhile return.

Accounting and user needs

Accounting seeks to satisfy the needs of a wide range of users. In relation to a particular business, there may be various groups which are likely to have an interest in financial aspects of it. (Although the points that will be made in this chapter and throughout this book may apply to a variety of organisations, such as nationalised industries, local authorities and charities, we are concentrating on private-sector businesses.)

The major users of financial information, for a business, are shown in Figure 1.1.

Activity 1.1

Why do each of the user groups identified need financial information relating to a business?

Your answer may be as follows:

User group	Use
Customers	To assess the ability of the business to continue in business and to supply the needs of the customers.
Suppliers	To assess the ability of the business to pay for the goods and services supplied.
Government	To assess how much tax the business should pay, whether it complies with agreed pricing policies, whether financial support is needed, and so on.
Owners	To assess how effectively the managers are running the business, and to make judgements about likely levels of risk and return in the future.
Lenders	To assess the ability of the business to meet its obligations and to pay interest and repay the principal sum.
Employees (non-management)	To assess the ability of the business to continue to provide employment and to reward employees for their labour.
Investment analysts	To assess the likely risks and returns associated with the business in order to determine its investment potential, and to advise clients accordingly.

Community representatives	To assess the ability of the business to continue to provide employment for the community and use community resources, to help fund environmental improvements, and so on.
Managers	To help them to make decisions and plans for the business, and to help them to exercise control to try to ensure that plans come to fruition. These decisions and plans would include those relating to financing (see below) and investment.
Competitors	To assess the threat posed by the business to their market share and profitability. To provide a benchmark by which to compare efficiency and performance.

This is not an exhaustive list. You may have thought of other reasons why each group would find accounting information useful.

Accounting as an information system

Accounting can be seen as an important part of the total information system within a business. People, both inside and outside the business, have to make decisions concerning the allocation of scarce economic resources. To ensure that these resources are allocated in an efficient and effective manner, users require economic information on which to base decisions. It is the role of the accounting system to provide that information. Thus we can view accounting as an information-gathering and communication system. The **accounting information system** is depicted in Figure 1.2. It has certain features that are common to all information systems within a business. These are:

* identifying and capturing relevant information (in this case financial information)
* recording the collected information in a systematic manner
* analysing and interpreting the collected information
* reporting the information in a manner that suits the need of users.

Given the decision-making emphasis of the text, we shall be concerned primarily with the final two elements of the process – the analysis and reporting of financial information. We are concerned with the way in which

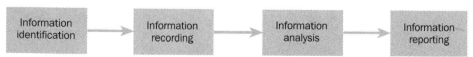

The figure shows the four sequential stages of an accounting information system. The first two stages are concerned with preparation, whereas the last two stages are concerned with using the information collected.

Figure 1.2 The accounting information system

information is used by, and is useful to, decision makers, rather than the way in which it is collected and recorded.

Accounting as a service function

Another way of viewing accounting is as a form of service. Accountants provide financial information to their 'clients', who are the various users identified earlier. The quality of the service provided will be determined by the extent to which the information needs of the various user groups have been met. It can be argued that, in order to meet the needs of users, financial information should possess certain key characteristics. These are:

✱ • *Relevance*. Financial information must have the ability to influence decisions. Unless this characteristic is present, there is really not any point in producing the information. The information may be relevant to the prediction of future events or relevant in helping to confirm past events.

✱ • *Reliability*. It should be free from any material error or bias. It should be capable of being relied on by users to represent what it is supposed to represent.

✱ • *Comparability*. Items that are basically the same should be treated in the same manner for measurement and presentation purposes.

✱ • *Understandability*. Financial reports should be expressed as clearly as possible, and should be capable of being understood by those at whom the information is aimed.

✱ • *Timeliness*. Financial information should be available in time for it to aid decision making.

The first two characteristics – relevance and reliability – are really what makes information useful. The last three characteristics – comparability, understand-ability and timeliness – will limit the usefulness of financial information by the extent to which they are missing. So, for example, information that is relevant to a particular decision may cease to be relevant if it is not produced in a timely fashion.

The characteristics listed above are sometimes in conflict, and so in practice it may be necessary to 'trade off' one characteristic against another. For example, a manager may require information on the current selling price of a unique cutting machine owned by the business in order to decide whether or not a recent offer for the machine should be accepted. Information concerning the current selling price is likely to be very relevant to the manager's decision but may not be very reliable, particularly as the machine is unique and there is likely to be little information available concerning market values.

Costs and benefits of accounting information

In the previous section, the five key characteristics of relevance, reliability, comparability, understandability and timeliness were identified. In fact, there is a sixth key characteristic that is also very important.

Activity 1.2

Suppose an item of information is capable of being provided. It is relevant to a particular decision, it is also reliable, comparable, and understandable by the decision maker concerned, and can be produced in a timely manner.

   Can you think of a reason why, in practice, you might choose not to provide the information?

The reason that you may decide not to provide the information is that you judge the cost of doing so to be greater than the potential benefit of having the information.

Suppose that you wish to buy a particular portable radio, which you have seen in a local shop for sale at £20. You believe that other local shops may have the same model of radio on offer for as little as £19. The only ways in which you can find out the prices at other shops are either to telephone them or visit them. Telephone calls cost money and involve some of your time. Visiting the shops may not involve the outlay of money, but more of your time will be involved. Is it worth the cost of finding out the price of the radio at various shops? The answer is, of course, that if the cost of discovering the price is less than the potential benefit, it is worth having that information.

Supplying accounting information to users is similar. The provision of accounting information costs money. If no accounting information were produced, no accounting staff would need to be employed. Salaries of accounting staff are normally only a part of the cost of producing accounting information. In order to be worth having, the potential benefits from having the information need to outweigh the cost of producing it. A real problem with making decisions about the relative cost and benefits of having accounting information is that the cost and benefit are normally very difficult, if not impossible, to identify with accuracy.

Going back to the portable radio, identifying the cost of finding the various selling prices before you actually set out to do so is problematical. It will probably involve considerations of the following factors:

- How many shops will you phone or visit?
- What will be the cost of each phone call?
- How long will it take you to make all of the phone calls or to visit all of the shops?
- How much do you value your time at?

The economic benefit of having the information on the price of radios is probably even harder to assess, the following probably being relevant:

- What is the cheapest price that you might be quoted for the radio?
- How likely is it that you will be quoted prices cheaper than £20?

As you can see, a decision on whether it is economically advantageous to discover other shops' prices for the radio is very difficult. It is possible to apply

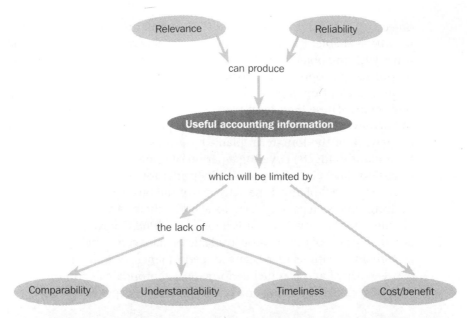

The figure shows that relevance and reliability are the key characteristics that determine usefulness (although more of one can mean less of the other). The level of usefulness, however, will be limited if comparability, understandability and timeliness are lacking, or if the cost exceeds the benefit.

Figure 1.3 The characteristics that influence the usefulness of accounting information

some 'science' to the decision, but a lot of subjective judgement is likely to be involved. It is normally exactly the same with decisions on producing accounting information in a business context.

No one would seriously advocate that the typical business should produce no accounting information. At the same time, no one would advocate that every item of information that could be seen as possessing one or more of the five key characteristics (relevance, reliability, comparability, understandability and timeliness) should be produced, irrespective of the cost of producing it (Figure 1.3).

Planning and control

We saw earlier that managers are important users of financial information. They need financial information to help them to plan and control the activities of the business. Planning and control can be seen as a sequence of logical steps that we shall now briefly describe; however, this topic will be considered in more depth in Chapter 9.

It is vitally important that businesses plan their future. Each business must have a clear view of where it is going and how it is going to get there. The first step in the planning process is to identify the objectives of the business. Objectives tend to be framed in broad terms and, once established, they are likely to remain in force for a long period, say ten years. To achieve the objectives that have been identified, a number of possible options (strategies) may be available. Each option must be considered carefully to see how closely it fits with the objectives that have been set, and to see whether the resources to pursue the options are available. Following this examination, the most appropriate option can be identified and used as the basis for preparing long-term plans. These long-term plans set out how the business will work towards the achievement of its objectives over a period of, say, five years. Within the framework of the long-term plans, a business will then usually prepare short-term plans (budgets) covering a period of one year. Their role is to convert the long-term plans into actionable blueprints for the immediate future.

However well planned the activities of the business may be, they will come to nothing unless steps are taken to achieve them. The process of ensuring that planned events actually occur is known as *control*. To exercise control, there must be a timely flow of information available to managers to help them compare actual performance with earlier planned performance. Where there are divergences between actual and planned performance, appropriate action must be taken. The planning, decision-making and control process is depicted in Figure 1.4.

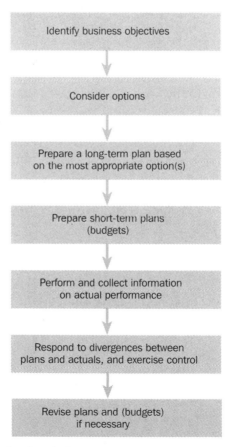

Figure 1.4 The planning and control process

Figure 1.4 sets out the key steps in the planning and control process. The starting point is to identify the business objectives: from there, it is possible to formulate plans. Once these plans have been established they can form the basis for controlling the activities of the business.

Accounting and finance has a vital role to play in each step of the planning and control process that has just been outlined. We shall see later that a key objective of private-sector businesses is to increase the wealth of their owners. It is important, therefore, that we have suitable financial indicators that can be used to set wealth-enhancement objectives. When considering the various options available to achieve the objectives of the business, financial information should also be relevant. By quantifying the likely costs and benefits associated with each option in financial terms, we should be able to see more clearly whether an option is worth pursuing.

Long-term plans, based on the most appropriate option, deal with the way in which business objectives will be met. Financial information should lie at the heart of these plans. It is important to set out the financing and investment requirements for the business and the expected levels of sales and expenses over the planning period. By doing so, the managers will have clear, quantifiable targets to be achieved. For similar reasons, financial information should be of vital importance in the development of short-term plans. As many aspects of planning will normally be couched in financial terms, information regarding actual performance, which is required to exercise control, should also be couched in financial terms. This will enable managers to compare more easily differences between planned and actual performance, and to assess the extent to which plans have been achieved. Where things have not gone according to plan, the size of the differences between planned and actual performance can help managers to set their priorities.

Business objectives

In the previous section, we mentioned that businesses seek to enhance the wealth of their owners. Throughout this book we shall assume that this is the main objective of a business. This may come as a surprise, as there are other objectives that a business may pursue that are related to the needs of others associated with the business. For example, a business may seek to provide good working conditions for its employees, or it may seek to conserve the environment for the local community. While a business may pursue these objectives, it is normally set up with a view to increasing the wealth of its owners, and in practice the behaviour of businesses over time appears to be consistent with this objective.

Does this mean that the needs of other groups associated with the business (employees, customers, suppliers, the community and so on) are not really important? The answer to this question is almost certainly 'No'. Satisfying the needs of other groups will often be consistent with the need to increase the wealth of the owners. A dissatisfied workforce, for example, may result in low productivity, strikes and so forth, which will in turn have an adverse effect on the wealth of the owners. Similarly, a business that upsets the local community by polluting the environment may attract bad publicity, resulting in a loss of customers and heavy fines.

In the case of large businesses, the owners are often divorced from day-to-day control of the business, and professional managers are employed to act on their behalf. This means that the wealth objectives of the owners should become the managers' objectives. However, there is always a risk that these managers will pursue their own interests, such as increasing their pay and 'perks' (for example, expensive cars and lavish offices) at the expense of the owners' interests. This can be a problem for the owners, which may be dealt with at least in part, by monitoring carefully the actions of managers through the use of regular financial reports. Thus accounting has an important role to play in helping the owners to assess whether the wealth enhancement objective is being pursued.

Why do I need to know anything about accounting and finance?

At this point you may be asking yourself 'Why do I need to study accounting and finance? I don't intend to become an accountant!' Well, from the explanation of what accounting and finance is about, which was given earlier in the chapter, it should be clear that the accounting/finance function within an organisation is a central part of its management information system. On the basis of information provided by the system, managers make decisions concerning the allocation of resources. Such decisions can have a profound effect on all those connected with the organisation. It is important, therefore, that *all* those who intend to work in organisations should have a fairly clear idea of certain important aspects of accounting and finance. These aspects include:

- how financial reports should be read and interpreted
- how financial plans are made
- how investment decisions are made
- how businesses are financed.

Many, perhaps most, students have a career goal of being a manager within an organisation – perhaps a personnel manager, marketing manager or IT manager. If you are one of these students, an understanding of accounting and finance is very important. When you become a manager, even a junior one, it is almost certain that you will have to use financial reports to help you to carry out your management tasks. It is equally certain that it is largely on the basis of financial information and reports that your performance as a manager will be judged.

As a manager, it is likely that you will be expected to help in forward planning for the organisation. This will often involve the preparation of forecast financial statements and setting of financial targets.

If you do not understand what the financial statements really mean and the extent to which the financial information is reliable, you will find yourself at a distinct disadvantage to others who know their way round the system. As a manager, you will also be expected to help decide how the limited resources available to the organisation should be allocated between competing options. This will require an ability to evaluate the costs and benefits of the different options available. Once again, an understanding of accounting and finance is important to carrying out this management task.

This is not to say that you cannot be an effective and successful personnel, marketing or computing manager unless you are a qualified accountant as well. It does mean, however, that you need to acquire a bit of 'street wisdom' in accounting and finance in order to succeed. This accounting and finance book is aimed at giving you just that.

Financial and management accounting

To provide information for the various user groups identified, accounting has been divided into two major areas: **management accounting** and **financial accounting**. Management accounting, as the name suggests, is concerned with providing managers with the information they require for the day-to-day running of the organisation. Financial accounting is concerned with providing the other users identified with information they will find useful.

The differences between the two types of accounting reflect the different audiences that they address. Briefly, the major differences are as follows:

- *Nature of the reports produced.* Financial accounting reports tend to be general-purpose reports. That is, they contain financial information that will be useful for a broad range of users and decisions. Management accounting reports, on the other hand, are often specific-purpose reports. That is, they are designed either with a particular decision in mind or for a particular manager.

- *Level of detail.* Financial accounting reports provide users with a broad overview of the position and performance of the business for a period. As a result, information is aggregated and detail is often lost. Management accounting reports, however, often provide managers with considerable detail to help them with a particular decision.

- *Restrictions.* Financial reporting for many businesses is subject to accounting regulations that seek to ensure that reports are produced following a standardised format. Because management accounting reports are for internal use only, there are no restrictions on the form and content of the reports.

- *Reporting interval.* For most businesses, financial accounting reports are produced on an annual basis. However, large companies may produce semi-annual reports, and a few produce quarterly reports. Management accounting reports may be produced as frequently as required by managers.

In many businesses, managers are provided with certain reports on a weekly or monthly basis, which allows them to check progress frequently.

- *Time horizon.* Financial accounting reports reflect the performance and position of the business to date. In essence, they are backward looking. Management accounting reports, on the other hand, often provide information concerning future performance as well as past performance. It is an over-simplification, however, to suggest that financial accounting reports never incorporate expectations concerning the future. Occasionally, businesses will release forecast information to other users in order to raise capital or to fight off unwanted takeover bids.

- *Range of information.* Financial accounting reports concentrate on information that can be quantified in monetary terms. Management accounting also produces such reports, but is also more likely to produce reports that contain information of a non-financial nature, such as measures of physical quantities of stocks and output. Financial accounting places greater emphasis on the use of objective, verifiable evidence when preparing reports. Management accounting reports may use information that is less objective and verifiable in order to provide managers with the information that they require.

We can see from the above that management accounting is less constrained than financial accounting. It may draw from a variety of sources, and use information that has varying degrees of reliability. The only real test to be applied when assessing the value of the information produced for managers is whether or not it improves the quality of decisions made.

Activity 1.3

Do you think this distinction between management accounting and financial accounting may be misleading?

Is there any overlap between the information needs of managers and the needs of other users?

The distinction between management and financial accounting suggests that there are differences between the information needs of managers and those of other users. While differences undoubtedly exist, there is also a good deal of overlap between the needs of managers and the needs of other users. For example, managers will at times be interested in receiving an historic overview of business operations of the sort provided to other users. Equally, the other users would be interested in receiving information relating to the future, such as the forecast level of profits, and non-financial information such as the state of the order book, product innovations and so on.

The distinction between the two areas reflects, to some extent, the differences in access to financial information. Managers have much more control over the form and content of information they receive. Other users have to rely on what managers are prepared to provide or what the financial reporting regulations state must be provided. Although the scope of financial accounting reports has increased over time, fears surrounding loss of competitive advantage and of user ignorance concerning the reliability of forecast data have led businesses to resist providing information, which is available for managers, to other users.

Broadly, Chapters 2 to 6 of this book deal with areas that are usually considered to be in the area of financial accounting, and the following three chapters are concerned with management accounting. The final three chapters are concerned with finance – that is, the raising and investing of funds.

SUMMARY

In this chapter we began by considering the nature and role of accounting and finance. We saw that accounting provides financial information to enable better decisions concerning a business to be made by a range of possible users. We saw that finance is also concerned with ensuring that better decisions are made but is particularly concerned with the financing and investing activities of the business. It was argued that, to be useful to users, accounting must possess certain characteristics, the most important of which are relevance and reliability. However, other characteristics – comparability, understandability and timeliness – will also play a part in ensuring that financial information is useful for decision makers. Managers are one of the most important groups of users of financial information, and we considered the vital role played by accounting in planning and controlling business activities.

Having provided an outline of accounting and finance, we discussed why an understanding of these subjects is likely to be relevant to your needs. It was argued that everyone connected with business should be a little 'street wise' about financial decision making. Finally, we saw that accounting has developed two main branches over the years – management accounting and financial accounting – and we explored the differences between these two branches.

✳ **Key terms**

accounting *p 1*	comparability *p 5*
finance *p 2*	understandability *p 5*
accounting information system *p 4*	timeliness *p 5*
relevance *p 5*	management accounting *p 11*
reliability *p 5*	financial accounting *p 11*

FURTHER READING

If you would like to explore in more depth topics covered in this text, we recommend the following books:

Atrill, P. and McLaney, E. *Accounting: an introduction*, Prentice Hall, 1998.

Elliott, B. and Elliott, J. *Financial accounting and reporting*, 3rd edn, Prentice Hall, 1999.

Horngren, C., Bhimani, A., Foster, G. and Datar, S. *Management and cost accounting*, Prentice Hall, 1999.

McLaney, E. *Business finance: theory and practice*, 5th edn, Pearson Education Ltd, 2000.

 ## REVIEW QUESTIONS

1.1 What is the purpose of producing accounting information?

1.2 What, in economic principle, should be the determinant of what accounting information is produced? Should economics be the only issue here? (Consider who are the users of accounting information.)

1.3 Why is timeliness an important characteristic of accounting information? Can you think of a potential conflict between the characteristics of timeliness and reliability?

1.4 Financial accounting statements tend to reflect past events. In view of this, how can they be of any assistance to a user in making a decision when decisions, by their very nature, can only be made about future actions?

2

Measuring and reporting financial position

In this chapter, we provide an overview of the major financial statements. We shall see how each of these statements contributes towards an assessment of the financial position and performance of a business. Following this overview, we begin a more detailed examination by turning our attention towards one of these financial statements – the balance sheet. We shall see how it is prepared, and we shall examine the principles underpinning this statement. We shall also consider its value for decision-making purposes.

Objectives

When you have completed this chapter you should be able to:

- explain the nature and purpose of the three major financial statements
- prepare a simple balance sheet and interpret the information that it contains
- discuss the accounting conventions underpinning the balance sheet
- discuss the limitations of the balance sheet in portraying the financial position of a business.

The major financial statements — an overview

The major financial statements are designed to provide a picture of the overall financial position and performance of the business. In order to provide this overall picture, the accounting system will normally produce three major financial reports on a regular recurring basis. The three financial statements are concerned with answering the following questions:

- What cash movements (that is, cash in and cash out) took place over a particular period?
- How much wealth (that is, profit) was generated by the business over a particular period?
- What is the accumulated wealth of the business at the end of a particular period?

These questions are addressed by the three financial statements, with each financial statement dealing with one of the questions. These three statements are:

* • the **cash flow statement**
* • the **profit and loss account**
* • the **balance sheet**.

Taken together, they provide an overall picture of the financial health of the business.

Perhaps the best way to introduce these financial statements is to look at an example of a very simple business. From this we shall be able to see the sort of information that each of the statements can usefully provide.

Example 2.1

Paul was unemployed and unable to find a job. He therefore decided to embark on a business venture in order to meet his living expenses. Christmas was approaching, and so he decided to buy gift wrapping paper from a local supplier and sell it on the corner of his local high street. He felt that the price of wrapping paper in the high street shops was excessive, and that this provided him with a useful business opportunity.

He began the venture with £40 in cash. On the first day of trading he purchased wrapping paper for £40 and sold three-quarters of his stock for £45 cash.

What cash movements took place during the first day of trading?

On the first day of trading a *cash flow statement*, showing the cash movements for the day, can be prepared as follows:

Cash flow statement for day 1

	£
Opening balance (cash introduced)	40
Add Cash from sales of wrapping paper	45
	85
Less Cash paid to purchase wrapping paper	40
Closing balance of cash	45

How much wealth (that is, profit) was generated by the business during the first day of trading?

A *profit and loss account* can be prepared to show the wealth (profit) generated on the first day. The wealth generated will represent the difference between the sales made and the cost of the goods (that is, wrapping paper) sold:

Profit and loss account for day 1

	£
Sales	45
Less Cost of goods sold (3/4 of £40)	30
Profit	15

Note that it is only the cost of the wrapping paper sold that is matched against the sales in order to find the profit, and not the whole of the cost of wrapping paper acquired. Any unsold stock (in this case $\frac{1}{4}$ of £40 = £10) will be charged against future sales.

What is the accumulated wealth at the end of the first day?

In order to establish the accumulated wealth at the end of the first day we can draw up a *balance sheet*. This will list the resources held at the end of the day:

Balance sheet at the end of day 1

	£
Cash (closing balance)	45
Stock of goods for resale ($\frac{1}{4}$ of £40)	10
Total business wealth	55

We can see from the above financial statements that each provides part of a picture that sets out the financial performance and position of the business. We begin by showing the cash movements. Cash is a vital resource, which is necessary for any business to function effectively. Cash is required to meet maturing obligations and to acquire other resources (such as stock). Cash has been described as the 'life blood' of a business, and movements in cash are usually given close scrutiny by users of financial statements.

However, it is clear that reporting cash movements alone would not be enough to portray the financial health of the business. The changes in cash over time do not give an insight into the profit generated. The profit and loss account provides us with information concerning this aspect of performance. For day 1, for example, we saw that the cash balance increased by £5, but the profit generated, as shown in the profit and loss account, was £15. The cash balance did not increase by the amount of the profit made because part of the wealth generated (£10) was held in the form of stocks.

To gain an insight into the total wealth of the business, a balance sheet is drawn up at the end of the day. Cash is only one form in which wealth can be held. In the case of this business, wealth is also held in the form of a stock of goods for resale. Hence, when drawing up the balance sheet, both forms of wealth held will be listed. In the case of a large business, there may be many other forms in which wealth will be held, such as land and buildings, equipment, motor vehicles, and so on.

Let us now continue with our example.

Example 2.1 (continued)

On the second day of trading, Paul purchased more wrapping paper for £20 cash. He managed to sell all of the new stock and half of the earlier stock for a total of £38.

The cash flow statement on day 2 will be as follows:

Cash flow statement for day 2

	£
Opening balance (from the end of day 1)	45
Add Cash from sales of wrapping paper	38
	83
Less Cash paid to purchase wrapping paper	20
Closing balance	63

The profit and loss account for day 2 will be as follows:

Profit and loss account for day 2

	£
Sales	38
Less Cost of goods sold (£20 $+\frac{1}{2}$ of £10)	25
Profit	13

The balance sheet at the end of day 2 will be:

Balance sheet at the end of day 2

	£
Cash (closing balance)	63
Stock of goods for resale ($\frac{1}{2}$ of £10)	5
Total business wealth	68

We can see that the total business wealth increased to £68 by the end of day 2. This represents an increase of £13 (that is, £68 − £55) over the previous day, which of course is the amount of profit made during day 2 as shown on the profit and loss account.

Activity 2.1

On the third day of his business venture, Paul purchased more stock for £47 cash. However, it was raining hard for much of the day and sales were slow. After Paul had sold half of his total stock for £32, he decided to stop trading until the following day.

Have a go at drawing up the three financial statements for day 3 of Paul's business venture.

Cash flow statement for day 3

	£
Opening balance (from the end of day 2)	63
Add Cash from sales of wrapping paper	32
	95
Less Cash paid to purchase wrapping paper	47
Closing balance	48

Profit and loss account for day 3

	£
Sales	32
Less Cost of goods sold ($\frac{1}{2}$ of £(47 + 5))	26
Profit	6

Balance sheet at the end of day 3

	£
Cash (closing balance)	48
Stock of goods for resale ($\frac{1}{2}$ of £(47 + 5))	26
Total business wealth	74

Note that the total business wealth increased by £6 (that is, the amount of the day's profit) even though the cash balance declined. This is because the business is holding more of its wealth in the form of stocks rather than cash, compared with the end of day 2.

It is important to recognise that the profit and loss account and cash flow statement are both concerned with measuring flows (of wealth and cash respectively) over time. The period of time may be one day, one month, one year, and so on. The balance sheet, however, is concerned with the financial position at a particular moment in time (the end of one day, one month, or whatever).

Figure 2.1 illustrates this point. The profit and loss account, cash flow statement and balance sheet, when taken together, are often referred to as the 'final accounts' of the business.

For external users of the accounts, these statements are normally backward looking, and are based on information concerning past events and transactions. This can be useful for users in providing feedback on past performance, and in identifying trends that provide clues to future performance. However, the statements can also be prepared using projected data to help assess likely future profits, cash flows and so on. The financial statements are normally prepared on a projected basis for internal decision-

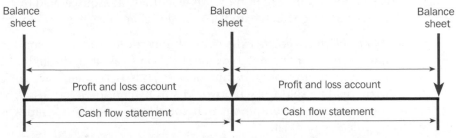

The figure shows how the profit and loss account and cash flow statement are concerned with measuring flows of wealth over time. The balance sheet, however, is concerned with measuring the stock of wealth at a particular moment in time.

Figure 2.1 The relationship between the balance sheet, the profit and loss account and the cash flow statement

making purposes only. Managers are usually reluctant to publish these projected statements for external users, as they may reveal valuable information to competitors.

Nevertheless, as external users have to make decisions about the future, projected financial statements prepared by managers are likely to be useful for this purpose. Managers are, after all, in a good position to assess future performance, and so their assessments are likely to provide a valuable source of information. In certain circumstances, such as raising fresh capital or resisting a hostile takeover bid, managers are prepared to depart from normal practice and issue projected financial statements to external users. Where publication does occur, some independent verification of the assumptions underlying the forecast statements is often provided by a firm of accountants to help lend credibility to the figures produced.

Now that we have an overview of the financial statements, we shall consider each statement in more detail. In Chapter 3 we shall look at the profit and loss account, and in Chapter 5 we shall go into more detail on the cash flow statement.

The balance sheet

The purpose of the balance sheet is simply to set out the financial position of a business at a particular moment in time. (The balance sheet is sometimes referred to as the *position statement*, because it seeks to provide the user with a picture of financial position.) We saw above that the balance sheet will reveal the forms in which the wealth of the business is held and how much wealth is held in each form. We can, however, be more specific about the nature of the balance sheet by saying that it sets out the **assets** of the business on the one hand, and the **claims** against the business on the other. Before looking at the balance sheet in more detail, we need to be clear about what these terms mean.

Assets

An asset, for accounting purposes, is essentially a resource held by the business that has certain characteristics. The major characteristics of an asset are:

- *A probable future benefit exists.* This simply means that the item is expected to have some future monetary value. This value can arise through its use within the business or through its hire or sale. Thus an obsolete piece of equipment that could be sold for scrap would still be considered an asset, whereas an obsolete piece of equipment that could not be sold for scrap would not be regarded as an asset.
- *The business has an exclusive right to control the benefit.* Unless the business has exclusive rights over the resource it cannot be regarded as an asset. Thus, for a business offering holidays on barges, the canal system may be a very valuable resource, but as the business will not be able to control the access of

others to the system, it cannot be regarded as an asset of the business. (However, the barges owned by the business would be regarded as assets.)

- *The benefit must arise from some past transaction or event.* This means that the transaction (or other event) giving rise to the business's right to the benefit must have already occurred, and will not arise at some future date. Thus an agreement by a business to purchase a piece of machinery at some future date would not mean the item is currently an asset of the business.
- *The asset must be capable of measurement in monetary terms.* Unless the item can be measured in monetary terms, with a reasonable degree of reliability the item will not be regarded as an asset for inclusion on the balance sheet. Thus the loyalty of customers may be extremely valuable to the business but is usually impossible to quantify and so will be excluded from the balance sheet.

We can see that these conditions will strictly limit the kind of items that may be referred to as 'assets' in financial statements. Certainly not all resources exploited by a business will be assets of the business. Once an asset has been acquired by a business, it will continue to be considered an asset until the benefits are exhausted or the business disposes of it in some way.

Activity 2.2

State which of the following items could appear on the balance sheet of business A as an asset. Explain your reasoning in each case.

1. £1,000 owing to business A by a customer who will never be able to pay.
2. The purchase of a licence from business B giving business A the right to produce a product designed by business B. Production of the new product under licence is expected to increase profits over the period in which the licence is held.
3. The hiring, by business A, of a new marketing director who is confidently expected to increase profits by over 30 per cent over the next three years.
4. The purchase of a machine that will save business A £10,000 per annum. It is currently being used by the business but has been acquired on credit and is not yet paid for.

Your answer to the above problems should be along the following lines:

1. Under normal circumstances a business would expect a customer to pay the amount owed. Such an amount is therefore typically shown as an asset under the heading 'debtors'. However, in this particular case the debtor is unable to pay. Hence the item is incapable of providing future benefits, and the £1,000 owing would not be regarded as an asset. Debts that are not paid are referred to as 'bad debts'.
2. The purchase of the licence would meet all of the conditions set out above and would therefore be regarded as an asset.
3. The hiring of a new marketing director would not be considered as the acquisition of an asset. One argument against its classification as an asset is that the organisation does not have exclusive rights of control over the director. (Nevertheless, it may have an exclusive right to the services that the director provides.) Perhaps a stronger argument

is that the value of the director cannot be measured in monetary terms with any degree of reliability.

4 The machine would be considered an asset even though it is not yet paid for. Once the organisation has agreed to purchase the machine, and has accepted it, the machine is legally owned by the organisation even though payment is still outstanding. (The amount outstanding would be shown as a claim, as we shall see below.)

The sorts of item that often appear as assets in the balance sheet of a business include:

- freehold premises
- machinery and equipment
- fixtures and fittings
- patents and trademarks
- debtors
- investments.

Activity 2.3

Can you think of three additional items which might appear as assets in the balance sheet of a business?

You may be able to think of a number of other items that could appear as an asset on the balance sheet of a business. Some items that you may have identified are:

- motor vehicles
- stock of goods
- computer equipment
- cash at bank
- cash in hand.

Note that an asset does not have to be a physical item – it may also be a non-physical right to certain benefits. Assets that have a physical substance and which can be touched are referred to as **tangible assets**. Assets that have no physical substance but which, nevertheless, provide expected future benefits are referred to as **intangible assets**.

Claims

A claim is an obligation on the part of the business to provide cash, or some other form of benefit, to an outside party. A claim will normally arise as a result of the outside party providing funds in the form of assets for use by the business. There are essentially two types of claim against an organisation:

- **Capital**. This represents the claim of the owner(s) against the business. This claim is sometimes referred to as the *owner's equity*. Some find it hard to understand how the owner can have a claim against the business, particularly when we consider the example of a sole-proprietor-type business where the owner *is*, in effect, the business. However, for accounting purposes, a clear distinction is made between the business (whatever its size) and the owner(s). The business is viewed as being quite separate from the owner, irrespective of whether it has a separate legal identity or not. This means that when financial statements are prepared, they are prepared for the business rather than for the owner(s). Viewed from this perspective, therefore, any funds contributed by the owner to help finance the business will be regarded as a claim against the business in its balance sheet.

✱ • **Liabilities**. Liabilities represent the claims of individuals and organisations, apart from the owner, that have arisen from past transactions or events such as supplying goods or lending money to the business.

Once a claim has been incurred by a business it will remain as an obligation until it is settled.

Now that the meaning of the terms *assets* and *claims* has been established we can go on and discuss the relationship between the two. This relationship is quite simple and straightforward. If a business wishes to acquire assets, it will have to raise the necessary funds from somewhere. It may raise the funds from the owner(s) or from other outside parties or from both. To illustrate the relationship let us take the example of a new business, as set out in Example 2.2 below.

Example 2.2

Jerry and Co. deposits £20,000 in a bank account on 1 March in order to commence business. Let us assume that the cash is supplied by the owner (£6,000) and a lender (£14,000). The raising of the funds in this way will give rise to a claim on the business by both the owner (capital) and the lender (liability). If a balance sheet of Jerry and Co. is prepared following the above transactions, the assets and claims of the business will appear as follows:

Jerry and Co.
Balance sheet as at 1 March

	£		£
Assets		*Claims*	
Cash at bank	20,000	Capital	6,000
		Liability – loan	14,000
	20,000		20,000

We can see from the balance sheet that has been prepared that the total claims are the same as the total assets. Thus:

$$\text{Assets} = \text{Capital} + \text{Liabilities}$$

This equation – which is often referred to as the *balance sheet equation* – will always hold true. Whatever changes may occur to the assets of the business or the claims against the business, there will be compensating changes elsewhere that will ensure that the balance sheet always 'balances'. By way of illustration, consider some further possible transactions for Jerry and Co. Assume that, after the £20,000 had been deposited in the bank, the following transactions took place:

2 March   Purchased a motor van for £5,000, paying by cheque.
3 March   Purchased stock-in-trade on one month's credit for £3,000.
4 March   Repaid £2,000 of the loan from the lender.
6 March   Owner introduced another £4,000 into the business bank account.

A balance sheet may be drawn up after each day in which transactions have taken place. In this way, the effect can be seen of each transaction on the assets and claims of the business. The balance sheet as at 2 March will be as follows:

Jerry and Co.
Balance sheet as at 2 March

	£		£
Assets		**Claims**	
Cash at bank (20,000 − 5,000)	15,000	Capital	6,000
Motor van	5,000	Liabilities – loan	14,000
	20,000		20,000

As can be seen, the effect of purchasing a motor van is to decrease the balance at the bank by £5,000 and to introduce a new asset – a motor van – onto the balance sheet. The total assets remain unchanged. It is only the 'mix' of assets that will change. The claims against the business will remain the same, as there has been no change in the funding arrangements for the business.

The balance sheet as at 3 March, following the purchase of stock, will be as follows:

Jerry and Co.
Balance sheet as at 3 March

	£		£
Assets		**Claims**	
Cash at bank	15,000	Capital	6,000
Motor van	5,000	Liabilities – loan	14,000
Stock	3,000	Liabilities – trade creditor	3,000
	23,000		23,000

The effect of purchasing stock has been to introduce another new asset (stock) onto the balance sheet. In addition, the fact that the goods have not yet been paid for means that the claims against the business will be increased by the £3,000 owed to the supplier, who is referred to as a *trade creditor* on the balance sheet.

Activity 2.4

Try drawing up a balance sheet for Jerry and Co. as at 4 March.

The balance sheet as at 4 March, following the repayment of part of the loan, will be as follows:

Jerry and Co.
Balance sheet as at 4 March

Assets	£	Claims	£
Cash at bank (15,000 – 2,000)	13,000	Capital	6,000
Motor van	5,000	Liabilities – loan (14,000 – 2,000)	12,000
Stock	3,000	Liabilities – trade creditor	3,000
	21,000		21,000

The repayment of £2,000 of the loan will result in a decrease in the balance at the bank of £2,000 and a decrease in the loan claim against the business by the same amount.

Activity 2.5

Try drawing up a balance sheet as at 6 March for Jerry and Co.

The balance sheet as at 6 March, following the introduction of more funds, will be as follows:

Jerry and Co.
Balance sheet as at 6 March

Assets	£	Claims	£
Cash at bank (13,000 + 4,000)	17,000	Capital (6,000 + 4,000)	10,000
Motor van	5,000	Liabilities – loan	12,000
Stock	3,000	Liabilities – trade creditor	3,000
	25,000		25,000

The introduction of more funds by the owner will result in an increase in the capital of £4,000 and an increase in the cash at bank by the same amount.

This example illustrates the point made earlier that the balance sheet equation (assets equals capital plus liabilities) will always hold true. This is because the equation reflects the fact that, if a business wishes to acquire assets, it must raise funds equal to the cost of those assets. These funds must be provided by the owners (capital), or by others (liabilities), or both. Hence the total cost of assets acquired should always equal the total capital plus liabilities.

It is worth pointing out that a business would not draw up a balance sheet after each day of transactions as shown in the example above. Such an approach is likely to be impractical, given even a relatively small number of transactions each day. A balance sheet for the business is usually prepared at the end of a defined reporting period. Determining the length of the reporting interval will involve weighing up the costs of producing the information against the perceived benefits of the information for decision-making purposes. In practice, the reporting interval will vary between businesses, and could be monthly, quarterly, half-yearly or annually. For external reporting purposes, an annual reporting cycle is the norm (although certain large companies report more frequently than this). However, for internal reporting purposes, many businesses produce monthly financial statements.

The effect of trading operations on the balance sheet

In the example we considered earlier, we dealt with the effect on the balance sheet of a number of different types of transactions that a business might undertake. These transactions covered the purchase of assets for cash and on credit, the repayment of a loan, and the injection of capital. However, one form of transaction, trading, has not yet been considered. In order to deal with the effect of trading transactions on the balance sheet let us return to our earlier example.

Example 2.2 (continued)

Let us return to the balance sheet that we drew up for Jerry and Co. as at 6 March. The balance sheet at that date was as follows:

Jerry and Co.
Balance sheet as at 6 March

Assets	£	Claims	£
Cash at bank	17,000	Capital	10,000
Motor van	5,000	Liabilities – loan	12,000
Stock	3,000	Liabilities – trade creditor	3,000
	25,000		25,000

Let us assume that, on 7 March, the business managed to sell all of the stock for £5,000 and received a cheque immediately from the customer for this amount. The balance sheet on 7 March, after this transaction has taken place, will be as follows:

Jerry and Co.
Balance sheet as at 7 March

Assets	£	Claims	£
Cash at bank (17,000 + 5,000)	22,000	Capital [10,000 + (5,000 – 3,000)]	12,000
Motor van	5,000	Liabilities – loan	12,000
Stock (3,000 – 3,000)	—	– trade creditor	3,000
	27,000		27,000

We can see that the stock (£3,000) has now disappeared from the balance sheet, but the cash at bank has increased by the selling price of the stock (£5,000). The net effect has therefore been to increase assets by £2,000 (that is £5,000 – £3,000). This increase represents the net increase in wealth (profit) that has arisen from trading. Also note that the capital of the business has increased by £2,000, in line with the increase in assets. This increase in capital reflects the fact that increases in wealth as a result of trading or other operations will be to the benefit of the owner and will increase his/her stake in the business.

Activity 2.6

What would have been the effect on the balance sheet if the stock had been sold on 7 March for £1,000 rather than £5,000?

The balance sheet on 7 March would be as follows:

Jerry and Co.
Balance sheet as at 7 March

Assets	£	Claims	£
Cash at bank (17,000 + 1,000)	18,000	Capital [10,000 + (1,000 – 3000)]	8,000
Motor van	5,000	Liabilities – loan	12,000
Stock (3,000 – 3,000)	—	– trade creditor	3,000
	23,000		23,000

As we can see, the stock (£3,000) will disappear from the balance sheet, but the cash at bank will rise only by £1,000. This will mean a net reduction in assets of £2,000. This reduction will be reflected in a reduction in the capital of the owner.

Thus we can see that any decrease in wealth (loss) arising from trading or other transactions will lead to a reduction in the owner's stake in the business. If the business wished to maintain the level of assets as at 6 March it would be necessary to obtain further funds from the owner or from lenders, or both.

What we have just seen means that the balance sheet equation can be extended as follows:

$$\text{Assets} = \text{Capital} + (-) \text{ Profit (Loss)} + \text{Liabilities}$$

The profit for the period is usually shown separately in the balance sheet as an addition to capital. Any funds introduced or withdrawn by the owner for living expenses or other reasons are also shown separately. By doing this we provide more comprehensive information for users of the financial statements. If we assume that the above business sold the stock for £5,000, as in the earlier example, and further assume that the owner withdrew £1,500 of the profit, the capital of the owner would appear as follows on the balance sheet:

	£
Capital	
Opening balance	10,000
Add Profit	2,000
	12,000
Less Drawings	1,500
Closing balance	10,500

If the drawings were in cash then the balance of cash would decrease by £1,500 in the balance sheet.

The classification of assets

To help users of financial information to locate items of interest easily on the balance sheet, it is customary to group assets and claims into categories. Assets are normally categorised as being either fixed or current. The distinction between these two categories is as follows:

✱ • **Fixed assets** are defined primarily according to the purpose for which they are held. Fixed assets are held with the intention of being used to generate wealth rather than being held for resale (although they may be sold by the business when there is no further use for the asset). They can be seen as the tools of the business. Fixed assets are normally held by the business on a continuing basis. The minimum period for which a fixed asset is expected to be held is not precisely defined, although one year is sometimes quoted.

Activity 2.7

Can you think of two examples of assets that may be classified as fixed assets within a particular business?

Examples of assets that are often defined as being fixed are:

• freehold premises
• plant and machinery
• motor vehicles
• patents.

This is not an exhaustive list. You may have thought of others.

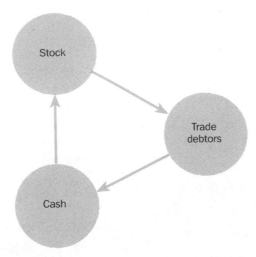

The figure shows how stock may be sold on credit to customers. When the customers pay, the trade debtors will be converted into cash, which can then be used to purchase more stocks, and so the cycle begins again.

Figure 2.2 The circulating nature of current assets

✱ • **Current assets** are assets that are not held on a continuing basis. They include cash itself and other assets that are expected to be converted to cash at some future point in time. Current assets are normally held as part of the day-to-day trading activities of the business. The most common current assets are stock, trade debtors (that is, customers who owe money for goods or services supplied on credit), and cash itself. The current assets mentioned are interrelated, and circulate within a business as shown in Figure 2.2. We can see that cash can be used to purchase stock, which is then sold as credit. When the trade debtors pay, the business receives an injection of cash, and so on.

It is important to appreciate that the classification of an asset may vary (that is, between fixed and current) according to the nature of the business being carried out. This is because the *purpose* for which a particular type of business holds a certain asset may vary. For example, a motor vehicle manufacturer will normally hold the motor vehicles produced for resale, and would therefore classify them as stock-in-trade. On the other hand, a business that uses motor vehicles for transportation purposes would classify them as fixed assets.

Activity 2.8

The assets of Kunalun and Co., a large metalworking business, are shown below:

- Cash at bank
- Fixtures and fittings
- Office equipment
- Motor vehicles
- Freehold factory premises

- Goodwill purchased from business taken over
- Plant and machinery
- Computer equipment
- Stock of work-in-progress (that is, partly completed goods)
- Short-term investments (that is, excess cash invested in the short term in order to generate income).

Which of the above do you think should be defined as fixed assets, and which should be defined as current assets?

Your answer to the above activity should be as follows:

Fixed assets	Current assets
Fixtures and fittings	Cash at bank
Office equipment	Stock of work-in-progress
Motor vehicles	Short-term investments
Freehold factory premises	
Goodwill purchased	
Plant and machinery	
Computer equipment	

The item 'goodwill purchased' in the list of fixed assets above requires some explanation. When a business takes over another business, the amount that is paid for the business taken over will often exceed the total value of the individual assets that have been acquired. This additional amount represents a payment for *goodwill*, which arises from such factors as the quality of products produced, the skill of the workforce, the relationship with customers, and so on. 'Qualitative' items such as these are normally excluded from the balance sheet as they are difficult to measure. However, when they have been acquired by a business at an agreed price, the amount paid provides an objective basis for measurement. Hence 'goodwill purchased' can be regarded as an asset and included on the balance sheet. Goodwill is regarded as a fixed asset as it is not held primarily for resale, and will be held on a continuing basis.

The classifications of claims

As we have already seen, claims are normally classified into capital (owner's claim) and liabilities (claims of outsiders). Liabilities are further classified into two groups:

* - **Long-term liabilities** represent those amounts due to outside parties that are not liable for repayment within the next 12 months after the balance sheet date.
* - **Current liabilities** represent amounts due for repayment to outside parties within 12 months of the balance sheet date.

Unlike assets, the purpose for which the liabilities are held is not an issue. It is only the period for which a liability is outstanding that is important. Thus a long-term liability will turn into a current liability when the settlement date comes within 12 months of the balance sheet date.

Activity 2.9

Can you think of examples of a long-term liability and a current liability?

Two examples of a long-term liability would be a long-term mortgage (that is, a loan secured on property) or long-term loan. Two examples of a current liability would be trade creditors (that is, amounts owing to suppliers for goods supplied on credit) and a bank overdraft (a form of bank borrowing that is repayable on demand).

Balance sheet formats

Now that the classification of assets and liabilities has been completed, it is possible to consider the format of the balance sheet. Although there is an almost infinite number of ways in which the same balance sheet information could be presented, there are in practice two basic formats. The first of these follows the style we adopted with Jerry and Co. earlier. A more comprehensive example of this style is shown below:

Brie Manufacturing
Balance sheet as at 31 December 2000

	£	£		£
Fixed assets			*Capital*	
Freehold premises		45,000	Opening balance	50,000
Plant and machinery		30,000	*Add* Profit	14,000
Motor vans		19,000		64,000
		94,000	Less Drawings	4,000
				60,000
			Long-term liabilities	
			Loan	50,000
Current assets			*Current liabilities*	
Stock-in-trade	23,000		Trade creditors	37,000
Trade debtors	18,000			
Cash at bank	12,000			
		53,000		
		147,000		147,000

Note that within each category of asset (fixed and current) the items are listed with the least liquid (furthest from cash) first, going down to the most liquid last. This is a standard practice, which is followed irrespective of the format used. Note also that the current assets are listed individually in the first

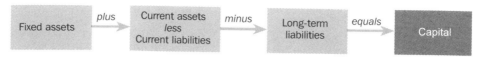

The figure sets out the structure for the vertical form of balance sheet layout.

Figure 2.3 The vertical layout for a balance sheet

column, and a subtotal of current assets (£53,000) is carried out to the second column to be added to the subtotal of fixed assets (£94,000). This convention is designed to make the balance sheet easier to read.

An obvious change to the format illustrated here is to show claims on the left and assets on the right. Some people prefer this approach because the claims can be seen as the source of finance for the business, and the assets show how that finance has been deployed. It could be seen as more logical to show sources first and uses second.

The format shown is sometimes referred to as the *horizontal layout*. However, in recent years, a more common form of layout for the balance sheet is the *narrative* or *vertical* form of layout. This format is really based on a rearrangement of the balance sheet equation. With the horizontal format above, the balance sheet equation is set out as:

**Fixed assets (FA) + Current assets (CA) =
Capital (C) + Long-term liabilities (LTL) + Current liabilities (CL)**

The vertical format merely rearranges this to:

$$FA + (CA - CL) - LTL = C$$

This rearranged equation is expressed in the format depicted in Figure 2.3.

We can therefore rearrange the balance sheet layout of Brie Manufacturing as follows:

Brie Manufacturing
Balance sheet as at 31 December 2000

	£	£
Fixed assets		
Freehold premises		45,000
Plant and machinery		30,000
Motor vans		19,000
		94,000
Current assets		
Stock-in-trade	23,000	
Trade debtors	18,000	
Cash at bank	12,000	
	53,000	
Less **Current liabilities**		
Trade creditors	37,000	
		16,000
Total assets *less* current liabilities		110,000

Less **Long-term liabilities**	
Loan	<u>50,000</u>
Net assets	<u><u>60,000</u></u>
Capital	
Opening balance	50,000
Add Profit	<u>14,000</u>
	64,000
Less Drawings	<u>4,000</u>
	<u><u>60,000</u></u>

Some people find this format easier to read than the horizontal format. It usefully highlights the relationship between current assets and current liabilities. We shall consider shortly why this relationship is an important one. The figure derived from deducting current liabilities from the current assets (£16,000 for Brie Manufacturing) is sometimes referred to as *net current assets* or *working capital*.

Self-assessment question 2.1

The following information relates to the Simonson Engineering Company as at 30 September 2000:

	£
Plant and machinery	25,000
Trade creditors	18,000
Bank overdraft	26,000
Stock-in-trade	45,000
Freehold premises	72,000
Long-term loans	51,000
Trade debtors	48,000
Capital at 1 October 1999	117,500
Cash-in-hand	1,500
Motor vehicles	15,000
Fixtures and fittings	9,000
Profit for the year to 30 September 2000	18,000
Drawings for the year to 30 September 2000	15,000

Required:
Prepare a balance sheet in the vertical format.

The balance sheet as a position at a point in time

As we have already seen, the balance sheet is a statement of the financial position of the business at *a specified point in time*. The balance sheet has been compared to a photograph. A photograph 'freezes' a particular moment in time and will only represent the events that occurred at that moment in time. Hence, events may be quite different immediately before and immediately after the photograph was taken. Similarly, the balance sheet represents a 'snapshot' of the business at a particular moment in time. When examining a balance sheet, therefore, it is important to establish the date at which it has been drawn up. This information should be prominently displayed in the balance sheet heading, as shown above. The more current the balance sheet date the better, when you are trying to assess the current financial position.

A business will normally prepare a balance sheet as at the close of business on the last day of its accounting year. In the UK, businesses are free to choose their accounting year. When making a decision on which year-end date to choose, commercial convenience can often be a deciding factor. Thus a business operating in the retail trade may choose to have a year-end date early in the calendar year (for example 31 January) because trade tends to be slack during that period and more staff time is available to help with the tasks involved with the preparation of the annual accounting statements (such as checking the amount of stock held). Since trade is slack, it is also a time when the amount of stock held by the business is likely to be untypically low as compared with other times of the year. Thus the balance sheet, though showing a fair view of what it purports to show, may not show a picture of what is more typically the position of the business over the year.

Accounting conventions and the balance sheet

Accounting is based on a number of rules or conventions that have evolved over time. They have evolved in order to deal with practical problems experienced by preparers and users, rather than to reflect some theoretical ideal. In preparing the balance sheets earlier, we have adhered to various * **accounting conventions**, although they have not been explicitly mentioned. Below we identify and discuss the major conventions that we have employed.

Business entity convention

For accounting purposes, the business and its owner(s) are treated as being quite separate and distinct. This is why owners are treated as being claimants against their own business in respect of their investment in the business. The * **business entity convention** must be distinguished from the legal position that may exist between businesses and their owners. For sole proprietorships and partnerships, the law does not make any distinction between the business and its owner(s). For limited companies, on the other hand, there is a clear legal distinction between the business and its owners. (As we shall see in Chapter 4, the limited company is regarded as having a separate legal existence.) For accounting purposes these legal distinctions are irrelevant, and the business entity convention applies to all businesses.

Money measurement convention

Accounting normally deals with only those items that are capable of being expressed in monetary terms. Money has the advantage that it is a useful common denominator with which to express the wide variety of resources held by a business. However, not all resources held by a business may be capable of being measured in monetary terms and so may be excluded from the balance sheet. The **money measurement convention**, therefore, limits the scope of accounting reports.

Activity 2.10

Can you think of resources held by a business that are not normally included on the balance sheet because they cannot be quantified in monetary terms?

In answering this activity you may have thought of the following:

- the quality of the workforce
- the reputation of the business's products
- the location of the business
- the relationship with customers
- the quality of management.

Accounting is a developing subject, and the boundaries of financial measurement can change. In recent years, attempts have been made to measure particular resources of a business that have been previously excluded from the balance sheet. For example, we have seen the development of human resource accounting, which attempts to measure the 'human assets' of the business. It is often claimed that employees are the most valuable 'assets' of a business. By measuring these assets and putting the amount on the balance sheet, it is sometimes argued that we would have a more complete picture of the financial position. For similar reasons, we have also seen attempts by certain large businesses to measure the value of brand names that they hold. However, some of the measurement methods proposed have been controversial, and often conflict with other accounting conventions. There are mixed views as to whether extending the boundaries of financial measurement will succeed in making the balance sheet a more useful representation of the financial position of a business.

Another approach to overcoming some of the limitations of money measurement is to publish a narrative financial statement. Rather than trying to 'quantify the unquantifiable', a narrative financial statement, which describes and explains key issues, could be published to help users assess financial health. Thus, in order to give a more complete picture of financial position, a narrative statement might incorporate a discussion of such matters as investment policy, financial structure and liquidity, as well as valuable resources that have not been quantified.

Historic cost convention

Assets are shown on the balance sheet at a value that is based on their **historic cost** (that is, acquisition cost). This method of measuring asset value has been adopted by accountants in preference to methods based on some form of current value. Many commentators find this particular convention difficult to support, as outdated historical costs are unlikely to help in the assessment of current financial position. It is often argued that recording assets at their current value would provide a more realistic view of financial position and would be relevant for a wide range of decisions. However, a system of measurement based on current values can present a number of problems.

Activity 2.11

Can you think of reasons why current value accounting may pose problems for both preparers and users of financial statements?

The term 'current value' can be defined in a number of ways. For example, it can be defined broadly as either the current replacement cost or the current realisable value (selling price) of an item. These two types of valuation may result in quite different figures being produced to represent the current value of an item. (Think, for example, of second-hand car values: there is often quite a difference between buying and selling prices.) In addition, the broad terms 'replacement cost' and 'realisable value' can be defined in different ways. We must therefore be clear about what kind of current value accounting we wish to use. There are also practical problems associated with attempts to implement any system of current value accounting. For example, current values, however defined, are often difficult to establish with any real degree of objectivity. This may mean that the figures produced are heavily dependent on the opinion of managers. Unless the current value figures are capable of some form of independent verification, there is a danger that the financial statements will lose their credibility among users.

By reporting assets at their historic cost, it is argued that more reliable information is produced. Reporting in this way reduces the need for subjective opinion, as the amount paid for a particular asset is usually a matter of demonstrable fact. However, information based on past costs may not always be relevant to the needs of users.

Later in the chapter we shall consider the valuation of assets in the balance sheet in more detail. We shall see that the historic cost convention is not always rigidly adhered to, and that departures from this convention often occur.

Going concern convention

✳ The **going concern convention** holds that the business will continue operations for the foreseeable future. In other words, there is no intention, or need, to liquidate the business. This convention is important because the value of fixed assets on a liquidation basis is often low in relation to the recorded values, and an expectation of winding up would mean that anticipated losses on sale should be fully recorded. However, where there is no expectation of liquidation, the value of fixed assets can continue to be shown at their recorded values (that is, based on historic cost). This convention therefore provides support for the historic cost convention under normal circumstances.

Dual aspect convention

Each transaction has two aspects, both of which will affect the balance sheet. Thus the purchase of a motor car for cash results in an increase in one asset (motor car) and a decrease in another (cash). The repayment of a loan results in the decrease in a liability (loan) and the decrease in an asset (cash/bank).

Activity 2.12

What are the two aspects of each of the following transactions?

- **Purchase £1,000 stock on credit.**
- **Owner withdraws £2,000 in cash.**
- **Sale of stock (purchased for £1,000) for £2,000 cash.**

Your answer should be as follows:

- Stock increases by £1,000, creditors increase by £1,000.
- Capital reduces by £2,000, cash reduces by £2,000.
- Assets show net increase of £1,000 (cash + £2,000, stock − £1,000), capital (profit) increases by £1,000.

✳ Recording the **dual aspect** of each transaction ensures that the balance sheet will continue to balance.

Prudence convention

✳ The **prudence convention** holds that financial statements should err on the side of caution. The prudence convention represents an attempt to deal with the uncertainty surrounding many events reported in the financial statements, and evolved to counteract the excessive optimism of some managers and owners which resulted, in the past, in an overstatement of financial position. Operation of this convention results in the recording of both actual and anticipated losses in full whereas profits are not recognised until they are realised (that is, there is reasonable certainty the profit will be received). When the prudence convention conflicts with another convention, it is prudence that will normally prevail. We shall see an example of this when we consider the valuation of current assets later in the chapter.

Activity 2.13

Can you think of a situation where certain users might find a prudent view of the financial position of a business will work to their disadvantage?

Applying the prudence convention can result in an understatement of financial position as unrealised profits are not recognised but anticipated losses are recognised in full. This may result in owners selling their stake in the business at a price that is lower than they would have received if a more 'realistic' approach to valuation were employed.

The degree of bias towards understatement may be difficult to judge. It is likely to vary according to the views of the individual carrying out the valuation.

Stable monetary unit convention

The **stable monetary unit convention** holds that money, which is the unit of measurement in accounting, will not change in value over time. However, in the UK and throughout much of the world, inflation has been a persistent problem over the years. This has meant that the value of money has declined in relation to other assets. In past years, high rates of inflation have resulted in balance sheets, which are drawn up on an historic cost basis, reflecting figures for assets that were much lower than if current values were employed. The value of freehold land and buildings, in particular, increased rapidly during much of the 1980s and during the late 1990s. Where this asset was held for some time by a business, there was often a significant difference between its original cost and the current market value. This led to the criticism that balance sheet values were seriously understated, and, as a result, some businesses broke away from the use of historic cost as the basis for valuing this particular asset. Instead, freehold land is periodically revalued in order to provide a more realistic statement of financial position. Although this represents a departure from accounting convention, it is a practice that has become increasingly common.

Activity 2.14

Refer to the vertical format balance sheet of Brie Manufacturing shown earlier. What would be the effect of revaluing the freehold land to a figure of £110,000 on the balance sheet?

The effect on the balance sheet would be to increase the freehold land to £110,000 and the gain on revaluation (that is, £110,000 − £45,000 = £65,000) would be added to the capital of the owner, as it is the owner who will benefit from the gain. The revised balance sheet would therefore be as follows:

Brie Manufacturing
Balance sheet as at 31 December 2000

	£	£
Fixed assets		
Freehold premises		110,000
Plant and machinery		30,000
Motor vans		19,000
		159,000
Current assets		
Stock-in-trade	23,000	
Trade debtors	18,000	
Cash at bank	12,000	
	53,000	
Less **Current liabilities**		
Trade creditors	37,000	
		16,000
Total assets less current liabilities		175,000
Less **Long-term liabilities**		
Loan		50,000
Net assets		125,000
Capital		
Opening balance		50,000
Add: Revaluation gain		65,000
Profit		14,000
		129,000
Less Drawings		4,000
		125,000

In practice, the revaluation of land and buildings often has a significant effect on the size of the balance sheet figures for tangible fixed assets. In past years, the effect on the balance sheet has usually been beneficial, as property has risen in value throughout much of the past three decades. However, during the early 1990s we witnessed a fall in property values, and we also witnessed some reluctance among those businesses that revalued their land and buildings upwards in earlier years, to make downward revaluations in recessionary years. A common reason cited was that the fall in value was considered to be only temporary.

Objectivity convention

✱ The **objectivity convention** seeks to reduce personal bias in financial statements. As far as possible, financial statements should be based on objective verifiable evidence rather than on matters of opinion.

Activity 2.15

Which of the above conventions does the objectivity convention support and which does it conflict with?

The objectivity convention provides further support (along with the going concern convention) for the use of historic cost as a basis of valuation. It can conflict, however, with the prudence convention, which requires the use of judgement in determining values.

The basis of valuation of assets on the balance sheet

It was mentioned earlier that, when preparing the balance sheet, the historic cost convention is normally applied for the reporting of assets. However, this point requires further elaboration as, in practice, it is not simply a matter of recording each asset on the balance sheet at its original cost. Below we consider the valuation procedures used for both current assets and fixed assets.

Current assets

Where the net realisable value (that is, selling price less any selling costs) of current assets falls below the cost of the assets, the former will be used as the basis of valuation instead. This reflects the influence of the prudence convention on the balance sheet. Current assets are short-term assets that are expected to be liquidated in the near future, and so any loss arising from a fall in value below their original cost is shown on the balance sheet.

Exhibit 2.1

The following extract from the published accounts for 1999 of National Power, a power-generating company, contains the following notes:

Current asset investments
Current asset investments are stated at the lower of cost and market value.

Stocks
Operating stocks of fuel and stores are valued at the lower of cost and net realisable value. They arc included as current assets.

Fixed assets

Many fixed assets, such as plant and machinery, motor vehicles, computer equipment and buildings, have a limited useful life. Ultimately, these assets will be used up as a result of wear and tear, obsolescence, and so on. The amount of a particular asset that has been used up over time, as a result of being employed by the business, is referred to as *depreciation*. The total depreciation relating to a fixed asset will normally be deducted from the cost of the asset on the balance sheet. This procedure is not really a contravention of the historic cost convention. It is simply recognition of the fact that a proportion of the fixed asset has been consumed in the process of generating benefits for the business. (The concept of depreciation is considered in more detail in the next chapter.)

There are, however, examples where the historic cost convention is contravened. We saw earlier that some assets *appreciate* in value over time. Freehold property was mentioned as an example of an asset that has appreciated in value a great deal in past years. As a result of this appreciation, it has become widespread practice to revalue freehold property by using current market values rather than historic cost. This practice not only contravenes the historic cost convention; it also contravenes the objectivity convention. This is because an opinion of what is the current market value is substituted for a cost figure (which is usually a matter of verifiable fact).

In recent years, we have also seen some large businesses attempt to place a value on their product brands (for example, Rank Hovis McDougall plc). Product brands may be very valuable to a business as they can generate customer loyalty, which in turn can lead to increased sales. This brand loyalty is often built up through many years of promotional and advertising expenditure. However, such expenditure may be difficult to trace, and so some form of current valuation is often used as the basis for including brand names on the balance sheet. (It should be said that the practice of including internally generated brands on the balance sheet is a controversial issue in accounting. Some doubt exists as to whether the value of brands can be established with a reasonable degree of reliability, and this in turn brings into question their inclusion on the balance sheet.)

Thus we can see that there are exceptions to the rule that assets are recorded at their historic cost. Moreover, the list of exceptions appears to be growing. In recent years the balance sheets of many businesses have increasingly reflected a mixture of valuation approaches. This trend is a matter of concern for the accountancy profession, as users are unlikely to find a variety of valuation methods very helpful when trying to assess financial position.

Interpreting the balance sheet

We have seen that the conventional balance sheet has a number of limitations. This has led some users of financial information to conclude that the balance sheet has little to offer in the way of useful information. However, this is not necessarily the case. The balance sheet can provide useful insights into the financing and investing activities of a business. In particular, the following aspects of financial position can be examined.

- *The liquidity of the business.* This is the ability of the business to meet its short-term obligations (current liabilities) from its liquid (cash and near-cash) assets. One of the reasons why the vertical format for the balance sheet is preferred by many users of accounts is the fact that it highlights the liquidity of the business: the current assets are directly compared with the current liabilities. Liquidity is particularly important because business failures occur when the business cannot meet its maturing obligations, whatever the root cause of that inability may be.

- *The 'mix' of assets held by the business.* The relationship between fixed assets and current assets is important. Businesses with too much of their funds tied up in fixed assets could be vulnerable to financial failure. This is because fixed assets are typically not easy to turn into cash in order to meet short-term obligations. Converting many fixed assets into cash may well lead to substantial losses for the business, because such assets are not always worth, on the open market, what the business paid to acquire them or what they are worth to the business. For example, a specialised piece of equipment may have little value to any other business, yet it could be worth a great deal to the business that owns it.

- *The financial structure of the business.* The relative proportion of total finance contributed by the owners and outsiders can be calculated to see whether the business is heavily dependent on outside financing. Heavy borrowing can bring with it a commitment to pay large interest charges and make large capital repayments at regular intervals. These are legally enforceable obligations, which can be a real burden as they have to be paid irrespective of the financial position of the business. Funds raised from the owners of the business, on the other hand, do not impose such obligations on the business.

The interpretation of the balance sheet will be considered in more detail in Chapter 6.

Self-assessment question 2.2

Consider the following balance sheet of a manufacturing business:

Russell Manufacturing Company
Balance sheet as at 30 April 2000

	£	£	£
Fixed assets			
Freehold premises			88,000
Plant and machinery			46,000
Motor vehicles			13,000
Fixtures and fittings			14,000
			161,000
Current assets			
Stock-in-trade		48,000	
Trade debtors		44,000	
Cash in hand		12,000	
		104,000	

	£	£	£
Less **Current liabilities**			
Trade creditors	24,000		
Bank overdraft	18,000		
		42,000	
Net current assets			62,000
Total assets less current liabilities			223,000
Long-term liabilities			
Loan			160,000
Net assets			63,000
Capital			
Opening balance			42,000
Add Profit			32,000
			74,000
Less Drawings			11,000
			63,000

Required:
What can you deduce about the financial position of the business from the information contained in the balance sheet shown above?

SUMMARY

In this chapter we took an overview of the three major financial statements – the balance sheet, the profit and loss account, and the cash flow statement. We saw how each of these statements contributes towards a picture of financial performance and position for a business. We then went on to consider the balance sheet in some detail. We saw that this statement shows the assets of the business and the claims against those assets at a particular moment in time. It is a statement of financial position; however, it can be argued that it is not a complete statement of financial position. There are certain valuable resources held by the business that cannot be accommodated easily within conventional accounting definitions and measurement methods. We examined the conventions of accounting that underpin the balance sheet, and saw how these place limits on the usefulness of the balance sheet in assessing current financial position.

In the following chapter we shall consider another of the three major financial statements: the profit and loss account.

REVIEW QUESTIONS

2.1 An accountant prepared a balance sheet for a business using the horizontal layout. In the balance sheet, the capital of the owner was shown next to the liabilities. This confused the owner, who argued: 'My capital is my major asset and so should be shown as an asset on the balance sheet.' How would you explain this misunderstanding to the owner?

2.2 'The balance sheet shows how much a business is worth.' Do you agree with this statement? Discuss.

2.3 Can you think of a more appropriate name for the balance sheet?

2.4 In recent years there have been attempts to place a value on the 'human assets' of a business in order to derive a figure that can be included on the balance sheet. Do you think humans should be treated as assets? Would 'human assets' meet the conventional definition of an asset for inclusion on the balance sheet?

EXAMINATION-STYLE QUESTIONS

Questions 2.5–2.8 are more advanced than 2.1–2.4. Those questions with a coloured number have answers at the back of the book.

2.1 While on holiday in Bridlington, Helen had her credit cards and purse stolen from a beach while she was swimming. She was left with only £40, which she had left in her hotel room, but had three days of her holiday remaining. She was determined to continue her holiday, and decided to make some money in order to be able to complete her holiday. She decided to sell orange juice to holidaymakers using the local beach. On day 1 she purchased 80 cartons of orange juice at £0.50 each for cash and sold 70 of these at £0.80 each. On the following day she purchased 60 cartons for cash at £0.50 each and sold 65 at £0.80 each. On the third and final day she purchased another 60 cartons for cash at £0.50 each. However, it rained and, as a result, business was poor. She managed to sell 20 at £0.80 each but sold off the rest of her stock at £0.40 each.

Required:
Prepare a profit and loss account and cash flow statement for each day's trading, and prepare a balance sheet at the end of each day's trading.

2.2 On 1 March 2000 Joe Conday started a new business. During March he carried out the following transactions:

March 1 Deposited £20,000 in a bank account.
     2 Purchased fixtures and fittings for £6,000 cash, and stock £8,000 on credit.
     3 Borrowed £5,000 from a relative and deposited it in the bank.
     4 Purchased a motor car for £7,000 cash and withdrew £200 for own use.
     5 Another motor car costing £9,000 was purchased. The motor car purchased on 4 March was given in part exchange at a value of £6,500. The balance of purchase price for the new car was paid in cash.
     6 Conday won £2,000 in a lottery and paid the amount into the business bank account. He also repaid £1,000 of the loan.

Required:
(a) Draw up a balance sheet for the business at the end of each day using the horizontal format.
(b) Show how the balance sheet you have prepared as at 6 March 2000 would be presented in the vertical format. (Present the balance sheet in good form.)

2.3 The following is a list of assets and claims of a manufacturing business at a particular point in time:

	£
Bank overdraft	22,000
Freehold land and buildings	245,000
Stock of raw materials	18,000
Trade creditors	23,000
Plant and machinery	127,000
Loan from Industrial Finance Corporation	100,000
Stock of finished goods	28,000
Delivery vans	54,000
Trade debtors	34,000

Required:
Write out a balance sheet in the standard vertical format incorporating these figures.
Hint: There is a missing item that needs to be deduced and inserted.

2.4 The following is a list of the assets and claims of Crafty Engineering Ltd at 30 June 2000:

	£000
Creditors	86
Motor vehicles	38
Loan from Industrial Finance Corporation	260
Machinery and tools	207
Bank overdraft	116
Stock-in-trade	153
Freehold premises	320
Debtors	185

(Note that the capital figure is missing and needs to be deduced.)

Required:
(a) Prepare the balance sheet of the business as at 30 June 2000 from the above information using the vertical format.
(b) Discuss the significant features revealed by this financial statement.

2.5 The balance sheet of a business at the start of the week is as follows:

Assets	£	Claims	£
Freehold premises	145,000	Capital	203,000
Furniture and fittings	63,000	Bank overdraft	43,000
Stock-in-trade	28,000	Trade creditors	23,000
Trade debtors	33,000		
	£269,000		£269,000

During the week the following transactions take place:

- Sold stock for £11,000 cash. This stock had cost £8,000.
- Sold stock for £23,000 on credit. This stock had cost £17,000.
- Received cash from trade debtors totalling £18,000.
- The owners of the business introduced £100,000 of their own money, which was placed in the business bank account.
- The owners brought a motor van, valued at £10,000, into the business.
- Bought stock-in-trade on credit for £14,000.
- Paid trade creditors £13,000.

Required:
Show the balance sheet at the end of the week after all of these transactions have been reflected.

3

Measuring and reporting financial performance

INTRODUCTION

In this chapter the profit and loss account will be examined. We shall see how this statement is prepared and what insights it provides concerning financial performance. We shall also consider some of the key measurement problems to be faced when preparing this statement.

Objectives

Having completed this chapter you should be able to:

- discuss the nature and purpose of the profit and loss account

- prepare a profit and loss account from relevant financial information and interpret the results

- discuss the main measurement issues that must be considered when preparing the profit and loss account

- explain the main accounting conventions underpinning the profit and loss account.

The profit and loss account (income statement)

In the previous chapter, we examined the nature and purpose of the balance sheet. We saw that this statement was concerned with setting out the financial position of a business at a particular moment in time. However, it is not usually enough for users to have information relating only to the amount of wealth held by a business at one moment in time. Businesses exist for the primary purpose of generating wealth, or profit, and it is the profit generated *during a period* that is the main concern of many users. Although the amount of profit generated is of particular interest to the owners of a business, other groups such as managers, employees and suppliers will also have an interest in the profit-making ability of the business. The purpose of the profit and loss account – or income statement, as it is sometimes called – is to measure and report how much **profit** (wealth) the business has generated over a period.

The measurement of profit requires that the total revenues of the business, generated during a particular period, be calculated. **Revenue** is simply a measure of the inflow of assets (such as cash, or amounts owed to a business by debtors) or the reduction in liabilities that arise as a result of trading operations. Different forms of business enterprise will generate different forms of revenue. Some examples of the different forms that revenue can take are as follows:

- sales of goods (for example, of a manufacturer)
- fees for services (for example, of a solicitor)
- subscriptions (for example, of a club)
- interest received (for example, of an investment fund).

Activity 3.1

The following represent different forms of business enterprise:

1 Accountancy practice
2 Squash club
3 Bus company
4 Newspaper
5 Finance company
6 Songwriter
7 Retailer
8 Magazine publisher.

Can you identify the major source(s) of revenue for each type of business enterprise?

Your answer to this activity should be along the following lines:

Type of business	Main source(s) of revenue
1 Accountancy practice	Fees for services
2 Squash club	Subscriptions, court fees
3 Bus company	Ticket sales, advertising
4 Newspaper	Newspaper sales, advertising
5 Finance company	Interest received on loans
6 Songwriter	Royalties, commission fees
7 Retailer	Sale of goods
8 Magazine publisher	Magazine sales and advertising

As you can see, it is quite possible for a business to have more than one source of revenue.

The total expenses relating to the period must also be calculated. An **expense** represents the outflow of assets (or increase in liabilities) that is incurred as a result of generating revenues. The nature of the business will again determine the type of expenses that will be incurred. Examples of some of the more common types of expenses are:

- the cost of buying goods that are subsequently sold – known as *cost of sales* or *cost of goods sold*
- salaries and wages
- rent and rates
- motor vehicle running expenses
- insurances
- printing and stationery
- heat and light
- telephone and postage, and so on.

The profit and loss account for a period simply shows the total revenue generated during a particular period and deducts from this the total expenses incurred in generating that revenue. The difference between the total revenue and total expenses will represent either profit (if revenues exceed expenses) or loss (if expenses exceed revenues). Thus, we have:

Profit (loss) for the period = Total revenue for the period
less **Total expenses incurred**
in generating the revenue

Relationship between the profit and loss account and balance sheet

The profit and loss account and balance sheet should not be viewed in any way as substitutes for one another. Rather they should be seen as performing different functions. The balance sheet is, as stated earlier, a statement of the financial position of a business at a single moment in time – a 'snapshot' of the stock of wealth held by the business. The profit and loss account, on the other hand, is concerned with the *flow* of wealth over a period of time. The two statements are closely related. The profit and loss account can be viewed as linking the balance sheet at the beginning of the period with the balance sheet at the end of the period. Thus, at the commencement of business, a balance sheet will be produced to reveal the opening financial position. After an appropriate period, a profit and loss account will be prepared to show the wealth generated over the period. A balance sheet will also be prepared to reveal the new financial position at the end of the period covered by the profit and loss account. This balance sheet will incorporate the changes in wealth that have occurred since the previous balance sheet was drawn up.

We saw in the previous chapter that the effect of making a profit (loss) on the balance sheet means that the balance sheet equation can be extended as follows:

Assets = Capital +(−) Profit (Loss) + Liabilities

The amount of profit or loss for the period is shown separately in the balance sheet as an adjustment to capital.

The above equation can be extended to:

$$\text{Assets} = \text{Capital} + (\text{Revenues} - \text{Expenses}) + \text{Liabilities}$$

In theory, it would be possible to calculate profit and loss for the period by making all adjustments for revenues and expenses through the capital account. However, this would be rather cumbersome. A better solution is to have an 'appendix' to the capital account in the form of a profit and loss account. By deducting expenses from the revenues for the period, the profit and loss account derives the profit (loss) for adjustment in the capital account. This figure represents the net effect of operations for the period. Providing this 'appendix' means that a detailed and more informative view of performance is presented to users.

The format of the profit and loss account

The format of the profit and loss account will vary according to the type of business to which it relates. In order to illustrate a profit and loss account, let us consider the case of a retail business (that is, a business that purchases goods in their completed state and resells them). This type of business usually has straightforward operations, and as a result the profit and loss account is relatively easy to understand.

The following example sets out a typical format for the profit and loss account of a retail business:

Hi-Price Stores
Trading and profit and loss account for the year ended 31 October 2000

	£	£
Sales		232,000
Less Cost of sales		154,000
Gross profit		78,000
Add Interest received from investments		2,000
		80,000
Less Salaries and wages	24,500	
Rent and rates	14,200	
Heat and light	7,500	
Telephone and postage	1,200	
Insurance	1,000	
Motor vehicle running expenses	3,400	
Loan interest	1,100	
Depreciation – fixtures and fittings	1,000	
Depreciation – motor van	600	
		54,500
Net profit		25,500

* The first part of the statement is concerned with calculating the **gross profit** for the period. The trading revenue, which arises from selling the goods, is the first item that appears. Deducted from this item is the trading expense, which is the cost of acquiring the goods sold during the period. The difference between the trading revenue and trading expense is referred to as *gross profit*. This represents the profit from simply buying and selling goods without taking into account any other expenses or revenues associated with the business. This first part of the statement, which is concerned with the calculation of gross profit, is referred to as the *trading account* or *trading section*. The remainder of the statement is referred to as the *profit and loss account*. Hence the heading of

* **trading and profit and loss account** that is shown above. (You may often find, however, that the term *profit and loss account* is used to describe the whole of this statement.)

Having calculated the gross profit, any additional revenues of the business are then added to this figure. In the above example, interest from investments represents an additional revenue. From this subtotal of gross profit and additional revenues, the other expenses (overheads) that have to be incurred in order to operate the business (salaries and wages, rent and rates and so on) are

* deducted. The final figure derived is the **net profit** for the period. This net profit figure represents the wealth generated during the period that is attributable to the owner(s) of the business and which will be added to their capital in the balance sheet. As can be seen, net profit is a residual – that is, the amount left over after deducting all expenses incurred in generating the sales for the period.

The profit and loss account – some further aspects

Having set out the main principles involved in preparing a profit and loss account, we need to consider some further points.

Cost of sales

* Deducing the **cost of sales** figure, as shown above, can vary between businesses. In some businesses, the cost of sales is identified at the time a sale has been made. For example, the more sophisticated supermarkets tend to have point-of-sale (checkout) devices that not only record each sale but simultaneously pick up the cost of the particular sale. Businesses that sell a relatively small number of high-value items (for example, an engineering business that produces custom-made equipment) also tend to match each sale with the cost of the goods sold at the time of the sale. However, some businesses (for example, small retailers) do not usually find it practical to match each sale to a particular cost of sale figure as the accounting period progresses. They find it easier to deduce the cost of sales figure at the end of the accounting period.

To understand how this is done it is important to recognise that the cost of sales figure represents the cost of goods that were *sold* during the period, rather than the cost of goods *purchased* during the period. Part of the goods purchased during a period may remain in stock and not be sold until a later period. In order to derive the cost of sales for a period, it is necessary to know the amount of opening stocks and closing stocks for the period and the cost of goods purchased during the period.

The opening stocks for the period plus the goods purchased during the period will represent the total goods available for resale. The closing stocks will represent that portion of the total goods available for resale that remain unsold at the end of the period. Thus the cost of goods actually sold during the period must be the total goods available for resale *less* the stocks remaining at the end of the period. This calculation is sometimes shown on the face of the trading account as follows:

	£	£
Sales		232,000
Less Cost of sales		
Opening stock	40,000	
Plus Goods purchased	189,000	
	229,000	
Less Closing stock	75,000	154,000
Gross profit		78,000

The trading account above is simply an expanded version of the earlier trading account for Hi-Price Stores using additional information concerning stock balances and purchases for the year.

Classification of expenses

The classifications for the revenue and expense items, as with the classification of various assets and claims in the balance sheet, is often a matter of judgement by those who design the accounting system. In the profit and loss account above, for example, the insurance expense could have been included with telephone and postage under a single heading – say general expenses. Such decisions are normally based on how useful a particular classification will be to users. However, for businesses that trade as limited companies, there are statutory rules that dictate the classification of various items appearing in the accounts for external reporting purposes. These rules will be discussed in Chapter 4.

Activity 3.2

The following information relates to the activities of H & S Retailers for the year ended 30 April 2000:

	£
Motor vehicle running expenses	1,200
Rent received from subletting	2,000
Closing stock	3,000
Rent and rates payable	5,000

	£
Motor vans	6,300
Annual depreciation – motor vans	1,500
Heat and light	900
Telephone and postage	450
Sales	97,400
Goods purchased	68,350
Insurance	750
Loan interest payable	620
Balance at bank	4,780
Salaries and wages	10,400
Opening stock	4,000

Prepare a trading and profit and loss account for the year ended 30 April 2000.
(*Hint*: **Not all items shown above should appear on this statement.**)

Your answer to this activity should be as follows:

H & S Retailers
Trading and profit and loss account for the year ended 30 April 2000

	£	£
Sales		97,400
Less Cost of sales		
Opening stock	4,000	
Plus Purchases	68,350	
	72,350	
Less Closing stock	3,000	69,350
Gross profit		28,050
Rent received		2,000
		30,050
Less		
Salaries and wages	10,400	
Rent and rates	5,000	
Heat and light	900	
Telephone and postage	450	
Insurance	750	
Motor vehicle running expenses	1,200	
Loan interest	620	
Depreciation – motor van	1,500	
		20,820
Net profit		9,230

In the case of the balance sheet, we saw that the information could be presented in either a horizontal format or a vertical format. This is also true of the trading and profit and loss account. Where a horizontal format is used, expenses are listed on the left-hand side and revenues on the right-hand side, the difference being either net profit or net loss. The vertical format has been used above as it is easier to understand and is now almost always used.

The reporting period

We have seen already that for reporting to those outside the business, a financial reporting cycle of one year is the norm, although some large businesses will produce a half-yearly, or interim, financial statement to provide more frequent feedback on progress. However, for those who manage a business, it is important to have much more frequent feedback on performance. Thus it is quite common for profit and loss accounts to be prepared on a quarterly or monthly basis in order to show the progress made during the year.

Profit measurement and the recognition of revenue

A key issue in the measurement of profit concerns the point at which revenue is recognised. It is possible to recognise revenue at different points in the production/selling cycle, and the particular point chosen could have a significant effect on the total revenues reported for the period.

Activity 3.3

A manufacturing business sells goods on credit (that is, the customer is allowed to pay some time after the goods have been received). Below are four points in the production/selling cycle at which revenue might be recognised by the business:

1 when the goods are produced
2 when an order is received from a customer
3 when the goods are delivered to the customer, and accepted by them
4 when the cash is received from the customer.

A significant amount of time may elapse between these different points. At what point do you think the business should recognise revenue?

Although you may have come to a different conclusion, the point at which we normally recognise revenue is 3 above. The reasons for this are explained below.

The *realisation convention* in accounting is designed to solve the revenue recognition problem (or at least to provide some consistency). This convention states that revenue should be recognised only when it has been realised. Normally, realisation is considered to have occurred when:

- the activities necessary to generate the revenue (for example, delivery of goods, carrying out of repairs, etc.) are substantially complete
- the amount of revenue generated can be objectively determined
- there is reasonable certainty that the amounts owing from the activities will be received.

Activity 3.4

Look back at the various points in the production/selling cycle at which revenue might be recognised as set out in the previous activity. At which of these points do you think the criteria for realisation will be fulfilled for the manufacturing business?

The criteria will probably be fulfilled when the goods are passed to the customers and are accepted by them. As we mentioned earlier, this is the normal point of recognition when goods are sold on credit. It is also the point at which there is a legally enforceable contract between the parties.

❋ The **realisation convention** in accounting means that a sale on credit is usually recognised *before* the cash is ultimately received. Thus the total sales figure shown in the profit and loss account may include sales transactions for which the cash has yet to be received. The total sales figure in the profit and loss account will therefore be different from the total cash received from sales.

Not all businesses will wait to recognise revenue until *all* of the work necessary to generate the revenue is complete. A construction business, for example, that is engaged in a long-term project such as building a dam, will not usually wait until the contract is complete. Were it to wait, this could mean that no revenue would be recognised by the business until several years after the work first commenced. Instead, the business will normally recognise a proportion of the total value of the contract when an agreed stage of the contract has been completed. This approach to revenue recognition is really a more practical interpretation of the realisation convention, rather than a deviation from it.

Profit measurement and the recognition of expenses

Having decided on the point at which revenue is recognised, we must now turn
❋ to the issue of the recognition of expenses. The **matching convention** in accounting is designed to provide guidance concerning the recognition of expenses. This convention states that expenses should be matched to the revenues that they helped to generate. In other words, expenses must be taken into account in the same profit and loss account in which the associated sale is recognised. Applying this convention may mean that a particular expense reported in the profit and loss account for a period may not be the same figure as the cash paid in respect of that item during the period. The expense reported may be either more or less than the cash paid during the period. Let us consider two examples that illustrate this point.

When the expense for the period is more than the cash paid during the period

Suppose that sales staff are paid a commission of 2 per cent of sales generated, and that total sales during the period amounted to £300,000. This will mean that the commission to be paid in respect of the sales for the period will be £6,000. Let us say, however, that by the end of the period the sales commission paid to staff was £5,000. If the business took no action on this and reported only the amount paid, it would mean that the profit and loss account would not reflect the full expense for the year. This would contravene the *matching convention* because not all of the expenses associated with the revenues of the period would have been matched in the profit and loss account. This will be remedied as follows:

- Sales commission expense in the profit and loss account will include the amount paid *plus* the amount outstanding (that is, £6,000 = £5,000 + £1,000).
- The amount outstanding (£1,000) represents an outstanding liability at the balance sheet date and will be included under the heading 'accruals' or **accrued expenses** in the balance sheet. As this item will have to be paid within 12 months of the balance sheet date, it will be treated as a current liability.

Ideally, all expenses should be matched to the period in which the sales to which they relate are reported. However, it is often difficult to match closely certain expenses to sales in the same way that we have matched sales commission to sales. It is unlikely, for example, that electricity charges incurred can be linked directly to particular sales in this way. As a result, the electricity charges incurred will normally be matched to the *period* to which they relate.

Suppose a business has reached the end of its accounting year and has only been charged electricity for the first three quarters of the year (amounting to £1,900), simply because the electricity company has yet to send out bills for the quarter that ends on the same date as the business's year end. In this situation, an estimate should be made of the electricity expense outstanding (that is, the bill for the last three months of the year is estimated). This figure (let us say the estimate is £500) is dealt with as follows:

- Electricity expense in the profit and loss account will include the amount paid, plus the amount of the estimate (that is, £1,900 + £500 = £2,400) in order to cover the whole year.
- The amount of the estimate (£500) represents an outstanding liability at the balance sheet date, and will be included under the heading 'accruals' or 'accrued expenses' in the balance sheet. As this item will have to be paid within 12 months of the balance sheet date, it will be treated as a current liability.

The above treatment will have the desired effect of increasing the electricity expense to the 'correct' figure for the year in the profit and loss account, presuming that the estimate is reasonably accurate. It will also have the effect of showing that, at the end of the accounting year, the business owed the amount of the last quarter's electricity bill. Dealing with the outstanding amount in this way reflects the dual aspect of the item, and will ensure that the balance sheet equation is maintained.

Let us say the estimate for outstanding electricity was correct. How will the payment of the electricity bill be dealt with?

When the electricity bill is eventually paid, it will be dealt with as follows:

- Reduce cash by the amount of the bill.
- Reduce the amount of the accrued expense as shown on the balance sheet.

If there is a slight error in the estimate, a small adjustment (either negative or positive depending on the direction of the error) can be made to the following year's expense. Dealing with the estimation error in this way is not strictly correct, but the amount is likely to be insignificant.

Activity 3.6

Can you think of other expenses, apart from electricity charges, that cannot be linked directly to sales and for which matching will therefore be done on a time basis?

You may have thought of the following examples:

- rent and rates
- insurance
- interest payments
- licences.

This is not an exhaustive list. You may have thought of others.

When the amount paid during the year is more than the full expense for the period

Suppose a business pays rent for its premises quarterly in advance (on 1 January, 1 March, 1 June and 1 September) and that, on the last day of the accounting year (31 December), it pays the next quarter's rent to the following 31 March (£400), which is a day earlier than required. This would mean that a total of five quarters' rent was paid during the year. If the business reports the cash paid in the profit and loss account, this would be more than the full expense for the year. This treatment would also contravene the matching convention because a higher figure than the expenses associated with the revenues of the year appears in the profit and loss account.

The problem is overcome by dealing with the rental payment as follows:

- Reduce cash to reflect the full amount of the rent paid during the year (that is, 5 × £400 = £2,000).
- Show the rent for four quarters as the appropriate expense in the profit and loss account (that is, 4 × £400 = £1,600).

✱ • Show the quarter's rent paid in advance (£400) as a **prepaid expense** on the asset side of the balance sheet.

The prepaid expense will appear as a current asset in the balance sheet, under the heading 'prepayments'.

In the next period, this prepayment will cease to be an asset and become an expense in the profit and loss account of that period. This is because the rent prepaid relates to that period and will be 'used up' during that period.

In practice, the treatment of accruals and prepayments will be subject to the
✱ **materiality convention** in accounting. This convention states that, where the amounts involved are immaterial, we should consider only what is expedient. This may mean that an item will be treated as an expense in the period in which it is paid, rather than being strictly matched to the revenues to which it relates. For example, a business may find that, at the end of an accounting period, there is a bill of £5 owing for stationery used during the year. The time and effort involved in recording this as an accrual would have little effect on the measurement of profit or financial position for a business of any size, and so it would be ignored when preparing the profit and loss account for the period. The bill would, presumably, be paid in the following period and therefore be treated as an expense of that period.

Profit and cash

The foregoing sections on revenues and expenses reveal that revenues do not usually represent cash received, and expenses are not the same as cash paid. As a result, the net profit figure (that is, total revenue minus total expenses) will not normally represent the net cash generated during a period. It is therefore important to distinguish between profit and liquidity. Profit is a measure of achievement, or productive effort, rather than a measure of cash generated. Although making a profit will increase wealth, we have already seen in the previous chapter that cash is only one form in which that wealth may be held.

Profit measurement and the calculation of depreciation

✱ The expense of **depreciation**, which appeared in the profit and loss account above, requires further explanation. Fixed assets (with the exception of freehold land) do not have a perpetual existence. They are eventually used up in the process of generating revenues for the business. In essence, depreciation is an attempt to measure that portion of the cost of a fixed asset that has been used up in generating the revenues recognised during a particular period. The depreciation charge is considered to be an expense of the period to which it relates.

To calculate a depreciation charge for a period, four factors have to be considered:

- the cost of the asset
- the useful life of the asset
- the residual value of the asset
- the depreciation method.

The cost of the asset

This will include all costs incurred by the business to bring the asset to its required location and to make it ready for use. Thus, in addition to the costs of acquiring the asset, any delivery costs, installation costs (for example, plant) and legal costs incurred in the transfer of legal title (for example, freehold property) will be included as part of the total cost of the asset. Similarly, any costs incurred in improving or altering an asset in order to make it suitable for its intended use within the business will also be included as part of the total cost.

Activity 3.7

Andrew Wu (Engineering) Ltd purchased a new motor car for its marketing director. The invoice received from the motor car supplier revealed the following:

	£	£
New BMW 325i		26,350
Delivery charge	80	
Alloy wheels	660	
Sun roof	200	
Petrol	30	
Number plates	130	
Road fund licence	155	1,255
		27,605
Part exchange – Reliant Robin		1,000
Amount outstanding		26,605

What is the total cost of the new car?

The cost of the new car will be as follows:

	£	£
New BMW 325i		26,350
Delivery charge	80	
Alloy wheels	660	
Sun roof	200	
Number plates	130	1,070
		27,420

These costs include delivery costs and number plates as they are a necessary and integral part of the asset. Improvements (alloy wheels and sun roof) are also regarded as part of the total cost of the motor car. The petrol costs and road fund licence, however, represent a cost of operating the asset rather than a part of the total cost of acquiring the asset and making it ready for use: hence these amounts will be charged as an expense in the period incurred (although part of the cost of the licence may be regarded as a prepaid expense in the period incurred).

The part exchange figure shown is part payment of the total amount outstanding, and is not relevant to a consideration of the total cost.

The useful life of the asset

An asset has both a *physical life* and an *economic life*. The physical life of an asset will be exhausted through the effects of wear and tear and/or the passage of time. It is possible, however, for the physical life to be extended considerably through careful maintenance, improvements, and so on. The economic life of an asset is determined by the effects of technological progress and changes in demand. After a while, the benefits of using the asset may be less than the costs involved. This may be because the asset is unable to compete with newer assets, or because it is no longer relevant to the needs of the business. The economic life of an asset may be much shorter than its physical life. For example, a computer may have a physical life of eight years and an economic life of three years. It is the economic life of an asset that will determine the expected useful life for the purpose of calculating depreciation. Forecasting the economic life of an asset, however, may be extremely difficult in practice. Both the rate at which technology progresses and shifts in consumer tastes can be swift and unpredictable.

Residual value (disposal value)

✴ When a business disposes of a fixed asset that may still be of value to others, some payment may be received. This payment will represent the **residual value**, or *disposal value*, of the asset. To calculate the total amount to be depreciated with regard to an asset, the residual value must be deducted from the cost of the asset. The likely amount to be received on disposal is, once again, often difficult to predict.

Depreciation method

Once the amount to be depreciated (that is, the cost of the asset less the residual value) has been estimated, the business must select a method of allocating this depreciable amount over the useful life of the fixed asset. Although there are various ways in which the total depreciation may be allocated and a depreciation charge for a period derived, there are really only two methods that are commonly used in practice.

✴ The first of these is known as the **straight-line method**. This method simply allocates the amount to be depreciated evenly over the useful life of the asset. In other words, an equal amount of depreciation will be charged for each year the asset is held.

Example 3.1

To illustrate this method, consider the following information:

Cost of machine	£40,000
Estimated residual value at the end of its useful life	£1,024
Estimated useful life	4 years

To calculate the depreciation charge for each year, the total amount to be depreciated must be calculated. This will be the total cost *less* the estimated residual value: that is, £40,000 – £1,024 = £38,976. Having done this, the annual depreciation charge can be derived by dividing the amount to be depreciated by the estimated useful life of the asset of four years. The calculation is therefore:

$$\frac{£38,976}{4} = £9,744$$

Thus the annual depreciation charge that appears in the profit and loss account in relation to this asset will be £9,744 for each of the four years of the asset's life.

The amount of depreciation relating to the asset will be accumulated for as long as it is held. This accumulated amount will be deducted from the cost of the asset on the balance sheet. Thus, for example, at the end of the second year the accumulated depreciation will be £9,744 × 2 = £19,488, and the asset details will appear on the balance sheet as follows:

	£	£
Machine at cost	40,000	
Less Accumulated depreciation	19,488	
		20,512

The balance of £20,512 shown above is referred to as the *written-down value* or *net book value* of the asset. It represents that portion of the cost of the asset that has still to be written off. This figure does *not* represent the current market value, which may be quite different.

The straight-line method derives its name from the fact that the written-down value of the asset at the end of each year, when graphed against time, will result in a straight line, as shown in Figure 3.1.

＊ The second approach to calculating depreciation for a period is referred to as the **reducing balance method**. This method applies a fixed percentage rate of depreciation to the written-down value of an asset each year. The effect of this will be high annual depreciation charges in the early years and lower charges in the later years. To illustrate this method let us take the same information used in our earlier example. Let us, however, use a fixed percentage (60 per cent) of the written-down value to determine the annual depreciation charge.

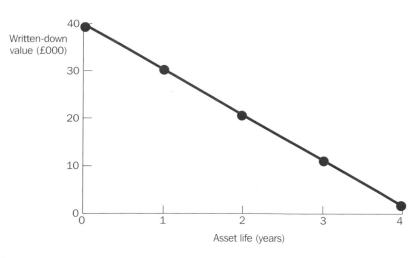

The figure shows that the written-down value of the asset declines by a constant amount each year. This is because the straight-line method provides a constant depreciation charge each year. The result, when plotted on a graph, is a straight line.

Figure 3.1 Graph of written-down value against time using the straight-line method

The calculations will be as follows:

	£
Cost of machine	40,000
Year 1 Depreciation charge (60%* of cost)	24,000
Written-down value (WDV)	16,000
Year 2 Depreciation charge (60% WDV)	9,600
Written-down value	6,400
Year 3 Depreciation charge (60% WDV)	3,840
Written-down value	2,560
Year 4 Depreciation charge (60% WDV)	1,536
Residual value	1,024

*Deriving the fixed percentage to be applied requires the use of the following formula:

$$P = (1 - \sqrt[n]{R/C}) \times 100\%$$

where: P = the depreciation percentage;
  n = the useful life of the assets (in years);
  R = the residual value of the asset;
  C = the cost of the asset.

The fixed percentage rate will, however, be given in all examples used in this text.

We can see that the pattern of depreciation is quite different for the two methods. If we plot the written-down value of the asset, which has been derived using the reducing balance method, against time, the result will be as shown in Figure 3.2.

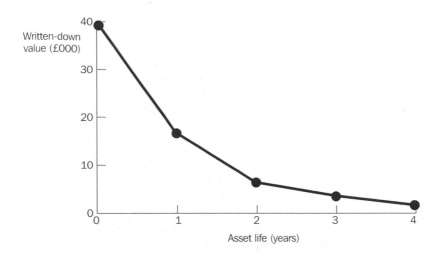

The figure shows that, under the reducing balance method, the written-down value of an asset falls by a larger amount in the earlier years than in the later years. This is because the depreciation charge is based on a fixed-rate percentage of the written-down value.

Figure 3.2 Graph of written-down value against time using the reducing balance method

Activity 3.8

Assume that the machine used in the example above was owned by a business that made a profit *before* depreciation of £20,000 for each of the four years in which the asset was held.

Calculate the net profit for the business for each year under each depreciation method, and comment on your findings.

Your answer should be as follows:

Straight-line method

	(a) Profit before depreciation £	(b) Depreciation £	(a−b) Net profit £
Year 1	20,000	9,744	10,256
Year 2	20,000	9,744	10,256
Year 3	20,000	9,744	10,256
Year 4	20,000	9,744	10,256

Reducing balance method

	(a) Profit before depreciation	(b) Depreciation	(a−b) Net profit/ (loss)
	£	£	£
Year 1	20,000	24,000	(4,000)
Year 2	20,000	9,600	10,400
Year 3	20,000	3,840	16,160
Year 4	20,000	1,536	18,464

The above calculations reveal that the straight-line method of depreciation results in a constant net profit figure over the four-year period. This is because both the profit before depreciation and the depreciation charge are constant over the period. The reducing balance method, however, results in a changing profit figure over time. In the first year a net loss is reported, and thereafter a rising net profit is reported.

Although the *pattern* of net profit over the period will be quite different, depending on the depreciation method used, the *total* net profit for the period will remain the same. This is because both methods of depreciating will allocate the same amount of total depreciation over the four-year period. It is only the amount allocated *between years* that will differ.

In practice, the use of different depreciation methods may not have such a dramatic effect on profits as suggested in the activity above. Where a business replaces some of its assets each year, the total depreciation charge calculated under the reducing balance method will reflect a range of charges (from high through to low), as assets will be at different points in the replacement cycle. This could mean that the total depreciation charge may not be significantly different from the total depreciation charge that would be derived under the straight-line method.

Selecting a depreciation method

How does a business choose which depreciation method to use for a particular asset? The most appropriate method should be the one that best matches the depreciation expense to the revenues that it helped generate. The business may therefore decide to undertake an examination of the pattern of benefits flowing from the asset. Where the benefits are likely to remain fairly constant over time (buildings, for example), the straight-line method may be considered appropriate. Where assets lose their efficiency over time and the benefits decline as a result (for example, certain types of machinery), the reducing balance method may be considered more appropriate. However, other approaches to selecting a depreciation method are also used in practice.

The accountancy profession has developed an accounting standard to deal with the problem of depreciation. As we shall see in Chapter 4, the purpose of accounting standards is to narrow the areas of difference in accounting between businesses by producing statements on best accounting practice. Unfortunately, the standard provides no clear statement on the suitability of the various methods of depreciation available. It simply states that management should select the depreciation method that is most appropriate to a particular asset and its use in the business. The standard does, however, require that limited companies disclose, in their financial statements, the methods of depreciation employed and either the depreciation rates applied or the useful lives of the assets.

Exhibit 3.1

An example of the type of disclosure required concerning depreciation policies is provided below. This is an extract from the 1999 published accounts of National Power, a power-generating company:

Tangible fixed assets

Depreciation is calculated so as to write down the cost of tangible fixed assets to their residual value evenly over their estimated useful lives. Estimated useful lives are reviewed periodically, taking into account commercial and technological obsolescence as well as normal wear and tear, provision being made for any permanent diminution in value

The depreciation charge is based on the following estimates of useful lives:

	Years
Power stations under operating leases (primary lease term)	7
Combined cycle gas turbine power stations	20
Other power stations	20–40
Non-operational buildings	40
Fixtures, fittings, tools and equipment	4–5
Computer equipment and software	3–4
Hot gas path CCGT turbine blades	4

Freehold land is not depreciated

In the case of certain intangible fixed assets such as research and development expenditure, determining the correct period over which the benefits extend may be extremely difficult. In practice, there are different approaches to dealing with this problem. Some businesses adopt a prudent view and write off such assets immediately, whereas others may write off the assets over time.

Depreciation and the replacement of fixed assets

A view often heard is that the purpose of depreciation is to provide for the replacement of an asset when it reaches the end of its useful life. However, this is *not* the purpose of depreciation as conventionally defined. It was mentioned earlier that depreciation represents an attempt to allocate the cost (less any residual value) of an asset over its expected useful life. The resulting depreciation charge in each period represents an expense, which is then used in the calculation of net profit for the period. Calculating the depreciation charge for a period is therefore necessary for the proper measurement of

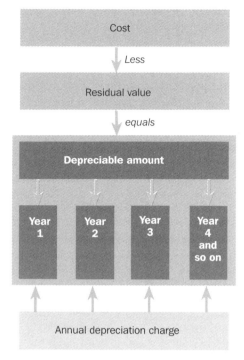

The figure shows how an annual depreciation charge is derived. The cost of an asset less the residual value will represent the amount to be depreciated. This amount is depreciated over the useful life of the asset using an appropriate depreciation method.

Figure 3.3 Calculating an annual depreciation charge

financial performance, and must be done whether or not the business intends to replace the asset in the future.

If there is an intention to replace the asset, the depreciation charge in the profit and loss account will not ensure that liquid funds are set aside by the business specifically for this purpose. Although the effect of a depreciation charge is to reduce net profit, and therefore to reduce the amount available for distribution to owners, the amounts retained within the business as a result may be invested in ways that are unrelated to the replacement of the specific assets.

Activity 3.9

Suppose that a business sets aside liquid funds, equivalent to the depreciation charge each year, with the intention of using this to replace the asset at the end of its useful life. Will this ensure that there will be sufficient funds available for this purpose?

No. Even if funds are set aside each year that are equal to the depreciation charge for the year, the total amount accumulated at the end of the asset's useful life may be insufficient for replacement purposes. This may be because inflation or technological advances have resulted in an increase in the replacement cost.

Depreciation and judgement

When reading the above sections on depreciation it may have struck you that accounting is not so precise and objective as is sometimes suggested. There are areas where subjective judgement is required, and depreciation provides a good illustration of this.

Activity 3.10

What kind of judgements must be made to calculate a depreciation charge for a period?

In answering this activity, you may have thought of the following:

- the cost of the asset (for example, deciding whether to include interest charges or not)
- the expected residual or disposal value of the asset
- the expected useful life of the asset
- the choice of depreciation method.

Making different judgements on these matters would result in a different pattern of depreciation charges over the life of the asset, and therefore in a different pattern of reported profits. However, under- or overestimations that are made in relation to the above will be adjusted for in the final year of an asset's life, and so the total depreciation charge (and total profit) over the asset's life will not be affected by estimation errors.

Profit measurement and the valuation of stocks

The way in which we measure the value of stock is important, as the amount of stock sold during a period will affect the calculation of net profit, and the remaining stock held at the end of the period will affect the portrayal of financial position. In the last chapter, we saw that historic cost is the basis for valuing assets, and so you may think that stock valuation should not be a difficult issue. However, in a period of *changing prices*, the valuation of stock can be a problem.

Consider the example of a business that supplies coal to factories and which has the following transactions during a period:

		Tonnes	Cost per tonne
May 1	Opening stock	1,000	£10
2	Purchased	5,000	£11
3	Purchased	8,000	£12
		14,000	
6	Sold	9,000	
	Closing stock	5,000	

The business must determine the cost of the stock sold during the period and the cost of the stock remaining at the end of the period. However, it may be difficult to match precisely particular purchases with sales. When stocks are acquired, they may enter a common pool and become indistinguishable from earlier stocks purchased. In which case, how do we know which stocks were sold and which remain?

Where it is difficult to trace particular stock movements, or where the costs in doing so outweigh the benefits, the solution is often to make an assumption concerning the physical flow of stocks through the business. This will enable the business to identify which stocks have been sold and which are still being held. The two most common assumptions used are:

* • **First in, first out (FIFO):** that is, the earliest stocks held are the first to be sold.
* • **Last in, first out (LIFO):** that is, the latest stocks held are the first to be sold.

These assumptions need not correspond to the *actual* flow of stocks through the business. They simply provide a useful and convenient way of deriving cost figures.

A further approach to deriving the cost of stocks is to assume that stocks entering the business lose their separate identity, and any issues of stock reflect the average cost of the stocks that are held. **Weighted average cost (AVCO)** is based on this idea. The weights used in deriving the average cost figure are the quantities of each batch of stock purchased.

Let us now use the information contained in the above example to calculate the cost of goods sold and closing stock figures for the business.

First in, first out

Using this approach, the first 9,000 tonnes purchased are assumed to be those that are sold. The remainder will comprise the closing stock and are assumed to be the later purchases. Thus we have:

		Cost of sales			Closing stock		
		No. of tonnes	Cost per tonne	Total	No. of tonnes	Cost per tonne	Total
			£	£		£	£
May	1	1,000	10	10,000			
	2	5,000	11	55,000			
	3	3,000	12	36,000	5,000	12	60,000
	Cost of sales			101,000	Closing stock		60,000

Last in, first out

Using this approach, the later purchases will be the first to be sold and the earlier purchases will comprise the closing stock. Thus we have:

	Cost of sales			Closing stock		
	No. of tonnes	Cost per tonne	Total	No. of tonnes	Cost per tonne	Total
		£	£		£	£
May 3	8,000	12	96,000			
2	1,000	11	11,000	4,000	11	44,000
1				1,000	10	10,000
	Cost of sales		107,000	Closing stock		54,000

Weighted average cost (AVCO)

Using this approach, a weighted average cost will be determined, which will be used to derive both the cost of goods sold and the cost of the remaining stocks held. Thus we have:

	Purchases		
	No. of tonnes	Cost per tonne	Total
		£	£
May 1	1,000	10	10,000
2	5,000	11	55,000
3	8,000	12	96,000
	14,000		161,000

Average cost = £161,000/14,000
= £11.5

	Cost of sales			Closing stock		
	No. of tonnes	Cost per tonne	Total	No. of tonnes	Cost per tonne	Total
		£	£		£	£
	9,000	11.5	103,500	5,000	11.5	57,500

Activity 3.11

Suppose the 9,000 tonnes of stock were sold for £15 per tonne.

(a) Calculate the gross profit for the period under each of the three methods.
(b) What observations concerning the portrayal of financial position and performance can you make about each method when prices are rising?

Your answer should be along the following lines:

Gross profit calculation

	FIFO	LIFO	AVCO
	£000	£000	£000
Sales (9,000 @ £15)	135.0	135.0	135.0
Cost of sales (see above)	101.0	107.0	103.5
Gross profit	34.0	28.0	31.5
	£000	£000	£000
Closing stock figure	60.0	54.0	57.5

The above figures reveal that FIFO will give the highest gross profit during a period of rising prices. This is because sales are matched with the earlier (and cheaper) purchases. LIFO will give the lowest gross profit as sales are matched against the more recent (and dearer) purchases. The AVCO method will normally give a figure that is between these two extremes.

The closing stock figure in the balance sheet will be highest with the FIFO method. This is because the cost of goods still held will be based on the more recent (and dearer) purchases. LIFO will give the lowest closing stock figure as the goods held in stock will be based on the earlier (and cheaper) stocks purchased. Once again, the AVCO method will normally give a figure that is between these two extremes.

Activity 3.12

Assume that prices are falling rather than rising. How would your observations concerning the portrayal of financial performance and position be different for the various stock valuation methods?

When prices are falling, the position of FIFO and LIFO is reversed. FIFO will give the lowest gross profit as sales are matched against the earlier (and dearer) goods purchased. LIFO will give the highest gross profit as sales are matched against the more recent (and cheaper) goods purchased. AVCO will give a cost of sales figure between these two extremes. The closing stock figure in the balance sheet will be lowest under FIFO as the cost of stock will be based on the more recent (and cheaper) stocks purchased. LIFO will provide the highest closing stock figure, and AVCO will provide a figure between the two extremes.

It is important to recognise that the different stock valuation methods will only have an effect on the reported profit *between years*. The figure derived for closing stock will be carried forward and matched with sales in a later period. Thus, if the cheaper purchases of stocks are matched to sales in the current period, it will mean that the dearer purchases will be matched to sales in a later period. Over the life of the business, therefore, the total profit will be the same whichever valuation method has been used.

Stock valuation – some further issues

We saw in the previous chapter that the closing stock figure will appear as part of the current assets of the business, and that the convention of prudence requires that current assets be valued at the lower of cost and net realisable value. (The net realisable value of stocks is the estimated selling price less any further costs that may be necessary to complete the goods and any costs involved in selling and distributing the goods.) This rule may mean that the valuation method applied to stocks will switch each year depending on whether cost or net realisable value is the lower. In practice, however, the cost of the stocks held is usually below the current net realisable value – particularly during a period of rising prices. It is, therefore, the cost figure that will normally appear in the balance sheet.

Activity 3.13

Can you think of any circumstances where the net realisable value will be lower than the cost of stocks held, even during a period of generally rising prices?

The net realisable value may be lower where:

- goods have deteriorated or have become obsolete
- there has been a fall in the market price of the goods
- the goods are being used as a 'loss leader'
- bad purchasing decisions have been made.

The accountancy profession has produced an accounting standard to deal with the issue of stock valuation. This standard supports the lower of cost and net realisable value rule and states that, when comparing the cost with the net realisable value, each item of stock should be compared separately. If this is not practical, categories of similar stock should be grouped together. The standard also identifies a number of methods of arriving at the cost of stocks that are acceptable. Although FIFO and AVCO are regarded as acceptable, the LIFO approach is not. The LIFO approach is also unacceptable to the Inland Revenue for taxation purposes. As a result, LIFO is rarely used in the United Kingdom, although it is in widespread use in the United States.

Stock valuation and depreciation provide two examples where the **consistency convention** must be applied. This convention holds that when a particular method of accounting is selected to deal with a transaction, this method should be applied consistently over time. Thus it would not be acceptable to switch from, say, FIFO to AVCO between periods (unless there are exceptional circumstances that make this appropriate). The purpose of this convention is to try to ensure that users are able to make valid comparisons between periods.

Activity 3.14

Stock valuation provides a further example where subjective judgement is required to derive the figures for inclusion in the financial statements. Can you identify the main areas where judgement is required?

The main areas are:

- the choice of cost method (FIFO, LIFO, AVCO)
- deciding which items should be included in the cost of stocks (particularly for work-in-progress and the finished goods of a manufacturing business)
- deriving the net realisable value figure for stocks held.

Profit measurement and the problem of bad and doubtful debts

Most businesses sell goods on credit. When credit sales are made, the revenue is usually recognised as soon as the goods are passed to, and accepted by, the customer. Recording the dual aspect of a credit sale will involve:

- increasing the sales; and
- increasing debtors

by the amount of the credit sale.

However, with this type of sale, there is always the risk that the customer will not pay the amount due. Where it is reasonably certain that the customer will not eventually pay, the debt is considered to be 'bad', and this must be taken into account when preparing the financial statements.

Activity 3.15

What would be the effect of not taking into account the fact that a debt is bad, when preparing the financial statements, on the portrayal of financial performance and position?

The effect would be to overstate the assets (debtors) on the balance sheet and to overstate profit in the profit and loss account, as the sale (which has been recognised) will not result in any future benefits arising.

To provide a more realistic picture of financial performance and position, * the **bad debt** must be 'written off'. This will involve:

- reducing the debtors; and
- increasing expenses (by creating an expense known as 'bad debts written off') by the amount of the bad debt. The matching convention requires that the bad debt is written off in the same period as that in which the sale that gave rise to the debt is recognised.

Note that, when a debt is bad, the accounting response is not simply to cancel the original sale. If we did this, the profit and loss account would not be so informative. Reporting the bad debts as an expense can be extremely useful in the evaluation of management performance.

At the end of the accounting period, it may not be possible to identify, with reasonable certainty, all the bad debts that have been incurred during the period. It may be that some debts appear doubtful, but only at some later point in time will the true position become clear. The uncertainty that exists does not mean that, when preparing the financial statements, we should ignore the possibility that some of the debtors outstanding will eventually prove to be bad. It would not be prudent to do so, nor would it comply with the need to match expenses to the period in which the associated sale is recognised. As a result, the business will normally try to identify all those debts that, at the end of the period, can be classified as 'doubtful' (that is, there is a possibility that they may eventually prove to be bad). This can be done by examining individual accounts of debtors or by taking a proportion of the total debtors outstanding based on past experience. Once a figure has been derived, a

✳ **provision for doubtful debts** can be created. This provision will be:

- shown as an expense in the profit and loss account; and
- deducted from the total debtors figure in the balance sheet.

By doing this, we take full account, in the appropriate accounting period, of those debtors where there is a risk of non-payment. This accounting treatment of doubtful debts will be in addition to the treatment of bad debts described earlier.

The following example illustrates the reporting of bad and doubtful debts.

Example 3.2

Desai Enterprises has debtors of £350,000 at the end of the accounting year to 30 June 2000. Investigation of these debtors reveals that £10,000 are likely to prove irrecoverable and that a further £30,000 are doubtful.

Extracts from the profit and loss account are shown below.

Profit and loss account (extracts) for the year ended 30 June 2000

	£
Bad debts written off	10,000
Provision for doubtful debts	30,000

Balance sheet (extracts) as at 30 June 2000

	£
Debtors	340,000*
Less Provision for doubtful debts	30,000
	310,000

(* that is, £350,000 − £10,000)

The provision for doubtful debts is of course an estimate, and it is quite likely that the actual amount of debts that ultimately prove to be bad will be different from the estimate. Let us say that, during the next accounting period, it was discovered that £26,000 of the debts that were considered to be doubtful proved to be irrecoverable. These debts must now be written off as follows:

- Reduce debtors by £26,000.
- Reduce provision for doubtful debts by £26,000.

However, a provision for doubtful debts of £4,000 will still remain. This amount represents an overestimate made when creating the provision in the profit and loss account for the year to 30 June 2000. As the provision is no longer needed, it should be eliminated. Remember that the provision was created by charging an expense in the profit and loss account for the year to 30 June 2000. As the expense was too high, the amount of the overestimate should be 'written back' in the next accounting period. In other words, it will be treated as revenue for the year to 30 June 2001. This will mean:

- reducing the provision for doubtful debts by £4,000
- increasing revenues by £4,000.

Ideally, of course, the amount should be written back to the profit and loss account for the year ended 30 June 2000. However, it is too late to do this.

Activity 3.16

Clayton Conglomerates had debts outstanding at the end of the accounting year to 31 March 2001 of £870,000. The chief accountant believed that £40,000 of those debts were irrecoverable and that a further £60,000 were doubtful. In the subsequent period, it was found that an overestimate had been made of the extent of the doubtful debts and that only £45,000 of the doubtful debts actually proved to be bad.

Show the relevant extracts in the profit and loss account for both 2001 and 2002 to report the bad debts written off and provision for doubtful debts. Also show the relevant balance sheet extract as at 30 June 2001.

Your answer should be as follows:

Profit and loss account (extracts) for the year ended 31 March 2001

	£
Bad debts written off	40,000
Provision for doubtful debts	60,000

Profit and loss account (extracts) for the year ended 31 March 2002

	£
Provision for doubtful debts written back (revenue)	15,000*

*This figure will usually be netted off against any provision created for doubtful debts in respect of 2002.

Balance sheet (extracts) as at 31 March 2001

	£
Debtors	830,000
Less Provision for doubtful debts	60,000
	770,000

Activity 3.17

Bad and doubtful debts represent further areas where judgement is required in deriving expenses figures for a particular period. What will be the effect of different judgements concerning the amount of bad and doubtful debts on the profit for a particular period and on the total profit reported over the life of the business?

Judgement is often required in order to derive a figure for bad debts incurred during a period. There may be situations where views will differ concerning whether or not a debt is irrecoverable. The decision concerning whether or not to write off a bad debt will have an effect on the expenses for the period, and hence on the reported profit. However, over the life of the business, the total reported profit will not be affected as incorrect judgements in one period will be adjusted for in a later period. Suppose, for example, that a debt of £100 was written off in a period, and that, in a later period, the amount owing was actually received. The increase in expenses of £100 in the period in which the bad debt was written off would be compensated for by an increase in revenues of £100 when the amount outstanding was finally received (bad debt recoverable). If, on the other hand, the amount owing of £100 was never written off in the first place, the profit for the two periods would not be affected by the bad debt adjustment, and would therefore be different, but the total profit for the two periods would be the same.

The same situation would apply where there are differences in judgements concerning doubtful debts.

Let us now try to bring together some of the points that we have raised in this chapter through a self-assessment question.

Self-assessment question 3.1

TT Limited is a new business that started trading on 1 January 2000. The following is a summary of transactions that occurred during the first year of trading:

1 The owners introduced £50,000 of capital, which was paid into a bank account opened in the name of the business.
2 Premises were rented from 1 January 2000 at an annual rental of £20,000. During the year, rent of £25,000 was paid to the owner of the premises.

3 Rates on the premises were paid during the year as follows:
   For the period 1 January 2000 to 31 March 2000   £500
   For the period 1 April 2000 to 31 March 2001   £1,200
4 A delivery van was bought on 1 January for £12,000. This is expected to be used in the business for four years and then to be sold for £2,000.
5 Wages totalling £33,500 were paid during the year. At the end of the year, the business owed £630 of wages for the last week of the year.
6 Electricity bills for the first three quarters of the year were paid totalling £1,650. After 31 December 2000, but before the accounts had been finalised for the year, the bill for the last quarter arrived showing a charge of £620.
7 Stock-in-trade totalling £143,000 was bought on credit.
8 Stock-in-trade totalling £12,000 was bought for cash.
9 Sales on credit totalled £152,000 (cost £74,000).
10 Cash sales totalled £35,000 (cost £16,000).
11 Receipts from trade debtors totalled £132,000.
12 Payments to trade creditors totalled £121,000.
13 Van running expenses paid totalled £9,400.

At the end of the year it was clear that a trade debtor who owed £400 would not be able to pay any part of the debt. The business uses the straight-line method for depreciating fixed assets.

Required:
Prepare a balance sheet as at 31 December 2000 and a profit and loss account for the year to that date. (Use the outline financial statements produced below to help you.)

TT Limited
Balance sheet as at 31 December 2000

	£	£	£
Fixed assets			
Motor van			
Current assets			
Stock-in-trade			
Trade debtors			
Prepaid expenses			
Cash			
	___		
Less *Current liabilities*			
Trade creditors			
Accrued expenses			
	___	___	___
Capital			
Original			▬
Add Retained profit			
			▬

Profit and loss account for the year ended 31 December 2000

	£	£
Sales		
Less Cost of sales		___
Gross profit		
Less Rent		
Rates		
Wages		
Electricity		
Bad debts		
Van expenses		
Van depreciation	___	___
Net profit for the year		___

Interpreting the profit and loss account

When a profit and loss account is presented to users it is sometimes the case that the only item with which they will be concerned will be the final net profit figure, or *bottom line* as it is sometimes called. Although the net profit figure is a primary measure of performance, and its importance is difficult to overstate, the profit and loss account contains other information that should also be of interest. In order to evaluate business performance effectively, it is important to find out how the final net profit figure was derived. Thus the level of sales, the nature and amount of expenses incurred, and the profit in relation to sales are important factors in understanding the performance of the business over a period. The analysis and interpretation of financial statements is considered in detail in Chapter 6. However, it may be useful at this point to consider some of the ways in which users will use the information contained within the profit and loss account.

Example 3.3

Consider the profit and loss account set out below:

Patel Wholesalers
Trading and profit and loss account for the year ended 31 March 2000

	£	£
Sales		460,500
Less Cost of sales		345,800
Gross profit		114,700
Less		
Salaries and wages	45,900	
Rent and rates	15,300	

	£	£
Telephone and postage	1,400	
Motor vehicle expenses	3,900	
Loan interest	4,800	
Depreciation – Motor van	2,300	
Depreciation – Fixtures and fittings	2,200	
		75,800
Net profit		38,900

To evaluate performance the following points might be considered:

- The sales figure represents an important measure of output, and can be compared with the sales figures of earlier periods and the planned sales figure for the current period in order to assess the achievement of the business.
- The gross profit figure can be related to the sales figure in order to find out the profitability of the goods that are sold. In the statement shown above we can see that the gross profit is about 25 per cent of the sales figure, or, to put it another way, for every £1 of sales generated the gross profit is 25p. This level of profitability may be compared with past periods, with planned levels of profitability, or with comparable figures of similar businesses.
- The expenses of the business may be examined and compared with past periods, and so on, in order to evaluate operating efficiency. Individual expenses can be related to sales to assess whether the level of expenses is appropriate. Thus, for example, in the above statement the salaries and wages represent almost 10 per cent of sales or, for every £1 of sales generated, 10p is absorbed by employee costs.
- Net profit can also be related to sales. In the statement shown above, net profit is about 8 per cent of sales. Thus for every £1 of sales the owners of the business benefit by 8p. Whether or not this is acceptable will again depend on making the kind of comparisons referred to earlier. Net profit as a percentage of sales can vary substantially between different types of business. There is usually a trade-off to be made between profitability and sales volume. Some businesses are prepared to accept a low net profit percentage in return for generating a high volume of sales. At the other extreme, some businesses may prefer to have a high net profit percentage but accept a relatively low volume of sales. For example, a supermarket may fall into the former category while a trader in luxury cars may fall into the latter category.

Chan Exporters
Trading and profit and loss account for the year ended 31 May 2001

	£	£
Sales		840,000
Less Cost of sales		620,000
Gross profit		220,000
Less		
Salaries and wages	92,000	
Selling and distribution expenses	44,000	
Rent and rates	30,000	
Bad debts written off	86,000	
Telephone and postage	4,000	
Insurance	2,000	
Motor vehicle expenses	8,000	
Loan interest	5,000	
Depreciation – Motor van	3,000	
Depreciation – Fixtures and fittings	4,000	
		278,000
Net profit (loss)		(58,000)

In the previous year sales were £640,000. The gross profit was £200,000 and the net profit was £37,000.

Required:
Analyse the performance of the business for the year to 31 May 2001 insofar as the information allows.

SUMMARY

In this chapter we have considered the profit and loss account. We have examined the main principles underpinning this statement, and we have looked at various measurement issues connected with the determination of profit. We have seen that the profit and loss account seeks to measure *accomplishment* during a period, rather than the cash generated. Thus revenues and expenses are not the same as cash received and cash paid, and net profit does not normally reflect the net cash flows for the period. Although cash flows are important to the assessment of business performance, these are dealt with in a separate financial statement.

Although accountants try to be objective when measuring profit, there are certain areas where they have to rely on subjective judgement. Three of these areas – depreciation, stock valuation and bad debts – were examined in some detail. We saw that different judgements can lead to quite different calculations of profit between years.

Key terms

profit *p 47*	materiality convention *p 58*
revenue *p 48*	depreciation *p 58*
expense *p 48*	residual value *p 60*
gross profit *p 51*	straight-line method *p 60*
trading and profit and loss	reducing balance method *p 61*
account *p 51*	first in, first out (FIFO) *p 68*
net profit *p 51*	last in, first out (LIFO) *p 68*
cost of sales *p 51*	weighted average cost (AVCO)
realisation convention *p 55*	*p 68*
matching convention *p 55*	consistency convention *p 71*
accrued expenses *p 56*	bad debt *p 72*
prepaid expense *p 58*	provision for doubtful debts *p 73*

REVIEW QUESTIONS

3.1 'Although the profit and loss account is a record of past achievement, the calculations required for certain expenses involve estimates of the future.' What is meant by this statement? Can you think of examples where estimates of the future are used?

3.2 'Depreciation is a process of allocation and not valuation.' What do you think is meant by this statement?

3.3 What is the convention of consistency? Does this convention help users in making more valid comparison *between* businesses?

3.4 'An asset is similar to an expense.' Do you agree?

EXAMINATION-STYLE QUESTIONS

Questions 3.4 and 3.5 are more advanced than questions 3.1–3.3. Those with a coloured number have answers at the back of the book.

3.1 You have heard the following statements made. Comment critically on them.

(a) 'Capital only increases or decreases as a result of the owners putting more cash into the business or taking some out.'
(b) 'An accrued expense is one that relates to next year.'
(c) 'Unless we depreciate this asset we shall be unable to provide for its replacement.'
(d) 'There is no point in depreciating the factory building. It is appreciating in value each year.'

3.2 Singh Enterprises has an accounting year to 31 December. On 1 January 2000 the business purchased a machine for £10,000. The machine had an expected life of four years and an estimated residual value of £2,000. On 1 January 2001 the business purchased another machine for £15,000. This machine had an expected useful life of five years and an estimated residual value of £2,500. On 31 December 2002 the business sold the first machine purchased for £3,000.

Required:
Show the relevant profit and loss extracts and balance sheet extracts for 2000, 2001 and 2002.

3.3 The owner of a business is confused, and comes to you for help. The financial statements for his business, prepared by an accountant, for the last accounting period revealed an increase in profit of £50,000. However, during the accounting period the bank balance declined by £30,000. What reasons might explain this apparent discrepancy?

3.4 Spratley Ltd is a builders' merchant. On 1 September the business had 20 tonnes of sand in stock at a cost of £18 per tonne and at a total cost of £360. During the first week in September, the business purchased the following amounts of sand:

September	Tonnes	Cost per tonne
		£
2	48	20
4	15	24
6	10	25

On 7 September the business sold 60 tonnes of sand to a local builder.

Required:
Calculate the cost of goods sold and the closing stock figures from the above information using the following stock costing methods:

(a) first in, first out
(b) last in, first out
(c) weighted average cost.

3.5 The following is the balance sheet of TT Ltd at the end of its first year of trading (from Self-assessment question 3.1):

TT Limited
Balance sheet as at 31 December 2000

	£	£	£
Fixed assets			
Motor van: Cost			12,000
Depreciation			2,500
			9,500

	£	£	£
Current assets			
Stock-in-trade	65,000		
Trade debtors	19,600		
Prepaid expenses*	5,300		
Cash	750		
		90,650	
Less **Current liabilities**			
Trade creditors	22,000		
Accrued expenses**	1,250		
		23,250	
			67,400
			£76,900
Capital			
Original			50,000
Retained profit			26,900
			£76,900

* The prepaid expenses consisted of rates (£300) and rent (£5,000).
** The accrued expenses consisted of wages (£630) and electricity (£620)

During 2001, the following transactions took place:

1 The owners withdrew capital in the form of cash of £20,000.
2 Premises continued to be rented at an annual rental of £20,000. During the year, rent of £15,000 was paid to the owner of the premises.
3 Rates on the premises were paid during the year as follows:
    For the period 1 April 2001 to 31 March 2002 £1,300
4 A second delivery van was bought on 1 January for £13,000. This is expected to be used in the business for four years and then to be sold for £3,000.
5 Wages totalling £36,700 were paid during the year. At the end of the year, the business owed £860 of wages for the last week of the year.
6 Electricity bills for the first three-quarters of the year and £620 for the last quarter of the previous year were paid totalling £1,820. After 31 December 2001, but before the accounts had been finalised for the year, the bill for the last quarter arrived showing a charge of £690.
7 Stock-in-trade totalling £67,000 was bought on credit.
8 Stock-in-trade totalling £8,000 was bought for cash.
9 Sales on credit totalled £179,000 (cost £89,000).
10 Cash sales totalled £54,000 (cost £25,000).
11 Receipts from trade debtors totalled £178,000.
12 Payments to trade creditors totalled £71,000.
13 Van running expenses paid totalled £16,200.

Required:
Prepare a balance sheet as at 31 December 2001 and a profit and loss account for the year to that date.

4

Accounting for limited companies

INTRODUCTION

In the United Kingdom most businesses, except the very smallest, trade in the form of limited companies. In this chapter we shall examine the nature of limited companies and how they differ in practical terms from sole proprietorships. This will involve us considering the manner in which finance is provided by the owners. It will also require us to consider the legal and other rules that surround the way in which companies must account to their owners and to other interested parties.

Objectives

When you have completed your study of this chapter you should be able to:

- discuss the nature of the limited company
- outline and explain the particular features and restrictions of the owners' claim, in the context of limited companies
- describe and explain the statutory rules that surround accounting for limited companies
- outline and explain the non-statutory rules that surround accounting for limited companies.

The nature of limited companies

✳ A **limited company** is an artificial legal person. That is to say that a company has many of the rights and obligations that 'real' people have. With the rare exceptions of those that are created by Act of Parliament or by Royal Charter, all UK companies are created as a result of the Registrar of Companies, accepting that the necessary formalities have been met, entering the name of the new company on the Registry of Companies. The Registrar of Companies is an officer of the Department of Trade and Industry. The necessary formalities are the very simple matters of filling in a few forms and paying a modest registration fee. Thus, in the United Kingdom, companies can be formed very easily and cheaply (for about £100).

Normally, companies are owned by at least two people. The owners are usually known as *members* or *shareholders*. The ownership of a company is normally divided into a number, frequently a large number, of **shares**, each of equal size. Each shareholder owns one or more shares in the company.

A limited company is legally separate from those who own and manage it. This fact leads to two important features of the limited company: perpetual life and limited liability.

Perpetual life

The life of the company is not related to the lives of the individuals who own or manage it. When an owner of part of the shares of the company dies, that person's shares pass to the beneficiary of his or her estate. Shares may be sold by an existing shareholder to another person who wishes to become a shareholder.

Limited liability

Since the company is a legal person in its own right, it must take responsibility for its own debts and losses. This means that once the shareholders have paid what they have agreed to pay for the shares, their obligation to the company, and to the company's creditors, is satisfied. Thus shareholders can limit their losses to that which they have paid or agreed to pay for their shares. This is of great practical importance to potential shareholders, since they know that what they can lose, as part owners of the business, is limited.

Contrast this with the position of sole proprietors or partners, the owners or part-owners of unincorporated businesses. Here there is not the opportunity that shareholders have to 'ring fence' the assets that they choose not to put into the business. If a sole proprietary business finds itself in a position where liabilities exceed the business assets, the law gives unsatisfied creditors the right to demand payment out of, what the sole proprietor may have regarded as, 'non-business' assets. Thus the sole proprietor could lose everything – house, car, the lot. This is because the law sees Jill, the sole proprietor, as being the same as Jill the private individual. The shareholder, by contrast, can lose only the amount invested in the company. Legally the business operated as a limited company, in which Jack owns shares, is not the same as Jack himself. This is true even where Jack and his close associates own all of the shares in the company.

Activity 4.1

We have just said that the fact that shareholders can limit their losses to that which they have paid or agreed to pay for their shares is of great practical importance to potential shareholders.

Can you think of any practical benefit to a private sector economy, in general, of this ability of shareholders to limit losses?

Business is a risky venture – in some cases a very risky one. People with money to invest will tend to be more content to do so where they know the limit of their liability. This means that more businesses will tend to be formed and that existing ones will find it easier to raise additional finance from existing and/or additional part-owners. This is good for the private-sector economy, since businesses will tend to form and expand more readily. Thus the wants of society are more likely to be met where limited liability exists.

✳ Though **limited liability** has this advantage to the providers of capital, the shareholders, it is not necessarily to the advantage of all others who have a stake in the business. Limited liability is attractive to shareholders because they can, in effect, walk away from the unpaid debts of the company, if the contribution of the shareholders has not been sufficient to meet those debts. This is likely to make any individual or another business, contemplating advancing credit, wary of dealing with the limited company. This can be a real problem for smaller, less established companies. For example, suppliers may insist on cash payment before delivery. Alternatively, a supplier may require a personal guarantee from a major shareholder that the debt will be paid before allowing a company trade credit. In such cases the supplier will circumvent the company's limited liability status by establishing the personal liability of an individual. Larger, more established companies tend to build up the confidence of suppliers. It is mainly to warn individuals and other businesses contemplating dealing with a limited company that the liability of the owners (shareholders) of that company is limited, that this fact must be indicated in the name of the company. As we shall see later in the chapter, there are other safeguards for those dealing with a limited company, in that the extent to which shareholders may withdraw their investment from the company is restricted.

Another important safeguard for those dealing with a limited company is that all limited companies must produce annual accounts (profit and loss account, balance sheet and cash flow statement), and in effect make these available to the public. Part of this chapter will be concerned with the rules surrounding the accounts of limited companies.

Management of companies – the role of directors

A limited company may have legal personality, but it is not a human being capable of making decisions and plans about the business and exercising control over it. These management tasks must be undertaken by human beings. The most senior level of management of a company is the board of directors.

✳ The shareholders elect **directors** (by law there must be at least one director) to manage the company on a day-to-day basis, on behalf of those shareholders. In a small company, the board may be the only level of management, and may consist of all of the shareholders. In larger companies the board may consist of ten or so directors, out of many thousands of shareholders. The directors need not even be shareholders. Below the board of directors could be several layers of management comprising thousands of people.

Whatever the size of the company, the directors are responsible to the shareholders, and to some extent to the world at large, for the conduct of the company. The directors' term of office is limited, and they must stand for election at the end of that term if they wish to continue in office.

Public and private companies

When a company is registered with the Registrar of Companies, it must be registered as either a public or a private company.

✳ The main practical difference between these is that a **public company** can ✳ offer its shares for sale to the general public, but a **private company** is restricted from doing so. A public limited company must signal its status to all interested parties by having the words 'public limited company' or their abbreviation 'plc' in its name. For a private limited company, the word 'limited' or 'Ltd' must appear as part of its name.

Private limited companies tend to be smaller businesses where the ownership is divided between relatively few shareholders, who are usually fairly close to one another – for example a family company. Numerically, there are vastly more private limited companies in the UK than there are public ones, but since the public ones tend to be individually larger, they probably represent a much more important group economically. Many private limited companies are no more than the vehicle through which businesses that are little more than sole proprietorships operate.

Regarding accounting requirements, there is no distinction between private and public companies.

Capital (owners' claim) of limited companies

The owner's claim of a sole proprietorship is normally encompassed in one figure on the balance sheet, usually labelled 'capital'. With companies, this is usually a little more complicated, though in essence the same broad principles apply. With a company the owners' claim is divided between shares – that is,
✳ the original investment – on the one hand, and **reserves** – that is, profits and gains subsequently made – on the other. There is also the possibility that there will be shares of more than one type and reserves of more than one type. Thus within the basic divisions of share capital and reserves there may well be further subdivisions. This probably seems quite complicated. Shortly we shall consider the reasons for these subdivisions, and all should become clearer.

The basic division

When a company is first formed, those who take steps to form it, usually known as the 'promoters' of the company, will decide how much needs to be raised by the potential shareholders to set up the company with the necessary assets to operate.

Example 4.1

Let us imagine that several people get together and decide to form a company to start up a new business. They estimate that the company will need £50,000 to obtain the necessary assets to operate the business. Between them they raise the cash, which they use to buy shares in the company with a **nominal or par value**, that is, a face value, of £1 each.

At this point the balance sheet of the company would be:

Balance sheet as at 31 March 2000

	£
Net assets (all in cash)	50,000
Capital and reserves	
Share capital	
50,000 shares of £1 each	50,000

The company now buys the necessary fixed assets and stock-in-trade and starts to trade. During the first year, the company makes a profit of £10,000. This, by definition, means that the owners' claim expands by £10,000. During the year the shareholders (owners) make no drawings of their capital, so at the end of the year the summarised balance sheet looks like this:

Balance sheet as at 31 March 2001

	£
Net assets (various assets less liabilities)	60,000
Capital and reserves	
Share capital	
50,000 shares of £1 each	50,000
Reserves (revenue reserve)	10,000
	60,000

The profit is shown in a *reserve*, known as a **revenue reserve**, because it arises from generating revenues (making sales). Note that we do not simply add the profit to the share capital. We must keep the two amounts separate (to satisfy company law). The reason for this is that there is a legal restriction on the maximum drawings of capital (or **dividends**) that the owners can make. This is defined by the amount of revenue reserves, so it is helpful to show these separately. We shall look at why there is this restriction, and how it works, later in the chapter.

Share capital

Shares represent the basic units of ownership of a business. All companies issue **ordinary shares**. The ordinary shares of a company are often referred to

✻ collectively as the **equity** of the company. The nominal value of the shares is at the discretion of the people who start up the company. For example, if the initial capital is to be £50,000, this could be two shares of £25,000 each, five million shares of one penny each or any other combination that gives a total of £50,000. Each share must have equal value.

Activity 4.2

The initial capital requirement for a new company is £50,000. There are to be two equal shareholders. Would you advise them to issue two shares of £25,000? Why, or why not?

Such large-denomination shares tend to be unwieldy. Suppose that one of the shareholders wanted to sell his or her shares. S/he would have to find one buyer. If there were shares of smaller denomination, it would be possible to sell part of the shareholding to various potential buyers. Similarly it would be possible to sell just part of the holding and retain part.

In practice, £1 is the normal maximum nominal value for shares. Shares of £0.25 and £0.50 each are probably the most common.

✻ Some companies also issue other classes of shares, **preference shares** being the most common. Preference shares guarantee that *if a dividend is paid*, the preference shareholders will be entitled to the first part of it up to a maximum value. This maximum is normally defined as a fixed percentage of the nominal value of the preference shares. If, for example, a company issues 10,000 preference shares of £1 each with a dividend rate of 6 per cent, this means that the preference shareholders are entitled to receive the first £600 of any dividend that is paid by the company for a year. The excess over £600 goes to the ordinary shareholders. Normally, any undistributed profits and gains accrue to the ordinary shareholders. Thus the ordinary shareholders are the primary risk-takers. Their potential rewards reflect this risk. Power normally resides in the hands of the ordinary shareholders. Normally, only the ordinary shareholders are able to vote on issues that affect the company, such as who the directors should be.

It is open to the company to issue shares of various classes, perhaps with some having unusual and exotic conditions, but in practice it is rare to find other than straightforward ordinary and preference shares.

Though a company may have different classes of shares whose holders have different rights, within each class all shares must be equally treated. The rights of the various classes of shareholders, as well as other matters relating to a particular company, are contained in that company's set of rules, known as the *articles and memorandum of association*. A copy of these rules is in effect available to the public, because one must be lodged with the Registrar of Companies, to be available for public access.

Reserves

Reserves are profits and gains that have been made by the company and which still form part of the shareholders' (owners') claim, because they have not been paid out to the shareholders. Profits and gains tend to lead to cash flowing into the company. It might be worth mentioning here that retained profits represent overwhelmingly the largest source of new finance for UK companies – more than share issues and borrowings combined, for most companies. These ploughed-back profits create most of the typical company's reserves. As well as reserves, the shareholders' claim consists of share capital.

Activity 4.3

Are reserves amounts of cash?
Can you think of a reason why this is an odd question?

To deal with the second point first, it is an odd question because reserves are a claim, or part of one, whereas cash is an asset. So reserves cannot be cash.

Reserves are classified as either revenue reserves or capital reserves. As we have already seen, revenue reserves arise from trading profit. They also arise from gains made on the disposal of fixed assets.

 Capital reserves arise for two main reasons: issuing shares at above their nominal value (for example issuing £1 shares at £1.50), and revaluing (upwards) fixed assets. Where a company issues shares at above their nominal value, UK law requires that the excess of the issue price over the nominal value is shown separately.

Activity 4.4

Can you think why shares might be issued at above their nominal value?

Hint: This would not usually happen when a company is first formed and the initial shares are being issued.

Once a company has traded and has been successful, the shares would normally be worth more than the nominal value at which they were issued. If additional shares are to be issued to new shareholders to raise finance for further expansion, unless they are issued at a value higher than the nominal value, the new shareholders will be gaining at the expense of the original ones.

Example 4.2

Based on future prospects, the net assets of a company are worth £1.5 million. There are currently 1 million ordinary shares in the company. The company wishes to raise an additional £0.6 million of cash for expansion and has decided to raise it by issuing new shares. If the shares are issued for £1 each, that is 600,000 shares, the number of shares will increase to 1.6 million and their total value will be £2.1 million (i.e 1.5 + 0.6). This means that the value of the shares after the new issue will be £1.3125 each (i.e. £2.1/1.6). So the original shareholders will have lost £0.1875 per share (i.e. £1.5 − £1.3125) and the new ones will have gained £0.3125 a share. The new shareholders will, no doubt, be delighted with this; the original ones will be less ecstatic.

Things could be made fair between the two sets of shareholders by issuing the new shares at £1.50 each. In this case the £1 per share nominal value will be included with share capital in the balance sheet. The £0.50 per share premium will be shown as a capital reserve known as the **share premium** account. It is not clear why UK company law insists on the distinction between nominal share values and the premium. Certainly other countries, with a very similar set of laws governing the corporate sector, do not see the necessity to distinguish between share capital and share premium, but show the total value at which shares are issued as one comprehensive figure on the company balance sheet.

Altering the nominal value of shares

The point has already been made that the people who start up a new company may make their own choice of the nominal or par value of the shares. This value need not be permanent. At a later date the shareholders can decide to change it.

Bonus shares

It is always open to the company to take reserves of any kind (capital or revenue) and turn them into share capital. The new shares are known as **bonus shares**. Issues of bonus shares are quite frequently encountered in practice.

Example 4.3

The summary balance sheet of a company is as follows:

Balance sheet as at 31 March 2000

	£
Net assets (various assets less liabilities)	128,000
Capital and reserves	
Share capital	
50,000 shares of £1 each	50,000
Reserves	78,000
	128,000

The company decides that it will issue, to existing shareholders, one new share for every share owned by each shareholder. The balance sheet immediately following this will appear as follows:

Balance sheet as at 31 March 2000

	£
Net assets (various assets less liabilities)	128,000
Capital and reserves	
Share capital	
100,000 shares of £1 each (50,000 + 50,000)	100,000
Reserves (78,000 − 50,000)	28,000
	128,000

Activity 4.5

A shareholder of the company in Example 4.3 owned 100 shares in the company before the bonus issue. How will things change for this shareholder, as a result of the bonus issue, as regards the number of shares owned and as regards the value of the shareholding?

The answer should be that the number of shares will double, from 100 to 200. Now the shareholder owns one five-hundreth of the company (200/100,000). Before the bonus issue, the shareholder also owned one five-hundreth of the company (100/50,000). The company's assets and liabilities have not changed one bit as a result of the bonus issue, so logically one five-hundreth of the value of the company should be identical to what it was before. Thus each share is worth half as much.

A bonus issue simply takes one part of the owners' claim (part of a reserve) and puts it into another part of the owners' claim (share capital).

Activity 4.6

Can you think of any reasons why a company might want to make a bonus issue if it has no economic consequence?

We think that there are three possible reasons:

- To lower the value of each share, without reducing the shareholders' collective or individual wealth.
- To provide the shareholders with a 'feelgood factor'. It seems to be believed that shareholders like bonus issues, because it appears to make them better off, though in practice it should not affect their wealth.
- Where reserves arising from operating profits and/or realised gains on the sale of fixed assets are used to make the bonus issue, it has the effect of taking part of that portion of the owners' claim that could be drawn by the shareholders, as drawings (or dividends), and locking it up. We shall see, a little later in this chapter, that there are severe restrictions on the extent to which shareholders may make drawings from their capital. An individual or organisation contemplating lending money to the company may insist that the dividend payment possibilities are restricted as a condition of making the loan. This point will be explained in a little more detail later.

Rights issues

 Rights issues are made when companies that have been established for some time raise additional share capital for expansion, or even to solve a liquidity problem (cash shortage) by issuing additional shares for cash. Company law gives existing shareholders the first right of refusal on these new shares. So the new shares would be offered to existing shareholders, in proportion to their existing holding. Thus existing shareholders are each given the 'right' to buy some new shares. Only where the existing shareholders agree to waive their right would the shares be offered to the investing public generally.

The company (that is, the existing shareholders) would typically prefer that the shares are bought by existing shareholders in any case, irrespective of the legal position. This is because:

- the ownership (and, therefore, control) of the company remains in the same hands; and
- the costs of making the issue (advertising, complying with various company law requirements) tend to be less if the shares are to be offered to existing shareholders.

To encourage existing shareholders to take up their 'rights' to buy some new shares, those shares are virtually always offered at a price below the current market price of the existing ones.

Activity 4.7

In Example 4.2, the point was illustrated that issuing new shares at below their current worth was to the advantage of the new shareholders at the expense of the old ones.
In view of this, does it matter that rights issues are almost always made at below the current value of the shares?

The answer is that it does not matter, *in these particular circumstances*. This is because, in a rights issue, the existing shareholders and the new shareholders are exactly the same people. Not only this, but the new shares will be held by the shareholders in the same proportion as they held the existing shares. Thus a particular shareholder will be gaining on the new shares exactly as much as he or she is losing on the existing ones. Thus, in the end, no one is better or worse off as a result of the rights issue being made at a discount.

You should be clear that a rights issue is a totally different thing from a bonus issue. Rights issues result in an asset (cash) being transferred from shareholders to the company. Bonus issues involve no transfer of assets in either direction.

Transferring share ownership – the role of the Stock Exchange

The point has already been made that shares in companies may be transferred from one owner to another without this change of share ownership having any direct impact on the company's business, nor on the shareholders not involved with the particular transfer. With major companies, the desire of some existing shareholders to sell their shares coupled with the desire of others to buy those shares has led to the existence of a formal market in which the shares can be bought and sold. The Stock Exchange (of the United Kingdom and the Republic of Ireland), and similar organisations around the world, are simply market-places in which shares in major companies are bought and sold. Prices are determined by the law of supply and demand. Supply and demand are themselves determined by investors' perceptions of the future economic prospects of the companies concerned.

Activity 4.8

If, as has been pointed out above, the change in ownership of the shares of a particular company does not directly affect that company, why would a particular company welcome the fact that its shares are traded in a recognised market?

The main reason is that investors are generally very reluctant to pledge their money unless they can see some way in which they can turn their investment back into cash. In theory, the shares of a particular company may be very valuable, as a result of the company having a very bright economic future, but unless this value is capable of being realised in cash, the benefit to the shareholders is dubious. After all, you cannot spend shares; you generally need cash.

This means that potential shareholders are much more likely to be prepared to buy new shares from the company (thus providing the company with new finance) where they can see a way of liquidating their investment (turning it into cash), as and when they wish to. The Stock Exchanges provide the means of liquidation.

Though the buying and selling of 'second-hand' shares does not provide the company with cash, the fact that the buying and selling facility exists will make it easier for the company to raise new share capital when it needs to do so.

Exhibit 4.1 (see page 94) shows the notes to the balance sheet, as at 1 May 1999, of Greene King plc, the brewer and pub owner based in Bury St. Edmunds. Note that the company has just one class of shares and four types of reserve.

Long-term loans and other sources of finance

While we are looking at the role of the company's owners in financing the company, it might be worth briefly considering other sources of finance used by companies. Many companies borrow money on a long-term basis, perhaps on a ten-year contract. Lenders may be banks and other professional providers of loan finance. Many companies raise loan finance in such a way that small investors, including private individuals, are able to lend small amounts. This is particularly the case with the larger, Stock Exchange listed, companies. They do

✱ this by making a *loan stock* or **debenture** issue, which, though large in total, can be taken up in small slices by individual investors, both private individuals and investing institutions, such as pension funds and insurance companies. In

Notes to the accounts for the fifty-two weeks ended 1 May 1999

Called-up share capital

	1999 £m	1998 £m
Ordinary shares of 25p each		
Authorised – 80 million shares (1998 – 80 million)	20.0	20.0
Issued – 60.9 million shares (1998 – 60.5 million)	15.2	15.1

Movements in shareholders' funds

	Share capital £m	Share premium £m	Revaluation reserve £m	Other reserve £m	Profit and loss account £m	Total £m
Group						
At 2 May 1998	15.1	90.0	103.5	(84.1)	160.3	285.7
Transfers	—	—	—	84.1	(84.1)	—
At 2 May 1998 (restated)	15.1	90.9	103.5	—	76.2	285.7
Retained profit	—	—	—	—	23.8	23.8
Share capital issued	0.1	2.4	—	—	—	2.5
Property revaluations	—	—	5.2	—	—	5.2
Transfer	—	—	(0.2)	—	0.2	—
At 1 May 1999	15.2	93.3	108.5	—	100.2	317.2

some cases, these slices of loans can be bought and sold through the Stock Exchange. This means that investors do not have to wait for the full term of the loan to obtain repayment, but can sell their slice of the loan to another would-be lender at intermediate points in the term of the loan. Some of the features of loan financing, particularly the possibility that loan stock may be marketable on the Stock Exchange, can lead to a confusion that loan stock are shares by another name. You should be clear that this is not the case. It is the shareholders who own the company and who therefore share in its losses and profits. Loan stock holders lend money to the company under a legally binding contract, which normally specifies the rate of interest, the interest payment dates and the date of repayment of the loan itself. Usually long-term loans are secured on assets of the company.

Long-term financing of companies can be depicted as in Figure 4.1.

Companies may also borrow finance on a short-term basis, perhaps from a bank as an overdraft. Most companies buy goods and services on a month or two's credit, as is normal in business-to-business transactions. This is, in effect, an interest-free loan.

It is important to the prosperity and stability of the company that it strikes a suitable balance between finance provided by the shareholders (equity) and loan financing. This topic will be explored in Chapter 6.

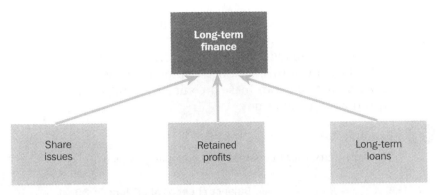

Companies derive their long-term financing needs from three sources: new share issues, retained profits, and long-term borrowing. For the typical company, the sum of the first two (known as *equity finance*) exceeds the third. Retained profit usually exceeds either of the other two, in terms of the amount of finance raised in most years.

Figure 4.1 Sources of long-term finance for the typical company

Restriction of the right of shareholders to make drawings of capital

Limited companies are required by law to distinguish between that part of their capital (shareholders' claim) which may be withdrawn by the shareholders and that part which may not be.

The withdrawable part is that which has arisen from trading profits and from realised profits on the disposal of fixed assets (to the extent that tax payments, on these profits and gains, and previous drawings have not extinguished this part of the capital). This withdrawable element of the capital is *revenue reserves*.

The non-withdrawable part normally consists of that which arose from funds injected by shareholders buying shares in the company and that which arose from upward revaluations of company assets which still remain in the company: that is, *share capital* and *capital reserves*.

Activity 4.9

Can you think of the reason why limited companies are required to distinguish different parts of their capital, whereas sole proprietorship businesses are not?

The reason for this is the limited liability that company shareholders enjoy, but which owners of unincorporated businesses do not. If a sole proprietor withdraws all of the owner's claim or even an amount in excess of this, the position of the creditors of the business is not weakened since they can legally enforce their claims against the sole trader as an individual. With a limited company, where the business and the owners are legally separate, such a legal right to enforce claims against individuals does not exist. However, to protect the company's creditors, the law insists that a specific part of the capital of a company cannot legally be withdrawn by the shareholders.

The law does not specify how large the non-withdrawable part of a particular company's capital should be, simply that anyone dealing with the company should be able to tell from looking at the company's balance sheet how large it is. In the light of this, a particular prospective lender, or supplier of goods or services on credit, can make a commercial judgement as to whether to deal with the company or not.

 Example 4.4

The summary balance sheet of a company is as follows:

Balance sheet as at 30 June 2000

	£
Net assets (fixed and current assets less short-term liabilities)	43,000
Capital and reserves	
Share capital	
20,000 shares of £1 each	20,000
Reserves (revenue)	23,000
	43,000

A bank has been asked to make a £25,000 long-term loan to the company. If the loan were to be made, immediately following, the balance sheet would appear as follows:

Balance sheet as at 30 June 2000

	£
Net assets (fixed and current assets less short-term liabilities (43,000 + 25,000))	68,000
Less Creditor: amounts falling due after more than one year	25,000
	43,000
Capital and reserves	
Share capital	
20,000 shares of £1 each	20,000
Reserves (revenue)	23,000
	43,000

As things stand, there are net assets to a total balance sheet value of £68,000 to meet the bank's claim of £25,000. It would be perfectly legal, however, for the company to pay a dividend of £23,000. The balance sheet would then appear as follows:

	£
Net assets (fixed and current assets less short-term liabilities (68,000 − 23,000))	45,000
Less Creditor: amounts falling due after more than one year	25,000
	20,000

Capital and reserves

Share capital

20,000 shares of £1 each   20,000

Reserves (revenue (23,000 − 23,000))   —

                                          20,000

This leaves the bank in a very much weaker position, in that there are now net assets with a balance sheet value of £45,000 to meet a claim of £25,000. Note that the difference between the amount of the bank loan and the net assets always equals the capital and reserves total. Thus the capital and reserves represent a 'margin of safety' for creditors. The larger the amount of the owners' claim that is withdrawable by the shareholders, the smaller is the potential margin of safety for creditors.

It is important to remember that company law says nothing about how large this margin of safety must be. It is left as a matter of the commercial judgement of the company concerned as to what is desirable. The larger it is, the easier will the company find it to persuade potential lenders to lend and suppliers to supply goods and services on credit.

Activity 4.10

Would you expect a company to pay all of its revenue reserves as a dividend? What factors might be involved with a dividend decision?

It would be very rare for a company to pay all of its revenue reserves as a dividend; a legal right to do so does not necessarily make it a good idea. Most companies see ploughed-back profits as a major, usually the major, source of new finance.

The factors that influence the dividend decision are likely to include:

- The availability of cash to pay a dividend: it would not be illegal to borrow to pay a dividend, but it would be unusual and, possibly, imprudent.
- The needs of the business for finance for investment.
- Possibly a need for the directors to create good relations with investors, who may regard a dividend as a positive feature.

You may have thought of others.

The law is quite specific that it is illegal, under normal circumstances, for shareholders to withdraw that part of their claim which is represented by shares and capital reserves. This means that potential creditors of the company know the maximum amount of the shareholders' claim that can be drawn by the shareholders.

Figure 4.2 shows the important division between that part of the shareholders' claim which can be withdrawn as a dividend and that part which cannot.

Earlier in the chapter, the point was made that a potential creditor may

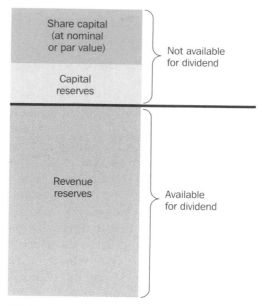

Total equity finance of limited companies consists of share capital, capital reserves and revenue reserves. Only the revenue reserves (which arise from realised profits and gains) can be used to fund a dividend. In other words, the maximum legal dividend is the amount of the revenue reserves.

Figure 4.2 Availability for dividends of various parts of the shareholders' claim

insist that some revenue reserves are converted to bonus shares (or *capitalised*) to increase the margin of safety, as a condition of granting a loan.

Perhaps it is worth pointing out, as a practical footnote to Example 4.4, that most potential long-term lenders would seek to have their loan secured against a particular asset of the company, particularly an asset such as freehold property. This would give them the right to seize the asset concerned, sell it and satisfy their claim, should the company default. Lenders often place restrictions, or *covenants*, on the borrowing company's freedom of action, as a condition of granting the loan. The covenants typically restrict the level of risk to which the company, and the lender's asset, is exposed.

Activity 4.11

Can you think of any circumstances in which a company could allow the non-withdrawable part of its capital to be reduced, yet remain within the law?

It can be reduced, but only as a result of the company sustaining trading losses or losses on disposal of fixed assets that exceed the amount of the withdrawable portion of the company's capital. It cannot be reduced by shareholders making drawings.

Drawings are usually made in the form of a dividend paid by the company to the shareholders, in proportion to the number of shares owned by each one.

The summarised balance sheet of Bonanza Ltd is as follows:

Balance sheet as at 31 December 2000

	£
Net assets (various assets less liabilities)	235,000
Capital and reserves	
Share capital	
100,000 shares of £1 each	100,000
Share premium account	30,000
Revaluation reserve	37,000
Profit and loss account balance	68,000
	235,000

1 Without any other transactions occurring at the same time, the company made a one-for-five rights share issue at £2 per share payable in cash (all shareholders took up their rights) and, immediately after, made a one-for-two bonus issue.

   Show the balance sheet immediately following the bonus issue, assuming that the directors wanted to retain the maximum dividend payment potential for the future.

2 Explain what external influence might cause the directors to choose not to retain the maximum dividend payment possibilities.

3 Show the balance sheet immediately following the bonus issue, assuming that the directors wanted to retain the *minimum* dividend payment potential for the future.

4 What is the maximum dividend that could be paid before and after the events described in point 1 above if the minimum dividend payment potential is achieved?

5 Lee owns 100 shares in Bonanza Ltd before the events described in point 1. Assuming that the net assets of the company have a value equal to their balance sheet value, show how these events will affect Lee's wealth.

6 Looking at the original balance sheet of Bonanza Ltd, shown above, what four things do we know about the company's status and history that are not specifically stated on the balance sheet?

The profit and loss account and balance sheet of limited companies

As we might expect, the financial statements of a limited company are, in essence, identical to those of a sole proprietor. There are, however, some differences of detail, and we shall now consider these.

Set out below are the profit and loss account and balance sheet of a limited company:

Da Silva plc

Profit and loss account for the year ended 31 December 2000

	£m	£m
Sales		840
Less Cost of sales		520
Gross profit		320
Less Operating expenses		
Wages and salaries	98	
Heat and light	18	
Rent and rates	24	
Motor vehicle expenses	20	
Insurance	4	
Printing and stationery	12	
Depreciation	45	
Audit fee	4	
		225
Operating profit		95
Less Interest payable		10
Profit before tax		85
Tax on profit		24
Profit after tax		61
Less Transfer to general reserve	20	
Proposed dividend	25	
		45
Unappropriated profit carried forward		16

Balance sheet as at 31 December 2000

	£m	£m
Fixed assets		
Land and buildings		132
Plant and machinery		171
		303
Current assets		
Stock	65	
Debtors	112	
Cash	36	
	213	
Less Creditors: amounts falling due within 12 months		
Creditors	74	
Corporation tax	12	
Proposed dividend	25	
	111	
Net current assets (working capital)		102
Total assets less current liabilities		405

	£m	£m
Less Creditors: amounts		
falling due in more than 12 months		
10% debentures		100
Net assets		305
Share capital		
Ordinary shares of £0.50 each		200
Reserves		
Share premium account	30	
General reserve	50	
Profit and loss account	25	
		105
		305

You may well feel that the most striking thing about these statements is the extent to which they look exactly the same as those that you have been used to with sole proprietors. This is correct; the differences are small. Let us go through and pick up these differences.

The profit and loss account

- *Layout.* The profit from trading activities, before interest payable (or receivable), is separately identified as 'operating profit'. Also, after interest has been deducted to find the profit for the year, the statement does not end there as it would were this the profit and loss account of a sole proprietor. The statement goes on to show how the profit has been appropriated between funds set aside to meet the tax on the profit, to pay a dividend to shareholders, and to make a transfer to a general (revenue) reserve. This last part of the statement is known as the 'appropriation account'.
- *Audit fee.* As we shall see later in this chapter, companies are normally required to have their financial statements audited by an independent firm of auditors, for which they are charged a fee. Though it is open to all sole proprietors to have their accounts audited, very few do so. This is therefore an expense that will normally be present in the profit and loss account of a company, but not that of a sole proprietor.
- *Tax.* As separate legal entities, companies are required to be responsible for their own tax on profit. The calculation of the tax would be based on the profit for the year.
- *Dividend.* This is the amount of dividend that will be paid to the shareholders. This is in the nature of drawings of capital by the owners of the company. The fact that the dividend is 'proposed' means that the cash had not yet been paid at 31 December 2000 (the year-end). Sometimes shareholders receive a dividend before the end of the year. With many companies they receive an 'interim' dividend, part way through the year, and a 'final' one shortly after the year end.

- *Transfer to general reserve.* What is left over of the year's profit, after tax and dividends have been accounted for, is retained, normally to be reinvested ('ploughed back') into the operations of the company. For this company the amount left is £36 million (that is, £61 million – £25 million). This could all have gone to increasing the profit and loss balance in the balance sheet. As is quite common in practice, however, an amount (£20 million for this company) has been transferred to a general reserve.

It is not totally clear why directors decide to make such transfers, since the funds concerned remain part of the revenue reserves, still available for dividend. The most plausible explanation seems to be that directors feel that taking funds out of the profit and loss account and placing them in a 'reserve' indicates an intention to retain the funds permanently in the company and not to use them to pay a dividend. Of course the balance on the profit and loss account is also a reserve, but that fact is not indicated in its title.

The balance sheet

- *Corporation tax.* The amount that appears in short-term liabilities represents 50 per cent of the tax on the profit of the year 2000. It is half of the tax charge that appears in the profit and loss account; the other 50 per cent will already have been paid. The remaining 50 per cent will be paid shortly following the balance sheet date. These payment dates are set down by law.
- *Dividend.* The dividend that was proposed in the profit and loss account also appears under short-term liabilities, also to be paid early in the new accounting year.
- *Share capital and reserves.* We have already discussed this area at length earlier in the chapter. Before the year end, the general reserve balance must have stood at £30 million, to be enhanced to its final level by the transferred appropriation of the year 2000 profit. Similarly, the profit and loss account balance must have been £9 million, just before the year end. As was mentioned above, the general reserve and the profit and loss account balance are identical in all respects; they both arise from retained profits, and are both available for dividend.

The directors' duty to account – the role of company law

As we have already seen, it is not usually possible for all of the shareholders to be involved in the general management of the company, nor do most of them wish to be involved, so they elect directors to act on their behalf. It is both logical and required by company law that directors are accountable for their actions in respect of their stewardship of the company's assets.

In this context directors are required by law:

- to maintain appropriate accounting records;
- to prepare an annual profit and loss account, a balance sheet that shows a

---

Exhibit 4.2

Statement of directors' responsibilities

Company law requires the directors to prepare financial statements for each financial year which give a true and fair view of the state of affairs of the company and group and of the profit or loss for that period. In preparing those financial statements, the directors are required to:

- select suitable accounting policies and then apply them consistently
- make judgements and estimates that are reasonable and prudent
- state whether applicable accounting standards have been followed, subject to any material departures disclosed and explained in the financial statements.

The directors are responsible for keeping proper accounting records which disclose with reasonable accuracy at any time the financial position of the company and the group and to enable them to ensure that the financial statements comply with the Companies Act 1985. They have general responsibility for taking such steps as are reasonably open to them to safeguard the assets of the company and the group and to prevent and detect fraud and other irregularities.

'true and fair' view of events, and a directors' report, and to make these available to all shareholders and to the public at large.

Exhibit 4.2 is an extract from the 1999 annual accounts of Monsoon plc, the fashion retailer. This statement sets out what the directors regard as their responsibilities for the annual accounts.

The relevant rules are embodied in the Companies Acts 1985 and 1989. Company law goes quite a long way in prescribing in detail the form and content of the accounting statements that the directors must publish. A copy of each year's accounts must be made available to all of the company's shareholders. The accounts must also be made available to the general public. This is achieved by the company submitting a copy to the Registrar of Companies (Department of Trade and Industry), who allows anyone who wishes to do so to inspect these accounts.

It must be strongly emphasised that there is absolutely no difference of principle between the profit and loss account and balance sheet of a company and those of a sole proprietor, which you have already met. Company accounts look a bit different in detail, for example, because of the need to divide the owners' claim into categories (share capital, share premium account, revenue reserves etc), which is not relevant for sole proprietors.

The role of accounting standards in company accounting

✱ **Accounting standards** (sometimes called *financial reporting standards*) are rules and guidelines, established by the UK accounting profession, which should be followed by preparers of the annual accounts of companies. They do not strictly have the same status as company law. Accounting standards do, however, define what is meant by a true and fair view, in various contexts and circumstances. Since company law requires that accounting statements show a true and fair view, this gives accounting standards an important place in company accounts preparation.

When UK accounting standards were first introduced in the 1970s, the committee responsible for developing them saw the role of accounting standards as being to 'narrow the difference and variety of accounting practice by publishing authoritative statements on best accounting practice which will, whenever possible, be definitive'. This continues to reflect the role of accounting standards.

International accounting standards

The internationalisation of business has led to a need for some degree of international harmonisation of accounting rules. It can no longer be assumed that the potential users of the accounts of a company whose head office is in the United Kingdom are familiar with UK accounting standards. Whichever user group we care to think of – employees, suppliers, customers, shareholders – some members of that group are quite likely to be residents of another country. It is to be expected that the trend towards internationalisation of business will continue.

These facts have led to the need for international accounting standards and the creation of the International Accounting Standards Committee (IASC). The IASC has issued a number of standards, but there is a problem. It is difficult to reconcile international differences in accounting procedures, which has tended to mean that the international standards have been slow to emerge. They have also tended to be fairly permissive of variations in practice.

The role of the Stock Exchange in company accounting

The Stock Exchange extends the accounting rules for those companies that are listed as being eligible to have their shares traded there. These extensions include the following requirements:

- summarised interim (half-year) accounts in addition to the statutorily required annual accounts
- a geographical analysis of turnover
- details of holdings of more than 20 per cent of the shares of other companies.

Figure 4.3 illustrates the sources of accounting rules with which larger UK companies must comply.

Auditors

Shareholders, in all but the very smallest companies, are required to elect a
✳ qualified and independent person or, more usually, a firm, to act as **auditors**.

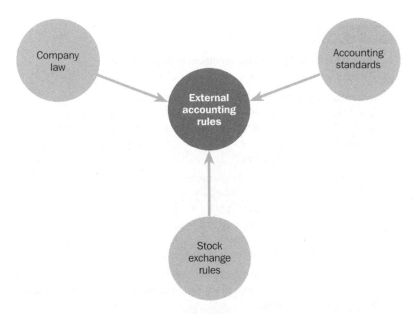

Company law provides the basic framework of company accounting regulation. This is augmented by the accounting standards, which have virtually the force of law. The Stock Exchange has its own additional rules for the companies listed by it.

Figure 4.3 Sources of accounting regulations for a UK limited company listed on the Stock Exchange

The main duty of auditors is to make a report as to whether, in their opinion, the accounting statements do that which they are supposed to do, namely, show a true and fair view and comply with statutory and accounting standard requirements. To put themselves in a position where they can conscientiously make such a statement, the auditors must scrutinise the annual accounting statements, prepared by the directors, and the evidence on which those statements are based. The auditors' opinion must be included with the accounting statements that are sent to the shareholders and to the Registrar of Companies.

The relationship between the shareholders, the directors and the auditors is illustrated in Figure 4.4.

Figure 4.4 shows that the shareholders elect the directors to act on their behalf in the day-to-day running of the company. The directors are required to 'account' to the shareholders on the performance, position and cash flows of the company, on an annual basis. The shareholders also elect auditors whose role it is to give the shareholders an impression of the extent to which they can regard the accounting statements prepared by the directors as reliable.

Exhibit 4.3 is the auditors' report for Monsoon plc. The statement appeared with the annual accounts of Monsoon for the year ended 29 May 1999.

Report of the auditors to the members of Monsoon plc

We have audited the financial statements on pages 15 to 33.

Respective responsibilities of directors and auditors

The directors are responsible for preparing the Annual Report, including as described on page 13, the financial statements. Our responsibilities, as independent auditors, are established by statute, the Auditing Practices Board, the Listing Rules of the London Stock Exchange and our profession's ethical guidance.

We report to you our opinion as to whether the financial statements give a true and fair view and are properly prepared in accordance with the Companies Act. We also report to you if, in our opinion, the directors' report is not consistent with the financial statements, if the company has not kept proper accounting records, if we have not received all the information and explanations we require for our audit, or if information specified by law or the Listing Rules regarding directors' remuneration and transactions is not disclosed.

We read the other information contained in the Annual Report and consider the implications for our report if we become aware of any apparent misstatements or material inconsistencies with the financial statements.

We review whether the statement on page 10 reflects the company's compliance with those provisions of the Combined Code specified for our review by the London Stock Exchange, and we report if it does not. We are not required to form an opinion on the effectiveness of the group's corporate governance procedures or its internal controls.

Basis of opinion

We conducted our audit in accordance with Auditing Standards issued by the Auditing Practices Board. An audit includes examination, on a test basis, of evidence relevant to the amounts and disclosures in the financial statements. It also includes an assessment of the significant estimates and judgements made by the directors in the preparation of the financial statements, and of whether the accounting policies are appropriate to the company's circumstances, consistently applied and adequately disclosed.

We planned and performed our audit so as to obtain all the information and explanations which we considered necessary in order to provide us with sufficient evidence to give reasonable assurance that the financial statements are free from material misstatement, whether caused by fraud or other irregularity or error. In forming our opinion we also evaluated the overall adequacy of the presentation of information in the financial statements.

Opinion

In our opinion the financial statements give a true and fair view of the state of affairs of the company and the group at 29 May 1999 and of the profit and cash flows of the group for the period then ended and have been properly prepared in accordance with the Companies Act 1985.

PricewaterhouseCoopers
Chartered Accountants and
Registered Auditors
London
1 September 1999

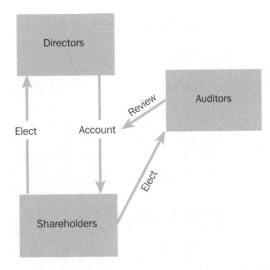

The directors are appointed by the shareholders to manage the company on the shareholders' behalf. The directors are required to report each year to the shareholders, by means principally of accounting statements, on the company's performance and position. To give greater confidence in the reports, the shareholders also appoint auditors to investigate the reports and express an opinion on their reliability.

Figure 4.4 **The relationship between the shareholders, the directors and the auditors**

Self-assessment question 4.2

This question requires you to adjust some figures on a set of company accounts. It should prove useful practice for the material that you covered in Chapters 2 and 3, as well as helping you to become familiar with the accounts of a company.

Presented below is a draft set of simplified accounts for Pear Limited for the year ended 30 September 2000.

Pear Limited
Profit and loss account for the year ended 30 September 2000

	£000	£000
Turnover		1,456
Cost of sales		768
Gross profit		688
Less Expenses		
Salaries	220	
Depreciation	249	
Other operating costs	131	600
Operating profit		88
Interest payable		15
Profit before taxation		73
Taxation at 30%		22
Profit after taxation		51

Balance Sheet as at 30 September 2000

	£000	£000
Fixed assets		
Cost	1,570	
Depreciation	(690)	
		880
Current assets		
Stocks	207	
Debtors	182	
Cash at bank	21	
	410	
Less Creditors: amounts due within one year		
Trade creditors	88	
Other creditors	20	
Taxation	22	
Bank overdraft	105	
	235	
Net current assets		175
Less Creditors: amounts due after more than one year		
10% Debenture – repayable 2005		(300)
		755
Capital and reserves		
Share capital		300
Share premium account		300
Retained profit at beginning of year	104	
Profit for year	51	155
		755

The following additional information is available:

1 Depreciation has not been charged on office equipment with a written-down value of £100,000. This class of assets is depreciated at 12 per cent per annum using the reducing balance method.

2 A new machine was purchased, on credit, for £30,000 and delivered on 29 September but has not been included in the financial statements.

3 An invoice for a sale on credit to the value of £18,000 for September has been omitted from the accounts. (The cost of sales is stated correctly.)

4 A dividend has been proposed of £25,000.

5 The interest payable on the debenture for the second half year has not been included in the accounts.

6 An invoice for electricity to the value of £2,000 for the quarter ended 30 September 2000 arrived on 4 October and has not been included in the accounts.

7   The charge for taxation will have to be amended to take account of the above information. Make the simplifying assumptions that (i) the tax charge is based strictly on the profit before taxation and (ii) it is payable shortly after the end of the year.

Required:
Prepare a revised set of financial statements for the year ended 30 September 2000 incorporating the additional information in points 1–7 above.

SUMMARY

In this chapter we have reviewed the position of limited companies, particularly in the context of accounting. Limited companies have their own legal status, which leads to many of their peculiarities, including the close attention that the law pays to company accounting. There are strict limits on the extent to which companies are allowed to make payments to their owners, the shareholders, as 'drawings' of capital. The Companies Acts set out carefully drafted rules regarding the form and content of the annual accounts. These statutory rules are interpreted and augmented by accounting standards, a set of rules established by the accounting profession. Auditors, who are independent of the company, report on whether the directors have fulfilled their statutory duty to prepare accounts that show 'a true and fair view' of the company's performance and position.

✳ Key terms

limited company *p 83*	ordinary shares *p 87*
shares *p 84*	equity *p 88*
limited liability *p 85*	preferences shares *p 88*
directors *p 85*	capital reserves *p 89*
public company *p 86*	share premium *p 90*
private company *p 86*	bonus shares *p 90*
reserves *p 86*	rights issues *p 92*
nominal value *p 87*	debenture *p 93*
revenue reserve *p 87*	accounting standards *p 103*
dividends *p 87*	auditors *p 104*

? REVIEW QUESTIONS

4.1   How does the liability of a limited company differ from the liability of a real person, in respect of amounts owed to others?

4.2   Some people are about to form a company, as a vehicle through which to run a new business. What are the advantages to them of forming a private limited company rather than a public one?

4.3 What is a reserve, in the context of the owners' claim of a limited company?

4.4 What is a preference share?

? EXAMINATION-STYLE QUESTIONS

Questions 4.4 and 4.5 are more advanced than 4.1–4.3. Those with a coloured number have an answer at the back of the book.

4.1 Briefly explain each of the following expressions, which you have seen in the accounts of a limited company:

(a) reserve
(b) nominal value of shares
(c) rights issue.

4.2 Briefly explain each of the following expressions, which you have seen in the accounts of a limited company:

(a) dividend
(b) debenture; and
(c) share premium account.

4.3 (a) Describe briefly the role played by each of the following in the publication of financial statements for public limited companies:

(i) the Companies Act 1985
(ii) the Accounting Standards Board
(iii) the Stock Exchange.

(b) Comment on the differences between the published financial statements of a company and its internal management accounts.

4.4 Comment on the following quotation:

> Limited companies can set a limit on the amount of debts that they will meet. They tend to have reserves of cash, as well as share capital, and they can use these reserves to pay dividends to the shareholders. Many companies have preference as well as ordinary shares. The preference shares give a guaranteed dividend. The shares of many companies can be bought and sold on the Stock Exchange; a shareholder selling shares can represent a useful source of new capital to the company. The auditors are appointed by the directors to check the books and prepare the annual accounts. Accounting standards, produced by the government, set out the basic framework for the annual accounts of companies. The basic requirement of company accounts is that they should provide 'a correct and accurate view' of the company's affairs.

4.5 Rose Limited operates a small chain of retail shops, which sell high-quality teas and coffees. Approximately half of sales are on credit. Abbreviated and unaudited accounts are given below:

Rose Limited

Profit and loss account for the year ended 31 March 2000

	£000	£000
Sales		12,080
Cost of sales		6,282
Gross profit		5,798
Labour costs	2,658	
Depreciation	625	
Other operating costs	1,003	
		4,286
Net profit before interest		1,512
Interest payable		66
Net profit before tax		1,446
Tax payable		506
Net profit after tax		940
Dividend payable		300
Retained profit for year		640
Retained profit brought forward		756
Retained profit carried forward		1,396

Balance sheet as at 31 March 2000

	£000	£000
Fixed assets		2,728
Current assets:		
Stocks	1,583	
Debtors	996	
Cash	26	
	2,605	
Creditors: amounts due within one year		
Trade creditors	1,118	
Other creditors	417	
Tax	506	
Dividends	300	
Overdraft	296	
	2,637	
Net current assets		(32)
Creditors: amounts due after more than one year		
Secured loan (2005)		(300)
		2,396
Share capital		
(50p shares, fully paid)		750
Share premium		250
Retained profit		1,396
		2,396

Since the unaudited accounts for Rose Limited were prepared, the following information has become available:

1 An additional £74,000 of depreciation should have been charged on fixtures and fittings.
2 Invoices for credit sales on 31 March 2000 amounting to £34,000 have not been included; cost of sales is not affected.
3 Stocks, which had been purchased for £2,000, have been damaged and are unsaleable.
4 Fixtures and fittings to the value of £16,000 have been delivered just before 31 March 2000, but these assets were not included in the accounts and the purchase invoice had not been processed.
5 Wages for Saturday-only staff, amounting to £1,000, have not been paid for the final Saturday of the year.
6 Tax is payable at 30 per cent of net profit before tax. Make the simplifying assumption that tax is payable shortly after the end of the year.

Required:

Prepare a balance sheet and profit and loss account for Rose Limited for the year ended 31 March 2000, incorporating the information in points 1–6 above.

5

Measuring and reporting cash flows

INTRODUCTION

Despite the undoubted value of the profit and loss account as a means of assessing the effect on a business's wealth of its trading activities, it has increasingly been recognised that the approach taken in preparing the profit and loss account can mask problems, or potential problems, of cash flow shortages. This is because in the profit and loss account we concern ourselves not with cash receipts and payments, but with revenues and expenses. This is principally because large expenditures on such things as fixed assets and stocks do not necessarily have an immediate effect on the profit and loss account. You may recall from Chapter 2, when we were considering the business of Paul, the wrapping paper seller, that the profit and loss account and the cash flow statement showed quite different information. Cash is important because, in practice, without it no business can operate. Companies are required to produce a cash flow statement as well as the more traditional profit and loss account and balance sheet. In this chapter we consider the deficiencies of these traditional statements, in the context of assessing cash flow issues. We go on to consider how the cash flow statement is prepared and how it may be interpreted.

Objectives

When you have completed this chapter you should be able to:

- discuss the crucial importance of cash to a business
- explain the nature of the cash flow statement and discuss how it can be helpful in identifying cash flow problems
- prepare a cash flow statement
- interpret a cash flow statement.

The importance of cash and cash flow

Simpler organisations, such as small clubs and other not-for-profit associations, limit their accounting activities to a record of cash receipts and cash payments.

✳ Periodically (normally annually), a summary of all cash transactions – the **cash flow** – for the period is produced for the members. The summary would show one single figure for each category of payment or receipt, for example membership subscriptions. This summary is usually the basis of decision making for the club and the main means of the committee's fulfilling its moral duty to account to the club members. This is usually found to be sufficient for such organisations.

Activity 5.1

Most organisations, including most businesses and many not-for-profit organisations, do not simply rely on a summary of cash receipts and payments, but produce a profit and loss type of statement. Can you remember the difference between a receipts and payments statement and a profit and loss account? Can you think why simple organisations do not feel the need for a profit and loss type of statement?

The difference between the two is that while a receipts and payments summary confines itself to cash movements, an accruals-based (that is, profit and loss type) statement is concerned with movements in wealth. Increases and decreases in wealth do not necessarily involve cash. A business making a sale (a revenue) increases its wealth, but if the sale is made on credit no cash changes hands – not at the time of the sale, at least. Here the increase in wealth is reflected in another asset – an increase in trade debtors. If an item of stock is the subject of the sale, the business incurs an expense in order to make the sale; wealth is lost to the business through the reduction in stock. Here an expense has been incurred, but no cash has changed hands. There is also the important distinction for profit-seeking organisations that the participants are going to be very concerned with wealth generation, not just with cash generation.

For an organisation with any significant level of complexity, a cash receipts and payments summary would not tell the participants all that they would want to know. An 'accruals-based' statement is necessary.

A simple organisation may just collect subscriptions from its members, perhaps raise further cash from activities, and spend cash on pursuing the purposes of the club, for example making payments to charity. Here everything that accounting is capable of reflecting is reflected in a simple cash receipts and payments statement. The club has no stock. There are no fixed assets. All transactions are for cash, rather than on credit.

Clearly organisations that are more complicated than simple clubs need to produce a profit and loss account that reflects movements in wealth, and the net increase (profit) or decrease (loss) for the period concerned. Until the mid-1970s in the UK, there was not generally felt to be any need for businesses to produce more than a profit and loss account and balance sheet. It seemed to be believed that all that shareholders and other interested parties needed to know, in accounting terms, about a business could be taken more or less directly from those two statements. This view seemed to be based partly on the implicit belief that if a business were profitable, then automatically it would have plenty of cash. Though in the very long run this is likely to be true, it is not necessarily true in the short to medium term.

Activity 5.2

The following is a list of business/accounting events. In each case, state the effect (increase, decrease or no effect) on both cash and profit:

	Effect	
	on profit	*on cash*
1 Repayment of a loan	_____	_____
2 Making a sale on credit	_____	_____
3 Buying a fixed asset for cash	_____	_____
4 Receiving cash from a trade debtor	_____	_____
5 Depreciating a fixed asset	_____	_____
6 Buying some stock for cash	_____	_____
7 Making a share issue for cash	_____	_____

You should have come up with the following:

	Effect	
	on profit	*on cash*
1 Repayment of a loan	none	decrease
2 Making a sale on credit	increase	none
3 Buying a fixed asset for cash	none	decrease
4 Receiving cash from a trade debtor	none	increase
5 Depreciating a fixed asset	decrease	none
6 Buying some stock for cash	none	decrease
7 Making a share issue for cash	none	increase

The explanations of these responses are as follows:

1. Repaying the loan requires that cash is paid to the creditors. Thus two figures in the balance sheet will be affected, but not the profit and loss account.
2. Making a sale on credit will increase the sales figure and probably profit (unless the sale was made for a price that precisely equalled the expenses involved). No cash will change hands, however, at this point.
3. Buying a fixed asset for cash obviously reduces the cash balance of the business, but its profit figure is not affected.
4. Receiving cash from a debtor increases the cash balance and reduces the debtors' balance. Both of these figures are on the balance sheet. The profit and loss account is unaffected.
5. Depreciating a fixed asset means that an expense is recognised. This causes the value of the asset, as it is recorded on the balance sheet, to fall by an amount equal to the amount of the expense.
6. Buying some stock for cash means that the value of the stock will increase and the cash balance will decrease by a similar amount. Profit is not affected.
7. Making a share issue for cash increases the owners' claim and increases the cash balance; profit is unaffected.

In 1991 a financial reporting standard, FRS 1, emerged that requires all but the smallest companies to produce and publish, in addition to the profit and loss account and balance sheet, a statement that reflects movements in cash. The reason for introducing this requirement was the increasing belief that, despite their usefulness, the profit and loss account and balance sheet do not concentrate sufficiently on liquidity. It was believed that the accruals-based nature of the profit and loss account tended to obscure the question of how and where the business was generating the cash that it needs to continue its operations.

Why is cash so important?

To businesses that are pursuing a goal that is concerned with profit/wealth, why is cash so important? Activity 5.1 illustrated the fact that cash and profit do not go hand in hand, so why the current preoccupation with cash? After all, cash is just an asset that a business needs to help it to function. The same could be said of stock or fixed assets.

The reason for the importance of cash is that people and organisations will not normally accept other than cash in settlement of their claims against the business. If a business wants to employ people it must pay them in cash. If it wants to buy a new fixed asset to exploit a business opportunity, the seller of the asset will normally insist on being paid in cash, probably after a short period of credit. When businesses fail, it is their inability to find the cash to pay claimants that really drives them under. These factors lead to cash being the pre-eminent business asset, and therefore the one that analysts and others watch most carefully in trying to assess the ability of the business to survive and/or to take advantage of commercial opportunities as they arise.

The cash flow statement

The cash flow statement is, in essence, a summary of the cash receipts and payments over the period concerned. All payments of a particular type, for example cash payments to acquire additional fixed assets, are added together to give just one figure that appears in the statement. The net total of the statement is the net increase or decrease of the cash of the business over the period. The statement is basically an analysis of the business's cash movements for the period. The cash flow statement is now accepted, with the profit and loss account and balance sheet, as one of the standard accounting statements.

The relationship between the three statements is shown in Figure 5.1. The balance sheet reflects the combination of assets (including cash) and claims (including the owners' capital) of the business *at a a particular point in time*. Both the cash flow statement and the profit and loss account explain the *changes over a period* to two of the items in the balance sheet, namely cash and owners' claim respectively. In practice, this period is typically the business's accounting year.

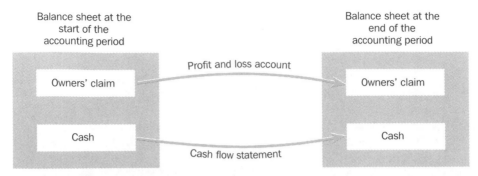

Balance sheet at the start of the accounting period

Balance sheet at the end of the accounting period

Profit and loss account

Owners' claim → Owners' claim

Cash → Cash

Cash flow statement

The balance sheet shows the position, at a particular point in time, of the business's assets and claims. The profit and loss account explains how, over a period between two balance sheets, the owners' claim figure in the first balance sheet has altered as a result of trading operations to become the figure in the second balance sheet. The cash flow statement also looks at changes over the accounting period, but this statement explains the alteration in the cash balances shown in the two consecutive balance sheets.

Figure 5.1 The relationship between the balance sheet, the profit and loss account and the cash flow statement

The standard layout of the cash flow statement is summarised in Figure 5.2. The explanations of terms in Figure 5.2 are as follows:

✱ • **Net cash flow from operating activities**. This is the net inflow or outflow from trading operations. It is equal to the sum of cash receipts from trade debtors (and cash sales where relevant) less the sums paid to buy stock, to pay rent, to pay wages and so on. Note that it is the amounts of cash received and paid, not the revenue and expense, that feature in the cash flow statement. It is, of course, the profit and loss account that deals with the expenses and revenues.

✱ • **Returns from investment and servicing of finance**. This category deals with payments made to suppliers of fixed return finance to reward them for the use of their money. Fixed return finance includes preference shares and interest-bearing loans, and the rewards are preference dividends and interest respectively. Similarly this part of the statement deals with cash that the business receives as interest and dividends from investments (in loans and shares) that it has made. The object of distinguishing between payments and receipts arising from financing and investment outside the business and money deriving from normal operating activities is presumably to enable the reader of the statement to separate the cash flow arising from these somewhat different types of activity.

Note that dividends paid by a business to its ordinary shareholders are dealt with later in the statement.

Note also that the word 'servicing' in this context refers to rewarding suppliers of finance for the use of their money. If they are not rewarded, they will not normally allow it to be used.

✱ • **Taxation**. This is fairly obvious, but you should be clear that the amounts shown here are payments and receipts of tax made during the period

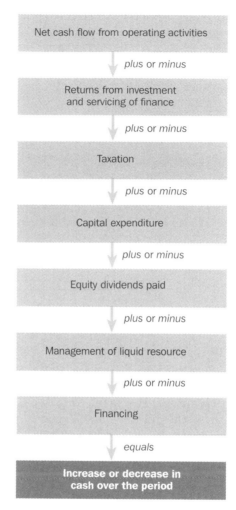

Figure 5.2 Standard layout of the cash flow statement

covered by the statement. Companies normally pay tax on their profits in four equal instalments. Two of these are during the year concerned, and the other two are during the following year. Thus by the end of each accounting year one half of the tax will have been paid, and the remainder will appear as a current liability at the end of the year, to be paid off during the following year. During any particular year, therefore, the tax payment would normally equal 50 per cent of the previous year's tax charge and 50 per cent of that of the current year.

❋ • **Capital expenditure**. This part of the statement is concerned with cash payments made to acquire additional fixed assets and with cash receipts from the disposal of fixed assets. These fixed assets could be loans made by the business or shares in another business bought by the business, as well as the more usual fixed assets such as buildings, machinery and so on.

*   • **Equity dividends paid**. This is cash dividends paid to the business's own ordinary shareholders (equity holders) during the period covered by the statement. Businesses frequently declare a dividend that is shown in one year's profit and loss account but which is not paid until the following year, being treated as a current liability until it is paid. This means that the dividend 'for the year' is often not paid until the following year.

*   • **Management of liquid resources**. This part of the statement deals with cash receipts and payments arising from the acquisition and disposal of readily disposable investments, which the business did not or does not intend to hold for any other reason than to find a profitable depository for what will probably be a short-term cash surplus. Readily disposable investments of this type will typically be investments in shares of businesses listed on the Stock Exchange, and government bills (short-term loans to the government).

*   • **Financing**. This part of the statement is concerned with the long-term financing of the business. So we are considering borrowings (other than very short term) and finance from share issues. This category is concerned with repayment/redemption of finance as well as with the raising of it.

*   • *Increase or decrease in cash over the period*. Naturally the total of the statement must be the net increase or decrease in cash over the period covered by the statement. 'Cash' here means notes and coins in hand and deposits in banks and similar institutions that are accessible to the business within 24 hours' notice, without incurring a penalty for premature withdrawal.

Example 5.1 sets out the statement according to the requirements of FRS 1. The headings printed in bold type are required specifically, and are the primary categories into which cash payments and receipts for the period must be analysed. Note that in Example 5.1 there is a subtotal in the statement after 'capital expenditure'. This is to highlight the extent to which the cash flows of the period, which arise from the 'normal' activities of the business (operations, servicing loans, tax and capital investment), cover the dividend on ordinary shares paid during the period.

Similarly there is a subtotal after the ordinary share dividend paid. The reason for drawing this subtotal is to highlight the extent to which the business has relied on additional external finance to support its trading and other normally recurring operations. It is claimed that, before the requirement for businesses to produce the cash flow statement, some businesses were able to obscure the fact that they were only able to continue their operations as a result of a series of borrowings and/or share issues. It is no longer possible to obscure such actions.

The effect on a business's cash balance of its various activities is shown in Figure 5.3. The activities that affect cash are analysed in the same way as is required by FRS 1. Note that the arrows in the figure show the *normal* direction of cash flow for the typical healthy, profitable business in a typical year.

Normally 'operating activities' provide positive cash flow: that is, they help to increase the business's cash resources. In fact, for UK businesses, cash

 **Example 5.1**

Propulsion plc
Cash flow statement for the year ended 31 December 2000

	£m	£m
Net cash inflows from operating activities		55
Returns from investment and servicing of finance		
Interest received	1	
Interest paid	(2)	
Net cash outflow from returns on investment and servicing of finance		(1)
Taxation		
Corporation tax paid	(4)	
Net cash outflow for taxation		(4)
Capital expenditure		
Payments to acquire intangible fixed assets	(6)	
Payments to acquire tangible fixed assets	(23)	
Receipts from sales of tangible fixed assets	4	
Net cash outflow for capital expenditure		(25)
		25
Equity dividends		
Dividend on ordinary shares	(10)	
Net cash outflow for equity dividends		(10)
		15
Management of liquid resources		
Disposal of treasury bills	3	
Net cash inflow from management of liquid resources		3
Financing		
Repayments of debenture stock	(6)	
Net cash outflow for financing		(6)
Increase in cash		12

generated from normal trading, even after deducting tax, interest and dividends, is overwhelmingly the most important source of new finance for most businesses in most time periods.

Various activities of the business each have their own effect on its cash balance, either positive or negative. The increase or decrease in the cash balance over a period will be the sum of these individual effects, taking account of the direction (cash in or cash out) of each activity's effect on cash.

Note that the direction of the arrow shows the normal direction of the cash flow in respect of each activity. In certain circumstances each of these arrows could be reversed in direction: for example, in some circumstances the business might be eligible to claim a repayment of tax instead of having to pay it. Only with 'management of liquid resources' will there not be a 'normal' direction of the cash flow.

Figure 5.3 Diagrammatic representation of the cash flow statement

Activity 5.3

Last year's cash flow statement for Angus plc showed a negative cash flow from operating activities. What could be the reason for this, and should the business's management be alarmed by it? (*Hint*: We think that there are two broad possible reasons for a negative cash flow.)

The two reasons are:

- The business is unprofitable. This leads to more cash being paid out to employees, suppliers of goods and services and so on, than is received from debtors in respect of sales. This would be particularly alarming, because a major expense for most businesses is depreciation of fixed assets. Since depreciation does not lead to a cash flow, it is not considered in cash flow from operating activities. Interest paid on any money borrowed by the business would not be included here either, because it is taken into account under 'servicing of finance'. Thus a negative operating cash flow might well indicate a very much larger trading loss – in other words a significant loss of the business's wealth.

- The other reason might be less alarming. A business that is expanding its activities (level of sales) would tend to spend quite a lot of cash, relative to the amount of cash coming in from sales. This is because it will probably be expanding its stockholdings to accommodate the increased demand. In the first instance, it would not necessarily benefit, in cash flow terms, from all of the additional sales. Normally, a business may well have to have the stock in place before additional sales could be made. Even when the additional sales are made, the sales would normally be made on credit, with the cash inflow lagging behind the sale. This would be particularly likely to be true of a new business, which would be expanding stocks and other assets from zero. Expansion typically causes cash flow strains for the reasons just explained. This can be a particular problem because the business's increased profitability might encourage a feeling of optimism, which could lead to necessary concern not being shown for the cash flow problem.

To continue with our consideration of the 'normal' direction of cash flows, normally a business would pay out more to service its loan finance than it receives from financial investments (loans made and shares owned) that it has itself made.

Companies pay tax on profits, so the cash flow would be from the company to the Inland Revenue, where the company is profitable, or there would not be a cash flow where the company is making a loss. Where a company makes a trading loss following a period of having paid tax on profits, it would be entitled to set the current loss against past profits and obtain a refund of past tax paid as a result. Thus there might be a positive cash flow from taxation.

Investing activities can give rise to positive cash flows when a business sells some fixed assets. Because most types of fixed asset wear out, and because businesses tend to seek to expand their asset base, the normal direction of cash in this area is out of the business: that is, negative.

Financing can go in either direction, depending on the financing strategy at the time. Since businesses seek to expand, there is a general tendency for this area to lead to cash coming into the business rather than leaving it.

Deducing net cash inflows from operating activities

The first category of cash flow that appears in the statement, and the one that is typically the most important for most businesses, is the cash flow from operations. There are two approaches that can be taken to deriving the figure for inclusion in the statement: the direct approach and the indirect approach.

The direct method

✱ In the **direct method** an analysis is undertaken of the cash records of the business for the period, picking out all payments and receipts relating to operating activities. These are summarised to give the net figure for inclusion in the cash flow statement. This could be a time-consuming and laborious activity, though it could be done by computer. Not many businesses adopt this approach.

The indirect method

The **indirect method** is the more popular method. It relies on the fact that, broadly, sales give rise to cash inflows, and expenses give rise to outflows. Broadly, therefore, net profit will be equal in amount to the net cash inflow from operating activities. Since businesses have to produce a profit and loss account in any case, information from it can be used to deduce the cash inflow from operating activities.

Within a particular accounting period it is not strictly true that net profit equals the net cash inflow from operating activities, however. Take sales, for example. When sales are made on credit, the cash receipt occurs some time after the sale. This means that sales made towards the end of an accounting year will be included in that year's profit and loss account, but most of the cash from those sales will flow into the business, and should be included in the cash flow statement, in the following year. Fortunately it is easy to deduce the cash received from sales if we have the relevant profit and loss account.

Activity 5.4

How can we deduce the cash inflow from sales using the profit and loss account and balance sheet for the business?

The balance sheet will tell us how much was owed in respect of credit sales at the beginning and end of the year (trade debtors). The profit and loss account tells us the sales figure. If we adjust the sales figure by the increase or decrease in trade debtors over the year, we deduce the cash from sales for the year.

Example 5.2

The sales figure for the year is £34 million. The trade debtors were £4 million at the beginning of the year, but had increased to £5 million by the end of the year.

Basically the debtors figure is affected by sales and cash receipts. It is increased when a sale is made and decreased when cash is received from a debtor. If, over the year, the sales and the cash receipts had been equal, the debtors figures would have been equal. Since the debtors figure increased, it must mean that less cash was received than sales were made. Thus the cash receipts from sales must be £33 million $(34 - (5 - 4))$.

Put slightly differently, we can say that as a result of sales, assets of £34 million flowed into the business during the year. If £1 million of this went to increasing the asset of trade debtors, this leaves only £33 million that went to increase cash.

The same general point is true in respect of nearly all of the other items that are taken into account in deducing the operating profit figure. The exception is depreciation. This is not necessarily associated with any movement in cash during the accounting period.

All of this means that if we take the operating profit (that is, the profit before interest and tax) for the year, add back the depreciation charged in arriving at that profit, and adjust this total by movements in stock, debtors and creditors, we have the effect on cash.

Example 5.3

The relevant information from the accounts of Dido plc for last year is as follows:

	£m
Net operating profit	122
Depreciation charged in arriving at net operating profit	34
At the beginning of the year	
Stock	15
Debtors	24
Creditors	18
At the end of the year	
Stock	17
Debtors	21
Creditors	19

The cash flow from operating activities is derived as follows:

		£m
Net operating profit		122
Add Depreciation		34
Net inflow of working capital from operations		156
Less Increase in stock		2
		154
Add Decrease in debtors	3	
Increase in creditors	1	4
Net cash inflow from operating activities		158

Thus the net increase in working capital, as a result of trading, was £156 million. Of this, £2 million went into increased stocks. More cash was received from debtors than sales were made, and less cash was paid to creditors than purchases of goods and services on credit. Both of these had a favourable effect on cash, which increased by £158 million.

The indirect method of deducing the net cash flow from operating activities is summarised in Figure 5.4.

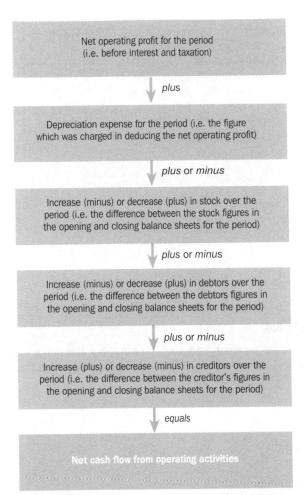

Figure 5.4 The indirect method of deducing the net cash flow from the operating activities

Activity 5.5

The relevant information from the accounts of Pluto plc for last year is as follows:

	£m
Net operating profit	165
Depreciation charged in arriving at net operating profit	41
At the beginning of the year:	
Stock	22
Debtors	18
Creditors	15
At the end of the year	
Stock	23
Debtors	21
Creditors	17

What figure should appear in the cash flow statement for 'net cash inflow from operating activities'?

Net cash flow from operating activities:

	£m	£m
Net operating profit		165
Add Depreciation		41
Net increase in working capital from operations		206
Less Increase in stock	1	
Increase in debtors	3	4
		202
Add Increase in creditors		2
Net cash inflow from operating activities		204

We can now go on to take a look at the preparation of a complete cash flow statement – see Example 5.4.

 Example 5.4

Torbryan plc's profit and loss account for the year ended 31 December 2000 and the balance sheets as at 31 December 1999 and 2000 are as follows:

Profit and loss account for the year ended 31 December 2000

	£m	£m
Turnover		576
Cost of sales		307
Gross profit		269
Distribution costs	65	
Administrative expenses	26	91
		178
Other operating income		21
		199
Interest receivable and similar income		17
		216
Interest payable and similar charges		23
		193
Tax on profit or loss on ordinary activities		46
Profit on ordinary activities after taxation		147
Retained profit brought forward from last year		16
		163
Transfer to general reserve	60	
Proposed dividend on ordinary shares	50	110
Retained profit carried forward		53

Balance sheets as at 31 December 1999 and 2000

	1999 £m	2000 £m
Fixed assets		
Intangible assets:		
Patents and trade marks	44	37
Tangible assets:		
Land and buildings	241	310
Plant and machinery	110	125
Fixtures, fittings, tools and equipment	155	163
	550	635
Current assets		
Stocks	44	41
Debtors:		
Trade debtors	115	123
Prepayments and accrued income	6	16
Cash at bank and in hand	2	3
	167	183
Creditors: amounts falling due within one year		
Bank overdraft	30	9
Trade creditors	44	39
Corporation tax	16	23
Dividend proposed	40	50
Accrued expenses	11	15
	141	136
Net current assets	26	47
Total assets less current liabilities	576	682
Creditors: amounts falling due after more than one year		
Debenture loans	400	250
	176	432
Capital and reserves		
Called-up ordinary share capital	150	200
Share premium account	–	40
Revaluation reserve	–	69
General reserves	10	70
Profit and loss account	16	53
	176	432

During 2000, the company spent £40 million on additional plant and £55 million on additional fixtures. There were no other fixed asset acquisitions or disposals. The cash flow statement would be as follows:

Torbryan plc

Cash flow statement for the year ended 31 December 2000

	£m	£m
Net cash inflows from operating activities		262
(see note 1 below)		
Returns from investment and servicing of finance		
Interest received	17	
Interest paid	(23)	
Net cash outflow from returns on investment and servicing of finance		(6)
Taxation		
Corporation tax paid (note 3)	(39)	
Net cash outflow for taxation		(39)
Capital expenditure		
Payments to acquire tangible fixed assets	(95)	
Net cash outflow for capital expenditure		(95)
		122
Equity dividends paid		
Dividends paid (note 2)	(40)	
Net cash outflow for dividends		(40)
		82
Management of liquid resources		—
Financing		
Repayments of debenture stock (note 4)	(150)	
Issue of ordinary shares (note 5)	90	
Net cash outflow for financing		60
Net increase in cash		22

To see how this relates to the cash of the business at the beginning and end of the year it is useful to show a reconciliation as follows:

Analysis of cash during the year ended 31 December 2000

	£m
Balance at 1 April 1999	(28)
Net cash inflow	22
Balance at 31 December 2000	(6)

To explain where the opening and closing balances came from, another reconciliation can be shown, as follows:

Analysis of cash balances as shown in the balance sheet

	2000	1999	Change in year
	£m	£m	£m
Cash at bank and in hand	3	2	
Bank overdrafts	(9)	(30)	
	(6)	(28)	22

Notes

1 Calculation of net cash inflow from operating activities

	£m	£m
Net operating profit (from the profit and loss account)		199
Add Depreciation		
Patents and trade marks (44 − 37)*	7	
Plant etc (110 + 40 − 125)*	25	
Fixtures etc. (155 + 55 − 163)*	47	79
		278
Less Increase in debtors (123 − 115)	8	
Increase in prepayments (16 − 6)	10	
Decrease in creditors (44 − 39)	5	23
		255
Add Decrease in stocks (44 − 41)	3	
Increase in accrued expenses (15 − 11)	4	7
		262

* Since there were no disposals, the depreciation charges must be the difference between the start and end of the year fixed asset values, adjusted by the cost of any additions. For example:

	£m
Plant etc. at book value, at 1. 1. 2000	110
Add additions	40
	150
Less depreciation (balancing figure)	25
Plant etc, at book value, at 31.12.2000	125

2 Dividends

Since all of the dividend for 2000 was unpaid at the end of 2000, it seems that the business pays just one final dividend each year, some time after the year end. Thus it is the 1999 dividend that will actually have led to a cash outflow in 2000.

3 Taxation

Tax is paid by companies 50 per cent during their accounting year and the other 50 per cent in the following year. Thus the 2000 payment would have been half the tax on the 1999 profit (that is, the figure that would have appeared in the current liabilities at the end of 1999), plus half of the 2000 tax charge (that is, $16 + (\frac{1}{2} \times 46) = 39$).

4 Debentures

It has been assumed that the debentures were redeemed for their balance sheet value. This is not always the case however.

5 Shares

The share issue raised £90 million, of which £50 million went into the share capital total on the balance sheet and £40 million into share premium.

6 Revaluation reserve

It seems that land and buildings were revalued during the year. This would not have affected cash.

Exhibit 5.1 is the cash flow statement of United Biscuit Holdings plc for the year ended 2 January 1999. United Biscuits manufactures foods and confectioneries. These include Penguin bars, McVities Jaffa Cakes, Hula Hoops, Jane Asher desserts and Linda McCartney prepared dishes.

Exhibit 5.1

Cash flow statement of United Biscuits (Holdings) plc for the year ended 2 January 1999

	£m
Net cash inflow from operating activities	149.7
Net cash outflow from returns on investments and servicing of finance	(11.1)
Tax paid	(31.5)
Net cash outflow from capital expenditure and financial investment	(87.8)
Net cash inflow/(outflow) from acquisitions and disposals	110.2
Dividends paid	(54.2)
Cash inflow before use of liquid resources and financing	75.3
Net cash (inflow)/outflow from management of liquid resources	(52.4)
Net cash outflow/(inflow) from financing	136.0
Decrease in cash in the period	(8.3)
	75.3

What does the cash flow statement tell us?

The cash flow statement tells us how the business has generated cash during the period and where that cash has gone. Since cash is properly regarded as the lifeblood of just about any business, this is potentially very useful information.

Tracking the sources and uses of cash over several years could show financing trends that a reader of the statements could use to help to make predictions about likely future behaviour of the company.

Looking specifically at the cash flow statement for Torbryan plc, in Example 5.4, we can see the following:

- Net cash flow from operations was strong, much larger than the profit figure. This would be expected because depreciation is deducted in arriving at profit. There was a general tendency for working capital to absorb some cash. This would not be surprising had there been an expansion of activity (sales output) over the year. From the information supplied, we do not know whether there was an expansion or not.

- There were net outflows of cash in servicing of finance, payment of tax and increasing fixed assets.
- There seems to be a healthy figure of net cash flow after equity dividends.
- There was a fairly major outflow of cash to redeem some debt finance, partly offset by the proceeds of a share issue.
- The net effect was a rather healthier-looking cash position in 2000 than was the case in 1999.

Chapter 6 deals, in a more analytical manner, with the interpretation of cash flow statements.

Self-assessment question 5.1

Touchstone plc's profit and loss accounts for the years ended 31 December 1999 and 2000 and the balance sheets as at 31 December 1999 and 2000 are as follows:

Profit and loss accounts for the years ended 1999 and 2000

	1999 £m	2000 £m
Turnover	173	207
Cost of sales	(96)	(101)
Gross profit	77	106
Distribution costs	(18)	(22)
Administrative expenses	(25)	(26)
	34	58
Other operating income	3	4
	37	62
Interest receivable and similar income	1	2
	38	64
Interest payable and similar charges	(2)	(4)
	36	60
Tax on profit or loss on ordinary activities	(8)	(16)
Profit on ordinary activities after taxation	28	44
Retained profit brought forward from last year	16	30
	44	74
Dividend (proposed and paid) on ordinary shares	(14)	(18)
Retained profit carried forward	30	56

Balance sheets as at 31 December 1999 and 2000

	1999 £m	2000 £m
Fixed assets		
Tangible assets:		
Land and buildings	94	110
Plant and machinery	53	62
	147	172

Current assets		
Stocks	25	24
Treasury bills	–	15
Debtors	16	26
Cash at bank and in hand	4	4
	45	69
Creditors: amounts falling due within one year		
Trade creditors	26	23
Corporation tax	4	8
Dividend proposed	12	14
	42	45
Net current assets	3	24
Total assets less current liabilities	150	196
Creditors: amounts falling due after more than one year		
Debenture loans (10%)	20	40
	130	156
Capital and reserves		
Called-up ordinary share capital	100	100
Profit and loss account	30	56
	130	156

Included in 'cost of sales', 'distribution costs' and 'administration expenses', depreciation was as follows:

	1999	2000
	£m	£m
Land and buildings	5	6
Plant and machinery	6	10

There were no fixed asset disposals in either year.

In both years an interim dividend was paid in the year in whose profit and loss account it was shown and a final dividend just after the end of the year concerned.

Required:

Prepare a cash flow statement for the business for 2000.

SUMMARY

Users of accounting information find it very useful to have a statement that highlights how a business generated cash, how it used cash, and the resultant effect on its cash resources over a period, typically one year. The cash flow statement does this. The cash flow statement contrasts with the profit and loss account to the extent that the former shows cash movements, whereas the latter shows changes in business wealth (not just that which is represented by cash) as a result just of trading activities. The statement used by UK businesses is of the form and content laid down by FRS 1. This standard requires that cash flows are analysed among those arising from trading operations, those that are concerned with dividends received and interest paid and received, those that relate to payments of tax, those that are caused by acquiring and disposing of fixed assets, those that relate to management of short-term investments, and those that arise from additions to or redemption of long-term finance.

Key terms

cash flow *p 114*
net cash flow from operating
    activities *p 117*
returns from investment and
    servicing of finance *p 117*
taxation *p 117*
capital expenditure *p 118*

equity dividends paid *p 119*
management of liquid resources
    p 119
financing *p 119*
direct method *p 122*
indirect method *p 123*

REVIEW QUESTIONS

5.1 The typical business outside the service sector has about 50 per cent more of its resources tied up in stock than in cash, yet there is no call for a 'stock flow statement' to be prepared. Why is cash regarded as more important than stock?

5.2 What is the difference between the direct and indirect methods of deducing cash flow from operating activities?

5.3 Taking each of the categories of the cash flow statement in turn, in which direction would you normally expect the cash flow to be?

  (a) Cash flow from operations
  (b) Cash flow from returns from investments and servicing of finance
  (c) Cash flow from taxation
  (d) Cash flow from capital expenditure
  (e) Cash flow from equity dividends
  (f) Cash flow from management of liquid resources
  (g) Cash flow from financing

5.4 What causes the net profit for the year not to equal the net cash inflow?

Questions 5.3–5.5 are more advanced than 5.1 and 5.2. Those with coloured numbers have answers at the back of the book.

5.1 How will each of the following events ultimately affect the amount of cash:

(a) An increase in the level of stock-in-trade.
(b) A rights issue of ordinary shares.
(c) A bonus issue of ordinary shares.
(d) Writing off the value of some stock-in-trade.
(e) The disposal of a large number of the business's shares by a major shareholder.
(f) Depreciating a fixed asset

5.2 The following information has been taken from the accounts of Juno plc for last year and the year before last:

		£m
Net operating profit	last year	187
	year before last	156
Depreciation charged in arriving at net operating profit		
	last year	55
	year before last	47
Stock held at the end of	last year	31
	year before last	27
Debtors at the end of	last year	23
	year before last	24
Creditors at the end of	last year	17
	year before last	15

Required:
What is the cash flow from operations figure for Juno plc for last year?

5.3 Torrent plc's profit and loss account for the year ended 31 December 2000 and the balance sheets as at 31 December 1999 and 2000 are as follows:

Profit and loss account

	£m	£m
Turnover		623
Cost of sales		353
Gross profit		270
Distribution costs	71	
Administrative expenses	30	101
		169
Other operating income		13
		182
Interest receivable and similar income		14
		196

	£m	£m
Interest payable and similar charges		26
		170
Tax on profit on ordinary activities		36
Profit on ordinary activities after taxation		134
Retained profit brought forward from last year		53
		187
Transfer to general reserve	40	
Proposed dividend on ordinary shares	60	100
Retained profit carried forward		87

Balance sheets as at 31 December 1999 and 2000

	1999	2000
	£m	£m
Fixed assets		
Intangible assets:		
Patents and trademarks	37	32
Tangible assets:		
Land and buildings	310	310
Plant and machinery	125	102
Fixtures, fittings, tools and equipment	163	180
	635	624
Current assets		
Stocks	41	35
Debtors		
Trade debtors	123	132
Prepayments and accrued income	16	13
Cash at bank and in hand	2	5
	182	185
Creditors: amounts falling due within one year		
Bank overdraft	8	34
Trade creditors	39	30
Corporation tax	23	18
Dividend proposed	50	60
Accrued expenses	15	11
	135	153
Net current assets	47	32
Total assets less current liabilities	682	656
Creditors: amounts falling due after more than one year		
Debenture loans	250	150
	432	506

	1999	2000
	£m	£m
Capital and reserves		
Called-up ordinary share capital	200	300
Share premium account	40	—
Revaluation reserve	69	9
General reserves	70	110
Profit and loss account	53	87
	432	506

During 2000, the business spent £67 million on additional fixtures etc. There were no other fixed asset acquisitions or disposals.

There was no share issue for cash during the year.

Required:

Prepare the cash flow statement for Torrent plc for the year ended 31 December 2000, including the supplementary statements.

5.4 Seaton plc's profit and loss accounts for the years ended 31 December 2000 and 2001 and the balance sheets as at 31 December 2000 and 2001 are as follows:

Profit and loss account

	2000	2001
	£m	£m
Turnover	207	153
Cost of sales	(101)	(76)
Gross profit	106	77
Distribution costs	(22)	(20)
Administrative expenses	(26)	(28)
	58	29
Other operating income	4	--
	62	29
Interest receivable and similar income	2	--
	64	29
Interest payable and similar charges	(4)	(4)
	60	25
Tax on profit or loss on ordinary activities	(16)	(6)
Profit on ordinary activities after taxation	44	19
Retained profit brought forward from last year	30	56
	74	75
Dividends on ordinary shares (paid and proposed)	(18)	(18)
Retained profit carried forward	56	57

Balance sheets as at 31 December 2000 and 2001

	2000 £m	2001 £m
Fixed assets		
Tangible assets:		
Land and buildings	110	130
Plant and machinery	62	56
	172	186
Current assets		
Stocks	24	25
Debtors	26	25
Cash at bank and in hand	19	1
	69	51
Creditors: amounts falling due within one year		
Bank overdraft	–	3
Trade creditors	23	20
Corporation tax	8	3
Dividend proposed	14	14
	45	40
Net current assets	24	11
Total assets less current liabilities	196	197
Creditors: amounts falling due after more than one year		
Debenture loans (10%)	40	40
	156	157
Capital and reserves		
Called-up ordinary share capital	100	100
Profit and loss account	56	57
	156	157

Included in 'cost of sales', 'distribution costs' and 'administration expenses', depreciation was as follows:

	2000 £m	2001 £m
Land and buildings	6	10
Plant and machinery	10	12

There were no fixed asset disposals in either year.
In both years an interim dividend was paid in the year in whose profit and loss account it was shown and a final dividend just after the end of the year concerned.

Required:
Prepare a cash flow statement for the business for 2001.

5.5 The following are the accounts for Nailsea plc for the year ended 30 June 2000 and 2001:

Profit and loss accounts for years ended 30 June

	2001	2000
	£m	£m
Sales	2,280	1,230
Operating costs	(1,618)	(722)
Depreciation	(320)	(270)
Operating profit	342	238
Interest	(27)	—
Profit before tax	315	238
Tax	(140)	(110)
Profit after tax	175	128
Dividend	(85)	(80)
Retained profit for year	90	48

Balance sheets as at 30 June

	2001		2000	
	£m	£m	£m	£m
Fixed assets (see below)		2,640		2,310
Current assets				
Stock	450		275	
Debtors	250		100	
Bank	83		—	
	783		375	
Less **Creditors due within one year**				
Bank overdraft	—		32	
Creditors	190		130	
Taxation	70		55	
Dividend	85		80	
	345		297	
Net current assets		438		78
		3,078		2,388
Less **Creditors falling due after more than one year**				
9% Debentures (2006)		300		—
		2,778		2,388
Share capital (fully paid £1 shares)		1,600		1,400
Share premium account		300		200
Retained profits		878		788
		2,778		2,388

Schedule of fixed assets

	Land & buildings £m	Plant & machinery £m	Total £m
Cost			
At 1 July 2000	1,500	1,350	2,850
Additions	400	250	650
At 30 June 2001	1,900	1,600	3,500
Depreciation			
At 1 July 2000	–	540	540
Charge for year at 20%	–	320	320
At 30 June 2001	–	860	860
Net book value at 30 June 2001	1,900	740	2,640

Required:

Prepare a cash flow statement for Nailsea plc for the year ended 30 June 2001.

Analysis and interpretation of financial statements

INTRODUCTION

In this chapter we shall consider the analysis, interpretation and evaluation of financial statements. We shall see how financial ratios can help in developing a financial profile of a business. We shall also consider problems that are encountered when applying this technique.

Objectives

When you have completed this chapter you should be able to:

- identify the major categories of ratios that can be used for analysis purposes
- calculate important ratios for determining the financial performance and position of a business, and explain the significance of the ratios calculated
- explain the importance of gearing to a business and its owners
- discuss the limitations of ratios as a tool of financial analysis.

Financial ratios

Financial ratios provide a quick and relatively simple means of examining the financial health of a business. A ratio simply relates one figure appearing in the financial statements to some other figure appearing in the financial statements (for example, net profit in relation to capital employed) or, perhaps, some resource of the business (for example, net profit per employee, sales per square metre of counter space, and so on).

Ratios can be very helpful when comparing the financial health of different businesses. Differences may exist between businesses in the scale of operations, and so a direct comparison of (say) the profits generated by each business may be misleading. By expressing profit in relation to some other measure (for example, sales), the problem of scale is eliminated. A business with a profit of, say, £10,000 and a sales turnover of £100,000 can be compared with a much larger business with a profit of, say, £80,000 and a sales turnover of £1,000,000 by the use of a simple ratio. The net profit to sales turnover ratio for the smaller company is 10 per cent ($[10,000/100,000] \times 100\%$) and the same ratio for the larger company will be 8 per cent ($[80,000/1,000,000] \times 100\%$). These ratios can be directly compared whereas comparison of the absolute profit figures would be less meaningful. The need to eliminate differences in scale through the use of ratios can also apply when comparing the performance of the same business over time.

By calculating a relatively small number of ratios, it is often possible to build up a reasonably good picture of the position and performance of a business. Thus it is not surprising that ratios are widely used by those who have an interest in businesses and business performance. Although ratios are not difficult to calculate, they can be difficult to interpret.

It is important to appreciate that ratios are really only the starting point for further analysis. They help to highlight the financial strengths and weaknesses of a business, but they cannot, by themselves, explain why certain strengths or weaknesses exist, or why certain changes have occurred. Only a detailed investigation will reveal these underlying reasons.

Ratios can be expressed in various forms, for example as a percentage, as a fraction, or as a proportion. The way a particular ratio is presented will depend on the needs of those who will use the information. Although it is possible to calculate a large number of ratios, only a relatively few, based on key relationships, may be helpful to the user. Many ratios that could be calculated from the financial statements (for example, rent payable in relation to current assets) may not be considered because there is no clear or meaningful relationship between the items.

There is no generally accepted list of ratios that can be applied to the financial statements, nor is there a standard method of calculating many ratios. Variations in both the choice of ratios and their calculation will be found in the literature and in practice. However, it is important to be consistent in the way in which ratios are calculated for comparison purposes. The ratios discussed below are those that are widely used because many consider them to be among the more important for decision-making purposes.

Financial ratio classification

Ratios can be grouped into certain categories, each of which reflects a particular aspect of financial performance or position. The following broad categories provide a useful basis for explaining the nature of the financial ratios to be dealt with.

- *Profitability.* Businesses come into being with the primary purpose of creating wealth for their owners. Profitability ratios provide an insight to the degree of success in achieving this purpose. They express the profits made (or figures bearing on profit, such as overheads) in relation to other key figures in the financial statements or to some business resource.
- *Efficiency.* Ratios may be used to measure the efficiency with which certain

resources have been utilised within the business. These ratios are also referred to as *activity* ratios.

- *Liquidity.* It is vital to the survival of a business for there to be sufficient liquid resources available to meet maturing obligations. Certain ratios may be calculated that examine the relationship between liquid resources held and creditors due for payment in the near future.
- *Gearing.* Gearing is an important issue, which managers must consider when making financing decisions. The relationship between the amount financed by the owners of the business and the amount contributed by outsiders has an important effect on the degree of risk associated with a business, as we shall see.
- *Investment.* Certain ratios are concerned with assessing the returns and performance of shares held in a particular business.

The need for comparison

Calculating a ratio by itself will not tell you very much about the position or performance of a business. For example, if a ratio revealed that the business was generating £100 in sales per square metre of counter space, it would not be possible to deduce from this information alone whether this level of performance was good, bad or indifferent. It is only when you compare this ratio with some 'benchmark' that the information can be interpreted and evaluated.

Activity 6.1

Can you think of any bases that could be used to compare a ratio you have calculated from the financial statements of a particular period?

In answering this activity you may have thought of the following bases:

- *Past periods.* By comparing the ratio you have calculated with the ratio of a previous period, it is possible to detect whether there has been an improvement or deterioration in performance. Indeed, it is often useful to track particular ratios over time (say five or ten years) in order to see whether it is possible to detect trends. However, the comparison of ratios from different time periods brings certain problems. In particular, there is always the possibility that trading conditions may have been quite different in the periods being compared. There is the further problem that, when comparing the performance of a single business over time, operating inefficiencies may not be clearly exposed. For example, the fact that net profit per employee has risen by 10 per cent over the previous period may at first sight appear to be satisfactory; however, this may not be the case if similar businesses have shown an improvement of 50 per cent for the same period. Finally, there is the problem that inflation may have distorted the figures on which the ratios are based. Inflation can lead to an overstatement of profit and an understatement of asset values.
- *Planned performance.* Ratios may be compared with the targets that management developed before the commencement of the period under review. The comparison of

planned performance with actual performance may therefore be a useful way of revealing the level of achievement attained. However, the planned levels of performance must be based on realistic assumptions if they are to be useful for comparison purposes.

- *Similar businesses.* In a competitive environment, a business must consider its performance in relation to those of other businesses operating in the same industry. Survival may depend on the ability to achieve comparable levels of performance. Thus a very useful basis for comparing a particular ratio is the ratio achieved by similar businesses during the same period. This basis is not, however, without its problems. Competitors may have different year-ends, and therefore trading conditions may not be identical. They may also have different accounting policies, which can have a significant effect on reported profits and asset values (for example, different methods of calculating depreciation, or different methods of valuing stock). Finally, it may be difficult to get hold of the accounts of competitor businesses. Sole proprietorships and partnerships, for example, are not obliged to publish their financial statements. In the case of limited companies, there is a legal obligation to publish accounts. However, a diversified company may not provide a detailed breakdown of activities sufficient for analysts to compare it with the activities of other businesses.

The key steps in financial ratio analysis

When employing financial ratios, a sequence of steps is carried out by the analyst. The first step involves identifying the key indicators and relationships that require examination. In order to carry out this step the analyst must be clear *who* the target users are and *why* they need the information. Different users of financial information are likely to have different information needs, which will in turn determine the ratios that they find useful. For example, shareholders are likely to be interested in their returns in relation to the level of risk associated with their investment. Thus profitability, investment and gearing ratios will be of particular interest. Long-term lenders are concerned with the long-term viability of the business. To help long-term lenders to assess this, the profitability ratios and gearing ratios of the business are also likely to be of particular interest. Short-term lenders, such as suppliers, may be interested in the ability of the business to repay the amounts owing in the short term. As a result the liquidity ratios should be of interest.

The next step in the process is to calculate ratios that are considered appropriate for the particular users and the purpose for which they require the information. The final step is interpretation and evaluation of the ratios. Interpretation involves examining the ratios in conjunction with an appropriate basis for comparison and any other information that may be relevant. The significance of the ratios calculated can then be established. Evaluation involves forming a judgement concerning the value of the information uncovered in the calculation and interpretation stage. While calculation is usually straightforward, interpretation and evaluation are more difficult,

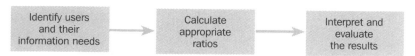

| Identify users and their information needs | → | Calculate appropriate ratios | → | Interpret and evaluate the results |

The three steps involve: first, identifying for whom and for what purpose the analysis and interpretation are required; second, selecting appropriate ratios and calculating them; and, finally, forming a judgement on the information produced.

Figure 6.1 Financial ratio analysis: the key steps

and often require high levels of skill. This skill can only really be acquired through much practice.

The three steps described are shown in Figure 6.1.

The ratios calculated

Probably the best way to explain financial ratios is to go through an example. Example 6.1 provides a set of financial statements from which we can calculate important ratios.

 Example 6.1

The following financial statements relate to Alexis plc, which owns a small chain of wholesale/retail carpet stores:

Balance sheets as at 31 March

	2000 £000	2000 £000	2001 £000	2001 £000
Fixed assets				
Freehold land and buildings at cost	451.2		451.2	
Less Accumulated depreciation	70.0	381.2	75.0	376.2
Fixtures and fittings at cost	129.0		160.4	
Less Accumulated depreciation	64.4	64.6	97.2	63.2
		445.8		439.4
Current assets				
Stock at cost	300.0		370.8	
Trade debtors	240.8		210.2	
Bank	3.4		3.0	
	544.2		584.0	
Creditors due within one year				
Trade creditors	(221.4)		(228.8)	
Dividends proposed	(40.2)		(60.0)	
Corporation tax due	(30.1)		(38.0)	
	(291.7)	252.5	(326.8)	257.2
		698.3		696.6
Creditors due beyond one year				
12% Debentures (secured)		200.0		60.0
		498.3		636.6

	2000		2001	
	£000	£000	£000	£000
Capital and reserves				
£0.50 Ordinary shares		300.0		334.1
General reserve		26.5		40.0
Retained profit		171.8		262.5
		498.3		636.6

Profit and loss accounts for the year ended 31 March

	2000		2001	
	£000	£000	£000	£000
Sales		2,240.8		2,681.2
Less Cost of sales				
Opening stock	241.0		300.0	
Purchases	1,804.4		2,142.8	
	2,045.4		2,442.8	
Less Closing stock	300.0	1,745.4	370.8	2,072.0
Gross profit		495.4		609.2
Wages and salaries	137.8		195.0	
Directors' salaries	48.0		80.6	
Rates	12.2		12.4	
Heat and light	8.4		13.6	
Insurance	4.6		7.0	
Interest payable	24.0		6.2	
Postage and telephone	3.4		7.4	
Audit fees	5.6		9.0	
Depreciation				
Freehold buildings	5.0		5.0	
Fixtures and fittings	27.0	276.0	32.8	369.0
Net profit before tax		219.4		240.2
Less Corporation tax		60.2		76.0
Net profit after tax		159.2		164.2
Add Retained profit brought forward		52.8		171.8
		212.0		336.0
Less				
Transfer to general reserve		–		(13.5)
Dividends proposed		(40.2)		(60.0)
Retained profit carried forward		171.8		262.5

Cash flow statement for the year ended 31 March

	2000		2001	
	£000	£000	£000	£000
Net cash inflow from operating activities		231.0		251.4
Returns on investments and servicing of finance				
Interest paid	(24.0)		(6.2)	
Net cash inflow (outflow) from returns on investments and servicing of finance		(24.0)		(6.2)
Taxation				
Corporation tax paid	(46.4)		(68.1)	
Tax paid		(46.4)		(68.1)
Capital expenditure				
Purchase of fixed assets	(121.2)		(31.4)	
Net cash inflow (outflow) from capital expenditure		(121.2)		(31.4)
Equity dividends				
Dividend on ordinary shares	(32.0)		(40.2)	
Net cash outflow for equity dividends		(32.0)		(40.2)
Management of liquid resources		—		—
Financing				
Issue of ordinary shares	20.0		34.1	
Repayment of loan capital	—	20.0	(140.0)	(105.9)
Increase (decrease) in cash and cash equivalents		27.4		(0.4)

The company employed 14 staff in 2000 and 18 in 2001.

All sales and purchases are made on credit.

The market value of the shares of the company at the end of each year was £2.50 and £3.50 respectively. The issue of equity shares during the year ended 31 March 2001 occurred at the beginning of the year.

Profitability

The following ratios may be used to evaluate the profitability of the business:

- return on ordinary shareholders' funds
- return on capital employed
- net profit margin
- gross profit margin.

Return on ordinary shareholders' funds (ROSF)

✱ The **return on ordinary shareholders' funds** compares the amount of profit for the period available to the owners with the owners' stake in the business. For a limited company, the ratio (which is normally expressed in percentage terms) is as follows:

$$\text{ROSF} = \frac{\textbf{Net profit after taxation and preference dividend (if any)}}{\textbf{Ordinary share capital plus reserves}} \times \textbf{100}$$

The net profit after taxation and any preference dividend is used in calculating the ratio, as this figure represents the amount of profit available to the owners. In the case of Alexis plc, the ratio for the year ended 31 March 2000 is:

$$\frac{159.2}{498.3} \times 100 = 31.9\%$$

Activity 6.2

Calculate the ROSF for Alexis plc for the year to 31 March 2001.

The ROSF for the following year will be as follows:

$$\text{ROSF} = \frac{164.2}{636.6} \times 100$$

$$= 25.8\%$$

Note that in calculating the ratios above, the figure for ordinary shareholders' funds as at the end of the year has been used. However, it can be argued that it is preferable to use an average figure for the year, as this would be more representative of the amount invested by owners during the period. The easiest approach to calculating the average amount invested by ordinary shareholders would be to take a simple average based on the opening and closing figures for the year. However, where these figures are not available, it is acceptable to use the year-end figures, provided that this approach is consistently adopted.

Return on capital employed (ROCE)

* The **return on capital employed** is a fundamental measure of business performance. This ratio expresses the relationship between the net profit generated by the business and the long-term capital invested in the business. The ratio is expressed in percentage terms and is as follows:

$$\text{ROCE} = \frac{\textbf{Net profit before interest and taxation}}{\textbf{Share capital + Reserves + Long-term loans}} \times \textbf{100}$$

Note, in this case, that the profit figure used in the ratio is the net profit *before* interest and taxation. This figure is used because the ratio attempts to measure the returns to all suppliers of long-term finance before any deductions for interest payable to lenders or payments of dividends to shareholders are made. For the year to 31 March 2000 the ratio for Alexis plc is:

$$ROCE = \frac{219.4 + 24.0}{698.3} \times 100$$

$$= 34.9\%$$

Activity 6.3

Calculate the ROCE for Alexis plc for the year to 31 March 2001.

For the year ended 31 March 2001 the ratio is:

$$ROCE = \frac{240.2 + 6.2}{696.6} \times 100$$

$$= 35.4\%$$

ROCE is considered by many to be a primary measure of profitability. It compares inputs (capital invested) with outputs (profit). This comparison is of vital importance in assessing the effectiveness with which funds have been deployed. Once again, an average figure for capital employed may be used where the information is available.

Net profit margin

* The **net profit margin ratio** relates the net profit for the period to the sales during that period. The ratio is expressed as follows:

$$\textbf{Net profit margin} = \frac{\textbf{Net profit before interest and taxation}}{\textbf{Sales}} \times \textbf{100}$$

The net profit before interest and taxation is used in this ratio as it represents the profit from trading operations before any costs of servicing long-term finance are taken into account. This is often regarded as the most appropriate measure of operational performance, for comparison purposes, as differences arising from the way in which a particular business is financed will not influence the measure. However, this is not the only way in which this ratio may be calculated in practice. The net profit after taxation is also used on occasions as the numerator (top part of the fraction).

For the year ended 31 March 2000 Alexis plc's net profit margin ratio (based on the net profit before interest and taxation) is:

$$\frac{243.4}{2,240.8} \times 100 = 10.9\%.$$

This ratio compares one output of the business (profit) with another output (sales). The ratio can vary considerably between types of business. For example, a supermarket will often operate on low prices and, therefore, low profit margins in order to stimulate sales and thereby increase the total amount of profit generated. A jeweller, on the other hand, may have a high net profit margin, but have a much lower level of sales volume. Factors such as the degree of competition, the type of customer, the economic climate and industry characteristics (such as the level of risk) will influence the net profit margins of a business.

Activity 6.4

Calculate the net profit margin for Alexis plc for the year to 31 March 2001.

The net profit margin for the year to 31 March 2001 will be:

$$\frac{246.4}{2,681.2} \times 100$$

$$= 9.2\%$$

Gross profit margin

✱ The **gross profit margin ratio** relates the gross profit of the business to the sales generated for the same period. Gross profit represents the difference between sales and the cost of sales. The ratio is therefore a measure of profitability in buying (or producing) and selling goods before any other expenses are taken into account. As cost of sales represents a major expense for retailing, wholesaling and manufacturing businesses, a change in this ratio can have a significant effect on the 'bottom line' (that is, the net profit for the year). The gross profit ratio is calculated as follows:

$$\textbf{Gross profit margin} = \frac{\textbf{Gross profit}}{\textbf{Sales}} \times 100$$

For the year to 31 March 2000 the ratio for Alexis plc is as follows:

$$\text{Gross profit margin} = \frac{495.4}{2,240.8} \times 100$$

$$= 22.1\%$$

Activity 6.5

Calculate the gross profit margin for Alexis plc for the year to 31 March 2001.

The gross profit margin for the year to 31 March 2001 is as follows:

$$\text{Gross profit margin} = \frac{609.2}{2,681.2} \times 100$$

$$= 22.7\%$$

The profitability ratios for the company over the two years can be set out as follows:

	2000	2001
	%	%
ROSF	31.9	25.8
ROCE	34.9	35.4
Net profit margin	10.9	9.2
Gross profit margin	22.1	22.7

Activity 6.6

What do you deduce from a comparison of the profitability ratios over the two years?

The gross profit margin shows a slight increase in 2001 over the previous year. This may be due to a number of reasons, such as an increase in selling prices and a decrease in the cost of sales. However, the net profit margin has shown a slight decline over the period. This means that operating expenses (wages, rates, insurance etc.) are absorbing a greater proportion of sales income in 2001 than in the previous year.

The net profit available to equity shareholders has risen only slightly over the period, whereas the share capital and reserves of the company have increased considerably (see the financial statements). The effect of this has been to reduce the ROSF. The ROCE has improved slightly in 2001. The slight decrease in long-term capital over the period and increase in net profit before interest and tax has resulted in a better return.

Efficiency

Efficiency ratios examine the ways in which various resources of the business are managed. The following ratios consider some of the more important aspects of resource management:

- average stock turnover period
- average settlement period for debtors
- average settlement period for creditors
- sales to capital employed
- sales per employee.

Average stock turnover period

Stocks often represent a significant investment for a business. For some types of business (for example, manufacturers), stocks may account for a substantial proportion of the total assets held. The **average stock turnover period** measures the average period for which stocks are being held. The ratio is calculated thus:

$$\text{Stock turnover period} = \frac{\text{Average stock held}}{\text{Cost of sales}} \times 365$$

The average stock for the period can be calculated as a simple average of the opening and closing stock levels for the year. However, in the case of a highly seasonal business, where stock levels may vary considerably over the year, a monthly average may be more appropriate.

In the case of Alexis plc the stock turnover period for the year ended 31 March 2000 is:

$$\frac{(241 + 300)/2}{1,745.4} \times 365$$

$$= 57 \text{ days (to nearest day)}$$

This means that, on average, the stock held is being 'turned over' every 57 days. A business will normally prefer a low stock turnover period to a high period, as funds tied up in stocks cannot be used for other purposes. In judging the amount of stock to carry, the business must consider such things as the likely future demand, the possibility of future shortages, the likelihood of future price rises, the amount of storage space available and the perishability of the product. The management of stocks will be considered in more detail in Chapter 11.

This ratio is sometimes expressed in terms of months rather than days. Multiplying by 12 rather than 365 will achieve this.

Activity 6.7

Calculate the average stock turnover period for Alexis plc for the year ended 31 March 2001.

The stock turnover period for the year to 31 March 2001 will be:

$$\frac{(300 + 370.8)/2}{2,072} \times 365$$

$$= 59 \text{ days}$$

Average settlement period for debtors

A business will usually be concerned with how long it takes for customers to pay the amounts owing. The speed of payment can have a significant effect on the cash flow of the business. The **average settlement period for debtors** calculates how long, on average, credit customers take to pay the amounts that they owe to the business. The ratio is as follows:

$$\text{Average settlement period} = \frac{\text{Trade debtors}}{\text{Credit sales}} \times 365$$

We are told that all sales made by Alexis plc are on credit, and so the average settlement period for debtors for the year ended 31 March 2000 is:

$$\frac{240.8}{2,240.8} \times 365$$

$$= 39 \text{ days.}$$

As no figures for opening debtors are available, the year-end debtors figure only is used. This is common practice.

Activity 6.8

Calculate the average settlement period for Alexis plc's debtors for the year ended 31 March 2001. (For the sake of consistency use the year-end debtors figure, rather than an average figure.)

The average settlement period for the year to 2001 is:

$$\frac{210.2}{2,681.2} \times 365$$

$$= 29 \text{ days}$$

A business will normally prefer a shorter average settlement period to a longer one as, once again, funds are being tied up that may be used for more profitable purposes. Although this ratio can be useful it is important to remember that it produces an *average* figure for the number of days for which debts are outstanding. This average may be badly distorted by, for example, a few large customers who are very slow payers.

Average settlement period for creditors

✱ The **average settlement period for creditors** measures how long, on average, the business takes to pay its trade creditors. The ratio is calculated as follows:

$$\textbf{Average settlement period} = \frac{\textbf{Trade creditors}}{\textbf{Credit purchases}} \times \textbf{365}$$

For the year ended 31 March 2000, Alexis plc's average settlement period is:

$$\frac{221.4}{1,804.4} \times 365$$

$$= 45 \text{ days}$$

Once again, the year-end figure rather than an average figure for creditors has been employed in the calculations.

Activity 6.9

Calculate the average settlement period for creditors for Alexis plc for the year ended 31 March 2001. (For the sake of consistency, use a year-end figure for creditors.)

The average settlement period is:

$$\frac{228.8}{2,142.8} \times 365$$

$$= 39 \text{ days}$$

This ratio provides an average figure which, like the average settlement period for debtors ratio, can be distorted by the payment period for one or two large suppliers.

As trade creditors provide a free source of finance for the business, it is perhaps not surprising that some businesses attempt to increase their average settlement period for trade creditors. However, such a policy can be taken too far and result in a loss of goodwill by suppliers. We shall return to the issues concerning the management of trade debtors and trade creditors in Chapter 11.

Sales to capital employed

✱ The **sales to capital employed ratio** (or asset turnover ratio) examines how effectively the assets of the business are being employed in generating sales revenue. The ratio is calculated as follows:

Sales to capital employed ratio

$$= \frac{\textbf{Sales}}{\textbf{Long-term capital employed (shareholders' funds + long-term loans)}}$$

For the year ended 31 March 2000 this ratio for Alexis plc is as follows:

$$\frac{2,240.8}{(498.3 + 200.0)}$$

$$= 3.2 \text{ times.}$$

Once again, year-end figures have been employed, although an average figure for total assets could also be used if sufficient information was available.

Activity 6.10

Calculate the sales to long-term capital employed ratio for Alexis plc for the year ended 31 March 2001. (For the sake of consistency, use a year-end figure for total assets.)

The sales to long-term capital employed ratio for the year ended 31 March 2000 will be:

$$\frac{2,681.2}{(636.6 + 60.0)}$$

$$= 3.8 \text{ times}$$

Generally speaking, a higher asset turnover ratio is preferred to a lower ratio. A higher ratio will normally suggest that assets are being used more productively in the generation of revenue. However, a very high ratio may suggest that the business is 'overtrading on its assets': that is, it has insufficient assets to sustain the level of sales achieved. When comparing this ratio between businesses, such factors as the age and condition of assets held, the valuation bases for assets and whether assets are rented or purchased outright can complicate interpretation.

A variation of this formula is to use the total assets less current liabilities (which is equivalent to long-term capital employed) in the denominator (lower part of the fraction) – the identical result is obtained.

Sales per employee

This ratio relates sales generated to a particular business resource. It provides a measure of the productivity of the workforce. The ratio is:

$$\text{Sales per employee} = \frac{\text{Sales}}{\text{Number of employees}}$$

For the year ended 31 March 2000 the ratio for Alexis plc is:

$$\frac{£2,240,800}{14}$$

$$= £160,057$$

It would also be possible to calculate sales per square metre of floor space in order to help assess productivity. This ratio is often used by retail businesses.

Activity 6.11

Calculate the sales per employee for Alexis plc for the year ended 31 March 2001.

The ratio for the year ended 31 March 2001 is:

$$\frac{£2,681,200}{18}$$

$$= £148,956$$

The activity ratios may be summarised as follows:

	2000	2001
Stock turnover period	57 days	59 days
Average settlement period for debtors	39 days	29 days
Average settlement period for creditors	45 days	39 days
Asset turnover	3.2 times	3.8 times
Sales per employee	£160,057	£148,956

A **Activity 6.12**

What do you deduce from a comparison of the efficiency ratios over the two years?

A comparison of the efficiency ratios between years provides a mixed picture. The average settlement period for both debtors and creditors has reduced. The reduction may have been the result of deliberate policy decisions, for example, tighter credit control for debtors, paying creditors promptly in order to maintain goodwill or to take advantage of discounts. However, it must always be remembered that these ratios, as is true of all ratios, are average figures and therefore may be distorted by a few exceptional amounts owed to, or owed by, the company.

The stock turnover period has shown a slight decrease over the period, but this may not be significant. Overall there has been an increase in the asset turnover ratio, which means that the sales have increased by a greater proportion than the net assets of the company. Sales per employee, however, have declined, and the reasons for this should be investigated.

The relationship between profitability and efficiency

In our earlier discussions concerning profitability ratios you will recall that return on capital employed (ROCE) is regarded as a key ratio by many businesses. The ratio is:

$$\text{ROCE} = \frac{\text{Net profit before interest and taxation}}{\text{Long-term capital employed}} \times 100$$

(where long-term capital companies share capital plus reserves plus long-term loans.) This ratio can be broken down into two elements, as shown in Figure 6.2. The first ratio is of course the net profit margin ratio, and the second ratio is the sales to capital employed ratio, which we discussed earlier.

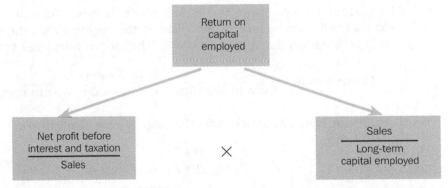

The ROCE ratio can be divided into two elements: net profit to sales, and sales to capital employed. By analysing ROCE in this way we can see the influence of both profitability and efficiency on this important ratio.

Figure 6.2 The main elements comprising the ROCE ratio

By breaking down the ROCE ratio in this manner, we highlight the fact that the overall return on funds employed within the business will be determined both by the profitability of sales and by efficiency in the use of capital.

 Example 6.2

Consider the following information concerning two different businesses operating in the same industry:

	Business A	Business B
Profit before interest and tax	£20m	£15m
Long-term capital employed	£100m	£75m
Sales	£200m	£300m

The ROCE for each business is identical (20 per cent). However, the manner in which the return was achieved by each business was quite different. In the case of Business A, the net profit margin is 10 per cent and the sales to capital employed ratio is 2 times (hence ROCE = 10% × 2 = 20%). In the case of Business B, the net profit margin is 5 per cent and the sales to capital employed ratio is 4 times (hence ROCE = 5% × 4 = 20%).

Example 6.2 demonstrates that a relatively low net profit margin can be compensated for by a relatively high sales to capital employed ratio, and a relatively low sales to capital employed ratio can be compensated for by a relatively high net profit margin. In many areas of retail and distribution (for example, supermarkets and delivery services) the net profit margins are quite low but the ROCE can be high, provided the assets are used productively.

Liquidity

Current ratio

❊ The **current ratio** compares the 'liquid' assets (that is, cash and those assets held that will soon be turned into cash) of the business with the short-term liabilities (creditors due within one year). The ratio is calculated as follows:

$$\text{Current ratio} = \frac{\text{Current assets}}{\text{Current liabilities (creditors due within one year)}}$$

For the year ended 31 March 2000 the current ratio of Alexis plc is:

$$\frac{544.2}{291.7}$$

$$= 1.9 \text{ times}$$

The ratio reveals that the current assets cover the current liabilities by 1.9 times. In some texts the notion of an 'ideal' current ratio (usually 2 times or

2:1) is suggested for businesses. However, this fails to take into account the fact that different types of business require different current ratios. For example, a manufacturing business will often have a relatively high current ratio because it is necessary to hold stocks of finished goods, raw materials and work-in-progress. It will also normally sell goods on credit, thereby incurring debtors. A supermarket chain, on the other hand, will have a relatively low ratio as it will hold only fast-moving stocks of finished goods and will generate mostly cash sales. (See exhibit 11.1 on p. 302.)

The higher the ratio, the more liquid the business is considered to be. As liquidity is of vital importance to the survival of a business, a higher current ratio is normally preferred to a lower ratio. However, if a business has a very high ratio this may suggest that funds are being tied up in cash or other liquid assets and are not being used as productively as they might otherwise be.

Activity 6.13

Calculate the current ratio for Alexis plc for the year ended 31 March 2001.

The current ratio for the year ended 31 March 2001 is:

$$\frac{584.0}{326.8}$$

$$= 1.8 \text{ times}$$

Acid test ratio

* The **acid test ratio** represents a more stringent test of liquidity. It can be argued that, for many businesses, the stock in hand cannot be converted into cash quickly. (Note that in the case of Alexis plc the stock turnover period was more than 50 days in both years.) As a result, it may be better to exclude this particular asset from any measure of liquidity. The acid test ratio is based on this idea and is calculated as follows:

$$\text{Acid test ratio} = \frac{\textbf{Current assets (excluding stock)}}{\textbf{Current liabilities (creditors due within one year)}}$$

The acid test ratio for Alexis plc for the year ended 31 March 2000 is:

$$\frac{(544.2 - 300)}{291.7}$$

$$= 0.8 \text{ times}$$

We can see that the 'liquid' current assets do not quite cover the current liabilities, and so the business may be experiencing some liquidity problems. In some types of business, however, where cash flows are strong, it is not unusual for the acid test ratio to be below 1.0 without causing particular liquidity problems. (See Exhibit 11.1 on p. 302.)

The current and acid test ratios for 2000 can be expressed as 1.9:1 and 0.8:1 respectively, rather than as a number of times. This form can be found in some texts. The interpretation of the ratios, however, will not be affected by this difference in form.

Activity 6.14

Calculate the acid test ratio for Alexis plc for the year ended 31 March 2001.

The acid test ratio for the year ended 31 March 2001 is:

$$\frac{(584.0 - 370.8)}{326.8}$$

$$= 0.7 \text{ times}$$

Both the current ratio and the acid test ratio derive the relevant figures from the balance sheet. As the balance sheet is simply a 'snapshot' of the financial position of the business at a single moment in time, care must be taken when interpreting the ratios. It is possible that the balance sheet figures are not representative of the liquidity position during the year. This may be due to exceptional factors, or simply to the fact that the business is seasonal in nature and the balance sheet figures represent the cash position at one particular point in the seasonal cycle only.

Operating cash flows to maturing obligations

✴ The **operating cash flows to maturing obligations ratio** compares the operating cash flows with the current liabilities of the business. It provides a further indication of the ability of the business to meet its maturing obligations. The ratio is calculated as follows:

$$\frac{\text{Operating cash flows}}{\text{Current liabilities}}$$

The higher this ratio, the better the liquidity of the business. This ratio has the advantage that the operating cash flows for a period usually provide a more reliable guide to the liquidity of a business than the current assets held at the balance sheet date. Alexis plc's ratio for the year ended 31 March 2000 is:

$$\frac{231.0}{291.7}$$

$$= 0.8 \text{ times}$$

This ratio indicates that the operating cash flows for the period are not sufficient to cover the current liabilities at the end of the period.

Activity 6.15

Calculate the operating cash flows to maturing obligations ratio for Alexis plc for the year ended 31 March 2001.

The ratio is

$$\frac{251.4}{326.8}$$

$$= 0.8 \text{ times}$$

The liquidity ratios for the two-year period may be summarised as follows:

	2000	2001
Current ratio	1.9	1.8
Acid test ratio	0.8	0.7
Operating cash flows to maturing obligations	0.8	0.8

Activity 6.16

What do you deduce from a comparison of the liquidity ratios over the two years?

The table above reveals a decrease in both the current ratio and the acid test ratio. These changes suggest a weakening liquidity position for the business. The company must monitor its liquidity carefully and be alert to any further deterioration in these ratios. The operating cash flows to maturing obligations ratio has not changed over the period. This ratio is quite low and reveals that the cash flows for the period do not cover the maturing obligations. This ratio should give some cause for concern.

Gearing

✱ **Gearing** occurs when a business is financed, at least in part, by contributions from outside parties. The level of gearing (that is, the extent to which a business is financed by outside parties) associated with a business is often an important factor in assessing risk. Where a business borrows heavily it takes on a commitment to pay interest charges and make capital repayments. This can be a significant financial burden, and can increase the risk of a business becoming insolvent. Nevertheless, it is the case that most businesses are geared to some extent.

Given the risks involved, you may wonder why a business would want to take on gearing. One reason may be that the owners have insufficient funds, and therefore the only way to finance the business adequately is to borrow from others. Another reason is that gearing can be used to increase the returns to owners. This is possible provided the returns generated from borrowed funds exceed the cost of paying interest. An example can be used to illustrate this point.

Example 6.3

Two companies, X Ltd and Y Ltd, commence business with the following long-term capital structures:

	X Ltd	Y Ltd
	£	£
£1 ordinary shares	100,000	200,000
10% loan	200,000	100,000
	300,000	300,000

In the first year of operations they both make a profit before interest and taxation of £50,000.

In this case X Ltd would be considered highly geared as it has a high proportion of borrowed funds in its long-term capital structure. Y Ltd is much lower geared. The profit available to the shareholders of each company in the first year of operations will be:

	X Ltd	Y Ltd
	£	£
Profit before interest and taxation	50,000	50,000
Interest payable	20,000	10,000
Profit before taxation	30,000	40,000
Taxation (say 25%)	7,500	10,000
Profit available to ordinary shareholders	22,500	30,000

The return on owners' equity for each company will be:

X Ltd	Y Ltd
$\dfrac{22,500}{100,000} \times 100$	$\dfrac{30,000}{200,000} \times 100$
$= 22.5\%$	$= 15\%$

We can see that X Ltd, the more highly geared company, has generated a better return on equity than Y Ltd.

An effect of gearing is that returns to equity become more sensitive to changes in profits. For a highly geared company, a change in profits can lead to a proportionately greater change in the returns to equity.

Activity 6.17

Assume that the profit before interest and tax was 20 per cent higher for each company than stated above. What would be the effect of this on owners' equity?

The revised profit available to the shareholders of each company in the first year of operations will be:

	X Ltd £	Y Ltd £
Profit before interest and taxation	60,000	60,000
Interest payable	20,000	10,000
Profit before taxation	40,000	50,000
Taxation (say 25%)	10,000	12,500
Profit available to ordinary shareholders	30,000	37,500

The return on owners' equity for each company will now be:

$$
\begin{array}{cc}
X\ Ltd & Y\ Ltd \\[4pt]
\dfrac{30,000}{100,000} \times 100 & \dfrac{37,500}{200,000} \times 100 \\[10pt]
= 30\% & = 18.75\%
\end{array}
$$

We can see that for X Ltd, the higher-geared company, the returns to equity have increased by 33 per cent, whereas for the lower-geared company the benefits of gearing are less pronounced. The increase in the returns to equity for Y Ltd has only been 25 per cent. The effect of gearing, of course, can work in both directions. Thus, for a highly geared company a small decline in profits may bring about a much greater decline in the returns to equity.

The effect of gearing is like the effect of two intermeshing cog wheels of unequal size (see Figure 6.3). The movement in the larger cog (profit before interest and tax) causes a more than proportionate movement in the smaller cog (returns to ordinary shareholders). The subject of gearing is discussed further in Chapter 12 on page 340.

Gearing ratio

✳ The **gearing ratio** measures the contribution of long-term lenders to the long-term capital structure of a business:

$$
\text{Gearing ratio} = \frac{\textbf{Long-term liabilities}}{\textbf{Share capital + Reserves + Long-term liabilities}} \times 100
$$

The gearing ratio for Alexis plc for the year ended 31 March 2000 is:

$$
\frac{200}{(498.3 + 200)} \times 100
$$

$$
= 28.6\%
$$

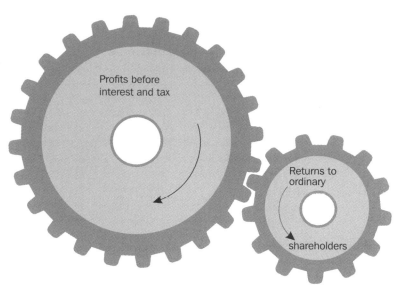

Profits before
interest and tax

Returns to
ordinary

shareholders

The two wheels are linked by the cogs, so that a relatively small circular movement in the large wheel (profit before interest and tax) leads to a relatively large circular movement in the small wheel (returns to ordinary shareholders).

Figure 6.3 The effect of financial gearing

This ratio reveals a level of gearing that would not normally be considered to be very high.

Activity 6.18

Calculate the gearing ratio of Alexis plc for the year ended 31 March 2001.

The gearing ratio for the following year will be:

$$\frac{60}{(636.6 + 60)} \times 100$$

$$= 8.6\%$$

This ratio reveals a substantial fall in the level of gearing over the year.

Interest cover ratio

❋ The **interest cover ratio** measures the amount of profit available to cover interest payable. The ratio may be calculated as follows:

$$\text{Interest cover ratio} = \frac{\textbf{Profit before interest and taxation}}{\textbf{Interest payable}}$$

The ratio for Alexis plc for the year ended 31 March 2000 is:

$$\frac{(219.4 + 24)}{24}$$

$$= 10.1 \text{ times}$$

This ratio shows that the level of profit is considerably higher than the level of interest payable. Thus a significant fall in profits could occur before profit levels failed to cover interest payable. The lower the level of profit coverage the greater the risk to lenders that interest payments will not be met.

Activity 6.19

Calculate the interest cover ratio of Alexis plc for the year ended 31 March 2001.

The interest cover ratio for the year ended 31 March 2001 is:

$$\frac{(240.2 + 6.2)}{6.2}$$

$$= 39.7 \text{ times}$$

Activity 6.20

What do you deduce from a comparison of the gearing ratios over the two years?

The gearing ratios are:

	2000	2001
Gearing ratio	28.6%	8.6%
Interest cover ratio	10.1times	39.7times

Both the gearing ratio and interest cover ratio have altered significantly in 2001. This is mainly due to the fact that a substantial part of the long-term loan was repaid during 2001. This repayment has had the effect of reducing the relative contribution of long-term lenders to the financing of the company and reducing the amount of interest payable.

The gearing ratio at 31 March 2001 would normally be considered to be very low, and might indicate that the business has some debt capacity (that is, it is capable of borrowing more if required). However, the availability of adequate security and profitability must also be taken into account before the debt capacity of a business can be properly assessed.

Investment ratios

There are various ratios available that are designed to help investors assess the returns on their investment. Below we consider some of these ratios.

Dividend per share

The **dividend per share** ratio relates the dividends announced during a period to the number of shares in issue during that period. The ratio is calculated as follows:

$$\text{Dividend per share} = \frac{\textbf{Dividends announced during the period}}{\textbf{Number of shares in issue}}$$

In essence, the ratio provides an indication of the cash return that an investor receives from holding shares in a company.

Although it is a useful measure, it must always be remembered that the dividends received will usually represent only a partial measure of return to investors. Dividends are usually only a proportion of the total earnings generated by the company and available to shareholders. A company may decide to plough back some of its earnings into the business in order to achieve future growth. These ploughed-back profits also belong to the shareholders, and should in principle increase the value of the shares held.

When assessing the total returns to investors we must take account of both the cash returns received *plus* any change in the market value of the shares held.

The dividend per share for Alexis plc for the year ended 31 March 2000 is:

$$\frac{40.2}{600 \text{ (i.e 300 @ £0.50)}} = 6.7\text{p.}$$

This ratio can be calculated for each class of share issued by a company. Alexis plc has only ordinary shares in issue and therefore only one dividend per share ratio can be calculated.

Activity 6.21

Calculate the dividend per share of Alexis plc for the year ended 31 March 2001.

Your answer to this activity should be as follows:

$$\frac{60.0}{668.2}$$

$$= 9.0\text{p}$$

Dividends per share can vary considerably between companies. A number of factors will influence the amount that a company is prepared to issue in the form of dividends to shareholders.

These factors include:

- the profit available for distribution to shareholders
- the future spending plans of the company
- the expectations of shareholders concerning the level of dividend payments
- the cash available.

Comparing dividend per share between companies is not always useful as there may be differences between the nominal value of shares issued. However, it is often useful to monitor the trend of dividends per share for a company over a period of time.

Dividend payout ratio

✳ The **dividend payout ratio** measures the proportion of earnings that a company pays out to shareholders in the form of dividends. The ratio is calculated as follows:

$$\text{Dividend payout ratio} = \frac{\textbf{Dividends announced for the year}}{\textbf{Earnings for the year available for dividends}} \times 100$$

In the case of ordinary shares, the earnings available for dividend will normally be the net profit after taxation and after any preference dividends announced during the period. This ratio is normally expressed as a percentage.

The dividend payout ratio for Alexis plc for the year ended 31 March 2000 is:

$$\frac{40.2}{159.2} \times 100$$

$$= 25.3\%$$

Activity 6.22

Calculate the dividend payout ratio of Alexis plc for the year ended 31 March 2001.

Your answer to this activity should be as follows:

$$\text{Dividend payout ratio} = \frac{60.0}{164.2} \times 100$$

$$= 36.5\%$$

Dividend yield ratio

✳ The **dividend yield ratio** relates the cash return from a share to its current market value. This can help investors to assess the cash return on their investment in the company. The ratio is:

$$\text{Dividend yield} = \frac{\textbf{Dividend per share}/(1 - t)}{\textbf{Market value per share}} \times 100$$

This ratio is also expressed as a percentage.

The numerator (the top part) of this ratio requires some explanation. In the United Kingdom, investors who receive a dividend from a company also receive a tax credit. This tax credit is equal to the amount of tax that would be payable on the dividends received by a lower-rate tax payer. As this tax credit can be offset against any tax liability arising from the dividends received, the dividends are effectively issued net of tax to lower-rate income tax payers.

Investors may wish to compare the returns from shares with the returns from other forms of investment. As these other forms of investment are often quoted on a 'gross' (that is, pre-tax) basis it is useful to 'gross up' the dividend to make comparison easier. This can be done by dividing the dividend per share by $(1 - t)$, where t is the lower rate of income tax.

Assuming a lower rate of income tax of 20 per cent, the dividend yield for Alexis plc for the year ended 31 March 2000 is:

$$\frac{6.7/(1 - 0.20)}{2.50} \times 100$$

$$= 3.4\%$$

Activity 6.23

Calculate the dividend yield for Alexis plc for the year ended 31 March 2001.

Your answer to this activity should be as follows:

$$\text{Dividend yield} = \frac{9.0/(1 - 0.20)}{3.50} \times 100$$

$$= 3.2\%$$

Earnings per share

* The **earnings per share** (EPS) value of a company relates the earnings generated by the company during a period and available to shareholders to the number of shares in issue. For equity (ordinary) shareholders, the amount available will be represented by the net profit after tax (less any preference dividend, where applicable). The ratio for equity shareholders is calculated as follows:

$$\text{Earnings per share} = \frac{\textbf{Earnings available to ordinary shareholders}}{\textbf{Number of ordinary shares in issue}}$$

In the case of Alexis plc, the earnings per share for the year ended 31 March 2000 will be as follows:

$$\frac{159.2}{600}$$

$$= 26.5\text{p}$$

This ratio is regarded by many investment analysts as a fundamental measure of share performance. The trend in earnings per share over time is used to help assess the investment potential of a company's shares.

Although it is possible to make total profits rise through ordinary shareholders investing more in the company, this will not necessarily mean that the profitability *per share* will rise as a result.

Activity 6.24

Calculate the earnings per share of Alexis plc for the year ended 31 March 2001.

The earnings per share for the year ended 31 March 2001 will be:

$$\text{Earnings per share} = \frac{164.2}{668.2}$$

$$= 24.6p$$

In this case, the new issue of shares occurred at the beginning of the financial year. Where an issue is made part way through the year, a weighted average of the shares in issue will be taken, based on the date at which the new share issue took place.

It is not usually very helpful to compare the earnings per share of one company with those of another. Differences in capital structure can render any such comparison meaningless. However, as for dividend per share, it can be very useful to monitor the changes that occur in this ratio for a particular company over time.

Operating cash flow per share

It can be argued that, in the short run at least, operating cash flows provide a better guide to the ability of a company to pay dividends and to undertake planned expenditures than the earnings figure. The **operating cash flow per share** is calculated as follows:

$$\frac{\textbf{Operating cash flows} - \textbf{preference dividends}}{\textbf{Number of ordinary shares in issue}}$$

The ratio for Alexis plc for the year ended 31 March 2000 is as follows:

$$\frac{231.0}{600.0}$$

$$= 38.5p$$

Activity 6.25

Calculate the operating cash flow (OCF) per share for Alexis plc for the year ended 31 March 2001.

Your answer should be as follows:

$$\text{OCF per share} = \frac{251.4}{668.2} = 37.6p$$

There has been a slight decline in this ratio over the two-year period.

For both years, the operating cash flow per share is higher than the earnings per share. This is not unusual. The effect of adding back depreciation to derive operating cash flows will usually ensure that a higher figure is derived.

Price/earnings ratio (P/E)

✳ The **price/earnings ratio** relates the market value of a share to the earnings per share. This ratio can be calculated as follows:

$$\text{Price/earnings ratio} = \frac{\text{Market value per share}}{\text{Earnings per share}}$$

The P/E ratio for Alexis Plc for the year ended 31 March 2000 will be:

$$\frac{£2.50}{26.5\text{p}}$$

$$= 9.4 \text{ times}$$

This ratio reveals that the capital value of the share is 9.4 times higher than its current level of earnings. The ratio is a measure of market confidence in the future of a company. The higher the P/E ratio the greater the confidence in the future earning power of the company and, consequently, the more investors are prepared to pay in relation to the earnings stream of the company.

P/E ratios provide a useful guide to market confidence concerning the future and can therefore be helpful when comparing different companies. However, differences in accounting conventions between businesses can lead to different profit and earnings per share figures, and this can distort comparisons.

Activity 6.26

Calculate the P/E ratio of Alexis plc for the year ended 31 March 2001.

Your answer to this activity should be as follows:

$$\text{P/E ratio} = \frac{£3.50}{24.6\text{p}}$$

$$= 14.2 \text{ times}$$

The investment ratios for Alexis plc over the two-year period are as follows:

	2000	2001
Dividend per share	6.7p	9.0p
Dividend payout ratio	25.3%	36.5%
Dividend yield ratio	3.4%	3.2%
Earnings per share	26.5p	24.6p
Operating cash flow per share	38.5p	37.6p
P/E ratio	9.4T	14.2T

Activity 6.27

What do you deduce from the investment ratios set out above?

There has been a significant increase in the dividend per share in 2001 as compared with the previous year. The dividend payout ratio reveals that this can be attributed, at least in part, to an increase in the proportion of earnings distributed to ordinary shareholders. However, the payout ratio for the year ended 31 March 2001 is still fairly low. Only about a third of earnings available for dividend is being distributed. The dividend yield has changed very little over the period, and remains fairly low at less than 4.0 per cent.

Earnings per share show a slight fall in 2001 when compared with the previous year. A slight fall also occurs in the operating cash flows per share. However, the price earnings ratio shows a significant improvement. The market is clearly much more confident about the future prospects of the business at 31 March 2001, than it had been 12 months earlier.

Exhibit 6.1

Investment ratios can vary significantly between companies and between industries. To give you some indication of the range of variations which occur, the average dividend yield ratios and average P/E ratios for listed businesses in 12 different industries are shown in Figures 6.4 and 6.5 respectively (see page 170).

Self-assessment question 6.1

A plc and B plc operate electrical wholesale stores in the south of England. The accounts of each company for the year ended 30 June 2001 are as follows:

Balance sheets as at 30 June 2001

	A plc		B plc	
	£000	£000	£000	£000
Fixed assets				
Freehold land and buildings at cost	436.0		615.0	
Less Accumulated depreciation	76.0	360.0	105.0	510.0
Fixtures and fittings at cost	173.4		194.6	
Less Accumulated depreciation	86.4	87.0	103.4	91.2
		447.0		601.2
Current assets				
Stock at cost	592.0		403.0	
Debtors	176.4		321.9	
Cash at bank	84.6		91.6	
	853.0		816.5	

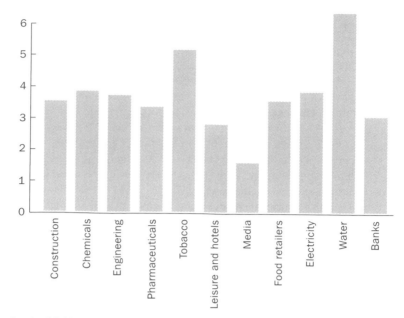

Average levels of dividend yield tend to vary from one industry to the next. Water companies tend to pay relatively large dividends, compared with their share price, whereas media companies pay relatively low ones.

Figure 6.4 Dividend yield ratios

Source: Constructed from data appearing in *Financial Times*, 2 December 1999

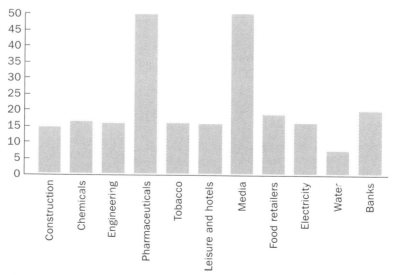

Average price/earnings ratios differ from one industry to the next, with media companies typically having relatively high share prices compared with their recent past earnings. Water companies are at the other end of the spectrum.

Figure 6.5 Price/earnings ratios

Source: Constructed from data appearing in *Financial Times*, 2 December 1999

	A plc		B plc	
	£000	£000	£000	£000
Creditors due within one year				
Trade creditors	(271.4)		(180.7)	
Dividends	(135.0)		(95.0)	
Corporation tax	(16.0)		(17.4)	
	(422.4)	430.6	(293.1)	523.4
		877.6		1,124.6
Creditors due beyond one year				
Debentures		190.0		250.0
		687.6		874.6
Capital and reserves				
£1 Ordinary shares		320.0		250.0
General reserves		355.9		289.4
Retained profit		11.7		335.2
		687.6		874.6

Trading and profit and loss accounts for the year ended 30 June 2001

	A plc		B plc	
	£000	£000	£000	£000
Sales		1,478.1		1,790.4
Less Cost of sales				
Opening stock	480.8		372.6	
Purchases	1,129.5		1,245.3	
	1,610.3		1,617.9	
Less Closing stock	592.0	1,018.3	403.0	1,214.9
Gross profit		459.8		575.5
Wages and salaries	150.4		189.2	
Directors salaries	45.4		96.2	
Rates	28.5		15.3	
Heat and light	15.8		17.2	
Insurance	18.5		26.8	
Interest payments	19.4		27.5	
Postage and telephone	12.4		15.9	
Audit fees	11.0		12.3	
Depreciation				
– Freehold buildings	8.8		12.9	
– Fixtures and fittings	17.7	327.9	22.8	436.1
Net profit before tax		131.9		139.4
Corporation tax		32.0		34.8
Net profit after taxation		99.9		104.6
Add retained profit brought forward		46.8		325.6
		146.7		430.2
Dividends proposed		135.0		95.0
Retained profit carried forward		11.7		335.2

All purchases and sales are on credit.

The market value of the shares in each company at the end of the year were £6.50 and £8.20 respectively.

Required:
For each company, calculate six different ratios that are concerned with liquidity, gearing and investment. What can you conclude from the ratios you have calculated?

Trend analysis

It is important to see whether there are trends occurring that can be detected from the use of ratios. Thus key ratios can be plotted on a graph to provide users with a simple visual display of changes occurring over time. The trends occurring within a company may be plotted against trends occurring within the industry as a whole for comparison purposes. An example of trend analysis is shown in Figure 6.6.

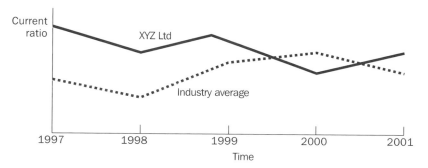

Figure 6.6 Graph plotting current ratio against time

Ratios and prediction models

Financial ratios, based on current or past performance, are often used to help predict the future, although both the choice of ratios and the interpretation of results are normally dependent on the judgement of the analyst. In recent years, however, attempts have been made to develop a more rigorous and systematic approach to the use of ratios for prediction purposes. In particular, researchers have shown an interest in the use of ratios to predict financial distress in a business. A number of methods and models employing ratios has now been developed that are claimed to predict future financial distress. Researchers have also developed ratio-based models with which to assess the supposed vulnerability of a business to takeover by another business. These areas, of course, are of interest to all those connected with the business. In the future, it is likely that further ratio-based models will be developed that predict other aspects of future performance.

Some companies publish certain key financial ratios as part of their annual accounts in order to help users identify important trends. These ratios may cover several years. The following ratios are included in the accounts of Beazer Group plc for 1999. Beazer's business is building residential properties.

	Year to 30 June 1995	Year to 30 June 1996	Year to 30 June 1997	Year to 30 June 1998	Year to 30 June 1999
Statistics					
Number of completions	6,679	5,979	7,177	7,776	7,509
Average sales price (£000)*	62	64	75	81	93
Operating margin**	12.7%	11.9%	12.2%	13.3%	13.1%
Interest cover (times)	N/A	N/A	20.4	16.8	9.1
Dividend cover (times)***	2.4	2.0	2.4	2.7	2.6
Gearing	N/A	8%	N/A	15%	14%
Return on capital employed	23%	17%	23%	25%	23%

* This is the average price per property sold during the year concerned.
** This is net profit/sales ($\times$ 100).
*** The dividend cover ratio is, basically, the converse of the dividend payout ratio considered earlier. The ratio is the earnings available for dividend divided by the dividends announced. It measures the extent to which dividends are covered by current earnings.

Limitations of ratio analysis

Although ratios offer a quick and useful method of analysing the position and performance of a business, they are not without their problems and limitations. Some of the more important limitations are considered below.

- *Quality of financial statements.* It must always be remembered that ratios are based on financial statements, and the results of ratio analysis are dependent on the quality of these underlying statements. Ratios will inherit the limitations of the financial statements on which they are based.
- *The restricted vision of ratios.* It is important not to rely exclusively on ratios, thereby losing sight of information contained in the underlying financial statements. Some items reported in these statements can be of vital importance in assessing position and importance. For example, the total sales, capital employed and profit figures may be useful in assessing changes in absolute size that occur over time, or differences in scale between businesses. Ratios do not provide such information. In comparing one figure with another, ratios measure *relative* performance and position, and therefore provide only part of the picture. Thus, when comparing two businesses, it will often be useful to assess the absolute size of profits, as well as the relative profitability of each business. For example, Company A may generate £1 million profit and have a ROCE of 15 per cent, and Company B may generate £100,000 profit and have a ROCE of 20 per cent. Although Company B has a higher level of *profitability*, as measured by ROCE, it generates lower total profits.

- *The basis for comparison.* We saw earlier that ratios require a basis for comparison in order to be useful. Moreover, it is important that the analyst compares like with like. When comparing businesses, however, no two businesses will be identical, and the greater the differences between the businesses being compared, the greater the limitations of ratio analysis. Furthermore, when comparing businesses, differences in such matters as accounting policies, financing policies and financial year-ends will add to the problems of evaluation.

- *Balance sheet ratios.* Because the balance sheet is only a 'snapshot' of the business at a particular moment in time, any ratios based on balance sheet figures, such as the liquidity ratios above, may not be representative of the financial position of the business for the year as a whole. For example, it is common for a seasonal business to have a financial year-end that coincides with a low point in business activity. Thus stocks and debtors may be low at the balance sheet date, and the liquidity ratios may also be low as a result. A more representative picture of liquidity can only really be gained by taking additional measurements at other points in the year.

SUMMARY

In this chapter, we saw that ratios can be used to analyse various aspects of the position and performance of a business. Used properly, they help to provide a quick thumbnail sketch of a business. However, they require a sound basis for comparison, and will only be as useful as the quality of the underlying financial statements permit. Though they can highlight certain strengths and weaknesses concerning financial performance and position, they do not identify underlying causes. This can be done only through a more detailed investigation of business practices and records.

✳ **Key terms**

return on ordinary shareholders'
    funds (ROSF)   *p 146*
return on capital employed
    (ROCE)   *p 147*
net profit margin ratio   *p 148*
gross profit margin ratio   *p 149*
average stock turnover period
    p 150
average settlement period for
    debtors   *p 151*
average settlement period for
    creditors   *p 152*
sales to capital employed ratio
    p 153

current ratio   *p 156*
acid test ratio   *p 157*
operating cash flows to maturing
    obligations ratio   *p 158*
gearing   *p 159*
gearing ratio   *p 161*
interest cover ratio   *p 162*
dividend per share   *p 164*
dividend payout ratio   *p 165*
dividend yield ratio   *p 165*
earnings per share   *p 166*
operating cash flow per share   *p 167*
price/earnings ratio   *p 168*

? REVIEW QUESTIONS

6.1 Some businesses operate on a low net profit margin (for example, a supermarket chain). Does this mean that the return on capital employed from the business will also be low?

6.2 What potential problems arise for the external analyst from the use of balance sheet figures in the calculation of financial ratios?

6.3 Two businesses operate in the same industry. One has a stock turnover period that is higher than the industry average, and the other has a stock turnover period which is lower than the industry average.
    Give three possible explanations for each ratio.

6.4 Identify and discuss three reasons why the P/E ratio of two companies operating within the same industry may differ.

EXAMINATION-STYLE QUESTIONS

Questions 6.4 and 6.5 are more advanced than 6.1–6.3. Those with a coloured number have an answer at the back of the book.

6.1 C. George (Western) Ltd has recently produced its accounts for the current year. The board of directors met to consider the accounts, and at this meeting concern was expressed that the return on capital employed had decreased from 14 per cent last year to 12 per cent for the current year.

The following reasons were suggested as to why this reduction in ROCE had occurred:

(i)   Increase in the gross profit margin.
(ii)   Reduction in sales.
(iii) Increase in overhead expenses.
(iv)   Increase in amount of stock held.
(v)   Repayment of a loan at the year end.
(vi)   Increase in the time taken for debtors to pay.

Required:
State, with reasons, which of the above might lead to a reduction in ROCE.

6.2 Business A and Business B are both engaged in retailing, but seem to take a different approach to this trade according to the information available. This information consists of a table of ratios, shown below.

Ratio	Business A	Business B
Return on capital employed (ROCE)	20%	17%
Return on owners equity (ROE)	30%	18%
Average settlement period for debtors	63 days	21 days
Average settlement period for creditors	50 days	45 days
Gross profit percentage	40%	15%
Net profit percentage	10%	10%
Stock turnover	52 days	25 days

Required:
(a)   Explain how each ratio is calculated.

(b)   Describe what this information indicates about the differences in approach between the two businesses. If one of them prides itself on personal service and one of them on competitive prices, which do you think is which and why?

6.3 Conday and Co. Ltd has been in operation for three years and produces antique reproduction furniture for the export market. The most recent set of accounts for the company is set out below:

Balance sheet as at 30 November

	£000	£000	£000
Fixed assets			
Freehold land and buildings at cost			228
Plant and machinery at cost		942	
Less Accumulated depreciation		180	762
			990
Current assets			
Stocks		600	
Trade debtors		820	
		1,420	
Less **Creditors: amounts falling due within one year**			
Trade creditors	665		
Taxation	48		
Bank overdraft	432	1,145	275
			1,265
Less **Creditors: amounts falling due in more than one year**			
12% debentures (note 1)			200
			1,065
Capital and reserves			
Ordinary shares of £1 each			700
Retained profits			365
			1,065

Profit and loss account for the year ended 30 November

	£000	£000
Sales		2,600
Less Cost of sales		1,620
Gross profit		980
Less Selling and distribution expenses (note 2)	408	
Administration expenses	174	
Finance expenses	78	660
Net profit before taxation		320
Corporation tax		95
Net profit after taxation		225
Proposed dividend		160
Retained profit for the year		65

Notes

1 The debentures are secured on the freehold land and buildings.
2 Selling and distribution expenses include £170,000 in respect of bad debts.

An investor has been approached by the company to invest £200,000 by purchasing ordinary shares in the company at £6.40 each. The company wishes to use the funds to finance a programme of further expansion.

Required:

(a) Analyse the financial position and performance of the company and comment on any features you consider to be significant.

(b) State, with reasons, whether or not the investor should invest in the company on the terms outlined.

6.4 The directors of Helena Beauty Products Ltd have been presented with the following abridged accounts:

Helena Beauty Products Ltd
Profit and loss account for the year ended 30 September

	2000		2001	
	£000	£000	£000	£000
Sales		3,600		3,840
Less Cost of sales				
Opening stock	320		400	
Purchases	2,240		2,350	
	2,560		2,750	
Less Closing stock	400	2,160	500	2,250
Gross profit		1,440		1,590
Less Expenses		1,360		1,500
Net profit		80		90

Balance sheet as at 30 September

	2000		2001	
	£000	£000	£000	£000
Fixed assets		1,900		1,860
Current assets				
Stock	400		500	
Debtors	750		960	
Bank	8		4	
	1,158		1,464	
Less *Creditors: amounts due*				
within one year	390	768	450	1,014
		2,668		2,874
Financed by				
£1 Ordinary shares		1,650		1,766
Reserves		1,018		1,108
		2,668		2,874

Required:
Using six ratios, comment on the profitability and efficiency of the business as revealed by the accounts shown above.

6.5 Threads Limited manufactures nuts and bolts, which are sold to industrial users. The abbreviated accounts for 2001 and 2000 are given below.

Profit and loss account for the year ended 30 June

	2001 £000	2001 £000	2000 £000	2000 £000
Sales		1,200		1,180
Cost of sales		(750)		(680)
Gross profit		450		500
Operating expenses	(208)		(200)	
Depreciation	(75)		(66)	
Interest	(8)		(–)	
		(291)		(266)
Profit before tax		159		234
Tax		(48)		(80)
Profit after tax		111		154
Dividend – proposed		(72)		(70)
Retained profit for year		39		84

Balance sheet as at 30 June

	2001 £000	2001 £000	2000 £000	2000 £000
Fixed assets		687		702
Current assets				
Stocks	236		148	
Debtors	156		102	
Cash	4		3	
	396		253	
Creditors: amounts due within one year				
Trade creditors	(76)		(60)	
Other creditors and accruals	(16)		(18)	
Dividend	(72)		(70)	
Tax	(24)		(40)	
Bank overdraft	(50)		(11)	
	(238)		(199)	
Net current assets		158		54
Creditors: amounts due after more than one year				
Bank loan		(50)		–
		795		756
Ordinary share capital of £1 (fully paid)		500		500
Retained profits		295		256
		795		756

Required:

(a) Calculate the following financial statistics for *both* 2001 and 2000, using end-of-year figures where appropriate:

    (i)   Return on capital employed

      (ii)   Net profit margin

      (iii)   Gross profit margin

      (iv)   Current ratio

      (v)   Liquid ratio (acid test ratio)

      (vi)   Day's debtors

      (vii) Day's creditors

      (viii) Stock turnover ratio

(b)   Comment on the performance of Threads Limited from the viewpoint of a company considering supplying a substantial amount of goods to Threads Limited on usual credit terms.

(c)   What action could a supplier take to lessen the risk of not being paid should Threads Limited be in financial difficulty?

Cost–volume–profit analysis

INTRODUCTION

This chapter is concerned with the relationship between volume of activity, costs and profit. Broadly, costs can be analysed between those costs that are fixed, relative to the volume of activity, and those that vary with the volume of activity. We shall consider how we can use knowledge of this relationship to make decisions and assess risk, particularly in the context of short-term decisions.

Objectives

On completion of this chapter you should be able to:

- distinguish between fixed costs and variable costs
- use knowledge of this distinction to deduce the break-even point for some activity
- make decisions on the use of spare capacity, using knowledge of the relationship between fixed and variable costs
- make decisions about the acceptance (or continuance) or rejection of a particular contract or activity, based on knowledge of the relationship between fixed and variable costs.

The behaviour of costs

∗ Costs represent the resources that have to be sacrificed to achieve a business objective. The objective may be to make a particular product, to render a particular service and so on. Costs may be broadly classified as:

- those that stay fixed (the same) when changes occur to the volume of activity; and
- those that vary according to the volume of activity.

∗ These are known as **fixed costs** and **variable costs** respectively.

We shall see in this chapter that knowledge of how much of each type of cost is associated with some particular activity can be of great value to the decision maker.

Fixed costs

The way in which fixed costs behave can be depicted as in Figure 7.1. The distance OF represents the amount of fixed costs, and this stays the same irrespective of the level of activity.

Activity 7.1

A business operates a small chain of hairdressing salons.
Can you give some examples of costs that are likely to be fixed for this business?

We came up with the following:

- rent
- insurance
- cleaning costs
- staff salaries.

Staff salaries and wages are sometimes discussed in books as being variable costs. In fact, they tend to be fixed. People are generally not paid according to the level of output, and it is not normal to sack staff when there is a short-term downturn in activity. If there is a long-term downturn in activity, or at least if it looks that way to management, redundancies may occur, with fixed cost savings. This, however, is true of all costs. If there is seen to be a likely reduction in demand the business may decide to close some branches and make rent cost savings. Thus 'fixed' does not mean set in stone for all time; it usually means fixed over the short to medium term.

As the level of output increases, the fixed costs stay exactly the same (OF).

Figure 7.1 Graph of fixed cost(s) against the level of activity

It is important to be clear that 'fixed', in this context, means only that the cost is not altered by changes in the level of activity. Fixed costs are likely to be affected by inflation. If rent (a typical fixed cost) goes up because of inflation, a fixed cost will have increased, but not because of a change in the level of activity.

The level of fixed costs does not stay the same, irrespective of the time period involved. Fixed costs are almost always *time-based*: that is, they vary with the length of time concerned. The rent charge for two months is normally twice that for one month. Thus fixed costs normally vary with time, but (of course) not with the level of output. You should note that when we talk of fixed costs being, say, £1,000, we must add the period concerned, say, £1,000 per month.

Activity 7.2

Do fixed costs stay the same irrespective of the level of output, even where there is a massive rise in the level of output?

Think in terms of the rent cost for the hairdressing business.

In fact, the rent is only fixed over a particular range (known as the 'relevant' range). If the number of people wanting to have their hair cut by the business increased, and the business wished to meet this increased demand, it would eventually have to expand its physical size. This might be achieved by opening additional branches, or perhaps by moving existing branches to larger premises in the same vicinity. It may be possible to cope with relatively minor increases in activity by using existing space more efficiently, or by having longer opening hours. If activity continued to expand, increased rent charges would seem inevitable. Thus, in practice, the situation described would look something like Figure 7.2.

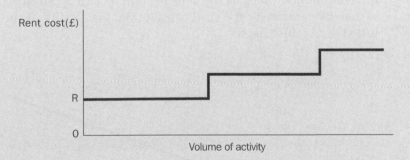

As the volume of activity increases from zero, the rent (a fixed cost) is unaffected. At a particular point, the volume of activity cannot increase further without additional space being rented. The cost of renting the additional space will cause a 'step' in the rent cost. The higher rent cost will continue unaffected if volume rises further until eventually another step point is reached.

Figure 7.2 Graph of rent cost against the level of activity

At lower levels of activity, the rent cost shown in Figure 7.2 would be OR. As the level of activity expands, the accommodation becomes inadequate and further expansion requires an increase in premises and, therefore, cost. This higher level of accommodation provision will enable further expansion to take place. Eventually, further costs will need to be incurred if further expansion is to occur. Fixed costs that behave like this are often referred to as **stepped fixed costs.**

Variable costs

Variable costs are costs that vary with the level of activity. In a manufacturing business, for example, this would include raw materials used.

Activity 7.3

Can you think of some examples of variable costs in the hairdressing business?

We can think of a couple:

- lotions and other materials used
- laundry costs to wash towels used to dry the hair of customers.

As with many types of business activity, variable costs of hairdressers tend to be relatively light in comparison with fixed costs: that is, fixed costs tend to make up the bulk of total costs.

Variable costs can be represented graphically as in Figure 7.3. At zero level of activity the cost is zero. The cost increases in a straight line as activity increases.

The straight line for variable cost on this graph implies that the cost of materials will normally be the same per unit of activity, irrespective of the level of activity concerned. We shall consider the practicality of this assumption a little later in this chapter.

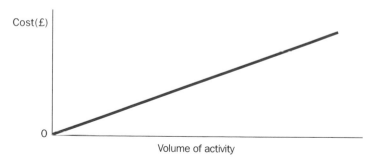

The graph shows that, at zero activity, there are no variable costs. However, as the level of activity increases, so does the variable cost.

Figure 7.3 Graph of variable costs against the level of activity

Semi-fixed (semi-variable) costs

 In some cases, costs have both an element of fixed and of variable cost about them. They can be described as **semi-fixed (semi-variable) costs**. An example might be the electricity cost for the hairdressing business. Some of this will be for heating and lighting, and this part is probably fixed, at least until the volume of activity expands to a point where longer opening hours or larger premises are necessary. The other part of the cost will vary with the level of activity. Here we are talking about such things as power for hairdryers, and so on.

Activity 7.4

Can you suggest another cost for a hairdressing business that is likely to be semi-fixed (semi-variable)?

Telephone charges have a rental element, which is fixed, and there may also be certain calls that have to be made irrespective of the volume of activity involved. However, increased business would be likely to lead to the need to make more telephone calls and hence increase call charges.

It is often not very obvious how much of each element a particular cost contains. It is usually necessary to look at past experience here. If we have data on what the electricity cost has been for various levels of activity, say the relevant data over several three-month periods (electricity is usually billed by the quarter), we can estimate the fixed and variable portions. This may be done graphically, as shown in Figure 7.4. We tend to use past data here purely

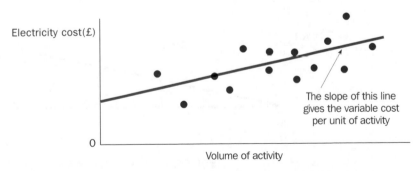

Here the electricity bill for a time period (for example, three months) is plotted against the volume of activity for that same period. This is done for a series of periods. A line is then drawn that best 'fits' the various points on the graph. From this line we can then deduce both the cost at zero activity (the fixed element) and the slope of the line (the variable element).

Figure 7.4 Graph of electricity cost against the level of activity

because it provides us with an estimate of future costs; past costs are not, of course, relevant for their own sake.

Each of the dots in the graph is a reading of the electricity charge for a particular level of activity (probably measured in terms of sales revenue). The diagonal line on the graph is the *line of best fit*. This means that, to us, this was the line that best seemed to represent the data. A better estimate can usually be made using a statistical technique (*least squares regression*), which does not involve drawing graphs and making estimates. In practice, it probably does not make too much difference which approach is taken.

From the graph we can say that the fixed element of the electricity cost is the amount represented by the vertical distance from the origin at zero (bottom left-hand corner) to the point where the line of best fit crosses the vertical axis of the graph. The variable cost per unit is the amount that the graph rises for each increase in the volume of activity.

Now that we have considered the nature of fixed and variable costs, we can go ✳ on to do something useful with that knowledge – carry out a **break-even analysis**.

Break-even analysis

If, in respect of a particular activity, we know the total fixed costs for a period and the total variable cost per unit, we can produce a graph like Figure 7.5.

Figure 7.5 shows a fixed cost area. Added to this is the variable cost, the wedge-shaped portion at the top of the graph. The uppermost line represents the total cost at any particular level of activity. This total is the vertical distance between the graph's horizontal axis and the uppermost line for the particular level of activity concerned. Logically enough, the total cost at zero activity is the amount of the fixed costs. This is because, even where there is nothing going on, the business will still be paying rent, salaries, and so on, at least in the short term. The fixed cost is augmented by the amount of the relevant variable costs, as the volume of activity increases.

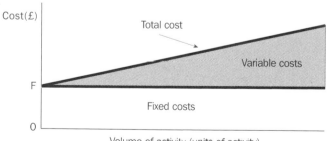

The bottom part of the graph represents the fixed cost element. To this is added the wedge-shaped top portion, which represents the variable costs. The two parts together represent total cost. At zero activity, the variable costs are zero, so total costs equal fixed costs. As activity increases so does total cost, but only because variable costs increase. We are assuming that there are no steps in the fixed costs.

Figure 7.5 Graph of total cost against level of activity

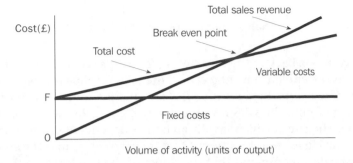

The sloping line starting at zero represents the sales revenue at various levels of activity. The point at which this finally catches up with the sloping total cost line, which starts at F, is the break-even point. Below this line a loss is made, above it a profit.

Figure 7.6 Break-even chart

If we superimpose onto this total cost graph a line representing total revenue
✱ for each level of activity, we obtain the **break-even chart** shown in Figure 7.6. Note that, at zero level of activity (zero sales), there is zero sales revenue. The profit (total sales revenue less total cost) at various levels of activity is the vertical distance between the total sales line and the total cost line at that
✱ particular level of activity. At **break-even point** there is no vertical distance between these two lines and thus there is no profit or loss; that is, the activity breaks even. Below break-even point a loss will be incurred; above break-even point there will be a profit. The further below break-even point, the higher the loss. The further above, the higher the profit.

As you may imagine, deducing break-even points by graphical means is a laborious business. It may have struck you that, since the relationships in the graph are all linear, it would be easy to calculate the break-even point.

We know that at break-even point (but not at any other point):

Total revenues = Total costs

That is,

Total revenues = Fixed costs + Total variable costs

If we call the number of units of output at break-even point b, then

b × Sales revenue per unit = Fixed costs + (b × Variable costs per unit)

Thus:

(b × Sales revenue per unit) − (b × Variable costs per unit) = Fixed costs

and:

b × (Sales revenue per unit − Variable costs per unit) = Fixed costs

giving:

$$b = \frac{\text{Fixed costs}}{\text{Sales revenue per unit} - \text{Variable costs per unit}}$$

If you look back at the break-even chart this seems logical. The total cost line starts off with an 'advantage' over the sales revenue line equal to the amount of the fixed costs. Because the sales revenue per unit is greater than the variable cost per unit, the sales revenue line will gradually catch up with the total cost line. The rate at which it will catch up is dependent on the relative steepness of the two lines, and the amount that it has to catch up is the amount of the fixed costs. Bearing in mind that the slopes of the two lines are the variable cost per unit and the selling price per unit, the above equation for calculating b looks perfectly logical.

Example 7.1

Cottage Industries Ltd makes baskets. The fixed costs of operating the workshop for a month total £500. Each basket requires materials that cost £2. Each basket takes two hours to make, and the business pays the basket-makers £3 an hour. The basket makers are all on contracts such that if they do not work for any reason, they are not paid. The baskets are sold to a wholesaler for £10 each.

What is the break-even point for basket-making for the business?

The break-even point (in number of baskets):

$$= \frac{\text{Fixed costs}}{(\text{Sales revenue per unit} - \text{Variable costs per unit})}$$

$$= £500/[£10 - (2 + 6)] = 250 \text{ baskets per month.}$$

Note that the break-even point must be expressed with respect to a period of time.

Activity 7.5

Can you think of reasons why the managers of a business might find it useful to know the break-even point of some activity that they are planning to undertake?

The usefulness of being able to deduce break-even point is that it makes it possible to compare the planned or expected level of activity with the break-even point and so make a judgement concerning the riskiness of the activity. Planning to operate only just above the level of activity necessary in order to break even may indicate that it is a risky venture, since only a small fall from the planned level of activity could lead to a loss.

Activity 7.6

Cottage Industries Ltd (see Example 7.1) expects to sell 500 baskets a month. The business has the opportunity to rent a basket-making machine. Doing so would increase the total fixed costs of operating the workshop for a month to £2,000. Using the machine would reduce the labour time to one hour per basket. The basket-makers would still be paid £3 an hour.

(a) How much profit would the business make each month from selling baskets (i) assuming that the basket-making machine is not rented and (ii) assuming that it is rented?
(b) What is the break-even point if the machine is rented?
(c) What do you notice about the figures that you calculate?

Estimated profit, per month, from basket-making:

	Without the machine		With the machine	
	£	£	£	£
Sales (500 × £10)		5,000		5,000
Less Materials (500 × £2)	1,000		1,000	
Labour (500 × 2 × £3)	3,000			
(500 × 1 × £3)			1,500	
Fixed costs	500		2,000	
		4,500		4,500
Profit		500		500

The break-even point (in number of baskets) with the machine:

$$= \frac{\text{Fixed costs}}{\text{Sales revenue per unit} - \text{Variable costs per unit}}$$

$$= £2,000/[£10 - (2+3)] = 400 \text{ baskets per month}$$

The break-even point without the machine is 250 baskets per month (see Example 7.1).
   There seems to be nothing to choose between the two manufacturing strategies regarding profit, at the estimated sales volume. There is, however, a distinct difference between the two strategies regarding the break-even point. Without the machine, the actual level of sales could fall by a half of that which is expected (from 500 to 250) before the business would fail to make a profit. With the machine however, a 20 per cent fall (from 500 to 400) would be enough to cause the business to fail to make a profit. On the other hand, for each additional basket sold above the estimated 500, an additional profit of only £2 (i.e. £10 − 2 − 6) would be made without the machine, whereas £5 (i.e. £10 − 2 − 3) would be made with the machine. (Note that knowledge of the break-even point and the planned level of activity gives some basis for assessing the riskiness of the activity.)

We shall take a closer look at the relationship between fixed costs, variable costs, break-even and the advice that we might give the management of Cottage Industries Ltd after we have briefly considered the notion of ✱ **contribution**.

Contribution

The bottom part of the break-even formula (sales revenue per unit – variable costs per unit) is known as the 'contribution' per unit. Thus for the basket-making activity, without the machine the contribution per unit is £2, and with the machine it is £5. This can be quite a useful figure to know in a decision-making context. It is known as contribution because it contributes to meeting the fixed costs, and if there is any excess, it also contributes to profit.

✱ The variable cost per unit will usually be equal to the **marginal cost**; that is, the additional cost of making one more basket. Where making one more will involve a step in the fixed costs, the marginal cost is not just the variable cost; it will include the increment, or step, in the fixed costs.

Profit–volume charts

✱ A slight variant of the break-even chart is the **profit–volume (PV) chart**. A typical PV chart is shown in Figure 7.7.

The profit–volume chart is obtained by plotting loss or profit against volume of activity. The slope of the graph is equal to the contribution per unit, since each additional unit sold decreases the loss, or increases the profit, by the sales revenue per unit less the variable cost per unit. At zero level of activity there are no contributions, so there is a loss equal to the amount of the fixed costs. As the level of activity increases, the amount of the loss gradually decreases until

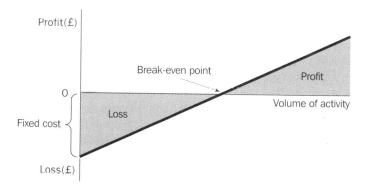

The sloping line is profit (loss) plotted against activity. As activity increases, so does total contribution (sales revenue less variable costs). At zero activity there are no contributions, so there will be a loss equal in amount to the total fixed costs.

Figure 7.7 Profit–volume chart

break-even point is reached. Beyond break-even point, profits increase as activity increases.

It may have occurred to you that the profit–volume chart does not tell us anything not shown by the break-even chart. Though it is true, information is perhaps more easily absorbed from the profit–volume chart. This is particularly true of the profit at any level of volume. This information is provided by the break-even chart as the vertical distance between the total cost and total sales revenue lines. The profit–volume chart, in effect, combines the total sales revenue and total variable cost lines, which means that profit (or loss) is plotted directly.

Margin of safety and operating gearing

✳ The **margin of safety** is the extent to which the planned level of output or sales lies above the break-even point. Going back to Activity 7.6, we saw that the following situation exists:

	Without the machine (number of baskets)	With the machine (number of baskets)
Expected level of sales	500	500
Break-even point	250	400
Difference (margin of safety):		
Number of baskets	250	100
Percentage of estimated level of sales	50%	20%

Activity 7.7

What advice would you give Cottage Industries Ltd about renting the machine, on the basis of the margin of safety figures?

It is a matter of personal judgement, which in turn is related to individual attitudes to risk, as to which strategy to adopt. Most people, however, would prefer the strategy of not renting the machine, since the margin of safety between the expected level of activity and the break-even point is much greater.

The relative margins of safety are directly linked to the relationship between the selling price per basket, the variable costs per basket, and the fixed costs per month. Without the machine the contribution (selling price less variable costs) per basket is £2. With the machine it is £5. On the other hand, without the machine the fixed costs are £500 a month; with the machine they are £2,000. This means that, with the machine, the contributions have more fixed costs to 'overcome' before the activity becomes profitable. On the other hand, the rate at which the contributions can overcome fixed costs is higher with the machine, because variable costs are lower. This means that one more, or one less, basket sold has a greater impact on profit than it does if the machine is not rented.

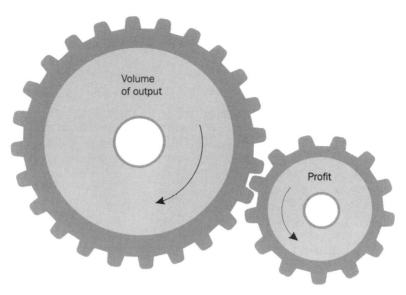

Where operating gearing is relatively high, as in the diagram, an amount of circular motion in the volume wheel causes a greater amount of circular motion in the profit wheel. An increase in volume would cause a disproportionately greater increase in profit. The equivalent would also be true of a decrease in activity, however.

Figure 7.8 The effect of operating gearing

The relationship between contribution and fixed costs is known as
✳ **operating gearing**. An activity with relatively high fixed costs compared with its variable costs is said to have high operating gearing. Thus, Cottage Industries Ltd is more highly operationally geared with the machine than it would be without the machine. Renting the machine increases the level of operating gearing quite dramatically because it causes an increase in fixed costs, but at the same time it leads to a reduction in variable costs per basket.

The reason why the word 'gearing' is used in this context is that, as with intermeshing gear wheels of different circumferences, a movement in one of the factors (volume of output) causes a more-than-proportionate movement in the other (profit) as illustrated by Figure 7.8.

We can demonstrate operating gearing with Cottage Industries Ltd's basket-making activities as follows:

	Without the machine			With the machine		
Volume	500	1,000	1,500	500	1,000	1,500
	£	£	£	£	£	£
Contributions*	1,000	2,000	3,000	2,500	5,000	7,500
Less Fixed costs	500	500	500	2,000	2,000	2,000
Profit	500	1,500	2,500	500	3,000	5,500

*£2 per basket without the machine and £5 per basket with it.

Note that, without the machine (low operating gearing), a doubling of the output from 500 to 1,000 units brings a trebling of the profit. With the machine (high operating gearing), doubling output causes profit to rise by six times.

Activity 7.8

In general terms, what types of business activity tend to be most highly operationally geared?

Hint: Cottage Industries Ltd might give you some idea.

In general, activities that are capital intensive tend to be more highly operationally geared, since renting or owning capital equipment gives rise to fixed costs and can also give rise to lower variable costs.

Weaknesses of break-even analysis

As we have seen, break-even analysis can provide some useful insights to the important relationship between fixed costs, variable costs and the volume of activity. It does, however, have its weaknesses. There are three general problems:

- *Non-linear relationships.* The normal approach to break-even analysis assumes that the relationships between sales revenues, variable costs and volume are strictly straight-line ones. In real life this is unlikely to be so.

  This is probably not a major problem, since break-even analysis is normally conducted in advance of the activity actually taking place. Our ability to predict future costs, revenues and so on is somewhat limited: hence what are probably minor variations from strict linearity are unlikely to be significant.
- *Stepped fixed costs.* Most fixed costs are not fixed over all volumes of activity. They tend to be 'stepped' in the way depicted in Figure 7.2. This means that, in practical circumstances, great care must be taken in making assumptions about fixed costs. The problem is particularly heightened because most activities will probably involve fixed costs of various types (rent, supervisory salaries, administration costs), all of which are likely to have steps at different points.
- *Multi-product businesses.* Most businesses do not offer just one product or service. This is a problem for break-even analysis since it raises problems of the effect of additional sales of one product or service on sales of another of the business's products or services. There is also the problem of identifying the fixed costs of one particular activity. Fixed costs tend to relate to more than one activity – for example, two activities may be carried out in the same rented premises. There are ways of dividing fixed costs between activities, but these tend to be arbitrary, which calls the value of the break-even analysis into question.

Marginal analysis

When we are trying to decide between two or more possible courses of action, and where economic costs and benefits are the decision-making criteria, *only costs that vary with the decision should be included in the decision analysis.* For example, a householder wants a house decorated. Two decorators have been asked to price the job. One of them will do the work for £250, the other one wants £300, in both cases on the basis that the householder will supply the materials. It is believed that the two decorators will do an equally good job. The materials will cost £200 irrespective of which decorator does the work. Assuming that the householder wants the house decorated at the lower cost, the two contractors' prices will be compared and a decision made on that basis. The cost of the materials is irrelevant because it will be the same in each case. It is only possible to distinguish rationally between courses of action on the basis of differences between them.

For many decisions that involve relatively small variations from existing practice and/or are for relatively limited periods of time, fixed costs are not relevant to the decision, because they will be the same irrespective of the decision made. This is because either:

- fixed costs tend to be impossible to alter in the short term; or
- managers are reluctant to alter them in the short term.

Suppose that a business occupies premises that it owns in order to carry out its activities. There is a downturn in demand for the service that the business provides, and it would be possible to carry on the business from smaller, cheaper premises. Does this mean that the business will sell its old premises and move to new ones overnight? Clearly it cannot mean this. This is partly because it is not usually possible to find a buyer for premises at very short notice, and it may be difficult to move premises quickly where there is, say, delicate equipment to be moved. Apart from external constraints on the speed of the move, management may feel that the downturn might not be permanent, and would thus be reluctant to take such a dramatic step as to deny itself the opportunity to benefit from a possible revival of trade.

The business's premises may provide one example of the more inflexible types of cost, but most fixed costs tend to be broadly similar in this context.

We shall now consider some decision-making areas where fixed costs can be regarded as irrelevant, and analyse decisions in those areas. The fact that the decisions that we are considering here are short term means that the objective of wealth enhancement will be promoted by pursuing a policy of seeking to generate as much net cash inflow as possible. In **marginal analysis** we concern ourselves just with costs and revenues that vary with the decision. This often means that fixed costs are ignored.

Accepting/rejecting special contracts

Activity 7.9

Cottage Industries Ltd has spare capacity in that it has spare basket-makers. An overseas retail chain has offered the business an order for 300 baskets at a price of £9 each.

Without considering any wider issues, should the business accept the order? (Assume that the business does not rent the machine.)

Since the fixed costs will be incurred in any case, they are not relevant to this decision. All we need to do is see whether the price offered will yield a contribution. If it will, the business will be better off by accepting the contract than by refusing it.

	£
Additional revenue per unit	9
Less Additional cost per unit	8
Additional contribution per unit	1

For 300 units, the additional contribution will be £300 (that is, 300 × £1). Since no fixed cost increase is involved, irrespective of what else is happening to the business, it will be £300 better off by taking this contract than by refusing it.

As ever with decision making, there are other factors that are either difficult or impossible to quantify which should be taken account of before reaching a final decision. In the case of Cottage Industries Ltd these could include the following.

- The possibility that spare capacity will have been 'sold off' cheaply when there is another potential customer who will offer a higher price, but, by which time, the capacity will be fully committed. It is a matter of commercial judgement as to how likely this will be.
- The problem that selling the same product, but at different prices, could lead to a loss of customer goodwill. The fact that each price will be to customers in different countries (that is, in different markets) may be sufficient to avoid this potential problem.
- If the business is going to suffer continually from being unable to sell its full production potential at the 'regular' price, it might be better, in the long run, to reduce capacity and make fixed cost savings. Using the spare capacity to produce marginal benefits may lead to the business failing to address this issue.
- On a more positive note, the business may see this as a way of breaking into the overseas market. This is something that might be impossible to achieve if the business charges its regular price.

The most efficient use of scarce resources

We tend to think in terms of the size of the market being the brake on output. That is to say that the ability of a business to sell will limit production, rather than the ability to produce will limit sales. In some cases, however, it is a limit on what can be produced that limits sales. Limited production might stem from a shortage of any factor of production – labour, raw materials, space, machinery and so on.

The most profitable combination of products will occur where the *contribution per unit of the scarce factor* is maximised.

Example 7.2

A business provides three different services, the details of which are as follows:

Service (code name)	AX107	AX109	AX220
	£	£	£
Selling price per unit	50	40	65
Variable cost per unit	25	20	35
Contribution per unit	25	20	30
Labour time per unit	5 hours	3 hours	6 hours

Within reason, the market will take as many units of each service as can be provided, but the ability to provide the service is limited by the availability of labour, all of which needs to be skilled. Fixed costs are not affected by the choice of service provided because provision of all three services uses the same production facilities.

The most profitable service is AX109 because it generates a contribution of £6.67 (£20/3) per hour. The other two generate only £5.00 each per hour (£25/5 and £30/6).

Your first reaction may have been that the business should provide only service AX220, because this is the one that yields the highest contribution per unit sold. If so, you are making the mistake of thinking of the ability to sell as being the limiting factor. If you are not convinced by the above analysis, take an imaginary number of available labour hours and ask yourself what is the maximum contribution (and, therefore, profit) that could be made by providing each service exclusively. Bear in mind that there is no shortage of anything else, including market demand, just a shortage of labour.

Activity 7.10

A business makes three different products, the details of which are as follows:

Product (code name)	B14	B17	B22
Selling price per unit (£)	25	20	23
Variable cost per unit (£)	10	8	12
Weekly demand (units)	25	20	30
Machine time per unit	4 hours	3 hours	4 hours

Fixed costs are not affected by the choice of product because all three products use the same machine. Machine time is limited to 148 hours a week.

Which combination of products should be manufactured if the business is to produce the highest profit?

Product (codename)	B14	B17	B22
	£	£	£
Selling price per unit	25	20	23
Variable cost per unit	10	8	12
Contribution per unit	15	12	11
Machine time per unit	4 hours	3 hours	4 hours
Contribution per machine hour	£3.75	£4.00	£2.75
Order of priority	2nd	1st	3rd

Therefore:

Produce   20 units of product B17 using   60 hours
          22 units of product B14 using   88 hours
                                             148 hours

This leaves unsatisfied the market demand for a further 3 units of product B14 and 30 units of product B22.

Activity 7.11

What steps could be contemplated that could lead to a higher level of contribution for the business in the last activity?

The possibilities for improving matters that occurred to us are as follows:

- Contemplate obtaining additional machine time. This could mean obtaining a new machine, subcontracting the machining to another business, or perhaps, squeezing a few more hours per week out of the business's own machine. Perhaps a combination of two or more of these is a possibility.
- Redesign the products in a way that requires less time per unit on the machine.
- Increase the price per unit of the three products. This might well have the effect of dampening demand, but the existing demand cannot be met at present, and it may be more profitable in the long run to make a greater contribution on each unit sold than to take one of the other courses of action to overcome the problem.

Activity 7.12

Going back to Activity 7.10, what is the maximum price that the business concerned would logically be prepared to pay to have the remaining B14s machined by a subcontractor, assuming that no fixed or variable costs would be saved as a result of not doing the machining 'in house'?

Would there be a different maximum if we were considering the B22s?

If the remaining three B14s were subcontracted at no cost, the business would be able to earn a contribution of £15, which it would not otherwise be able to gain. Any price up to £15 per unit would be worth paying a subcontractor to undertake the machining, therefore. Naturally, the business would prefer to pay as little as possible, but anything up to £15 would still make it worthwhile subcontracting the machining.

This would not be true of the B22s because they have a different contribution per unit; £11 would be the relevant figure in their case.

Make-or-buy decisions

Businesses are frequently confronted by the need to decide whether to produce the product or service that they sell themselves, or to buy it in from some other business. Thus a producer of electrical appliances might decide to subcontract the manufacture of one of its products to another business, perhaps because there is a shortage of production capacity in the producer's own factory, or because it believes it to be cheaper to subcontract than to make the appliance itself.

It might just be part of a product that is subcontracted. For example, the producer may have a component for the appliance made by another manufacturer. In principle, there is hardly any limit to the scope of make-or-buy decisions. Virtually any part, component or service that is required in production of the main product or service, or the main product or service itself, could be the subject of a make-or-buy decision. So, for example, the personnel function of a business, which is normally performed 'in house', could be subcontracted. At the same time, electrical power, which is typically provided by an outside electrical utility business, could be generated 'in house'.

 Example 7.3

Jones Ltd needs a component for one of its products. It can subcontract production of the component to a subcontractor who will provide the components for £20 each. The business can produce the components internally for total variable costs of £15 per component. Jones Ltd has spare capacity.

Should the component be subcontracted or produced internally?

The answer is that Jones Ltd should produce the component internally, since the variable cost of subcontracting is greater by £5 than the variable cost of internal manufacture.

 Activity 7.13

Shah Ltd needs a component for one of its products. It can subcontract production of the component to a subcontractor who will provide the components for £20 each. The business can produce the components internally for total variable costs of £15 per component.

Shah Ltd has no spare capacity, so it can only produce the component internally by reducing its output of another of its products. While it is making each component, it will lose contributions of £12 from the other product.

Should the component be subcontracted or produced internally?

The answer is to subcontract.

The relevant cost of internal production of each component is:

	£
Variable cost of production of the component	15
Opportunity cost of lost production of the other product	12
	27

This is obviously more costly than the £20 per component that will have to be paid to the subcontractor.

Activity 7.14

What factors, other than the immediately financially quantifiable, would you consider when making a make-or-buy decision?

We feel that there are two major factors:

1 The general problems of subcontracting:
   (a) loss of control of quality;
   (b) potential unreliability of supply.
2 Expertise and specialisation. It is possible for most businesses, with sufficient determination, to do virtually everything 'in house'. This may, however, require a level of skill and facilities that most businesses do not have nor feel inclined to acquire. Though it is true that most businesses could generate their own electricity, their managements tend to take the view that this is better done by a specialist generator business.

Closing or continuation decisions

It is quite common for businesses to account separately for each department or section, to try to assess the relative effectiveness of each one.

Example 7.4

Goodsports Ltd is a retail shop that operates through three departments, all in the same premises. The three departments occupy roughly equal areas of the premises. The trading results for the year just finished showed the following:

	Total	Sports equipment	Sports clothes	General clothes
	£000	£000	£000	£000
Sales	534	254	183	97
Costs	482	213	163	106
Profit/(loss)	52	41	20	(9)

It would appear that if the general clothes department were to close, the business would be more profitable, by £9,000 a year, assuming last year's performance to be a reasonable indication of future performance.

When the costs are analysed between those that are variable and those that are fixed, however, the following results are obtained:

	Total	Sports equipment	Sports clothes	General clothes
	£000	£000	£000	£000
Sales	534	254	183	97
Variable costs	344	167	117	60
Contribution	190	87	66	37
Fixed costs (rent etc)	138	46	46	46
Profit/(loss)	52	41	20	(9)

Now it is obvious that closing the general clothes department, without any other developments, would make the business worse off by £37,000 (the department's contribution). The department should not be closed, because it makes a positive contribution. The fixed costs would continue whether the department closed or not. As can be seen from the above analysis, distinguishing between variable and fixed costs can make the picture a great deal clearer.

Activity 7.15

In our consideration of the Goodsports Ltd example, it was stated that the general clothes department should not be closed 'without any other developments'.

What 'other developments' could affect this decision, making continuation either more attractive or less attractive?

The things that we could think of are as follows:

- Expansion of the other departments or replacing the general clothes department with a completely new activity. This would make sense only if the space currently occupied by the general clothes department could generate contributions totalling at least £37,000 a year.
- Subletting the space occupied by the general clothes department. Once again, this would need to generate a net figure of £37,000 a year to make it more financially beneficial than keeping the department open.

- There may be advantages in keeping the department open even if it generated no contribution (assuming no other use for the space). This is because customers may be attracted into the shop because it has general clothing and they may then buy something from one of the other departments. By the same token, the activity of a subtenant might attract customers into the shop. (On the other hand, it might drive them away!)

Self-assessment question 7.1

Khan Ltd can make three products (A, B and C) using the same machines. Various estimates for next year have been made as follows:

Product	A	B	C
	£/unit	£/unit	£/unit
Selling price	30	39	20
Variable material cost	15	18	10
Other variable production costs	6	10	5
Share of fixed overheads	8	12	4
	hours	hours	hours
Time per unit required on machines	2	3	1

Fixed overhead costs for next year are expected to total £40,000.

Required:

(a) If the business were to make only product A next year, how many units would it need to make in order to break even? (Assume for this part of the question that there is no effective limit to market size and production capacity.)

(b) If the business has maximum machine capacity for next year of 10,000 hours, in which order of preference would the three products come?

(c) If the maximum market for next year for the three products is as follows:

   product A   3,000 units
   product B   2,000 units
   product C   5,000 units

   what quantities of which product should the business make next year and how much profit would this be expected to yield?

SUMMARY

In this chapter we have seen that costs broadly divide into those that are fixed relative to the level of activity and those that are not affected by changes in the level of activity. Knowledge of how this distinction applies to any particular activity enables us to undertake break-even analysis: that is, deducing the break-even point for the activity. We have also seen that, for short-run decisions, all fixed costs (that is, costs that do not vary with the level of activity) can be assumed to be irrelevant, and all variable cost can be assumed to be relevant. This helps us to make decisions on the use of spare capacity, on the most effective use of scarce resources, on short-term make-or-buy decisions, and on decisions relating to the continuance or deletion of part of a business.

* **Key terms**

costs p 181	break-even point p 187
fixed costs p 181	contribution p 190
variable costs p 181	marginal cost p 190
stepped fixed costs p 184	profit–volume (PV) chart p 190
semi-fixed (semi-variable) costs p 185	margin of safety p 191
	operating gearing p 192
break-even analysis p 186	marginal analysis p 194
break-even chart p 187	

? REVIEW QUESTIONS

7.1 Define the terms *fixed cost* and *variable cost*.

7.2 What is meant by the *break-even point* for an activity? How is the break-even point calculated?

7.3 When we say that some business activity has *high operating gearing*, what do we mean?

7.4 If there is a scarce resource that is restricting sales, how will the business maximise its profit?

? EXAMINATION-STYLE QUESTIONS

Questions 7.4 and 7.5 are more advanced than questions 7.1–7.3. Those questions with a coloured number have answers at the back of the book.

7.1 The management of your company is concerned at its inability to obtain enough fully-trained labour to enable it to meet its present budget projection.

Product:	Alpha	Beta	Gamma	Total
	£	£	£	£
Direct costs				
Materials	6,000	4,000	5,000	15,000
Labour	9,000	6,000	12,000	27,000
Expenses	3,000	2,000	2,000	7,000
Allocated fixed costs	13,000	8,000	12,000	33,000
Total cost	31,000	20,000	31,000	82,000
Profit	8,000	9,000	2,000	19,000
Sales	39,000	29,000	33,000	101,000

The amount of labour likely to be available amounts to £20,000. You have been asked to prepare a statement ensuring that at least 50 per cent of the budget sales are achieved for each product, and the balance of labour is used to produce the greatest profit.

Required:
(a) Prepare a statement showing the greatest profit available from the limited amount of skilled labour available, within the constraint stated.
(b) Provide an explanation of the method you have used.
(c) Provide an indication of any other factors that need to be considered.

7.2 Lannion and Co is engaged in providing and marketing a standard cleaning service. Summarised results for the past two months reveal the following:

	October	November
Sales (units of the service)	200	300
Sales (£)	5,000	7,500
Operating profit (£)	1,000	2,200

There were no price changes of any description during these two months.

Required:
(a) Deduce the break-even point (in units of the service) for Lannion.
(b) State why the company might find it useful to know its break-even point.

7.3 A hotel group prepares accounts on a quarterly basis. The senior management is reviewing the performance of one hotel and making plans for 2001.

They have in front of them the results for 2000 (based on some actual results and some forecasts to the end of 2000):

Quarter	Sales	Profit/(loss)
	£	£
1	400,000	(280,000)
2	1,200,000	360,000
3	1,600,000	680,000
4	800,000	40,000
Total	4,000,000	800,000

The total estimated number of visitors (guest nights) for 2000 is 50,000. The results follow a regular pattern; there are no unexpected cost fluctuations beyond the seasonal trading pattern exhibited. The management intend to incorporate into their plans for 2001 an anticipated increase in unit variable costs of 10 per cent and a profit target for the hotel of £1million.

Required:
(a) Determine the total variable and total fixed costs of the hotel for 2000, by the use of a PV chart or by calculation.
Tabulate the provisional annual results for 2000 in total, showing variable and fixed costs separately. Show also the revenue and costs per visitor.

(b) (i) If there is no increase in visitors for 2001, what will be the required revenue rate per hotel visitor to meet the profit target?
(ii) If the required revenue rate per visitor is not raised above the 2000 level, how many visitors are required to meet the profit target?
(c) Outline and briefly discuss the assumptions that are contained within the accountants' typical PV or break-even analysis, and assess whether they limit its usefulness.

7.4 A company makes three products, A, B and C. All three products require the use of two types of machine: cutting machines and assembling machines. Estimates for next year include the following:

	Product A	Product B	Product C
Selling price (per unit)	£25.00	£30.00	£18.00
Sales demand (units)	2,500	3,400	5,100
Material cost (per unit)	£12.00	£13.00	£10.00
Variable production cost (per unit)	£7.00	£4.00	£3.00
Time required per unit on cutting machines	1.0 hours	1.0 hours	0.5 hours
Time required per unit on assembling machines	0.5 hours	1.0 hours	0.5 hours

Fixed overhead costs for next year are expected to total £42,000. It is the company's policy for each unit of production to absorb these in proportion to its total variable costs.

The company has cutting machine capacity of 5,000 hours per annum and assembling machine capacity of 8,000 hours per annum.

Required:
(a) State, with supporting workings, which products in which quantities the company should plan to make next year on the basis of the above information.
(b) State the maximum price per product that it would be worth the company paying a subcontractor to carry out that part of the work which could not be done internally.

7.5 Darmor Ltd has three products, which require the same production facilities. Information about their per-unit production costs are as follows:

Product	A	B	C
	£	£	£
Labour: Skilled	6	9	3
Unskilled	2	4	10
Materials	12	25	14
Variable overheads	3	7	7
Share of fixed overheads	5	10	10

All labour and materials are variable costs. Skilled labour is paid a basic rate of £6 an hour, and unskilled labour is paid a basic rate of £4 an hour. The labour costs per unit, shown above, are based on basic rates of pay. Skilled labour is scarce, which means that the company could sell more than the maximum that it is able to make of any of the three products.

Product A is sold in a regulated market, and the regulators have set a price of £30 per unit for it.

Required:

(a) State, with supporting workings, the price that must be charged for products B and C, such that the company would be indifferent between making and selling any of the three products.

(b) State, with supporting workings, the maximum rate of overtime premium that the company would logically be prepared to pay its skilled workers to work beyond the basic time.

Full costing

INTRODUCTION

In this chapter we are going to look at an approach to deducing the cost of a unit of output that takes account of all of the costs. This full-costing approach, as it is called, is very widely used in practice. The precise approach taken tends to depend on whether each unit of output is identical to the next or whether each unit has its own individual characteristics. It also tends to depend on whether the business accounts for overheads on a departmental basis or not. We shall look at how full costing is achieved, and then we shall consider its usefulness for management purposes. Finally, we shall examine activity-based costing, which, by taking a different approach to dealing with overheads, represents a variation on the traditional full-costing approach.

Objectives

When you have completed this chapter you should be able to:

- deduce the full cost of a unit of output in a single-product environment
- distinguish between direct and indirect costs and use this distinction to deduce the full cost of a job in a multi-product environment
- discuss the problem of charging overheads to jobs in a multi-product environment
- explain the role and nature of activity-based costing.

The nature of full costing

❋ With **full costing** we are concerned with all costs involved with achieving some objective, for example making a particular product. The logic of full costing is that all of the costs of running a particular facility, say a factory, are part of the cost of the output of that factory. For example, the rent may be a cost that will not alter merely because we make one more unit of production, but if the factory were not rented there would be nowhere for production to take place, so rent is an important element of the cost of each unit of output.

Full cost is the total amount of resources, usually measured in monetary terms, sacrificed to achieve a particular objective. It takes account of all resources sacrificed to achieve the objective. Thus, if the objective were to supply a customer with a service or product, delivery of the service or product to the customer's premises would normally be included as part of the full cost.

If a business is trying to set prices for its output that will lead to the business making a profit, the prices charged must cover all costs. As we shall see later, pricing is one of the uses to which full cost information is put in practice.

Deriving full costs in a single-product operation

The simplest case for which to deduce the full cost per unit is where the business only has one product line: that is, each unit of its product is identical. Here it is simply a question of adding up all the costs of production incurred in the period (materials, labour, rent, fuel and power and so on) and dividing this total by the total number of units of output for the period.

Activity 8.1

Rustic Breweries Ltd has just one product, a bitter beer that is marketed as 'Old Rustic'. During last month the company produced 7,300 pints of the beer. The costs incurred were as follows:

	£
Ingredients (hops and so on)	390
Fuel	85
Rent of brewery premises	350
Depreciation of brewery equipment	75
Labour	880

What is the full cost per pint of producing 'Old Rustic'?

This is found simply by taking all of the costs and dividing by the number of pints brewed:

£(390 + 85 + 350 + 75 + 880)/7,300 = £0.24 per pint.

There can be problems in deciding exactly how much cost was incurred. In the case of Rustic Breweries Ltd, for example, how is the cost of depreciation deduced? It is certainly an estimate, and so its reliability is open to question. Should we use the 'relevant' cost of the raw materials (almost certainly the replacement cost), or the actual price paid for the stock used? If it is worth calculating the cost per pint, it must be because this information will be used for some decision-making purpose, so the replacement cost is probably more logical. In practice, however, it seems that historic costs are more often used to deduce full costs.

There can also be problems in deciding precisely how many units of output there were. Brewing beer is not a very fast process. This means that, at any given moment, there is likely to be some beer that is in the process of being brewed. This, in turn, means that some of the costs incurred last month were in respect of some beer that was work-in-progress at the end of the month and are not therefore included in the output quantity of 7,300 pints. Similarly, part of the 7,300 pints was started and incurred costs in the previous month, yet all of those pints were included in the 7,300 pints that we used in our calculation of the cost per pint. Work-in-progress is not a serious problem, but account does need to be taken of it if reliable full cost information is to be obtained.

This approach to full costing, which can be taken with identical, or near identical units of output, is often referred to as **process costing**.

Multi-product operations

Where the units of output of the product, or service, are not identical, for the purposes for which full cost is used, it will not be acceptable to adopt the approach that we used with pints of 'Old Rustic' in Activity 8.1. It is clearly reasonable to ascribe an identical cost to units of output that are identical; it is not so where the units of output are obviously different. Whereas customers would expect to pay the same price for each pint of a particular type of beer that they buy, most people would not expect to pay the same price for each car repair carried out by a particular garage, irrespective of the complexity and size of the repair. So, while it is reasonable to price pints of beer equally because the pints are identical, it is not acceptable to price car repairs equally where they are widely different.

Direct and indirect costs

Where the units of output are not identical, we normally separate costs into two categories. These are:

* **Direct costs.** These are costs that can be identified with specific cost units. That is to say, the effect of the cost can be measured in respect of each particular unit of output. The main examples of these are direct materials and direct labour. Collecting direct costs is a simple matter of having a cost-recording system that is capable of capturing the cost of direct material used on each job and the cost, based on the hours worked and the rate of pay, of direct workers.

* **Indirect costs** (or **overheads**). These are all other costs: that is, those that cannot be directly measured in respect of each particular unit of output.

We shall use the terms 'indirect costs' and 'overheads' interchangeably for the remainder of this book. Overheads are sometimes known as **common costs** because they are common to all production of the production unit (for example factory or department) for the period.

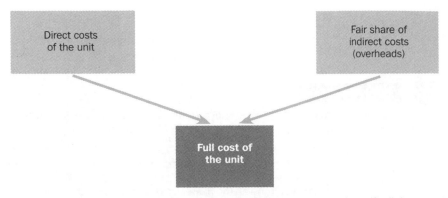

The full cost of any particular job is the sum of those costs that can be measured specifically in respect of the job (direct costs) and a share of those costs that create the environment in which production can take place, but which do not relate specifically to any particular job (overheads).

Figure 8.1 The relationship between direct costs and indirect costs

Job costing

✱ The term **job costing** is used to describe the way in which we identify the full cost per unit of output (job) where the units of output differ. To cost (that is, deduce the full cost of) a particular unit of output (job), we usually ascribe the direct costs to the job, which, by the definition of direct costs, is capable of being done. We then seek to 'charge' each unit of output with a fair share of indirect costs. This is shown graphically in Figure 8.1.

Activity 8.2

Sparky Ltd is a business that employs a number of electricians. The business undertakes a range of work for its customers, from repairing fuses, at one end of the range, to installing complete wiring systems in new houses, at the other.

In respect of a particular job done by Sparky Ltd, into which category, direct or indirect, would each of the following costs fall?

- the wages of the electrician who did the job
- depreciation (wear and tear) of the tools used by the electrician
- the salary of Sparky Ltd's accountant
- the cost of cable and other materials used on the job
- rent of the premises where Sparky Ltd stores its stock of cable and other materials.

Only the electrician's wages earned while working on the particular job and the cost of the actual materials used on the job are direct costs. This is because it is possible to measure how much time (and therefore the labour cost) was spent on the particular job and how much materials were used in the job.

All of the other costs are general costs of running the business and, as such, must form part of the full cost of doing the job, but they cannot be directly measured in respect of the particular job.

It is important to note that whether a cost is a direct one or an indirect one depends on the item being costed, the cost objective. People tend to refer to overheads without stating what the cost objective is; this is incorrect.

Activity 8.3

Into which category, direct or indirect, would each of the costs listed in Activity 8.2 fall if we were seeking to find the cost of operating the entire business of Sparky Ltd for a month?

The answer is that all of them will be direct costs, since they can all be related to, and measured in respect of, running the business for a month.

Naturally, broader-reaching cost units, such as operating Sparky Ltd for a month, tend to include a higher proportion of direct costs than do more limited ones, such as a particular job done by Sparky Ltd. As we shall see shortly, this makes costing broader cost units rather more straightforward than costing narrower ones, since direct costs are easier to deal with.

The collection of costs and the behaviour of costs

We saw in Chapter 7 that the relationship between fixed and variable costs is that, between them, they make up the full cost (or total cost, as it is usually known in the context of marginal analysis). This is illustrated in Figure 8.2.

The similarity of what is shown in Figure 8.2 to that which is depicted in Figure 8.1 might lead us to believe that there might be some relationship between fixed, variable, direct and indirect costs. More specifically, some people seem to believe, mistakenly, that variable costs and direct costs are the same and that fixed costs and overheads are the same. This is incorrect.

✱ The notions of fixed and variable are concerned entirely with **cost behaviour** in the face of changes to the volume of output. Directness of costs

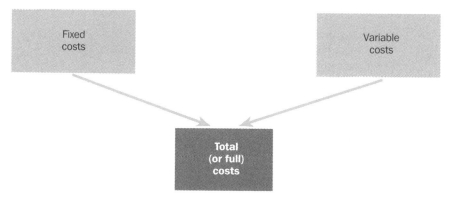

The total cost of a job is the sum of those costs that remain the same irrespective of the level of activity (fixed costs) and those that vary according to the level of activity (variable costs).

Figure 8.2 The relationship between fixed costs, variable costs and total costs

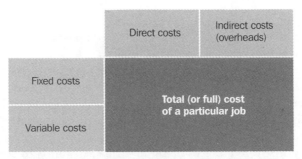

A particular job's full (or total) cost will be made up of some variable and some fixed cost elements. It will also be made up of some direct and some indirect (overhead) element.

Figure 8.3 The relationship between direct, indirect, variable and fixed costs of a particular job

is entirely concerned with collecting together the elements that make up full cost: that is, with the extent to which costs can be measured directly in respect of particular units of output or jobs. These are entirely different concepts. Though it may be true that there is a tendency for fixed costs to be indirect costs (overheads) and for variable costs to be direct costs, there is no direct link, and there are many exceptions to this tendency. For example, most operations have variable overheads. Labour, a major element of direct cost in most production contexts, is usually a fixed cost, certainly over the short term.

The relationship between the reaction of costs to volume changes, on the one hand, and how costs need to be gathered to deduce the full cost, on the other, in respect of a particular job is shown in Figure 8.3.

Total cost is the sum of direct and indirect costs. It is also the sum of fixed and variable costs. These two facts are independent of one another. Thus a particular cost may, for example, be fixed relative to the level of output, on the one hand, and be either direct or indirect on the other.

The notion of distinguishing between direct and indirect costs is related only to deducing full cost in a job costing environment. You may recall that when we were considering costing a pint of 'Old Rustic' beer earlier in Activity 8.1, whether particular elements of cost were direct or indirect was of absolutely no consequence. This was because all costs were shared equally between the pints of beer. Where we have units of output that are not identical, we have to look more closely at the make-up of the costs to achieve a fair measure of the total cost of a particular job.

Indirect costs of any activity must form part of the cost of each unit of output. By definition, however, they cannot be directly related to individual ✱ **cost units**. This raises a major practical issue: how are indirect costs to be apportioned to individual cost units?

It is reasonable to view the overheads as rendering a service to the cost units. A manufactured product can be seen as being rendered a service by the factory in which the product is made. In this sense, it is reasonable to charge each cost unit with a share of the costs of running the factory (rent, lighting, heating, cleaning, building maintenance, and so on). It also seems reasonable to relate the charge for the 'use' of the factory to the level of service that the product has received from the factory

The next step is the difficult one. How might the cost of running the factory, which is a cost of all production, be divided between individual products that are not similar in size and complexity of manufacture?

One possibility is sharing this overhead cost equally between each cost unit produced in the period. Most of us would not propose this method unless the cost units were close to being identical, in terms of the extent to which they had 'benefited' from the overheads.

If we are not to propose equal shares, we must identify something observable and measurable about the cost units that we feel provides a reasonable basis for distinguishing between one cost unit and the next in this context.

In practice, time spent working on the cost unit by direct labour is the basis that is most popular. It must be stressed that this is not the 'correct' way, and it certainly is not the only way. We could, for example, use relative size of products as measured by weight or by relative material cost. Possibly, we could use the relative lengths of time during which each unit of output was worked on by machines.

To see how job costing, as it is usually called, works let us consider Example 8.1.

Example 8.1

Johnson Ltd has overheads of £10,000 each month. Each month 2,500 direct labour hours are worked and charged to units of output (the business's products). A particular job undertaken by the business used direct materials costing £46. Direct labour worked on the job was 15 hours and the wage rate is £5 an hour. Overheads are charged to jobs on a direct labour hour basis. What is the full cost of the job?

First, let us establish the **overhead absorption (recovery) rate**, that is, the rate at which jobs will be charged with overheads. This is £4 (that is, £10,000/ 2,500) per direct labour hour.

Thus, the full cost of the job is:

	£
Direct materials	46
Direct labour (15 × £5)	75
	121
Overheads (15 × £4)	60
Full cost of the job	181

Note, in Example 8.1, that the number of labour hours (15 hours) appears twice in deducing the full cost: once to deduce the direct labour cost and the second time to deduce the overheads to be charged to the job. These are really two separate issues, though they are both based on the same number of labour hours.

Note also that if all of the jobs that are undertaken during the month are assigned overheads in a similar manner, all £10,000 of overheads will be charged to the jobs between them. Jobs that involve a lot of direct labour will be assigned a large share of overheads, and those that involve little direct labour will be assigned a small share of overheads.

Activity 8.4

Can you think of reasons why direct labour hours is regarded as the most logical basis for sharing overheads between cost units?

The reasons that occurred to us are as follows:

- Large jobs should logically attract large amounts of overheads because they are likely to have been rendered more 'service' by the overheads than small ones. The length of time that they are worked on by direct labour may be seen as a rough and ready way of measuring relative size, though other means of doing this may be found – for example, relative physical size.
- Most overheads are related to time. Rent, heating, lighting, fixed asset depreciation, supervisors' and managers' salaries and loan interest, which are all typical overheads, are all more or less time based. That is to say that the overhead cost for one week tends to be about half of that for a similar two-week period. Thus, a basis of apportioning overheads to jobs that takes account of how long the units of output benefited from the 'service' rendered by the overheads seems logical.
- Direct labour hours are capable of being measured in respect of each job. They will normally be measured to deduce the direct labour element of cost in any case. Thus, a direct labour hour basis of dealing with overheads is practical to apply in the real world.

It cannot be emphasised enough that there is no 'correct' way to apportion overheads to jobs. Overheads (indirect costs), by definition, do not naturally relate to individual jobs. If, nevertheless, we wish to take account of the fact that overheads are part of the cost of all jobs, we must find some acceptable way of including a share of the total overheads in each job. If a particular means of doing this is accepted by those who are affected by the full cost deduced, then the method is as good as any other method. Accounting is concerned only with providing useful information to decision makers. In practice, the method that gains the most acceptability as being useful is the direct labour hour method.

Activity 8.5

Marine Suppliers Ltd undertakes a range of work, including making sails for small sailing boats on a made-to-measure basis.
 The following costs are expected to be incurred by the company during the next month:

ISLE COLLEGE

Indirect labour cost	£9,000
Direct labour time	6,000 hours
Depreciation (wear and tear) of machinery	£3,000
Rent and rates	£5,000
Direct labour costs	£30,000
Heating, lighting and power	£2,000
Machine time	2,000 hours
Indirect materials	£500
Other miscellaneous indirect costs	£200
Direct materials cost	£3,000

The company has received an enquiry about a sail, and it is estimated that the sail will take 12 direct labour hours to make and will require 20 square metres of sailcloth, which costs £2 per square metre.

The company normally uses a direct labour hour basis of charging overheads to individual jobs.

What is the full cost of making the sail?

First it is necessary to identify which are the indirect costs and total them as follows:

	£
Indirect labour	9,000
Depreciation	3,000
Rent and rates	5,000
Heating, lighting and power	2,000
Indirect materials	500
Other miscellaneous indirect costs	200
Total indirect costs	19,700

(Note that this list does not include the direct costs. This is because we shall deal with the direct costs separately.)

Since the company uses a direct labour hour basis of charging overheads to jobs, we need to deduce the indirect cost or overhead recovery rate per direct labour hour. This is simply:

£19,700/6,000 = £3.28 per direct labour hour.

Thus, the full cost of the sail would be expected to be:

	£
Direct materials (20 × £2)	40.00
Direct labour (12 × (£30,000/6,000))	60.00
Indirect costs (12 × £3.28)	39.36
Total cost	139.36

Activity 8.6

Suppose that Marine Suppliers Ltd (Activity 8.5) used a machine hour basis of charging overheads to jobs. What would be the cost of the job detailed, if it is expected to take 5 machine hours (as well as 12 direct labour hours)?

The total overheads will of course be the same irrespective of the method of charging them to jobs. Thus, the overhead recovery rate, on a machine hour basis, will be:

£19,700/2,000 = £9.85 per machine hour

Thus, the full cost of the sail would be expected to be:

	£
Direct materials (20 × £2)	40.00
Direct labour (12 × (£30,000/6,000))	60.00
Indirect costs (5 × £9.85)	49.25
Total cost	149.25

A question now presents itself as to which of the two costs for this sail is the correct one, or simply the better one. The answer is that neither is the correct one, as was pointed out earlier. Which is the better one is a matter of judgement. This judgement is concerned entirely with usefulness of information, which in this context is probably concerned with the attitudes of those who will be affected by the figure used. Thus fairness, as it is perceived by those people, is likely to be the important issue.

Probably, most people would feel that the nature of the overheads should influence the choice of the basis of charging the overhead to jobs. Where, because the operation is a capital-intensive one, the overheads are dominated by those relating to machinery (depreciation, machine maintenance, power and so on), machine hours might be favoured. Otherwise direct labour hours might be preferred.

It could appear that one of these bases might be preferred to the other one simply because it apportions either a higher or a lower amount of overheads to a particular job. This would be irrational, however. Since the total overheads are the same irrespective of the method of charging the total to individual jobs, a method that gives a higher share of overheads to one particular job must give a lower share to the remaining jobs. There is one cake of fixed size. If one person is to be given a relatively large slice, the other people, between them, must receive relatively smaller slices. To illustrate further this issue of apportioning overheads, consider Example 8.2.

Example 8.2

A business expects to incur overheads totalling £20,000 next month. The total direct labour time worked is expected to be 1,600, hours and machines are expected to operate for a total of 1,000 hours.

During the month, the business expects to do just two large jobs. Information concerning each job is as follows:

	Job 1	Job 2
Direct labour hours	800	800
Machine hours	700	300

How much of the total overheads will be charged to each job if overheads are to be charged on:

(a) a direct labour hour basis; and
(b) a machine hour basis?

What do you notice about the two sets of figures that you calculate?

(a) *Direct labour hour basis*
Overhead recovery rate = £20,000/1,600 = £12.50 per direct labour hour.

Job 1   £12.50 × 800 = £10,000
Job 2   £12.50 × 800 = £10,000

(b) *Machine hour basis*
Overhead recovery rate = £20,000/1,000 = £20.00 per machine hour.

Job 1   £20.00 × 700 = £14,000
Job 2   £20.00 × 300 = £6,000

It is clear from this that the total overheads charged to jobs is the same (that is, £20,000) whichever method is used. So, whereas the machine hour basis gives Job 1 a higher share than does the direct labour hour method, the opposite is true for Job 2.

It is not possible to charge overheads on one basis to one job and on the other basis to the other job. This is because either total overheads will not be fully charged to the jobs, or the jobs will be overcharged with overheads. For example, the direct labour hour method for Job 1 (£10,000) and the machine hour basis for Job 2 (£6,000) will mean that only £16,000 of a total £20,000 of overheads will be charged to jobs. As a result, the objective of full costing, which is to charge all overheads to jobs done, will not be achieved. In this particular case, if selling prices are based on full costs, the business may not charge prices high enough to cover all of its costs.

Segmenting the overheads

As we have just seen, charging the same overheads to different jobs on different bases is not possible. It is possible, however, to charge one segment of the overheads on one basis and another segment, or other segments, on another basis.

Activity 8.7

Taking the same business as in Example 8.2, on closer analysis we find that of the overheads totalling £20,000 next month, £8,000 relate to machines (depreciation, maintenance, rent of the space occupied by the machines, and so on) and the remainder to more general overheads. The other information about the business is exactly as it was before.

How much of the total overheads will be charged to each job if the machine-related overheads are to be charged on a machine hour basis and the remaining overheads are charged on a direct labour hour basis?

Direct labour hour basis

Overhead recovery rate = £12,000/1,600 = £7.50 per direct labour hour.

Machine hour basis

Overhead recovery rate = £8,000/1,000 = £8.00 per machine hour.

Overheads charged to jobs

	Job 1 £	Job 2 £
Direct labour hour basis		
£7.50 × 800	6,000	
£7.50 × 800		6,000
Machine hour basis		
£8.00 × 700	5,600	
£8.00 × 300		2,400
Total	11,600	8,400

We can see from this that the total expected overheads of £20,000 is charged in total.

Segmenting the overheads in this way may well be seen as providing a better basis of charging overheads to jobs. This is quite often found in practice, usually by dividing a business into separate 'areas' for costing purposes, charging overheads differently from one area to the next.

Remember that there is no correct basis of charging overheads to jobs, so our frequent reference to the direct labour and machine hour bases should not be taken to imply that these are the correct methods. However, it should be said that these two methods do have something to commend them and are popular in practice. As we have already discussed, a sensible method does need to identify something about each job that can be measured and which distinguishes it from other jobs. There is also a lot to be said for methods that are concerned with time because most overheads are time related.

Dealing with overheads on a departmental basis

In general, all but the smallest businesses are divided into departments. Normally, each department deals with a separate activity.

The reasons for dividing a business into departments include the following:

- Many businesses are too large and complex to run as a single unit, and it is more practical to run them as a series of relatively independent units with each one having its own manager.
- Each department normally has its own area of specialism and is managed by a specialist.
- Each department can have its own accounting records that enable its performance to be assessed, which can lead to greater motivation among the staff.

Very many businesses deal with charging overheads to cost units on a department-by-department basis. They do this in the expectation that it will give rise to a fairer means of charging overheads. It is probably often the case that it does not lead to any great improvement in the fairness of the resulting full costs. Though it may not be of enormous benefit in many cases, it is probably not an expensive exercise to apply overheads on a departmental basis. Since costs are collected department by department for other purposes (particularly control), to apply overheads on a department-by-department basis is a relatively simple matter.

The departmental approach to deriving full costs works in the way depicted in Figure 8.4.

The job in Figure 8.4 starts life in the Preparation Department when some direct materials are taken from the stores and worked on by a Preparation Department direct worker. Thus the job will be charged with direct materials, direct labour and with a share of the Preparation Department's overheads. The

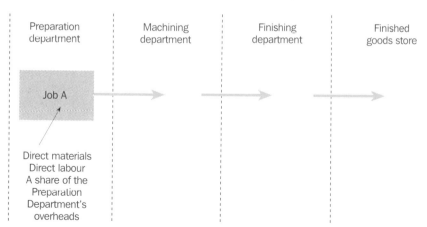

As the particular job passes through the three departments, where work is carried out on it, the job 'gathers' costs of various types.

Figure 8.4 A cost unit passing through the production process

job then passes into the Machining Department, already valued at the costs that it picked up in the Preparation Department. Further direct labour and, possibly, materials are added in the Machining Department, plus a share of that department's overheads. The job now passes into the Finishing Department, valued at the cost of the materials, labour and overheads that it accumulated in the first two departments. In the Finishing Department, further direct labour and, perhaps, materials are added, and the job picks up a share of that department's overheads. The job, now complete, passes into the finished goods store or is dispatched to the customer. The basis of charging overheads to jobs (for example direct labour hours) might be the same for all three departments, or it might be different from one department to another. In the present example, it is quite likely that machine-related costs dominate the Machining Department, so overheads might well be charged to jobs on a machine hour basis. The other two departments may well be labour intensive, and direct labour hours may be seen as being appropriate there.

The passage of the job through the departments can be compared to a snowball being rolled across snow: as it rolls, it picks up more and more snow.

Where costs are dealt with departmentally, each department is known as a **cost centre**. A cost centre can be defined as some physical area or some activity or function for which costs are separately identified. Charging direct costs to jobs, in a departmental system, is exactly the same as where the whole business is one single cost centre. It is simply a matter of keeping a record of:

- the number of hours of direct labour worked on the particular job and the grade of labour, assuming that there are different grades with different rates of pay;
- the cost of the direct materials taken from stores and applied to the job; and
- any other direct costs, for example some subcontract work, associated with the job.

This record-keeping will normally be done departmentally in a departmental system.

It is obviously necessary to identify the production overheads of the entire organisation on a departmental basis. This means that the total overheads of the business must be divided between the departments, such that the sum of the departmental overheads equals the overheads for the entire business. By charging all of their overheads to jobs, between them the departments will charge all of the overheads of the business to jobs.

Batch costing

The production of many types of goods and services, particularly goods, involves producing in a batch of identical, or nearly identical, units of output, but where each batch is distinctly different from other batches. For example, a theatre may put on a production whose nature, and therefore costs, are very different from those of other productions. On the other hand, ignoring differences in the desirability of the various types of seating, all of the individual units of output (tickets to see the production) are identical.

In these circumstances, we should normally deduce the cost per ticket by using a job costing approach (taking account of direct and indirect costs and so on) to find the cost of mounting the production and then simply divide this by the number of tickets expected to be sold to find the cost per ticket. This is ✳ known as **batch costing**.

Full cost as the break-even price

It may have occurred to you by now that if all goes according to plan (direct costs, overheads and the basis of charging overheads, for example direct labour hours, prove to be as expected), then selling the output for its full cost should cause the business to break even exactly. Therefore, whatever profit (in total) is loaded onto full cost to set actual selling prices will result in that level of profit being earned for the period.

The forward-looking nature of full costing

Though deducing full costs can be done after the work has been completed, it is often done in advance. In other words, costs are frequently predicted. Where, for example, full costs are needed as a basis on which to set selling prices, it is usually the case that prices need to be set before the customer will accept the job being done. Even where no particular customer has been identified, some idea of the ultimate price will need to be known before the manufacturer will be able to make a judgement as to whether potential customers will buy the product, and in what quantities. There is a risk, of course, that the actual outcome will differ from that which was predicted. If this occurs, corrections are subsequently made.

Self-assessment question 8.1

Promptprint Ltd, a printing business, has received an enquiry from a potential customer for a quotation for a job. The business pricing policy will be based on the plans for the next financial year shown below:

	£
Sales (billings to customers)	196,000
Materials direct	38,000
Labour direct	32,000
Variable overheads	2,400
Advertising (for business)	3,000
Depreciation	27,600
Administration	36,000
Interest	8,000
Profit (before tax)	49,000

A first estimate of the direct costs for the job is shown below:

	£
Direct materials	4,000
Direct labour	3,600

Based on the estimated direct costs:
(a) Prepare a recommended quote for the job based on the plans, commenting on your method.
(b) Comment on the validity of using financial plans in pricing and recommend any improvements you would consider desirable for the business pricing policy used in (a).

Activity-based costing (ABC)

What we have considered so far in this chapter is the traditional, and still very widely used, approach to job costing (deriving the full cost of output where one unit of output differs from another). This approach is to collect for each job those costs that can be unequivocally linked to, and measured in respect of, the particular job (direct costs). All other costs (overheads) are thrown into a pool of costs and charged to individual jobs according to some formula. Traditionally, this formula has been on the basis of the number of direct labour hours worked on each individual job.

This traditional approach to job costing developed when the notion of trying to cost industrial production first emerged, probably around the time of the Industrial Revolution. At that time, manufacturing industry was characterised by the following features:

- *Direct labour-intensive and direct labour-paced production.* Labour was at the heart of production. To the extent that machinery was used, it was to support the efforts of direct labour, and the speed of production was dictated by direct labour.
- *A low level of overheads relative to direct costs.* Little was spent on power, personnel services, machinery (therefore low depreciation charges) and other areas typical of the overheads of modern businesses.
- *A relatively uncompetitive market.* Transport difficulties, limited industrial production worldwide and lack of knowledge by customers of competitors' prices meant that businesses could prosper without being too scientific in pricing their output.

Since overheads represented a pretty small element of total costs, it was acceptable and practical to deal with overheads in a fairly arbitrary manner. Not too much effort was devoted to trying to control the cost of overheads because the rewards of better control were relatively small, certainly when compared with the rewards from controlling direct labour and material costs. It was also reasonable to charge overheads to individual jobs on a direct labour hour basis. Most of the overheads were incurred directly in the support of direct labour: providing direct workers with a place to work, heating and lighting that workplace, employing people to supervise the direct workers, and so on. At the same time, all production was done by direct workers, perhaps aided by machinery.

In more recent years, the world of industrial production has fundamentally altered. Much of it is now characterised by:

- *Capital-intensive and machine-paced production.* Machines are now at the heart of production. Most labour supports the efforts of machines, for example technically maintaining them, and the speed of production is dictated by machines.
- *A high level of overheads relative to direct costs.* Modern industry is characterised by very high depreciation, servicing and power costs. There are also high costs of a nature scarcely envisaged in the early days of industrial production, such as personnel and staff welfare costs. At the same time there are very low, sometimes no, direct labour costs. The proportion of total cost accounted for by direct materials has typically not altered too much, but more efficient production tends to lead to less waste and therefore less material cost, again tending to make overheads more dominant.
- *A highly competitive international market.* Industrial production, much of it highly sophisticated, is carried out worldwide. Transport, including fast air freight, is relatively cheap. Fax, telephone, e-mail and so on ensure that potential customers can quickly and cheaply know the prices of a range of suppliers. The market is therefore likely to be highly competitive. This means that businesses need to know their costs with a greater degree of accuracy than historically has been the case.

Whereas, in the past, overhead recovery rates were typically much less per direct labour hour than the actual rate paid to direct workers, it is now becoming increasingly common for overhead recovery rates to be a multiple of the hourly rate of pay. When production is dominated by direct labour paid £5 an hour it might be reasonable to have a recovery rate of £1 an hour. When, however, direct labour plays a relatively small part in production, to have overhead recovery rates of £50 per direct labour hour is likely to lead to very arbitrary costing. Just a small change in the amount of direct labour worked on a job could massively affect the cost deduced. This is not because the direct worker is massively well paid, but – for no better reason – overheads, not particularly related to labour, are charged on a direct labour hour basis.

The whole question of overheads, what causes them and how they are charged to jobs has, as a result of changes in the environment in which manufacturers operate, been receiving closer attention recently. Historically, businesses have been content to accept that overheads exist and to deal with them, for costing purposes, in as practical a way as possible. There has been a growing realisation that overheads do not just happen; they must be caused by something.

Example 8.3

Modern Producers Ltd has, like virtually all manufacturers, a stock storage area (stores). The costs of running the stores include a share of the factory rent and other establishment costs, such as heating and lighting. They also include salaries of staff employed to look after the stock, and the cost of financing the stock held in the stores.

The company has two product lines, product A and product B. Production of both of these uses raw materials that are held in the stores. Product A is only made specifically to customers' orders, the finished product being transferred direct from the production area to be dispatched to the customer. Product B is manufactured for stock. The company prides itself on its ability to supply this product in relatively large quantities instantly. As a consequence, much of the stores is filled with finished stocks of product B ready to be dispatched as an order is received.

Traditionally, the whole cost of operating the stores has been treated as a general overhead and included in the total of overheads that is charged to jobs, on a direct labour hour basis. This means that, when assessing the cost of products A and B, the cost of operating the stores has fallen on them according to the number of direct labour hours worked on each one. In fact, most of the stores cost should be charged to product B, since this product causes (and benefits from) the stores cost much more than is true of product A. Failure to account more precisely for the costs of running the stores is masking the fact that product B is not as profitable as it seems to be; it may even be leading to losses as a result of the relatively high cost of operating the stores that it causes, but which so far have been charged partly to product A.

Cost drivers

Realisation that overheads do not just occur, but are caused by activities, such
✱ as holding products in stores, that 'drive' the costs is at the heart of **activity-based costing** (ABC). The traditional approach is that direct labour hours are a
✱ **cost driver**, which probably used to be true. It is now recognised to be no longer the case.

There is a basic philosophical difference between the traditional and ABC approaches. Traditionally, we tend to think of overheads as rendering a service to cost units, the cost of which must be charged to those units. ABC sees overheads as being *caused* by cost units, and that those cost units must be charged with the costs that they cause.

Activity 8.8

Can you think of any other purpose that identification of the cost drivers serves, apart from deriving more accurate costs?

Identification of the activities that cause costs puts management in a position where it may well be able to control them.

The opaque nature of overheads has traditionally rendered them difficult to control, relative to the much more obvious direct labour and material costs. If, however, analysis of overheads can identify the cost drivers, questions can be asked about whether the activity that is driving costs is necessary at all, and whether the cost justifies the benefit. In our example, it may be a good marketing ploy that product B can be supplied immediately from stock, but there is a cost, and that cost should be recognised and assessed against the benefit.

Advocates of activity-based costing argue that most overheads can be analysed and cost drivers identified. If this is true, it means that it is possible to gain much clearer insights into the costs that are caused activity by activity. As a result, fairer and more accurate product costs can be identified, and costs can be controlled more effectively.

ABC in practice in manufacturing industry

In practice, ABC has not yet gained a real foothold in UK manufacturing industry. Colin Drury, Steve Braund, Paul Osborne and Mike Tayles, four accounting academics, undertook a survey of UK manufacturers and their management accounting procedures. This was published in 1993 by the Chartered Association of Certified Accountants. Exhibit 8.1 is a table of the results of this survey, relating to the current and intended introduction of ABC.

Exhibit 8.1

Existing use and attitudes to ABC in UK manufacturing industry

	All business units (N = 289) %	Smaller business units (N = 46) %	Larger business units (N = 45) %
No discussions have taken place regarding the introduction of ABC	45	63	35
A decision has been taken not to introduce ABC	5	7	2
Some consideration is being given to introducing ABC	37	28	40
It is intended to introduce ABC	9	2	16
ABC has been introduced	4	0	7

We can see that only 13 per cent of respondents had introduced ABC, or had a clear intention to do so. Some 37 per cent, however, were considering its introduction. Given that the survey took place in 1993, and that ABC was then a fairly recent development, it seems reasonable to conjecture that it is now a more widely used approach to dealing with overheads.

ABC and service industries

Much of the discussion of ABC so far in this chapter has concentrated on manufacturing industry, perhaps because early users of ABC were manufacturing businesses. In fact, ABC is possibly even more relevant to service industries because, in the absence of a direct materials element, its total costs are likely to be particularly heavily affected by overheads. There certainly is evidence that ABC has been adopted by some businesses that sell services rather than goods.

Activity 8.9

What is the difference in the way in which direct costs are accounted for when using ABC, relative to their treatment taking a traditional approach to full costing?

The answer is no difference at all. ABC is concerned only with the way in which overheads are charged to jobs to derive the full cost.

Criticisms of ABC

Critics of ABC argue that analysis of overheads in order to identify cost drivers is very time consuming and costly, and that the benefit of doing so, in terms of more accurate costing and the potential for cost control, does not justify the cost of carrying out the analysis.

ABC is also criticised for the same reason that full costing generally is criticised. This is that it does not provide very relevant information for decision making. This point will be addressed shortly.

Uses of full cost information

Why do we need to deduce full cost information? There are probably two main reasons:

- *For pricing purposes.* In some industries and circumstances, full costs are used as the basis of pricing. Here the full cost is deduced and a percentage is added on for profit. This is known as *cost plus* pricing. Garages, carrying out vehicle repairs, probably provide an example of this.

  In many circumstances, suppliers are not in a position to deduce prices on a cost plus basis, however. Where there is a competitive market, a supplier will probably need to accept the price that the market offers: that is, most suppliers are *price takers* not *price makers*.

- *For income measurement purposes.* You may recall from Chapter 3 that to provide a valid means of measuring a business's income it is necessary to match expenses with the revenues realised in the same accounting period. Where manufactured stock is made or partially made in one period but sold in the next, or where a service is partially rendered in one accounting period but the revenue is realised in the next, the full cost (including an appropriate share of overheads) must be carried from one accounting period to the next. Unless we are able to identify the full cost of work done in one period that is the subject of a sale in the next, the profit figures of the periods concerned will become meaningless. This will mean that users of accounting information will not have reliable means of assessing the effectiveness of the business, or parts of it. This second reason for needing full cost information can be illustrated by Example 8.4.

 Example 8.4

During the accounting year that ended on 31 December 2000, Engineers Ltd made a special machine for a customer. At the beginning of 2001, after having a series of tests successfully completed by a subcontractor, the machine was delivered to the customer. The company's normal practice (typical of most businesses and following the realisation convention) is to take account of sales when the product passes to the customer. The sale price of the machine was £25,000.

During the year 2000, materials costing £3,500 were used on making the machine and 1,200 hours of direct labour, costing £9,300, were worked on the machine. The company uses a direct labour hour basis of charging overheads to jobs, which is believed to be fair because most of its work is labour intensive. The total manufacturing overheads for the company for the year 2000 were £77,000, and the total direct labour hours worked were 22,000. Testing the machine cost £1,000.

How much profit or loss did the company make on the machine in 2000? How much profit or loss did the company make on the machine in 2001? At what value must the company carry the machine in its accounting system at the end of 2000, so that the correct profit will be recorded for each of the two years?

No profit or loss was made in 2000, following the company's (and the generally accepted) approach to recognising revenues (sales). If the sale were not to be recognised until 2001 it would be illogical (and in contravention of the matching convention) to treat the costs of making the machine as expenses until that time.

In 2001, the sale would be recognised and all of the costs, including a reasonable share of overheads, would be set against it in the 2001 profit and loss account, as follows:

	£	£
Sales price		25,000
Costs:		
Direct labour	9,300	
Direct materials	3,500	
Overheads (1,200 × (£77,000/22,000))	4,200	
Total incurred in year 2000	17,000	
Testing cost	1,000	
Total cost		18,000
Year 2001 profit from the machine		7,000

The machine needs to be shown as an asset of the company at £17,000 at 31 December 2000.

Unless all production costs are charged in the same accounting period as that in which the sale is recognised in the profit and loss account, distortions will occur that will render the profit and loss account much less useful. Thus it is necessary to deduce the full cost of any production undertaken completely or partially in one accounting period, but sold in a subsequent one.

Criticisms of full costing

Full costing is widely criticised because, in practice, it tends to use past costs and to restrict its consideration of future costs to outlay costs. It can be argued that past costs are irrelevant, irrespective of the purpose for which the information is to be used. This is basically because it is not possible to make decisions about the past, only about the future. Advocates of full costing would argue that it provides an informative long-run average cost.

Despite the criticisms that are made of full costing, it is, according to research evidence, very widely practised.

SUMMARY

In this chapter we have seen that many, perhaps most, businesses seek to identify the total or full cost of pursuing some objective, typically of a unit of output. Where all units of goods or service produced by a business are identical, this tends to be a fairly straightforward matter – a case of simply finding the total cost for a period and dividing by the number of units of output for the same period.

Where a business's output is of units that are not similar, it is necessary to take a less straightforward approach to the problem. Normally such businesses identify the direct costs of production: those costs that can be directly measured in respect of a particular unit of output. To these are added a share of the overheads according to some formula, which of necessity must to some extent be arbitrary. Survey evidence shows that direct labour hours is the most popular basis of charging overheads to cost units. Costing individual cost units in this way is known as job costing.

Activity-based costing is strongly advocated by many people as providing a more focused approach to applying overheads to jobs. It achieves this by identifying 'cost drivers' or activities that give rise to overhead costs.

Full cost information is widely used by businesses, but it is also widely criticised as not providing very helpful and relevant information.

Key terms

full costing *p 206*
process costing *p 208*
direct costs *p 208*
indirect costs *p 208*
overheads *p 208*
common costs *p 208*
job costing *p 209*
cost behaviour *p 210*

cost units *p 211*
overhead absorption (recovery)
  rate *p 212*
cost centre *p 219*
batch costing *p 220*
activity-based costing *p 223*
cost driver *p 223*

REVIEW QUESTIONS

8.1 What problem does the existence of work-in-progress cause in process costing?

8.2 What is the point of distinguishing direct costs from indirect ones?

8.3 Are direct costs and variable costs the same thing?

8.4 It is sometimes claimed that the full cost of pursuing some objective represents the long-run break-even selling price. Why is this said, and what does it mean?

EXAMINATION-STYLE QUESTIONS

None of these questions is at advanced level. Those with a coloured number have answers at the back of the book.

8.1 Distinguish between:

- job costing
- process costing
- batch costing.

What tend to be the problems specifically associated with each of these?

8.2 Bodgers Ltd operates a job costing system. Towards the end of each financial year, the overhead recovery rate (the rate at which overheads will be charged to jobs) is established for the forthcoming year.

(a) Why does the company bother to predetermine the recovery rate in the way outlined?

(b) What steps will be involved in predetermining the rate?

(c) What problems might arise with using a predetermined rate?

8.3 Many businesses charge overheads to jobs, in a job costing environment, on a departmental basis.

    What is the advantage that is claimed for charging overheads to jobs on a departmental basis, and why is it claimed?

What circumstances need to exist to make a difference to a particular job according to whether overheads are charged on a 'business-wide' basis or on a 'departmental' basis? (Note that the answer to this part of the question is not specifically covered in the chapter. You should nevertheless be able to deduce the reason from what you know.)

8.4 In a job costing system, it is necessary to divide the business up into departments. Fixed costs (or overheads) will be collected for each department. Where a particular fixed cost relates to the business as a whole, it must be divided between the departments. Usually this is done on the basis of area of floorspace occupied by each department relative to the entire business. When the total fixed costs for each department have been identified, this will be divided by the number of hours that were worked in each department to deduce an overhead recovery rate. Each job that was worked on in a department will have a share of fixed costs allotted to it according to how long it was worked on. The total cost for each job will therefore be the sum of the variable costs of the job and its share of the fixed costs. It is essential that this approach is taken in order to deduce a selling price for the firm's output.

You are required to prepare a table of two columns. In the first column you should show any phrases or sentences with which you do not agree (in the above statement), and in the second column you should show your reason for disagreeing with each one.

8.5 Pieman Products Ltd makes road trailers to the precise specifications of individual customers.

The following are predicted to occur during the forthcoming year, which is about to start:

Direct materials cost	£50,000
Direct labour costs	£80,000
Direct labour time	16,000 hours
Indirect labour cost	£25,000
Depreciation (wear and tear) of machinery etc.	£8,000
Rent and rates	£10,000
Heating, lighting and power	£5,000
Indirect materials	£2,000
Other indirect costs	£1,000
Machine time	3,000 hours

All direct labour is paid at the same hourly rate.

A customer has asked the company to build a trailer for transporting a racing motor cycle to races. It is estimated that this will require materials and components that will cost £1,150. It will take 250 direct labour hours to do the job, of which 50 will involve the use of machinery.

Required:
Deduce a logical cost for the job, and explain the basis of dealing with overheads that you propose.

9

Budgeting

INTRODUCTION

This chapter is concerned with budgets. Budgeting is an activity that most business managers see as one of the most crucial in which they are engaged. We shall consider the purpose of budgets and how they fit into the decision-making and planning process. We shall also consider how budgets are prepared. Lastly, we shall take a look at how budgets are used to help exercise control over the business to try to ensure that its objectives are achieved.

Objectives

On completion of this chapter you should be able to:

- define a budget and show how budgets, corporate objectives and long-term plans are related

- explain the interlinking of the various budgets within the business

- indicate the uses of budgeting, and construct various budgets, including the cash budget, from relevant data

- use a budget to provide a means of exercising control over the business.

Budgets, long-term plans and corporate objectives

We saw in Chapter 1 that it is vitally important that businesses develop plans for the future. Whatever a business is trying to achieve, it is unlikely to be successful unless its managers have clear in their minds what the future direction of the business is going to be. Thus the starting point is to identify, as precisely as possible, the long-term objectives to be pursued. Once this has been done, the various options available to fulfil these objectives should be evaluated. The most appropriate option(s) should be selected and plans developed on the basis of this selection.

Businesses typically produce a long-term plan, perhaps going five years into the future, and a short-term plan normally looking at the following 12 months.

The planning sequence can be shown graphically, as in Figure 9.1. We can see that the overall objectives are first defined; they are then translated into

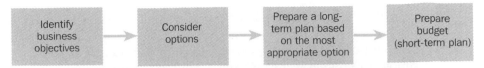

| Identify business objectives | → | Consider options | → | Prepare a long-term plan based on the most appropriate option | → | Prepare budget (short-term plan) |

The figure shows the planning sequence within a business. Once the objectives of the business have been identified, the various options that can fulfil these objectives must be evaluated. A long-term plan is then developed to achieve these objectives. The budget is a short-term plan for the business, which is prepared within the framework of the long-term plan.

Figure 9.1 Objectives, plans and budgets.

✱ long-term plans of action, whose achievement is through working towards short-term plans or **budgets**.

The long-term plan would define the general direction of the business over the next five or so years and would deal, in broad terms, with such matters as:

- the market that the business will seek to serve
- production/service rendering methods
- what the business will offer to its customers
- levels of profit and returns to shareholders sought
- financial requirements and financing methods
- personnel requirements
- bought-in goods and services requirements and sources.

The budget is essentially a financial plan for the short term. It is likely to be expressed mainly in financial terms, and is designed to convert the long-term plan into an actionable blueprint for the future. The budget will define precise targets for:

- sales and expenses
- cash receipts and payments
- short-term credit to be given or taken
- stock-in-trade requirements
- personnel requirements.

Clearly, the relationship between objectives, long-term plans and budgets is that the objectives, once set, are likely to last for quite a long time, perhaps throughout the life of the business (though changes can and do occur). A series of long-term plans identify how the objectives are to be pursued, and budgets identify how the long-term plan is to be fulfilled.

An analogy might be found in terms of someone enrolling on a course of study. His, or her, objective might be to have a working career that is rewarding in various ways. The person might have identified the course as the most effective way to work towards this objective. In working towards achievement of the objective, passing a particular stage of the course might be identified as the target for the forthcoming year. Here the intention to complete the entire course is analogous to a long-term plan, and passing each stage is analogous to the budget. Having achieved the 'budget' for the first year, the 'budget' for the second year becomes passing the second stage. It should be emphasised that planning is the role of management rather than of accountants. Traditionally, the role of the management accountant has been simply to provide technical advice and assistance to managers in order to help them plan. However, things are changing. Increasingly, the management accountant is seen as a member of the management team and, in this management role, is expected to contribute towards the planning process.

Time horizon of plans and budgets

It need not necessarily be the case that long-term plans are set for five years and that budgets are set for 12 months – it is up to the management of the business concerned – though these are fairly typical of the time periods found in practice. A business involved in certain industries, say information technology, may feel that five years is too long a planning period since new developments can, and do, occur virtually overnight. It also need not be the case that a budget is set for one year. However, this appears to be a widely used time horizon.

Activity 9.1

Can you think of any reason why most businesses prepare detailed budgets for the forthcoming year, rather than for a shorter or longer period?

The reason is probably that a year represents a long enough period for the budget preparation exercise to be worthwhile, yet short enough into the future for detailed plans to be made. As we shall see later in this chapter, the process of formulating budgets can be time consuming, but there are economies of scale: for example, preparing the budget for the next twelve months would not normally take twice as much time and effort as preparing the budget for the next six months.

The annual budget sets targets for the year for all levels of the business. It is usually broken down into monthly budgets that define monthly targets. In many cases the annual budget will, in any case, be built up from monthly figures. For example, the sales staff will be required to make sales targets for each month of the budget period.

There will always be some aspect of the business that will stop it achieving its objectives to the maximum extent. This is often a limited ability of the business to sell its products. Sometimes, it is some production shortage (labour, materials and plant) that is the **limiting factor**. It is important that the limiting factor is identified. Ultimately, most, if not all, budgets will be affected by the limiting factor, so if it can be identified at the outset, all managers can be informed of the restriction early in the process.

Budgets and forecasts

We saw earlier that a budget is a financial plan for a future period of time. Note particularly that a budget is a plan, not a forecast. To talk of a plan suggests an intention or determination to achieve the planned targets. Forecasts tend to be predictions of the future state of the environment.

Clearly forecasts are very helpful to the planner/budget setter. If a reputable forecaster has forecast the particular number of new cars to be purchased in the United Kingdom during next year, it will be valuable for a manager in a car manufacturing business to obtain this forecast figure when setting sales budgets. However, the forecast and the budget are distinctly different.

The interrelationship of various budgets

For a particular business, for a particular period, there is more than one budget. Each one will relate to a specific aspect of the business. It is generally considered that the ideal situation is that there should be a separate budget for each person who is in a managerial position, no matter how junior. The contents of all of the individual budgets are, in effect, summarised in **master budgets** which would typically be a budgeted income statement (profit and loss account) and balance sheet. However, the cash flow statement (in summarised form) may also be considered part of the master budget.

Figure 9.2 illustrates the interrelationship and interlinking of the individual budgets, in this particular case using a manufacturing business as an example. Starting at the top of Figure 9.2, the sales budget is usually the first budget to be prepared, as this will determine the overall level of activity for the forthcoming period. The finished stock requirement would be dictated largely by the level of sales; it would also be dictated by the policy of the business on finished stock holding. The requirement for finished stock would define the required production levels, which would in turn dictate the requirements of the individual production departments or sections. The demands of manufacturing, in conjunction with the business's policy on raw material stock holding, define the raw materials stock budget. The purchases budget will be dictated by the raw materials stock budget, which will, in conjunction with the policy of the business on creditor payment, dictate the trade creditors budget. One of the inputs into the cash budget will be from the trade creditors budget; another will be the trade debtors budget, which itself derives via the debtor policy of the business from the sales budget. Cash will also be affected by overheads and by direct labour costs (themselves linked to production) and by capital expenditure. The factors that affect policies on matters such as stock holding, debtor and creditor collection periods will be discussed in some detail in Chapter 10.

Assuming that the budgeting process takes the order just described, it might be found in practice that there is some constraint to achieving the sales target. For example, the production facilities of the business may be incapable of

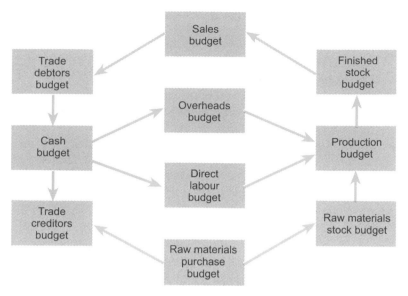

The figure shows the interrelationship of budgets for a manufacturing business. The starting point is usually the sales budget. The expected level of sales normally defines the overall level of activity for the business, and the other budgets will be drawn up in accordance with this. Thus, the sales budget will largely define the finished stock requirements, and from this we can define the production requirements and so on.

Figure 9.2 The interrelationship of various budgets

meeting the necessary levels of output to match the sales budget for one or more months. In this case, it might be reasonable to look at the ways of overcoming the problem. As a last resort, it might be necessary to revise the sales budget to a lower level to enable production to meet the target.

 Activity 9.2

Can you think of any ways in which a short-term shortage of production facilities might be capable of being overcome?

We thought of the following:

- Higher production in previous months and stockpiling to meet the higher demand period(s).
- Increasing the production facility might be possible, perhaps by working overtime and/ or acquiring (buying or leasing) additional plant.
- It may be possible to subcontract some production.
- It may be possible to encourage potential customers to change the timing of their buying by offering discounts, or other special terms, during the months that have been identified as being quiet.

You may well have thought of other approaches.

There will not only be the horizontal relationships between budgets that we have just looked at, but usually vertical ones as well. For example, the sales budget may be broken down into a number of subsidiary budgets, perhaps one for each regional sales manager. Thus the overall sales budget will be a summary of the subsidiary ones. The same may be true of virtually all of the other budgets, most particularly the production budget. Figure 9.2 gives a very simplified outline of the budgetary framework of the typical manufacturing business.

All of the operating budgets that we have just reviewed are set within the framework of the master budgets: that is, the budgeted profit and loss account and balance sheet.

The uses of budgets

Budgets are generally regarded as having four areas of usefulness described below:

- *They tend to promote forward thinking and the possible identification of short-term problems.* In the previous section of this chapter, we saw that a shortage of production capacity may be identified during the budgeting process. Making this discovery, in plenty of time, may leave a number of means of overcoming the problem open to exploration. Take, for example, the problem of a shortage of production at a particular part of the year. If the potential problem is picked up early enough, all of the suggestions in the answer to Activity 9.2 and, possibly, other ways of overcoming the problem can be explored and considered rationally. Budgeting should help to achieve this.
- *They can be used to help co-ordination between various sections of the business.* It is crucially important that the activities of the various departments and sections of the business are linked so that the activities of one department are complementary to those of another. For example, the activities of the purchasing/procurement department of a manufacturing business should dovetail with the raw materials needs of the production departments. If this is not the case, production could run out of stock, leading to expensive production stoppages. Alternatively, excessive stocks could be bought, leading to large and unnecessary stock holding costs.
- *They can motivate managers to better performance.* Having a stated task can motivate performance. It is thought by many people that simply to tell a manager to do his or her best is not very motivating, but to define a required level of achievement is likely to motivate. It is felt by some that managers are better motivated by being able to relate their particular role in the business to the overall objectives of the business. Since budgets are directly derived from corporate objectives, budgeting makes this possible.

It might seem that requiring managers to work towards predetermined targets will stifle skill, flair and enthusiasm. There is this danger if targets are badly set. If, however, the budgets are set in such a way as to offer challenging, yet achievable, targets, the manager is still required to show skill, flair and enthusiasm.

It is obviously not possible to allow managers to operate in an unconstrained environment. Having to operate in a way that matches the goals of the business is a price of working in an effective business.

✳ • *They can provide a basis for a system of control.* **Control** is concerned with ensuring that events conform to plans. If senior management wishes to control the performance of subordinates, it needs some standard or yardstick against which the performance can be compared and assessed. It is possible to compare current performance with that which happened last month or last year, or perhaps with what happens in another business. However, the most logical yardstick is often planned performance.

Activity 9.3

What is wrong with comparing actual performance with past performance or the performance of others in an effort to exercise control?

The answer is that there is no automatic reason to believe that what happened in the past, or is happening elsewhere, represents a sensible target for this year in this business. Considering what happened last year, and in other businesses, may help in the formulation of plans, but past events and the performance of others should not automatically be seen as the target.

If there are data available concerning the actual performance for a period (say a month) that can be compared with the planned performance, then a basis for
✳ control will have been established. Such a basis will enable the use of **management by exception**, a technique whereby senior managers can spend most of their time dealing with those of their subordinates who have failed to achieve the budget, and not having to spend too much time on those who are performing well. It also allows junior managers to exercise self-control, since by knowing what is expected of them and what they have actually achieved, they can assess how well they are performing and take steps to correct matters where they are failing to achieve.

We shall consider the effect of making plans, and being held accountable for their achievement, later in the chapter

An example of a budget – the cash budget

We shall now look in some detail at one particular budget, the cash budget. There are three reasons for using this as an example:

- It is at least as good an example as is any other budget.
- Most economic aspects of a business are reflected in cash sooner or later, so that the cash budget reflects the whole business more than any other single budget, for the typical business.

- Very small, unsophisticated businesses (for example, a corner shop) may feel that full-scale budgeting is not appropriate to their needs, but almost certainly they should prepare a cash budget as a minimum.

We shall also consider other budgets later in the chapter.

Since budgets are documents that are to be used only internally by the business, their style and format is a question of management choice, and will therefore vary from one business to the next. However, since managers, irrespective of the business, are likely to be using budgets for similar purposes, there is a tendency for some consistency of approach to exist across most businesses. We can probably say that, in most businesses, the cash budget would possess the following features:

1. The budget period would be broken down into sub-periods, typically months.
2. The budget would be in columnar form, with a column for each month.
3. Receipts of cash would be identified under various headings and a total for each month's receipts shown.
4. Payments of cash would be identified under various headings and a total for each month's payments shown.
5. The surplus of total cash receipts over payments, or of payments over receipts, for each month would be identified.
6. The running cash balance, which would be obtained by taking the balance at the end of the previous month and adjusting it for surplus or deficit of receipts over payments for the current month, would be identified.

Typically, all of the pieces of information in items 3 to 6 would be useful to management for one reason or another.

Probably the best way to deal with this topic is through an example.

Example 9.1

Suppliers Ltd is a wholesale business. The budgeted profit and loss account for the next six months is as follows:

	Jan £000	Feb £000	Mar £000	Apr £000	May £000	June £000
Sales	52	55	55	60	55	53
Cost of goods sold	30	31	31	35	31	32
Salaries and wages	10	10	10	10	10	10
Electricity	5	5	4	3	3	3
Depreciation	3	3	3	3	3	3
Other overheads	2	2	2	2	2	2
Total expenses	50	51	50	53	49	50
Net profit	2	4	5	7	6	3

The business allows all of its customers one month's credit (that is, goods sold in January will be paid for in February). Sales during December had been £60,000.

The business plans to maintain stocks at their existing level until sometime in March, when they are to be reduced by £5,000. Stocks will remain at this lower level indefinitely. Stock purchases are made on one month's credit (the December purchases were £30,000). Salaries, wages and 'other overheads' are paid in the month concerned. Electricity is paid quarterly in arrears in March and June. The business plans to buy and pay for a new delivery van in March. This will cost a total of £15,000, but an existing van will be traded in for £4,000 as part of the deal. The business expects to start January with £12,000 in cash.

Show the cash budget for the six months ending in June.

Solution

Cash budget for the six months ending 30 June:

	Jan £000	Feb £000	Mar £000	Apr £000	May £000	June £000
Receipts						
Debtors (note 1)	60	52	55	55	60	55
Payments						
Creditors (note 2)	30	30	31	26	35	31
Salaries and wages	10	10	10	10	10	10
Electricity			14			9
Other overheads	2	2	2	2	2	2
Van purchase			11			
Total payments	42	42	68	38	47	52
Cash surplus	18	10	(13)	17	13	3
Cash balance (note 3)	30	40	27	44	57	60

Notes

1 The cash receipts lag a month behind sales because customers are given a month in which to pay for their purchases.

2 In most months, the purchases of stock will equal the cost of goods sold. This is because the business maintains a constant level of stock. For stock to remain constant at the end of each month, the business must replace exactly the amount of stock that has been used. During March, however, the business plans to reduce its stock by £5,000. This means that stock purchases will be lower than stock usage in that month. The payments for stock purchases lag a month behind purchases because the business expects to be allowed a month to pay for what it buys.

3 Each month's cash balance is the previous month's figure plus the cash surplus (or minus the cash deficit) for the current month. The balance at the start of January is £12,000, according to the information provided earlier.

Activity 9.4

Looking at the cash budget of Suppliers Ltd (above), what conclusions do you draw, and what possible course of action do you recommend, regarding the cash balance over the period concerned?

For the size of the business, there appears to be a fairly large and increasing cash balance. Management might give consideration to putting some of the cash into an income-yielding deposit. Alternatively, it could be used to expand the trading activities of the business by, for example, increasing the investment in fixed assets.

Activity 9.5

Suppliers Ltd, the wholesale business that was the subject of Example 9.1, now wishes to prepare its cash budget for the second six months of the year. The budgeted profit and loss account for the second six months is as follows:

	July £000	Aug £000	Sept £000	Oct £000	Nov £000	Dec £000
Sales	57	59	62	57	53	51
Cost of goods sold	32	33	35	32	30	29
Salaries and wages	10	10	10	10	10	10
Electricity	3	3	4	5	6	6
Depreciation	3	3	3	3	3	3
Other overheads	2	2	2	2	2	2
Total expenses	50	51	54	52	51	50
Net profit	7	8	8	5	2	1

The business will continue to allow all of its customers one month's credit (that is, goods sold in July will be paid for in August).

The business plans to increase stocks from the 30 June level by £1,000 each month until, and including, September. During the following three months, stock levels will be decreased by £1,000 each month.

Stock purchases, which had been made on one month's credit until the June payment, will, starting with the purchases made in June, be made on two months' credit.

Salaries and wages and 'other overheads' will continue to be paid in the month concerned. Electricity is paid quarterly in arrears in September and December.

At the end of December, the business intends to pay off part of a loan. This payment is to be such that it will leave the business with a cash balance of £5,000 with which to start next year.

Remember, any information that you need relating to the first six months of the year, including the cash balance that is expected to be brought forward on 1 July, is given in Example 9.1.

Have a go at the cash budget for the six months ending in December.

Cash budget for the six months ending 31 December:

	July £000	Aug £000	Sept £000	Oct £000	Nov £000	Dec £000
Receipts						
Debtors	53	57	59	62	57	53
Payments						
Creditors (note 1)	–	32	33	34	36	31
Salaries and wages	10	10	10	10	10	10
Electricity			10			17
Other overheads	2	2	2	2	2	2
Loan repayment (note 2)						131
Total payments	12	44	55	46	48	191
Cash surplus	41	13	4	16	9	(138)
Cash balance	101	114	118	134	143	5

Notes

1 There will be no payment to creditors in July because the June purchases will be made on two months' credit, and will therefore be paid in August. The July purchases, which will equal the July cost of sales figure plus the increase in stock made in July, will be paid for in September, and so on.

2 The repayment is simply the amount that will cause the balance at 31 December to be £5,000.

Preparing other budgets

Though each one will have its own idiosyncrasies, other budgets will tend to follow the same sort of pattern as the cash budget. Take the *debtors budget* for example. This would normally show the planned amount owing from credit sales to the business at the beginning and at the end of each month, the planned total sales for each month, and the planned total cash receipts from debtors. The layout would be something like the following:

	Month 1	Month 2	and so on
	£	£	
Opening balance	X	X	
Sales	X	X	
	X	X	
Less Cash receipts	X	X	
Closing balance	X	X	

The opening and closing balances represent the amount planned to be owed (in total) to the business by debtors at the beginning and end of the month, respectively.

The layout of the *creditors budget* would be something like the following:

	Month 1	Month 2	and so on
	£	£	
Opening balance	X	X	
Purchases	X	X	
	X	X	
Less Cash payments	X	X	
Closing balance	X	X	

The opening and closing balances represent the amount planned to be owed (in total) by the business to creditors, at the beginning and end of the month respectively.

A *raw materials stock budget* (for a manufacturing business) would follow a similar pattern, as follows:

	Month 1 £ (or physical units	Month 2 £ (or physical units)	and so on
Opening balance	X	X	
Purchases	X	X	
	X	X	
Less Issues to production	X	X	
Closing balance	X	X	

The opening and closing balances represent the amount of stock, at cost, planned to be held by the business at the beginning and end of the period respectively.

The stock budget will normally be expressed in financial terms, but may also be expressed in physical terms (for example, kg or metres) for individual stock items.

A manufacturing business would normally produce both a raw materials stock budget and a finished stock budget. A *finished stock budget* (for a manufacturing business) would typically be as follows:

	Month 1 £ (or physical units)	Month 2 £ (or physical units)	and so on
Opening balance	X	X	
Finished stock transferred from production	X	X	
	X	X	
Less Finished stock sold	X	X	
Closing balance	X	X	

Activity 9.6

Have a go at preparing the debtors budget for Suppliers Ltd for the six months July to December (see Activities 9.4 and 9.5).

Debtors budget for the six months ended 31 December:

	July £000	Aug £000	Sept £000	Oct £000	Nov £000	Dec £000
Opening balance (note 1)	53	57	59	62	57	53
Sales	57	59	62	57	53	51
	110	116	121	119	110	104
Less Cash receipts	53	57	59	62	57	53
Closing balance	57	59	62	57	53	51

This could of course be set out in any manner that would have given the sort of information that management would require in respect of planned levels of debtors and associated transactions.

Note
1   The opening balances will be the sales figures for the previous month, since the business plans to allow its credit customers one month's credit.

Note how the debtors budget links to the cash budget; the cash receipts row of figures is the same. The debtors budget would similarly link to the sales budget. This is how the linking that was discussed earlier in this chapter, is achieved.

Activity 9.7

Have a go at preparing the creditors budget for Suppliers Ltd for the six months July to December (see Activity 9.4).

Hint: Remember that the creditor payment period alters from the June purchases onwards.

Creditors budget for the six months ending 31 December:

	July £000	Aug £000	Sept £000	Oct £000	Nov £000	Dec £000
Opening balance (note 1)	32	65	67	70	67	60
Purchases	33	34	36	31	29	28
	65	99	103	101	96	88
Less Cash payments (note 2)	–	32	33	34	36	31
Closing balance	65	67	70	67	60	57

This again could be set out in any manner that would have given the sort of information that management would require in respect of planned levels of creditors and associated transactions.

Notes

1　The opening balance for July will be the planned purchases figures for the previous month (June), since the business plans, until the June purchases, to take one month's credit from its suppliers. The opening balances for July to December will represent the planned purchases for the previous two months.

2　There will be no payment to creditors planned in July because creditors will be paid two months after the month of purchase, starting with the June purchases which will be paid for in August.

Self-assessment question 9.1

Antonio Ltd has planned production and sales for the next eight months as follows:

	Production units	Sales units
May	350	350
June	400	400
July	500	400
August	600	500
September	600	600
October	700	650
November	750	700
December	750	800
January	750	750

During the period, the business plans to advertise heavily to generate these increases in sales. Payments for advertising of £1,000 and £1,500 will be made in July and October respectively.

The selling price per unit will be £20 throughout the period. Forty per cent of sales are normally made on two months' credit. The other 60 per cent are settled within the month of the sale.

Raw material will be held in stock for one month before it is taken into production. Purchases of raw materials will be on one month's credit (buy one month, pay the next). The cost of raw material is £8 per unit of production.

Other direct production expenses, including labour, are planned to be £6 per unit of production. These will be paid in the month concerned.

Various production overheads, which during the period to 30 June had run at £1,800 per month, are expected to rise to £2,000 each month from 1 July to 31 October. These are expected to rise again from 1 November to £2,400 per month and to remain at that level for the foreseeable future. These overheads include a steady £400 each month for depreciation. Overheads are planned to be paid 80 per cent in the month of production and 20 per cent in the following month.

To help to meet the planned increased production, a new item of plant will be bought and will be delivered in August. The cost of this item is £6,600; the contract with the supplier will specify that this will be paid in three equal amounts in September, October and November.

Raw material stock is planned to be 500 units on 1 July. The balance at the bank the same day is planned to be £7,500.

You are required to draw up:

- a raw materials budget, showing both physical quantities, and financial values
- a creditors budget
- a cash budget

for the six months ending 31 December.

The cash budget reveals a potential cash deficiency during October and November. Can you suggest any ways in which a modification of plans could overcome this problem?

Using budgets for control – flexible budgets

Earlier in this chapter, the point was made that budgets can provide a useful basis for exercising control over the business. This is because control is usually seen as making events conform to a plan. Since the budget represents the plan, making events conform to it is the obvious way to try to control the business. Using budgets in this way is popular in practice.

As we saw in Chapter 1, for most businesses the routine is as shown in Figure 9.3.

These steps in the control process are probably fairly easy to understand. The point is that, if plans are drawn up sensibly, we have a basis for exercising control

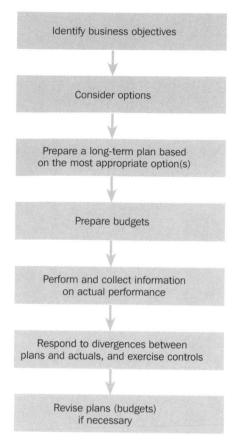

```
┌─────────────────────────────────────┐
│     Identify business objectives      │
└─────────────────────────────────────┘
                  │
                  ▼
┌─────────────────────────────────────┐
│           Consider options            │
└─────────────────────────────────────┘
                  │
                  ▼
┌─────────────────────────────────────┐
│     Prepare a long-term plan based    │
│     on the most appropriate option(s) │
└─────────────────────────────────────┘
                  │
                  ▼
┌─────────────────────────────────────┐
│            Prepare budgets            │
└─────────────────────────────────────┘
                  │
                  ▼
┌─────────────────────────────────────┐
│     Perform and collect information   │
│          on actual performance        │
└─────────────────────────────────────┘
                  │
                  ▼
┌─────────────────────────────────────┐
│     Respond to divergences between    │
│  plans and actuals, and exercise controls │
└─────────────────────────────────────┘
                  │
                  ▼
┌─────────────────────────────────────┐
│         Revise plans (budgets)        │
│              if necessary             │
└─────────────────────────────────────┘
```

The figure shows the planning and control sequence within a business. Once the objectives have been determined, the various options that can fulfil these objectives must be evaluated in order to prepare the long-term plan. The budget is a short-term plan set within the framework of the long-term plan. Control can be exercised through a comparison of budgeted and actual performance. Where a significant divergence emerges, some form of corrective action should be taken. If the budget figures prove to be based on incorrect assumptions about the future, it may be necessary to revise the budget.

Figure 9.3 The decision-making, planning and control process

over the business. This also requires that we have the means of measuring actual performance, in the same terms as those in which the budget is stated. If they are not in the same terms, comparison will not usually be possible.

Taking steps to exercise control means finding out where and why things did not go according to plan and seeking ways to put things right for the future. One of the reasons why things may not have gone according to plan is that the plans may, in reality, prove to be unachievable. In this case, if budgets are to be a useful basis for exercising control in the future, it may be necessary to revise the budgets for future periods to bring targets into the realms of achievability.

This last point should not be taken to mean that budget targets can simply be ignored if the going gets tough; rather that they should be flexible. Budgets may prove to be totally unrealistic targets, however, for a variety of reasons, including unexpected changes in the commercial environment (for example, an unexpected collapse in demand for services of the type in which the business deals). In this case, nothing whatsoever will be achieved by pretending that the targets can be met.

By having a system of budgetary control, via **flexible budgets** a position can be established where decision making and responsibility can be delegated to junior management, yet control can still be retained by senior management. This is because senior managers can use the budgetary control system to ascertain which junior managers are meeting targets and, therefore, working towards the objectives of the business. This enables a *management by exception* environment to be created. Here, senior management concentrates its energy on areas where things are not going according to plan (the exceptions – it is to be hoped). Junior managers who are performing to budget can be left to get on with the job.

Exhibit 9.1

Preparation of budgets in SMEs

A recent study of budgeting practice in small and medium-sized enterprises (SMEs) revealed that the most frequently prepared budget is the sales budget, followed by the budgeted profit and loss account and the overheads budget.

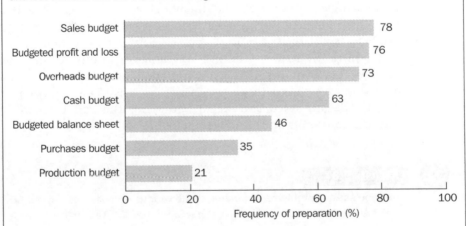

Source: Chittenden, F., Poutziouris, P. and Michaelis, N. *Financial management and working capital practices in UK SMEs*, Manchester Business School, 1998.

Comparison of the actual performance with the budget

Since the principal objective of most private sector businesses is to enhance their shareholders' wealth, and remembering that profit is the net increase in wealth as a result of trading, the most important budget target to meet is the profit target. In view of this, we shall begin with that aspect in our consideration of making the comparison between actuals and budgets. Example 9.2 shows the budgeted and actual profit and loss account for Baxter Ltd for the month of May.

Example 9.2

The following are the budgeted and actual profit and loss accounts for Baxter Ltd for the month of May:

	Budget	*Actual*
Output	1,000 units	900 units
(production and sales)		
	£	£
Sales	100,000	92,000
Raw materials	(40,000) (40,000 metres)	(36,900) (37,000 metres)
Labour	(20,000) (5,000 hours)	(17,500) (4,375 hours)
Fixed overheads	(20,000)	(20,700)
Operating profit	20,000	16,900

From Example 9.2, it is clear that the budgeted profit was not achieved. As far as May is concerned, this is a matter of history. However, the business (or at least one aspect of it) is out of control. Senior management must discover where things went wrong during May and try to ensure that they are not repeated in later months. Thus it is not enough to know that, overall, things went wrong; we need to know where and why. The approach taken is to compare the budgeted and actual figures for the various items (sales, raw materials and so on) in the above statement.

Activity 9.8

Can you see any problems in comparing the various items (sales, raw materials and so on) for the budget and the actual performance of Baxter Ltd in order to draw conclusions as to which aspects were out of control?

The problem is that the actual level of output was not as budgeted. The actual level of output was 10 per cent less than budget. This means that we cannot, for example, say that there was a labour cost saving of £2,500 (that is, £20,000 − £17,500) and conclude that all is well in that area.

Flexing the budget

One practical way to overcome our difficulty is to 'flex' the budget to what it would have been, had the planned level of output been 900 units rather than 1,000 units. **Flexing the budget** simply means revising it to that which it would have been had the planned level of output been some different figure.

In the context of control, the budget is usually flexed to reflect the volume which actually occurred. To be able to flex the budget we need to know which items are fixed and which are variable, relative to the level of output. Once we have this knowledge, flexing is a simple operation. We shall assume that sales revenue, material cost and labour cost vary strictly with volume. Fixed overheads, by definition, will not. Whether in real life labour cost does vary in this way is not so certain, but it will serve well enough as an assumption for our purposes.

On the basis of the assumptions regarding the behaviour of costs, the flexed budget would be as follows:

	Flexed budget	
Output	900 units	
(production and sales)		
	£	
Sales	90,000	
Raw materials	(36,000)	(36,000 metres)
Labour	(18,000)	(4,500 hours)
Fixed overheads	(20,000)	
Operating profit	16,000	

Putting the original budget, the flexed budget and the actual for May together, we obtain the following:

	Original budget	Flexed budget	Actual
Output	1,000 units	900 units	900 units
(production and sales)			
	£	£	£
Sales	100,000	90,000	92,000
Raw materials	(40,000)	(36,000)	(36,900)
Labour	(20,000)	(18,000)	(17,500)
Fixed overheads	(20,000)	(20,000)	(20,700)
Operating profit	20,000	16,000	16,900

We can now make a more valid comparison between budget (using the flexed figures) and actual. We can now see that there was a genuine labour cost saving, even after allowing for the output shortfall.

It may occur to you that we seem to be saying that it does not matter if there are volume shortfalls, because we just revise the budget and carry on as if nothing had happened. This must be an invalid approach, because losing sales means losing profit. The first point we must pick up, therefore, is the loss of profit arising from the loss of sales of 100 units of the product.

Activity 9.9

What will be the loss of profit arising from the sales shortfall, assuming that everything except sales volume was as planned?

The answer is simply the difference between the original and flexed budget profit figures. The only difference between these two profit figures is the assumed volume of sales; everything else was the same. Thus the figure is £4,000 (£20,000 − £16,000).

* The difference between the original and flexed budget profit figures is called the *sales volume variance*. It is an **adverse variance** because, taken alone, it has the effect of making the actual profit lower than that which was budgeted. A variance that will have the effect of increasing profit above that which is * budgeted is known as **favourable variance**. We can therefore say that a * **variance** is the effect of that factor on the budgeted profit. When looking at some particular aspect, such as sales volume, we assume that all other factors went according to plan. This is shown in Figure 9.4.

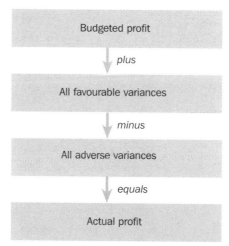

The variances represent the differences between the budgeted and actual profit, and can be used to reconcile the two profit figures.

Figure 9.4 Relationship between the budgeted and actual profit

Activity 9.10

What further does the senior management of Baxter Ltd need to know about the May sales volume variance?

It needs to know why the volume of sales fell below the budgeted figure. Only by discovering this information will management be in a position to try to see that it does not occur again.

Who should be asked about this sales volume variance? The answer would probably be the sales manager: the person who should know precisely why the departure from budget has occurred. This is not the same as saying that it was the sales manager's fault. The reason for the problem could easily have been that production was at fault in not having produced the budgeted production, meaning that there were not sufficient items to sell. What is not in doubt is that, in the first instance, it is the sales manager who should know the reason for the problem.

Activity 9.11

The budget and actual figures for Baxter Ltd for June are given below. They will be used as the basis for a series of activities, which you should work through as we look at variance analysis. Note that the company had budgeted for a higher level of output for June than it did for May.

	Budget for June	Actual for June
Output (production and sales)	1,100 units	1,150 units
	£	£
Sales	110,000	113,500
Raw materials	(44,000) (44,000 metres)	(46,300) (46,300 metres)
Labour	(22,000) (5,500 hours)	(23,200) (5,920 hours)
Fixed overheads	(20,000)	(19,300)
Operating profit	24,000	24,700

Try flexing the June budget, comparing it with the June actuals and find the sales volume variance.

	Flexed budget	Actual
Output (production and sales)	1,150 units	1,150 units
	£	£
Sales	115,000	113,500
Raw materials	(46,000) (46,000 metres)	(46,300) (46,300 metres)
Labour	(23,000) (5,750 hours)	(23,200) (5,920 hours)
Fixed overheads	(20,000)	(19,300)
Operating profit	26,000	24,700

The sales volume variance is £2,000 (favourable) (that is, £26,000 − £24,000). It is favourable because the original budget profit was lower than the flexed budget profit.

Going back to May, it is now a matter of comparing the actual figures with the flexed budget ones to find out the other causes of the £3,100 (that is, £20,000 − £16,900) profit shortfall.

Starting with the sales revenue figure, we can see that there is a difference of £2,000 (favourable) between the flexed budget and the actual figures. This can only arise from higher prices being charged than were envisaged in the original budget, because any variance arising from the volume difference has already been 'stripped out' in the flexing process. This is known as the *sales price variance*.

Activity 9.12

Using the figures in Activity 9.11, what is the sales price variance for June?

The sales price variance for June is £1,500 (adverse) (that is, £115,000 – £113,500).

In May, there was an overall or *total direct materials variance* of £900 (adverse). Who should be held accountable for this variance? The answer depends on whether the difference arises from excess usage of the raw material, in which case it is the production manager, or whether it is a higher-than-budgeted price per metre being paid, in which case it is the responsibility of the buying manager.

Fortunately, we have the means available to go beyond this total variance. We can see from the figures that there was a 1,000 metre excess usage of the raw material. All other things being equal, this alone would have led to a profit shortfall of £1,000, since clearly the budgeted price per metre is £1. The £1,000 (adverse) variance is known as the *direct materials usage variance*. Normally, this would be the responsibility of the production manager.

Activity 9.13

Using the figures in Activity 9.11, what was the direct materials usage variance for June?

The direct materials usage variance for June was £300 (adverse) [that is, (46,300 – 46,000) × £1].

The other aspect of direct materials is the *direct materials price variance*. Here we simply take the actual quantity bought and compare what should have been paid for it with what was actually paid for it. In May, for a quantity of 37,000 metres, the cost should have been £37,000; it was actually £36,900. Thus we have a favourable variance of £100.

Activity 9.14

Using the figures in Activity 9.11, what was the direct materials price variance for June?

The direct materials price variance for June was zero [that is, (46,300 – 46,300) × £1].

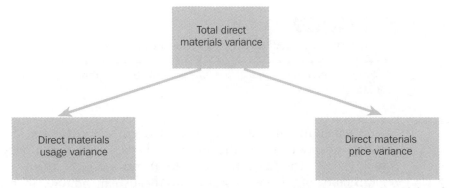

The total direct materials variance is the sum of the direct materials usage variance and the price variance, and can be analysed into those two.

Figure 9.5 The relationship between the total, usage and price variances for direct materials

As we have just seen, the total direct materials variance is the sum of the usage variance and the price variance. This is illustrated in Figure 9.5.

Direct labour variances are similar in form to those for raw materials. The *total direct labour variance* for May was £500 (that is, £18,000 – £17,500). Again, this information is not particularly helpful since the responsibility for the rate of pay lies primarily with the personnel manager, at least to the extent of being able to explain the variance. The number of hours taken to complete a particular quantity of output is, however, the responsibility of the production manager.

The *direct labour efficiency variance* compares the number of hours that would be allowed for the achieved level of production with the actual number of hours, and then costs the difference at the allowed hourly rate. Thus, for May, it was (4,500 – 4,375) × £4 = £500 (favourable). The variance is favourable because fewer hours were used than would have been allowed for the actual level of output.

Activity 9.15

Using the figures in Activity 9.11, what was the direct labour efficiency variance for June?

The direct labour efficiency variance for June was £680 (adverse) [that is, (5,920 – 5,750) × £4].

The *direct labour rate variance* compares the actual cost of the hours worked with the planned cost. For 4,375 hours worked in May, the allowed cost would be £17,500 (that is, 4,375 × £4). Since this is exactly the amount that was paid, there is no rate variance.

Using the figures in Activity 9.11, what was the direct labour rate variance for June?

The direct labour rate variance for June was £480 (favourable) [that is, (5,920 × £4) − 23,200].

The remaining area is that of fixed overheads. Here the *fixed overhead spending variance* is simply the difference between the flexed budget and the actual figures. For May, this was £700 (adverse). In theory, this is the responsibility of whoever controls overheads expenditure. In practice, this tends to be a very slippery area, and one that is notoriously difficult to control.

Using the figures in Activity 9.11, what was the fixed overhead spending variance for June?

The fixed overhead spending variance for June was £700 (favourable) [that is, £20,000 − £19,300].

We are now in a position to reconcile the original May budget profit with the actual one, as follows:

	£	£
Budgeted profit		20,000
*Add **Favourable variances***		
Sales price variance	2,000	
Direct materials price	100	
Direct labour efficiency	500	2,600
		22,600
*Less **Adverse variances***		
Sales volume	4,000	
Direct material usage	1,000	
Fixed overhead spending	700	5,700
Actual profit		16,900

Activity 9.18

Using the figures in Activity 9.11, try reconciling the original profit figure for June with the actual June figure.

	£	£
Budgeted profit		24,000
Add **Favourable variances**		
Sales volume	2,000	
Fixed overhead spending	700	
Direct labour rate	480	
		3,180
		27,180
Less **Adverse variances**		
Sales price	1,500	
Direct material usage	300	
Direct labour efficiency	680	
		2,480
Actual profit		24,700

Activity 9.19

The following are the budgeted and actual profit and loss accounts for Baxter Ltd for the month of July:

	Budget	**Actual**
Output	1,000 units	1,050 units
(production and sales)		
	£	£
Sales	100,000	104,300
Raw materials	(40,000) (40,000 metres)	(41,200) (40,500 metres)
Labour	(20,000) (5,000 hours)	(21,300) (5,200 hours)
Fixed overheads	(20,000)	(19,400)
Operating profit	20,000	22,400

Produce a reconciliation of the budgeted and actual operating profit, going into as much detail as possible with the variance analysis.

The original budget, the flexed budget and the actual are as follows:

	Original budget	**Flexed budget**	**Actual**
Output	1,000 units	1,050 units	1,050 units
(production and sales)			

	£	£	£
Sales	100,000	105,000	104,300
Raw materials	(40,000)	(42,000)	(41,200)
Labour	(20,000)	(21,000)	(21,300)
Fixed overheads	(20,000)	(20,000)	(19,400)
Operating profit	20,000	22,000	22,400

Reconciliation of the budgeted and actual operating profits for June

	£	£
Budgeted profit		20,000
Add Favourable variances:		
Sales volume (22,000−20,000)	2,000	
Direct material usage {[(1,050×40)−40,500]×£1}	1,500	
Direct labour efficiency {[(1,050×5)−5,200]×£4}	200	
Fixed overhead spending (20,000−19,400)	600	4,300
		24,300
Less Adverse variances:		
Sales price variance (105,000−104,300)	700	
Direct materials price [(40,500×£1)−41,200]	700	
Direct labour rate [(5,200×£4)−21,300]	500	1,900
Actual profit		22,400

Standard quantities and costs

The budget is a financial plan for a future period of time. It is built up from
✳ standards. **Standard quantities and costs** (or revenues) are those planned for
individual units of input or output. Thus standards are the building blocks of
the budget.

We can say about Baxter Ltd's operations that:

- The standard selling price is £100 per unit of output.
- The standard raw material cost is £40 per unit of output.
- The standard raw material usage is 40 metres per unit of output.
- The standard raw material price is £1 per metre (that is, per unit of input).
- The standard labour cost is £20 per unit of output.
- The standard labour time is 5 hours per unit of output.
- The standard labour rate is £4 per hour (that is, per unit of input).

The standards, like the budgets to which they are linked, represent targets and,
therefore, yardsticks by which actual performance is measured. They are derived
from experience of what is a reasonable quantity of input (for labour time and
materials usage) and from assessments of the market for the product (standard
selling price) and for the inputs (labour rate and material price). These should be
subject to frequent review and, where necessary, revision. It is vital, if they are to
be used as part of the control process, that they represent realistic targets.

Calculation of most variances is, in effect, based on standards. For example, the material usage variance is the difference between the standard materials usage for the level of output and the actual usage, costed at the standard materials price.

Standards can have uses other than in the context of budgetary control. The existence of what should be, and normally are, the various usages and costs associated with the operations of the business, provides decision makers with a ready set of information for their decision-making and income measurement purposes.

Reasons for adverse variances

A constant possible reason why variances occur is that the standards against which performance is being measured are not reasonable targets. This is certainly not to say that the immediate reaction to an adverse variance should be that the standard is unreasonably harsh. On the other hand, standards that are not achievable are useless.

Activity 9.20

The variances that we have considered are:

- sales volume
- sales price
- direct material usage
- direct materials price
- direct labour efficiency
- direct labour rate
- fixed overhead spending.

Ignoring the possibility that standards may be unreasonable, jot down any ideas that occur to you as possible practical reasons for adverse variances in each case.

The reasons that we thought of included the following:

Sales volume

- Poor performance by sales personnel.
- Deterioration in market conditions between the setting of the budget and the actual event.
- Lack of stock to sell as a result of some production problem.

Sales price

- Poor performance by sales personnel.
- Deterioration in market conditions between the setting of the budget and the actual event.

Direct materials usage

- Poor performance by production department staff, leading to high rates of scrap.
- Substandard materials, leading to high rates of scrap.
- Faulty machinery, causing high rates of scrap.

Direct materials price

- Poor performance by buying department staff.
- Change in market conditions between setting the standard and the actual event.

Labour efficiency

- Poor supervision.
- A low skill grade of worker taking longer to do the work than was envisaged for the correct skill grade.
- Low-grade materials, leading to high levels of scrap and wasted labour time.
- Problems with machinery, leading to labour time being wasted.
- Dislocation of materials supply, leading to workers being unable to proceed with production.

Labour rate

- Poor performance by the personnel function.
- Using a higher grade of worker than was planned.
- Change in labour market conditions between setting the standard and the actual event.

Fixed overheads

- Poor supervision of overheads.
- General increase in costs of overheads not taken into account in the budget.

There are many variances that it is possible to calculate, given the range of operations found in practice. We have considered just the most basic of them. They are all, however, based on similar principles.

Though we have tended to use the example of a manufacturing business to explain variance analysis, this should not be taken to imply that variance analysis is not equally applicable and useful in a service sector business.

Investigating variances

It is unreasonable to expect budget targets to be met precisely each month. Whatever the reason for a variance, finding it will take time, and time is costly. Given that small variances are almost inevitable, and that **investigating variances** can be expensive, management needs to establish a policy on which variances to investigate and which to accept. For example, for Baxter Ltd (the example used earlier in this chapter and the subject of Activities 9.8 to 9.19) the budgeted usage of materials during May was 40,000 metres at a cost of £1 per metre. Suppose that production had been the same as the budgeted quantity of output, but that 40,005 metres of material had actually been used. Would this adverse variance of £5 be investigated? Probably not. What though if the variance were £50 or £500 or £5,000?

Activity 9.21

What broad approach do you feel should be taken on whether to spend money investigating a particular variance?

The general approach to this policy must be concerned with cost and benefit. What benefit there is likely to be from knowing why a variance exists needs to be balanced against the cost of obtaining that information.

Knowing the reason for a variance can only have any value when it might provide management with the means to bring things back under control, so that future targets can be met. It should be borne in mind here that variances will normally either be zero, or very close to zero. This is to say that achieving targets, give or take small variances, should be normal.

Broadly, we can probably say the following:

- Significant adverse variances should be investigated because the continuation of the fault that they represent could be very costly. Management must decide what 'significant' means. A certain amount of science, in the form of statistical models, ultimately can be brought to bear in making this decision, but it must be a matter of managerial judgement as to what is significant. Perhaps a variance of 5 per cent from the budgeted figure would be deemed to be significant.
- Significant *favourable* variances should probably be investigated as well as those that are unfavourable. Though such variances would not cause such immediate management concern as adverse ones, they still represent things not going according to plan. If actual performance is significantly better than target, it may well mean that the target is unrealistically low.
- Insignificant variances, though not triggering immediate investigation, should be kept under review. For each aspect of operations, the cumulative sum of variances, over a series of control periods, should be zero, with small adverse variances in some periods being compensated by small favourable ones in other periods. This should be the case with variances that are caused by chance factors, which will not necessarily repeat themselves.

Where a variance is caused by a more systematic factor, which will repeat itself, the cumulative sum of the periodic variances will not be zero but an increasing figure. Where the increasing figure represents a set of adverse variances it may well be worth investigating the situation, even though the individual variances may be insignificant. Even where the direction of the cumulative total points to favourable variances, investigation may still be considered to be valuable.

Methods used to make decisions on investigation of variances

	% 'often' or 'always'
Decisions based on managerial judgement	75
Variance exceeds a specific monetary amount	41
Variance exceeds a given percentage of standard	36
Statistical models	3

Exhibit 9.2 is taken from the research of Drury, Braund, Osborne and Tayles, which was mentioned in Chapter 8. The table shows the methods used by respondents to the survey to make the decision on whether to investigate a particular variance.

It is interesting to note the large extent to which these decisions are made on the basis of some, presumably subjective, judgement rather than using a more systematic approach.

Compensating variances

❋ There is superficial appeal in the idea of **compensating variances**; that is, trading off linked favourable and adverse variances against each other without further consideration. For example, a sales manager believes that she could sell more of the product if prices were lowered, and that this would feed through to increased net operating profit.

Activity 9.22

What possible reason is there why the sales manager should not go ahead with the price reduction?

The change in policy will have ramifications for other areas of the business, including the following:

- The need for more goods to be available to sell. Production might not be able to supply this, and it might not be possible to buy the stock in from elsewhere, either.
- Increased sales would involve an increased need for finance to pay for increased production.

Thus 'trading off' variances is not automatically acceptable, without a more far-reaching consultation and revision of plans.

Necessary conditions for effective budgetary control

❋ It is obvious from what we have seen of **budgetary control** that if such control is to be successful, a system, or a set of routines, must be established to enable the potential benefits to be gained.

Activity 9.23

Jot down a list of points that you feel need to be included in any system, or routines, which will enable control through budgets to be effective.

(We have not specifically covered these points, but your common sense, and perhaps your background knowledge, should enable you to think of a few.)

There is no unequivocally correct answer to this activity. However, most businesses that operate successful budgetary control systems tend to share some common factors. These include the following:

- A serious attitude taken to the system by all levels of management, right from the very top.
- Clear demarcation between areas of managerial responsibility so that accountability can more easily be ascribed for any area that seems to be going out of control.
- Budget targets being reasonable, so that they represent a rigorous yet achievable target. This may be promoted by managers being involved in setting their own targets. It is argued that this can promote the managers' commitment and motivation.
- Established data collection, analysis and dissemination routines, which take the actual results, the budget figures, and calculate and report the variances.
- Reports aimed at individual managers, rather than general-purpose documents. This avoids managers having to wade through reams of reports to find the part that is relevant to them.
- Fairly short reporting periods, typically a month, so that things cannot go too far wrong before they are picked up.
- Variance reports being produced and disseminated shortly after the end of the relevant reporting period.
- Action being taken to get operations back under control if they are shown to be out of control.

Limitations of the traditional approach to control through variances and standards

Budgetary control, of the type that we have reviewed in this chapter, has obvious appeal and, judging by the wide extent of its use in practice, it has value as well. It is somewhat limited at times, however. Some of its limitations are as follows:

- Vast areas of most business and commercial activities simply do not have the same direct relationship between inputs and outputs as is the case with, say, level of output and the amount of raw materials used. Many of the expenses of a modern business are in areas such as training and advertising, where the expense is discretionary and not linked to the level of output in a direct way.
- Standards can quickly become out of date as a result of both technological change and price changes. This does not pose insuperable problems, but it does require that the potential problem is systematically addressed.

Standards that are unrealistic are, at best, useless. At worst, they could have adverse effects on performance. A buyer who knows that it is impossible to meet price targets, because of price rises, may have a reduced incentive to minimise costs.

- Sometimes factors that are outside the control of the manager concerned can affect the calculation of the variance for which that manager is held accountable. This is likely to have an adverse affect on the manager's performance. The situation can often be overcome by a more considered approach to the calculation of the variance, which results in that which is controllable by the manager being separated from that which is not.
- In practice, creating clear lines of demarcation between the areas of responsibility of various managers may be difficult. Thus, one of the prerequisites of good budgetary control is lost.

Behavioural aspects of budgetary control

Budgets, perhaps more than any other accounting statement, are prepared with the objective of affecting the attitudes and behaviour of managers. The point was made earlier in this chapter that budgets are intended to motivate managers. In practice, research evidence generally shows this to be true. More specifically:

- The existence of budgets generally tends to improve performance.
- Setting demanding, but achievable, budget targets tends to motivate better than less demanding targets. It seems that setting the most demanding targets that will be accepted by managers is a very effective way to motivate them.
- Unrealistically demanding targets tend to have an adverse effect on managers' performance.
- The participation of managers in setting their targets tends to improve motivation and performance. This is probably because those managers feel a sense of commitment to the targets and a moral obligation to achieve them.

It has been suggested that allowing managers to set their own targets will lead to 'slack' being introduced, so making achievement of the target that much easier. On the other hand, in an effort to impress, a manager may select a target that is not really achievable. These points imply that care must be taken in the extent to which managers have unfettered choice of their own targets. Evidence tends to suggest that where the managers work in an environment where they are expected to meet the budget targets represented in the budget, they will, almost irrespective of other factors, tend to try to introduce slack into the budget. Where there is a more relaxed attitude, or other factors (for example, staff morale) are considered alongside the analysis of variances, managers are less inclined to seek to build in slack.

Where a manager fails to meet a budget, care must be taken by that manager's senior in dealing with the failure. A harsh, critical approach may demotivate the manager. Adverse variances may imply that the manager needs help from the senior.

The existence of budgets gives senior managers a ready means to assess the performance of their subordinates. Where promotion or bonuses depend on the absence of variances, senior management must be very cautious.

Self-assessment question 9.2

Toscanini Ltd makes a standard product, which is budgeted to sell at £4.00 per unit, in a competitive market. It is made by taking a budgeted 0.4 kg of material, budgeted to cost £2.40/kg, and working on it by hand by an employee, paid a budgeted £4.00/hour, for a budgeted 12 minutes. Monthly fixed overheads are budgeted at £4,800. The output for May was budgeted at 4,000 units.

The actual results for May were as follows:

	£
Sales (3,500 units)	13,820
Materials (1,425 kg)	(3,420)
Labour (690 hours)	(2,690)
Fixed overheads	(4,900)
Actual operating profit	2,810

No stocks of any description existed at the beginning and end of the month.

Required:
(a) Deduce the budgeted profit for May, and reconcile it with the actual profit in as much detail as the information provided will allow.
(b) State which manager should be held accountable, in the first instance, for each variance calculated.
(c) Assuming that the standards were all well set in terms of labour times and rates and material usage and price, suggest at least one feasible reason for each of the variances that you identified in (a), given what you know about the company's performance for May.
(d) If it were discovered that the actual total world market demand for the company's product was 10 per cent lower than it had been estimated to be when the May budget was set, state how and why the variances, that you identified in (a) could be revised to provide information that would be potentially more useful.

SUMMARY

We began this chapter by considering the relationship between business objectives, long-term plans and budgets. We also considered how those short-term plans, or budgets, are derived. Next we discussed the role of budgeting and how budgets can be used to try to achieve the business objectives. We saw that budgets are set within the framework of the long-term plans and represent one step towards the realisation of the business objectives. After this we saw how budgets are prepared, and how budgets for different facets of the business can be made to coordinate.

The chapter then went on to examine the way in which budgets can be used to help management exercise control over the business. We saw how it is possible, by making a comparison between the actual outcomes and the original budgets, and carrying out further analysis, to identify areas of the business that are not performing according to plan.

Key terms

budgets *p 231*	adverse variance *p 248*
limiting factor *p 232*	favourable variance *p 248*
master budgets *p 233*	variance *p 248*
control *p 236*	standard quantities and costs *p 254*
management by exception *p 236*	investigating variances *p 256*
flexible budgets *p 245*	compensating variances *p 258*
flexing the budget *p 247*	budgetary control *p 258*

REVIEW QUESTIONS

9.1 Define a *budget*. How is a budget different from a forecast?

9.2 What were the four uses of budgets that were identified in the chapter?

9.3 What is meant by a *variance*?

9.4 What is the point in flexing the budget in the context of variance analysis? Does flexing imply that differences between budget and actual in the volume of output are ignored in variance analysis?

EXAMINATION-STYLE QUESTIONS

Questions 9.4 and 9.5 are more advanced than questions 9.1–9.3. Those with a coloured number have an answer at the back of the book.

9.1 You have overheard the following statements:

(a) 'A budget is a forecast of what is expected to happen in a business during the next year.'
(b) 'Budgets must be prepared with a column for each month so that you can see the whole year at a glance, month by month.'
(c) 'Budgets are OK but they stifle all initiative. No manager worth employing would work for a business which seeks to control through budgets.'
(d) 'Any sensible person would start with the sales budget and build up the other budgets from there.'

Required:
Critically discuss these statements, explaining any technical terms.

9.2 Finetime Ltd, a new business, started production on 1 April. Planned sales for the next eight months are as follows:

	Sales units
May	500
June	600
July	700
August	800
September	900
October	900
November	900
December	800
January	700

The selling price per unit will be a consistent £100, and all sales will be made on one month's credit. It is planned that sufficient finished goods stock for each month's sales should be available at the end of the previous month.

Raw material purchases will be such that there will be sufficient raw materials stock available at the end of each month to meet the following month's planned production precisely. This planned policy will operate from the end of April. Purchases of raw materials will be on one month's credit. The cost of raw material is £40 per unit of finished product.

The direct labour cost, which is variable with the level of production, is planned to be £20 per unit of finished production. Production overheads are planned to be £20,000 each month, including £3,000 for depreciation. Non-production overheads are planned to be £11,000 per month, of which £1,000 will be depreciation. Various fixed assets costing £250,000 will be bought and paid for during April.

Except where specified otherwise, assume that all payments take place in the same month as the cost is incurred.

The business will raise £300,000 in cash from a share issue in April.

Required:
Draw up:

- a finished stock budget, showing just physical quantities
- a raw materials stock budget, showing both physical quantities, and financial values
- a trade creditors budget
- a trade debtors budget
- a cash budget

for the six months ending 30 September.

9.3 Antonio plc makes product X, the standard cost of which is:

	£
Sales revenue	25
Direct labour (2 hours)	(5)
Direct materials (1 kg)	(10)
Fixed overheads	(3)
Standard profit	7

The budgeted output for March was 1,000 units of product X; the actual output was 1,100 units, which was sold for £28,200. There were no stocks of any description at either end of March.

The actual production costs were

	£
Direct labour (2,150 hours)	5,550
Direct materials (1,170 kg)	11,630
Fixed overheads	3,200

Calculate the variances for March as fully as you are able to from the available information, and use the variances calculated to reconcile the budgeted and actual profit figures.

9.4 Lewisham Ltd manufactures one product line – the Zenith. Sales of Zeniths over the next few months are planned as follows:

1 *Demand*

	units
July	180,000
August	240,000
September	200,000
October	180,000

Each Zenith sells for £3 each.

2 *Debtor receipts*
Debtors are expected to pay as follows:

70% during the month of sale
28% during the following month

The remainder of debtors are expected to go bad.

Debtors who pay in the month of sale are entitled to deduct a 2 per cent discount from the invoice price.

3 *Finished goods stocks*
Stocks of finished goods are expected to be 40,000 units at 1 July. The company's policy is that, in future, the stock at the end of each month should equal 20 per cent of the following month's planned sales requirements.

4 *Raw materials stock*
Stock of raw materials is expected to be 40,000 kg on 1 July. The company's

policy is that, in future, the stock at the end of each month should equal 50 per cent of the following month's planned production requirements. Each Zenith requires 0.5 kg of the raw material, which costs £1.50 per kg.

Raw materials are paid for in the month after purchase.

5 *Labour and overheads*

The direct labour cost of each Zenith is £0.50. The variable overhead element of each Zenith is £0.30. Fixed overheads, including depreciation of £25,000, total £47,000 per month.

All labour and overheads are paid during the month in which they arose.

6 *Cash in hand*

The company plans to have a bank balance (in funds) at 1 August of £20,000.

Required:

Prepare the following budgets:

(a) Finished stock budget (expressed in units of Zenith) for each of the three months July, August and September.

(b) Raw materials budget (expressed in kg of the raw material) for the two months July and August

(c) Cash budget for August and September.

9.5 Mowbray Ltd makes and sells one standard product, the standard costs of which are as follows:

	£
Direct materials: 3 kg at £2.50 per kg	7.50
Direct labour: 30 minutes at £4.50 per hour	2.25
Fixed overheads	3.60
	13.35
Selling price	20.00
Standard profit margin	6.65

The monthly production and sales are planned to be 1,200 units. The actual results for May were as follows:

	£	
Sales	18,000	
Less Direct materials	(7,400)	(2,800 kg used)
Direct labour	(2,300)	(510 hours)
Fixed overheads	(4,100)	
Operating profit	4,200	

There were no stocks of any description at either the start or the end of the month. As a result of poor sales demand during May, the company had reduced the price of all sales by 10 per cent.

Required:

Calculate the budgeted profit for May and reconcile it to the actual profit through variances, going into as much detail as is possible from the information available.

Capital investment decisions

INTRODUCTION

In this chapter we shall look at how businesses can make decisions involving investments in new plant, machinery, buildings and similar long-term assets. Though we shall be considering this topic in the context of businesses making decisions about the type of assets that were just mentioned, the general principles can equally well be applied to investments in the shares of companies, irrespective of whether the investment is being considered by a business or by a private individual.

Objectives

When you have completed your study of this chapter you should be able to:

• explain the nature and importance of investment decision making

• identify the four main investment appraisal methods used in practice

• use each method to reach a decision on a particular practical investment opportunity

• discuss the attributes and defects of each of the methods.

The nature of investment decisions

The essential feature of investment decisions, irrespective of who is to make the decision, is the time factor. Investment involves making an outlay of something of economic value, usually cash, at one point in time, which is expected to yield economic benefits to the investor at some other point in time. Typically, the outlay precedes the benefits. Also, the outlay is typically one large amount and the benefits arrive in a stream over a fairly protracted period.

Investment decisions tend to be of crucial importance to the investor because:

• *Large amounts of resources are often involved.* Many investments made by a business involve laying out a significant proportion of its total resources. If mistakes are made with the decision, the effects on the business could be significant, if not catastrophic.

- *It is often difficult and/or expensive to 'bail-out' of an investment once it has been undertaken.* It is often the case that investments made by a business are specific to its needs. For example, a manufacturing business may have a factory built that has been designed to accommodate the particular flow of production of that business. This may render the factory of rather limited second-hand value to another potential user with different needs. If the business found, after having made the investment, that the product that is being produced in the factory is not selling as well as was planned, the only possible course of action might be to close down production and sell the factory. This would probably mean that much less could be recouped from the investment in the factory than it had originally cost, particularly if the costs of design are included as part of the cost, as they logically should be.

Activity 10.1

When managers are making decisions involving capital investments, what should the decision seek to achieve?

The answer to this question must be that any decision must be made in the context of the objectives of the business concerned. For a private-sector business, this is likely to include increasing the wealth of the shareholders of the business through long-term profitability.

Methods of investment appraisal

Given the importance of investment decisions to the viability of the business, it is essential that proper screening of investment proposals takes place. An important part of this screening process is to ensure that appropriate methods of evaluating the profitability of investment projects are used.

Research shows that there are basically four methods used in practice by businesses throughout the world to evaluate investment opportunities.

They are:

- accounting rate of return (ARR)
- payback period (PP)
- net present value (NPV)
- internal rate of return (IRR).

It is possible to find businesses that use variants of these four methods. It is also possible to find businesses, particularly smaller ones, that do not use any formal appraisal method, but rely more on the 'gut feeling' of its managers. Most businesses, however, seem to use one of the four methods that we shall now review.

To help us to examine each of the four methods, it might be useful to consider how each of them would cope with a particular investment opportunity. Let us consider the following example.

Example 10.1

Billingsgate Battery Company has carried out some research that shows that it could manufacture and sell a product that the business has recently developed.

Production would require investment in a machine that would cost £100,000, payable immediately. Production and sales would take place throughout the next five years. At the end of that time, it is estimated that the machine could be sold for £20,000.

Production and sales of the product would be expected to occur as follows:

	Number of units
Next year	5,000
Second year	10,000
Third year	15,000
Fourth year	15,000
Fifth year	5,000

It is estimated that the new product can be sold for £12 a unit, and that the relevant material and labour costs will total £8 a unit.

To simplify matters, we shall assume that the cash from sales and for the costs of production are paid and received, respectively, at the end of each year. (This is clearly unlikely to be true in real life – money will have to be paid to employees on a weekly or a monthly basis, and customers will pay within a month or two of buying the product. On the other hand, it is probably not a serious distortion. It is a simplifying assumption that is often made in real life, and it will make things more straightforward for us now. You should be clear, however, that there is nothing about any of the four approaches that *demands* this assumption being made.)

Bearing in mind that each product sold will give rise to a net cash inflow of £4 (that is £12–£8), the cash flows (receipts and payments) over the life of the product will be as follows:

Time		£000
Immediately	Cost of machine	(100)
1 year's time	Net profit before depreciation (£4 × 5,000)	20
2 years' time	Net profit before depreciation (£4 × 10,000)	40
3 years' time	Net profit before depreciation (£4 × 15,000)	60
4 years' time	Net profit before depreciation (£4 × 15,000)	60
5 years' time	Net profit before depreciation (£4 × 5,000)	20
5 years' time	Disposal proceeds from the machine	20

Note that, broadly speaking, the net profit before deducting depreciation (that is, before non-cash items) equals the net amount of cash flowing into the business.

Having set up the example, we shall go on to look at the techniques used to assess investment opportunities and see how they deal with the decision in the example.

Accounting rate of return (ARR)

✳ The **accounting rate of return** method takes the average accounting profit that the investment will generate and expresses it as a percentage of the average investment in the project as measured in accounting terms.
Thus:

$$\text{ARR} = \frac{\text{Average annual profit}}{\text{Average investment to earn that profit}} \times 100\%$$

We can see that to calculate the ARR, we need to deduce two pieces of information:

- the annual average profit
- the average investment for the particular project.

The average profit before depreciation over the five years is £40,000 [that is (20 + 40 + 60 + 60 + 20)/5]. Assuming straight-line depreciation (that is, equal annual amounts), the annual depreciation charge will be £16,000 [that is, (100,000 − 20,000)/5]. Thus the average annual profit is £24,000 (that is, 40,000 − 16,000).
The average investment over the five years can be calculated as follows:

$$\text{Average investment} = \frac{\text{Cost of machine} + \text{disposal value}}{2}$$

$$= \frac{£100,000 + £20,000}{2}$$

$$= £60,000$$

Thus, the ARR of the investment is:

$$\text{ARR} = \frac{£24,000}{£60,000} \times 100\%$$

$$= 40\%$$

To decide whether the 40 per cent return is acceptable, we shall have to compare this percentage with the minimum required by the business.

Activity 10.2

Chaotic Industries is considering an investment in a fleet of ten delivery vans to take its products to customers. The vans will cost £15,000 each to buy, payable immediately. The annual running costs are expected to total £20,000 for each van (including the driver's salary). The vans are expected to operate successfully for six years, at the end of which period they will all have to be sold, with disposal proceeds expected to be about £3,000 per van. At present, the business uses a commercial carrier for all of its deliveries. It is expected that this carrier will charge a total of £230,000 each year for the next five years to undertake the deliveries.

What is the ARR of buying the vans? Note that cost savings are as relevant a benefit from an investment as are actual net cash inflows.

The vans will save the business £30,000 a year (that is, 230,000 − (20,000 × 10)), before depreciation, in total.

Thus, the inflows and outflows will be:

Time		£000
Immediately	Cost of vans	(150)
1 year's time	Net saving before depreciation	30
2 years' time	Net saving before depreciation	30
3 years' time	Net saving before depreciation	30
4 years' time	Net saving before depreciation	30
5 years' time	Net saving before depreciation	30
6 years' time	Net saving before depreciation	30
6 years' time	Disposal proceeds from the vans (10×3)	30

The total annual depreciation expense (assuming a straight-line approach) will be £20,000 (that is, (150,000 − 30,000)/6). Thus, the average annual saving, after depreciation, is £10,000 (that is, 30,000 − 20,000).

The average investment will be

$$\text{Average investment} = \frac{£150,000 + £30,000}{2}$$

$$= £90,000$$

Thus, the ARR of the investment is

$$\text{ARR} = \frac{£10,000}{£90,000} \times 100\% = 11.1\%$$

ARR and the return on capital employed (ROCE) ratio take the same approach to performance measurement. You may recall from Chapter 6 that ROCE is a popular means of assessing the performance of a business *after* the period has passed. However, ARR can be argued to be a useful means of assessing an investment opportunity *before* it takes place. In theory, if all investments made by Chaotic Industries (Activity 10.2) actually proved to have an ARR of 11.1 per cent, then the ROCE for that business should be 11.1 per cent. Since private-sector businesses are normally seeking to increase the wealth of their owners, ARR may seem to be a sound method of appraising investment opportunities. Profit can be seen as a net increase in wealth over a period, and relating it to the size of investment made to achieve it seems a logical approach.

A user of ARR would require that any investment undertaken by the business would be able to achieve a minimum ARR. Perhaps the minimum would be the rate that previous investments had achieved (as measured by ROCE). Perhaps it would be the industry-average ROCE.

Where there are competing projects that all seem capable of exceeding the minimum rate, the one with the higher or highest ARR would normally be selected.

ARR is said to have a number of advantages as a method of investment appraisal. It was mentioned earlier that ROCE is a widely-used measure of business performance. Shareholders use this ratio to evaluate management performance, and often the financial objective of a business will be expressed in terms of a target ROCE. It therefore seems sensible to use a method of investment appraisal that is consistent with this overall approach to measuring business performance. ARR is also a measure of profitability that many believe is the correct way to evaluate investments, and it produces a percentage figure of return that managers understand and feel comfortable with.

Activity 10.3

ARR suffers from a very major defect as a means of assessing investment opportunities. Can you reason out what this is?

Hint: The defect is not concerned with the ability of the decision maker to forecast future events, though this too can be a problem. Try to remember what was the essential feature of investment decisions that we identified at the beginning of this chapter,

The problem with ARR is that it almost completely ignores the time factor. In the Billingsgate Battery example, exactly the same ARR would have been computed under any of the following three scenarios:

Time		Original scenario £000	Scenario 2 £000	Scenario 3 £000
Immediately	Cost of machine	(100)	(100)	(100)
1 year's time	Net profit before depreciation	20	10	160
2 years' time	Net profit before depreciation	40	10	10
3 years' time	Net profit before depreciation	60	10	10
4 years' time	Net profit before depreciation	60	10	10
5 years' time	Net profit before depreciation	20	160	10
6 years' time	Disposal proceeds	20	20	20

Since the same total profit over the five years arises in all three of these cases, the average net profit after depreciation must be the same in each case. In turn, this means that each case will give rise to the same ARR of 40 per cent.

Given a financial objective of increasing the wealth of the business, any rational decision maker faced with these three scenarios as a choice between three separate investments would strongly prefer Scenario 3. This is because most of the benefits from the investment come in within 12 months of investing the £100,000 to establish the project. The original scenario would rank second, and Scenario 2 would come a poor third in the rankings. Any appraisal technique that is not capable of distinguishing between these three situations is seriously flawed.

Clearly the use of ARR can easily cause poor decisions to be made. We shall look in more detail at the reason for timing being so important, later in this chapter.

There are other defects associated with the ARR method. For investment appraisal purposes, it is cash flows rather than accounting profits that are important. Cash is the ultimate measure of the economic wealth generated. This is because it is cash that is used to acquire resources and for distribution to shareholders. Accounting profit is more appropriate for reporting purposes. It is a measure of productive effort for a particular reporting period such as a year or half-year. ARR also fails to take account of the fact that pounds received at a later date are worth less than pounds received at an earlier date.

The ARR method can also create problems when considering competing investments of different size.

Activity 10.4

Sinclair Wholesalers plc is currently considering opening a new sales outlet in Coventry. Two possible sites have been identified for the new outlet. Site A has a capacity of 30,000 sq. metres. It will require an average investment of £6 million, and will produce an average profit of £600,000 per annum. Site B has a capacity of 20,000 sq. metres. It will require an average investment of £4 million, and will produce an average profit of £500,000 per annum.

What is the ARR of each investment opportunity? Which site would you select, and why?

The ARR of Site A is £600,000/£6 million = 10 per cent. The ARR of Site B is £500,000/£4 million = 12.5 per cent. Thus, Site B has the higher ARR. However, in terms of the absolute profit generated, Site A is the more attractive. If the ultimate objective is to maximise the wealth of the shareholders of Sinclair Wholesalers plc, it would be better to choose Site A even though the percentage return is lower. It is the absolute size of the return rather than the relative (percentage) size that is important.

Payback period (PP)

* The **payback period** method seems to go some way to overcoming the timing problem of ARR, or at least at first glance it does.

It might be useful to consider PP in the context of the Billingsgate Battery example. You will recall that essentially the project's costs and benefits can be summarised as:

Time		£000
Immediately	Cost of machine	(100)
1 year's time	Net profit before depreciation	20
2 years' time	Net profit before depreciation	40
3 years' time	Net profit before depreciation	60
4 years' time	Net profit before depreciation	60
5 years' time	Net profit before depreciation	20
5 years' time	Disposal proceeds	20

Note that all of these figures are amounts of cash to be paid or received.

The payback period is the length of time it takes for the initial investment to be repaid out of the net cash inflows from the project. In this case, it will be nearly three years before the £100,000 outlay is covered by the inflows, still assuming that the cash flows occur at year-ends. The payback period can be derived by calculating the cumulative cash flows as follows:

Year		Net cash flows £000	Cumulative cash flows £000	
Immediately	Cost of machine	(100)	(100)	
1 year' time	Net profit before depreciation	20	(80)	(−100 + 20)
2 years' time	Net profit before depreciation	40	(40)	(−80 + 40)
3 years' time	Net profit before depreciation	60	20	(−40 + 60)
4 years' time	Net profit before depreciation	60	80	(20 + 60)
5 years' time	Net profit before depreciation	20	100	(80 + 20)
5 years' time	Disposal proceeds	20	120	(100 + 20)

We can see that the cumulative cash flows become positive in the third year. If we assume that the cash flows arise evenly over the year, the precise payback period would be:

$$2 \text{ years} + (40/60) = 2\tfrac{2}{3} \text{ years}$$

(where 40 represents the cash flow still required at the beginning of the third year to repay the initial outlay, and 60 is the projected cash flow during the third year). Again we must ask how to decide whether $2\tfrac{2}{3}$ years is acceptable. A manager using PP would need to have a minimum payback period in mind. For example, if Billingsgate Battery had a minimum payback period of three years it would accept the project, but it would not go ahead if its minimum payback period were two years. If there were two competing projects that both met the minimum payback period requirement, the decision maker should select the project with the shorter payback period.

Activity 10.5

What is the payback period of the Chaotic Industries project from Activity 10.2?

The inflows and outflows are expected to be:

Time		Net cash flows £000	Cumulative net cash flows £000
Immediately	Cost of vans	(150)	(150)
1 years' time	Net saving before depreciation	30	(120)
2 years' time	Net saving before depreciation	30	(90)
3 years' time	Net saving before depreciation	30	(60)
4 years' time	Net saving before depreciation	30	(30)
5 years' time	Net saving before depreciation	30	0
6 years' time	Net saving before depreciation	30	30
6 years' time	Disposal proceeds from the machine	30	60

The payback period here is five years; that is, it is not until the end of the fifth year that the vans will pay for themselves out of the savings that they are expected to generate.

The PP approach has certain advantages. It is quick and easy to calculate, and can be easily understood by managers. The logic of using PP is that projects that can recoup their cost quickly are economically more attractive than those with longer payback periods. PP is probably an improvement on ARR in respect of the timing of the cash flows. PP is not, however, the whole answer to the problem.

Activity 10.6

In what respect, in your opinion, is PP not the whole answer as a means of assessing investment opportunities? Consider the cash flows arising from three competing projects:

Time		Project 1 £000	Project 2 £000	Project 3 £000
Immediately	Cost of machine	(200)	(200)	(200)
1 year's time	Net profit before depreciation	40	10	80
2 years' time	Net profit before depreciation	80	20	100
3 years' time	Net profit before depreciation	80	170	20
4 years' time	Net profit before depreciation	60	20	200
5 years' time	Net profit before depreciation	40	10	500
5 years' time	Disposal proceeds	40	10	20

Hint: Again, the defect is not concerned with the ability of the manager to forecast future events. This is a problem, but it is a problem whatever approach we take.

Any rational manager would prefer Project 3 to either of the other two scenarios, yet PP sees all three of them as being equally attractive in that they all have a three-year payback period. The method cannot distinguish between those projects that pay back a significant amount before the three-year payback period and those that do not. Project 3 is by far the best bet because the cash flows come in earlier and they are greater in total, yet PP would not identify it as the best.

The cumulative cash flows of each project are set out in Figure 10.1.

Within the payback period, PP ignores the timing of the cash flows. Beyond the payback period, the method totally ignores both the size and the timing of the cash flows. While ignoring cash flows beyond the payback period neatly avoids the practical problems of forecasting cash flows over a long period, it means that relevant information may be ignored.

The PP approach is seen as a means of dealing with the problem of risk by favouring projects with a short payback period. However, this is a fairly crude approach to the problem. There are more systematic approaches to dealing with risk that can be used.

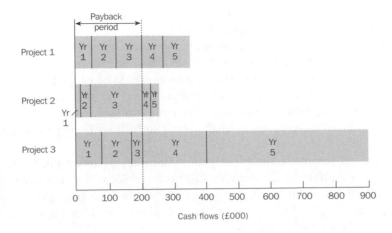

Payback period

The payback method of investment appraisal would view Projects 1, 2 and 3 as being equally attractive. In doing so the method completely ignores the fact that Project 3 provides the payback cash earlier in the three-year period *and* goes on to generate large benefits in later years.

Figure 10.1 The cumulative cash flows of each project

It seems that PP has the advantage of taking some note of the timing of the costs and benefits from the project, but it suffers from the disadvantage of ignoring relevant information. ARR ignores timing to a great extent, but it does take account of all benefits and costs. What we really need to help us to make sensible decisions is a method of appraisal that takes account of all of the costs and benefits of each investment opportunity, but which also makes a logical allowance for the timing of those costs and benefits.

Net present value (NPV)

✱ The **net present value** method provides us with what we really need.

Consider the Billingsgate Battery example, which can be summarised as follows:

Time		£000
Immediately	Cost of machine	(100)
1 year's time	Net profit before depreciation	20
2 years' time	Net profit before depreciation	40
3 years' time	Net profit before depreciation	60
4 years' time	Net profit before depreciation	60
5 years' time	Net profit before depreciation	20
5 years' time	Disposal proceeds	20

Given that the principal financial objective of the business is probably to increase wealth, it would be very easy to assess this investment if all of the cash flows were to occur now (all at the same time). All that we should need to do is to add up the benefits (total £220,000) and compare it with the cost (£100,000). This would lead us to the conclusion that the project should go ahead, because the business would be better off by £120,000. Of course, it is not as easy as this, because time is involved. The cash outflow (payment) will, if the project is undertaken, occur immediately. The inflows (receipts) will arise at a range of later times.

The time factor arises because normally people do not see £100 paid out now as equivalent in value to £100 receivable in a year's time. If you were to be offered £100 in 12 months, provided that you paid £100 now, you would not be prepared to do so, unless you wished to do someone (perhaps a friend or relation) a favour.

Activity 10.7

Why would you see £100 to be received in a year's time as unequal in value to £100 to be paid immediately? (There are basically three reasons.)

The reasons are:

- interest lost
- risk
- effects of inflation.

We shall now take a closer look at these three factors in turn.

Interest lost

If you are to be deprived of the opportunity to spend your money for a year, you could equally well be deprived of its use by placing it on deposit in a bank or building society. In this case, at the end of the year you could have your money back and have interest as well. Thus, unless the opportunity to invest will offer similar returns, you will be incurring an *opportunity cost*. An opportunity cost occurs where one course of action, for example making an investment in, say, a computer, deprives you of the opportunity to derive some benefit from an alternative action, for example putting the money in the bank.

From this we can see that any investment opportunity must, if it is to make you more wealthy, by taking it than by ignoring it, do better than the returns that are available from the next best opportunity. Thus, if Billingsgate Battery Company sees putting the money in the bank on deposit as the alternative to investment in the machine, the return from investing in the machine must be better than that from investing in the bank. If the bank offered a better return, the business would become more wealthy by putting the money on deposit.

Risk

Buying a machine to manufacture a product to be sold in the market, on the strength of various estimates made in advance of buying the machine, exposes the business to **risk**. Things may not turn out as expected.

It is important to remember that the decision whether or not to invest in the machine must be taken *before* any of these things are known. It is only after the machine has been purchased that we realise that the level of sales that had been estimated before the event is not going to be achieved. It is not possible to wait until we know for certain whether the market will behave as we expected before we buy the machine. We can study reports and analyses of the market. We can commission sophisticated market surveys, and these may give us more confidence in the likely outcome. We can advertise strongly and try to expand sales. Ultimately, however, we have to decide whether or not to jump off into the dark and accept the risk.

Normally, people expect to receive greater returns where they perceive risk to be a factor. Examples of this in real life are not difficult to find. One such example is the fact that a bank will tend to charge a higher rate of interest to a borrower whom the bank perceives to be more risky, than to one who can offer good security for the loan and who can point to a regular source of income.

Going back to Billingsgate Battery Company's investment opportunity, it is not enough to say that we would not advise making the investment unless the returns from it are higher than those from investing in a bank deposit. Clearly we would want returns above the level of bank deposit interest rates, because the logical equivalent investment opportunity to investing in the machine is not putting the money on deposit but making an alternative investment that seems to have a risk similar to that of the investment in the machine.

In practice, we tend to expect a higher rate of return from investment projects where the risk is perceived as being higher. How risky a particular project is, and, therefore how large this **risk premium** should be, are matters that are difficult to handle. In practice, it is necessary to make some judgement on these questions.

Inflation

If you are to be deprived of £100 for a year, when you come to spend that money it will not buy as much in the way of goods and services at it would have done a year earlier. Generally, you will not be able to buy as many tins of baked beans or loaves of bread or bus tickets for a particular journey as you could have done a year earlier. Clearly, the investor needs this loss of purchasing power to be compensated for if the investment is to be made. This is on top of a return that takes account of the returns that could have been gained from an alternative investment of similar risk.

*   In practice, interest rates observable in the market tend to take **inflation** into account. Rates that are offered to potential building society and bank depositors include an allowance for the rate of inflation that is expected in the future.

To summarise these factors, we can say that the logical investor, who is seeking to increase his or her wealth, will only be prepared to make investments that will compensate for the loss of interest and purchasing power of the money invested and for the fact that the returns that are expected may not materialise (risk). This is usually assessed by seeing whether the proposed investment will yield a return that is greater than the basic rate of interest (which would include an allowance for inflation) plus a risk premium.

These three factors (interest lost, risk and inflation) are set out in Figure 10.2.

The figure shows the three factors influencing the discount rate that were discussed earlier.

Figure 10.2 **The factors influencing the discount rate to be applied to a project**

Naturally, investors need at least the minimum returns before they are prepared to invest. However, it is in terms of the effect on their wealth that they should logically assess an investment project. Usually it is the investment with the highest percentage return that will make the investor most wealthy, but we shall see later in this chapter that this is not always the case. For the time being, therefore, we shall concentrate on wealth.

Let us now return to the Billingsgate Battery Company example. You will recall that the cash flows expected from this investment, were it to be made, are:

Time		£000
Immediately	Cost of machine	(100)
1 year's time	Net profit before depreciation	20
2 years' time	Net profit before depreciation	40
3 years' time	Net profit before depreciation	60
4 years' time	Net profit before depreciation	60
5 years' time	Net profit before depreciation	20
5 years' time	Disposal proceeds	20

Let us assume that instead of making this investment the business could make an alternative investment with similar risk and obtain a return of 20 per cent a year.

You will recall that we have concluded that it is not possible just to compare the basic figures listed above. It would therefore be useful if we could express each of these cash flows in similar terms so that we could make a direct comparison between the sum of the inflows over time and the immediate £100,000 investment. In fact, we can do this.

Activity 10.9

We know that Billingsgate Battery Company could alternatively invest its money at a rate of 20 per cent a year. How much do you judge the present (immediate) value of the expected first year receipt of £20,000 to be? In other words, if instead of having to wait a year for the £20,000, and being deprived of the opportunity to invest it at 20 per cent, you could have some money now, what sum to be received now would you regard as exactly equivalent to getting £20,000, but having to wait a year for?

We should obviously be happy to accept a lower amount if we could get it immediately than if we had to wait a year. This is because we could invest it at 20 per cent (in the alternative project). Logically, we should be prepared to accept the amount that with a year's income will grow to £20,000. If we call this amount PV (for present value) we can say:

$$PV + (PV \times 20\%) = £20,000$$

that is, the amount plus income from investing the amount for the year equals the £20,000.

If we rearrange this equation we find:

$$PV \times (1 + 0.2) = £20,000$$

Note that 0.2 is the same as 20 per cent, but expressed as a decimal.

Further rearranging gives:

$$PV = £20,000/(1 + 0.2)$$
$$PV = £16,667$$

Thus, rational investors who have the opportunity to invest at 20 per cent a year would not mind whether they have £16,667 now or £20,000 in a year's time. In this sense we can say that, given a 20 per cent investment opportunity, the present value of £20,000 to be received in one year's time is £16,667.

If we could derive the present value (PV) of each of the cash flows associated with the machine investment, we could easily make the direct comparison between the cost of making the investment (£100,000) and the various benefits that will derive from it in years 1 to 5. Fortunately we can do precisely this.

We can make a more general statement about the the PV of a particular cash flow. It is:

PV of the cash flow of year n = Actual cash flow of year n divided by $(1 + r)^n$

where n is the year of the cash flow (that is, how many years into the future) and r is the opportunity investing rate expressed as a decimal (instead of as a percentage).

We have already seen how this works for the £20,000 inflow for year 1. For year 2 the calculation would be:

$$\text{PV of year 2 cash flow (£40,000)} = £40,000/(1 + 0.2)^2$$

$$PV = £40,000/(1.2)^2 = £40,000/1.44 = £27,778$$

Thus the present value of the £40,000 to be received in two year's time is £27,778.

Activity 10.10

See if you can show that an investor would be indifferent to £27,778 receivable now, or £40,000 receivable in two years' time, assuming that there is a 20 per cent investment opportunity.

The reasoning goes like this:

	£
Amount available for immediate investment	27,778
Add Interest for year 1 (20% × 27,778)	5,556
	33,334
Add Interest for year 2 (20% × 33,334)	6,668
	40,002

(The extra £2 is only a rounding error.)

Thus because the investor can turn £27,778 into £40,000 in two years, these amounts are equivalent, and we can say that £27,778 is the present value of £40,000 receivable after two years (given a 20% rate of return).

Now let us deduce the present values of all of the cash flows associated with the machine project and hence the *net present value* of the project as a whole. The relevant cash flows and calculations are as follows:

Time	Cash flow	Calculation of PV	PV
	£000		£000
Immediately (time 0)	(100)	$(100)/(1 + 0.2)^0$	(100.00)
1 year's time	20	$20/(1 + 0.2)^1$	16.67
2 years' time	40	$40/(1 + 0.2)^2$	27.78
3 years' time	60	$60/(1 + 0.2)^3$	34.72
4 years' time	60	$60/(1 + 0.2)^4$	28.94
5 years' time	20	$20/(1 + 0.2)^5$	8.04
5 years' time	20	$20/(1 + 0.2)^5$	8.04
			24.19

(Note that $(1 + 0.2)^0 = 1$)

Once again, we must ask how we can decide whether the machine project is acceptable to the business. In fact, the decision rule is simple. If the NPV is positive we accept the project; if it is negative we reject the project. In this case, the NPV is positive, so we accept the project and buy the machine.

Investing in the machine will make the business £24,190 better off. What the above is saying is that the benefits from investing in this machine are worth a total of £124,190 today. Since the business can 'buy' these benefits for just £100,000 the investment should be made. If, however the benefits were below £100,000 they would be less than the cost of 'buying' them.

Activity 10.11

What is the *maximum* the Billingsgate Battery Company would be prepared to pay for the machine, given the potential benefits of owning it?

The company would be prepared to pay up to £124,190 since the wealth of the owners of the business would be increased up to this price – though the company would prefer to pay as little as possible.

Using discount tables

Deducing the present values of the various cash flows is a little laborious using the approach that we have just taken. To deduce each PV we took the relevant cash flow and multiplied it by $1/(1 + r)^n$. Fortunately, there is a quicker way.

* Tables exist that show values of this **discount factor** for a range of values of r and n. Such a table is appended at the end of this chapter on page 298. Take a look at it.

Look at the column for 20 per cent and the row for one year. We find that the factor is 0.833. Thus the PV of a cash flow of £1 receivable in one year is £0.833. So a cash flow of £20,000 receivable in one year's time is £16,667 (that is, 0.833 × £20,000), the same result as we found doing it longhand.

What is the NPV of the Chaotic Industries project from Activity 10.2, assuming a 15 per cent opportunity cost of finance (discount rate)? You should use the discount table on page 298.

Remember that the inflows and outflows are expected to be:

		£000
Immediately	Cost of vans	(150)
1 year's time	Net saving before depreciation	30
2 years' time	Net saving before depreciation	30
3 years' time	Net saving before depreciation	30
4 years' time	Net saving before depreciation	30
5 years' time	Net saving before depreciation	30
6 years' time	Net saving before depreciation	30
6 years' time	Disposal proceeds from the machine	30

The calculation of the NPV of the project is as follows:

Time	Cash flows £000	Discount factor (from the table)	Present value £000
Immediately	(150)	1.000	(150.00)
1 year's time	30	0.870	26.10
2 years' time	30	0.756	22.68
3 years' time	30	0.658	19.74
4 years' time	30	0.572	17.16
5 years' time	30	0.497	14.91
6 years' time	30	0.432	12.96
6 years' time	30	0.432	12.96
		Net present value	(23.49)

How would you interpret this result?

The fact that the project has a negative NPV means that the present value benefits from the investment are worth less than the cost of entering into it. Any cost up to £126,510 (the present value of the benefits) would be worth paying, but not £150,000.

The discount tables reveal how the value of £1 diminishes as its receipt goes further into the future. Assuming an opportunity cost of finance of 20 per cent per annum, £1 to be received immediately, obviously, has a present value of £1. However, as the time before it is to be received extends, the present value diminishes significantly, as is shown in Figure 10.3.

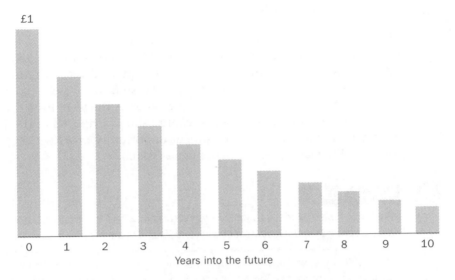

£1

Years into the future

The present value of a future receipt (or payment) of £1 depends on how far in the future it will occur. Those that will occur in the near future will have a larger present value than those whose occurrence is more distant in time.

Figure 10.3 Present value of £1 receivable at various times in the future, assuming an annual financing cost of 20 per cent

Why NPV is superior to ARR and PP

From what we have seen, NPV seems to be a better method of appraising investment opportunities than either ARR or PP. This is because it fully addresses each of the following issues:

- *The timing of the cash flows.* By discounting the various cash flows associated with each project according to when it is expected to arise, the fact that cash flows do not all occur simultaneously is taken into account by NPV. Associated with this is the fact that by discounting, using the opportunity cost of finance (that is, the return that the next best alternative opportunity would generate), the net benefit after financing costs have been met is identified (as the NPV of the project).
- *The whole of the relevant cash flows.* NPV includes all of the relevant cash flows, irrespective of when they are expected to occur. It treats them differently according to their date of occurrence, but they are all taken into account in the NPV, and they all have an influence on the decision.
- *The objectives of the business.* NPV is the only method of appraisal in which the output of the analysis has a direct bearing on the wealth of the business. (Positive NPVs enhance wealth; negative ones reduce it.) Since most private sector businesses seek to maximise shareholders' wealth, NPV is superior to the methods previously discussed.

Internal rate of return (IRR)

This is the last of the four major methods of investment appraisal that are found in practice. It is quite closely related to the NPV method in that, like NPV, it also involves discounting future cash flows. The **internal rate of return** is the discount rate that, when applied to the future cash flows of a project, will produce an NPV of precisely zero. In essence, it represents the yield from the project.

You will recall that when we discounted the cash flows of the Billingsgate Battery Company machine investment opportunity at 20 per cent, we found that the NPV was a positive figure of £24,190.

Activity 10.14

What does the NPV of the machine project (that is, £24,190 (positive)) tell us about the rate of return that the investment will yield for the business?

The fact that the NPV is positive when discounting at 20 per cent implies that the rate of return that the project generates is more than 20 per cent. The fact that the NPV is a pretty large figure implies that the actual rate of return is quite a lot above 20 per cent. We should expect increasing the size of the discount rate to reduce NPV, because a higher discount rate gives a lower discount factor. Thus future inflows are more heavily discounted, which will reduce their impact on the NPV.

It is somewhat laborious to deduce the IRR by hand, since it cannot usually be calculated directly. Thus iteration (trial and error) is the only approach.

Let us try a higher rate and see what happens, say 30 per cent:

Time	Cash flow	Discount factor	PV
	£000		£000
Immediately (time 0)	(100)	1.000	(100.00)
1 year's time	20	0.769	15.38
2 years' time	40	0.592	23.68
3 years' time	60	0.455	27.30
4 years' time	60	0.350	21.00
5 years' time	20	0.269	5.38
5 years' time	20	0.269	5.38
			(1.88)

In increasing the discount rate from 20 per cent to 30 per cent, we have reduced the NPV from £52,600 (positive) to £1,880 (negative). Since the IRR is the discount rate which will give us an NPV of exactly zero, we can conclude that the IRR of Billingsgate Battery Company's machine project is very slightly under 30 per cent. Further trials could lead us to the exact rate, but there is probably not much point, given the likely inaccuracy of the cash flow estimates. It is probably good enough, for practical purposes, to say that the IRR is about 30 per cent.

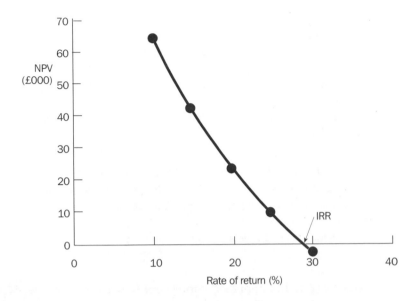

If the discount rate were zero, the NPV would be the sum of the net cash flows. In other words, no account would be taken of the time value of money. However, if we assume increasing discount rates, there is a corresponding decrease in the NPV of the project. When the NPV line crosses the horizontal axis there will be a zero NPV, and the point where it crosses is the IRR.

Figure 10.4 The relationship between the NPV and IRR methods

The relationship between the NPV method discussed earlier and the IRR is shown graphically in Figure 10.4 using the information relating to the Billingsgate Battery Company.

We can see that, where the discount rate is zero, the NPV will be the sum of the net cash flows. In other words, no account is taken of the time value of money. However, as the discount rate increases there is a corresponding decrease in the NPV of the project. When the NPV line touches the horizontal axis there will be a zero NPV, and that will also represent the IRR.

Activity 10.15

What is the internal rate of return of the Chaotic Industries project from Activity 10.2? You should use the discount table at the end of this chapter.

Hint: Remember that you already know the NPV of this project at 15 per cent.

Since we know (from a previous activity) that, at a 15 per cent discount rate, the NPV is a relatively large negative figure, our next trial is using a lower discount rate, say 10 per cent:

Time	Cash flows	Discount factor	Present value
	£000	(from the table)	£000
Immediately	(150)	1.000	(150.00)
1 year's time	30	0.909	27.27
2 years' time	30	0.826	24.78
3 years' time	30	0.751	22.53
4 years' time	30	0.683	20.49
5 years' time	30	0.621	18.63
6 years' time	30	0.565	16.95
6 years' time	30	0.565	16.95
		Net present value	(2.40)

We can see that NPV rose about £21,000 (£23,490 − £2,400) for a 5 per cent drop in the discount rate: that is, about £4,200 for each 1 per cent. We need to know the discount rate for a zero NPV: that is, a fall of a further £2,400. This logically would be roughly 0.6 per cent (that is, 2,400/4,200). Thus the IRR is close to 9.4 per cent. However, to say that the IRR is about 9 per cent is near enough for most purposes.

Users of the IRR approach should apply the following decision rules:

- For any project to be acceptable, it must meet a minimum IRR requirement. Logically, this minimum should be the opportunity cost of finance.
- Where there are competing projects (for example, the business can choose one of the projects only) the one with the higher or highest IRR would be selected.

IRR has certain attributes in common with NPV. All cash flows are taken into account, and their timing is logically handled. The main disadvantage with IRR is the fact that it does not address the question of wealth generation. It could therefore lead to the wrong decision being made. This is because IRR would, for example, always see a return of 25 per cent being preferable to a 20 per cent IRR, assuming an opportunity cost of finance of, say, 15 per cent. Though this may well lead to the project being taken that could most effectively increase wealth, it could nevertheless have the opposite effect. This is because IRR completely ignores the *scale of investment*. With a 15 per cent cost of finance, £1.5 million invested at 20 per cent would make you richer than £0.5 million invested at 25 per cent. IRR does not recognise this. It should be acknowledged that it is not usual for projects to be competing where there is such a large difference in scale. Even though the problem may be rare and, typically, IRR will give the same signal as NPV, a method (NPV) that is always reliable must be better to use than IRR.

A further problem with the IRR method is that it has difficulty handling projects with unconventional cash flows. In the examples studied so far, each project has a negative cash flow arising at the start of its life and then positive cash flows thereafter. However, in some cases, a project may have both positive and negative cash flows at future points in its life. Such a pattern of cash flows can result in the the IRR method providing more than one solution, or even no solution at all.

Some practical points

When dealing with questions relating to investment appraisal, there are several practical points that you should bear in mind:

- *Relevant costs.* As with all decision making, we should only take account of cash flows that vary according to the decision in our analysis. Thus cash flows that will be the same, irrespective of the decision under review, should be ignored. For example, overheads that will be incurred in equal amount whether the investment is made or not should be ignored, even though the investment could not be made without the infrastructure that the overhead costs create. Similarly, past costs should be ignored as they are not affected by, and do not vary with, the decision.
- *Opportunity costs.* Opportunity costs arising from benefits foregone must be taken into account. Thus, for example, when considering a decision concerning whether or not to continue to use a machine already owned by the business, for producing a new product, the realisable value of the machine may be an important opportunity cost.
- *Taxation.* Tax will usually be affected by an investment decision. The profits will be taxed, the capital investment may attract tax relief, and so on. Tax is levied on these at significant rates. This means that, in real life, unless tax is formally taken into account, the wrong decision could easily be made. In practice, some, if not all, of the taxation relating to the current year's profits may be paid in a later period. The timing of the tax outflow must be taken into account when preparing the cash flows for the project.
- *Cash flows not profit flows.* We have seen that for the NPV, IRR and PP methods, it is cash flows rather than profit flows that are relevant to the evaluation of investment projects. In a problem requiring the application of any of these methods you may be given details of the profits for the investment period, and will be required to adjust these in order to derive the cash flows. Remember, the net profit before depreciation is an approximation to the cash flows for the period, and so you should work back to this figure.

  When the data are expressed in profit rather than cash flow terms, an adjustment in respect of working capital may also be necessary. Some adjustment should be made to take account of changes in the net cash investment (or disinvestment) made in trade debtors, stock and creditors. For example, launching a new product may give rise to an increase in working capital, requiring an immediate outlay of cash. This outlay for additional working capital should be shown in your NPV calculations as part of the initial cost. However, the additional working capital will be released by the end of the life of the product. This disinvestment, resulting in an inflow of cash at the end of the life of the project, should also be taken into account in your calculations at the point at which it is received.

- *Interest payments.* When using discounted cash flow techniques, interest payments should not be taken into account in deriving the cash flows for the period. The discount factor already takes account of the costs of financing, so to take account of interest charges in deriving cash flows for the period would be double counting.

- *Other factors.* Investment decision making must not be viewed as simply a mechanical exercise. The results derived from a particular investment appraisal method will be only one input into the decision-making process. There may be broader issues connected to the decision that have to be taken into account, but which may be difficult or impossible to quantify. The reliability of the forecasts and the validity of the assumptions used in the evaluation will also have a bearing on the final decision.

Activity 10.16

The directors of Manuff (Steel) Ltd have decided to close one of its factories. There has been a reduction in the demand for the products made at the factory in recent years, and the directors of the company are not optimistic about the long-term prospects for these products. The factory is situated in the north of England, in an area where unemployment is high.

The factory is leased, and there are still four years of the lease remaining. The directors are uncertain as to whether the factory should be closed immediately or at the end of the period of the lease. Another company has offered to sublease the premises from Manuff (Steel) Ltd at a rental of £40,000 per annum for the remainder of the lease period.

The machinery and equipment at the factory cost £1,500,000, and has a written-down value of £400,000. In the event of immediate closure, the machinery and equipment could be sold for £220,000. The working capital at the factory is £420,000, and could be liquidated for that amount immediately, if required. Alternatively, the working capital can be liquidated in full at the end of the lease period. Immediate closure would result in redundancy payments to employees of £180,000.

If the factory continues in operation until the end of the lease period, the following operating profits (losses) are expected:

	Year 1	Year 2	Year 3	Year 4
	£000	£000	£000	£000
Operating profit (loss)	160	(40)	30	20

The above figures include a charge of £90,000 per year for depreciation of machinery and equipment. The residual value of the machinery and equipment at the end of the lease period is estimated at £40,000.

Redundancy payments are expected to be £150,000 at the end of the lease period if the factory continues in operation. The company has a cost of capital of 12 per cent. Ignore taxation.

Required:

(a) Calculate the incremental cash flows arising from a decision to continue operations until the end of the lease period rather than to close immediately.

(b) Calculate the net present value of continuing operations until the end of the lease period, rather than closing immediately.

(c) What other factors might the directors of the company take into account before making a final decision on the timing of the factory closure?

(d) State, with reasons, whether or not the company should continue to operate the factory until the end of the lease period.

Your answer to this activity should be as follows:

(a) *Incremental cash flows*

			Years		
	0	**1**	**2**	**3**	**4**
	£000	*£000*	*£000*	*£000*	*£000*
Operating cash flows		250	50	120	110
Sale of machinery	(220)				40
Redundancy costs	180				(150)
Sub-lease rentals		(40)	(40)	(40)	(40)
Working capital invested	(420)				420
	(460)	210	10	80	380
(b) Discount rate 12 per cent	1.00	0.89	0.80	0.71	0.64
Present value	(460)	186.9	8.0	56.8	243.2
Net present value	34.9				

(c) Other factors that may influence include:

- *The overall strategy of the company.* The company may need to set the decision within a broader context. It may be necessary to manufacture the products made at the factory because they are an integral part of the company's product range. The company may wish to avoid redundancies in an area of high unemployment for as long as possible.
- *Flexibility.* A decision to close the factory is probably irreversible. If the factory continues, however, there may be a chance that the prospects for the factory will brighten in the future.
- *Creditworthiness of sublessee.* The company should investigate the creditworthiness of the sublessee. Failure to receive the expected sublease payments would make the closure option far less attractive.
- *Accuracy of forecasts.* The forecasts made by the company should be examined carefully. Inaccuracies in the forecasts or any underlying assumptions may change the expected outcomes.

(d) The NPV of the decision to continue operations rather than close immediately is positive. Hence shareholders would be better off if the directors took this course of action. The factory should therefore continue in operation rather than close down. This decision is likely to be welcomed by employees, as unemployment is high in the area.

Self-assessment question 10.1

Beacon Chemicals plc is considering the erection of a new plant to produce a chemical named X14. The new plant's capital cost is estimated at £100,000, and if its construction is approved now, the plant can be erected and commence production by the end of 2002. £50,000 has already been spent on research and development work. Estimates of revenues and costs arising from the operation of the new plant appear below:

	2003	2004	2005	2006	2007
Sales price (£ per unit)	100	120	120	100	80
Sales volume (units)	800	1,000	1,200	1,000	800
Variable costs (£ per unit)	50	50	40	30	40
Fixed costs (£000)	30	30	30	30	30

If the new plant is erected, sales of some existing products will be lost, and this will result in a loss of contribution of £15,000 per year over its life.

The accountant has informed you that the fixed costs include depreciation of £20,000 per annum on new plant. They also include an allocation of £10,000 for fixed overheads. A separate study has indicated that if the new plant were built, additional overheads, excluding depreciation, arising from its construction would be £8,000 per year. The plant would require additional working capital of £30,000.

For the purposes of your initial calculations ignore taxation.

Required:

(a) Deduce the relevant annual cash flows associated with building and operating the plant.
(b) Deduce the payback period.
(c) Calculate the net present value using a discount rate of 8 per cent.

Hint: You should deal with the investment in working capital by treating it as a cash outflow at the start of the project and an inflow at the end.

Investment appraisal in practice

Many surveys have been conducted in the UK into the methods of investment appraisal used in practice. They have tended to show the following features:

- businesses using more than one method to assess each investment decision, increasingly so over time
- an increased use of the discounting methods (NPV and IRR) over time, with these two becoming the most popular in recent years
- continued popularity of ARR and payback period, despite their theoretical shortcomings and the rise in popularity of the discounting methods
- a tendency for larger businesses to use the discounting methods and to use more than one method in respect of each decision.

Exhibit 10.1

Method	Percentage of businesses using the method
Net present value	80
Internal rate of return	81
Payback period	70
Accounting rate of return	56

Source: Arnold, G.C. and Hatzopoulos, P. 'Investment and finance decision making in large, medium and small UK companies'. Unpublished, but cited in Arnold, G.C. *Corporate financial management* (Financial Times, Pitman Publishing 1998).

Exhibit 10.1 shows the results of the most recent (1997) survey conducted of UK businesses regarding their use of investment appraisal methods.

Activity 10.17

How do you explain the popularity of the payback method, given the theoretical limitations discussed earlier in this chapter?

A number of possible reasons may explain this finding:

- PP is easy to understand and use.
- It can avoid the problems of forecasting far into the future.
- It gives emphasis to the early cash flows when there is greater certainty concerning their accuracy.
- It emphasises the importance of liquidity. Where a business has liquidity problems, a short payback period for a project is likely to appear attractive.

The importance of payback may suggest a lack of sophistication among managers concerning investment appraisal. This criticism is most often made against managers of smaller business. In fact, other surveys have found that smaller businesses were much less likely to use discounted cash flow methods (NPV and IRR) than larger businesses.

The sum of percentage usage for each appraisal method is 287 per cent, which indicates that many businesses use more than one method to appraise investments. It is therefore possible that payback is used by some businesses as an initial screening device, and that projects that pass successfully through this stage are then subject to more sophisticated discounted cash flow analysis. Exhibit 10.1 suggests that most businesses use one of the two discounted cash flow methods.

IRR may be as popular as NPV, despite IRR's theoretical weaknesses, because it expresses outcomes in percentage terms rather than absolute terms. This form of expression appears to be more acceptable to managers. This may be because managers are used to using percentage figures as targets (for example, return on capital employed).

SUMMARY

In this chapter we have considered how managers might approach the problem of assessing investment opportunities. We saw that there are basically four methods that are used to any significant extent in practice:

- accounting rate of return
- payback period
- net present value
- internal rate of return.

The first two of these are very seriously flawed by their failing to take full account of the time dimension of investment. Assuming that the objective of making investments is to enhance the wealth of the business, the NPV method is, theoretically, by far the best of the four methods, in that it rationally and fully takes account of all relevant information. Since IRR is fairly similar to NPV, it tends to give similar signals to those provided by NPV. IRR does suffer from a fundamental theoretical flaw, which can lead to it giving misleading signals on some occasions. We concluded the chapter by considering some more practical aspects of using the appraisal methods.

 Key terms

accounting rate of return (ARR)
 p 269
payback period (PP) *p 272*
net present value (NPV) *p 275*
risk *p 277*

risk premium *p 277*
inflation *p 278*
discount factor *p 281*
internal rate of return *p 284*

 REVIEW QUESTIONS

10.1 Why is the net present value method of investment appraisal considered to be theoretically superior to other methods of investment appraisal found in the literature?

10.2 The payback method has been criticised for not taking the time value of money into account. Could this limitation be overcome? If so, would this method then be preferable to the NPV method?

10.3 Research indicates that the IRR method is a more popular method of investment appraisal than the NPV method. Why might this be?

10.4 Why are cash flows rather than profit flows used in the IRR, NPV and PP methods of investment appraisal?

EXAMINATION-STYLE QUESTIONS

Questions 10.4 and 10.5 are more advanced than 10.1–10.3. Those with a coloured number have an answer at the back of the book.

10.1 The directors of Mylo Ltd are currently considering two mutually exclusive investment projects. Both projects are concerned with the purchase of new plant. The following data are available for each project:

	Project	
	1	2
	£	£
Cost (immediate outlay)	100,000	60,000
Expected annual net profit (loss):		
Year 1	29,000	18,000
2	(1,000)	(2,000)
3	2,000	4,000
Estimated residual value of the plant	7,000	6,000

The company has an estimated cost of capital of 10 per cent, and employs the straight-line method of depreciation for all fixed assets when calculating net profit. Neither project would increase the working capital of the company. The company has sufficient funds to meet all capital expenditure requirements.

Required:
(a) Calculate for each project:
  (i) The net present value.
  (ii) The approximate internal rate of return.
  (iii) The payback period.
(b) State which, if any, of the two investment projects the directors of Mylo Ltd should accept, and why.
(c) State, in general terms, which method of investment appraisal you consider to be most appropriate for evaluating investment projects, and why.

10.2 C. George (Controls) Ltd manufactures a thermostat that can be used in a range of kitchen appliances. The manufacturing process is, at present, semi-automated. The equipment used costs £540,000, and has a written-down (balance sheet) value of £300,000. Demand for the product has been fairly stable, and output has been maintained at 50,000 units per annum in recent years.

The following data, based on the current level of output, have been prepared in respect of the product:

	Per unit £	£
Selling price		12.40
Less		
Labour	3.30	
Materials	3.65	
Overheads: Variable	1.58	
Fixed	1.60	
		10.13
Profit		2.27

Although the existing equipment is expected to last for a further four years before it is sold for an estimated £40,000, the company has recently been considering purchasing new equipment that would completely automate much of the production process. The new equipment would cost £670,000 and would have an expected life of four years, at the end of which it would be sold for an estimated £70,000. If the new equipment is purchased, the old equipment could be sold for £150,000 immediately.

The assistant to the company accountant has prepared a report to help assess the viability of the proposed change, which includes the following data:

	Per unit £	£
Selling price		12.40
Less		
Labour	1.20	
Materials	3.20	
Overheads: Variable	1.40	
Fixed	3.30	
		9.10
Profit		3.30

Depreciation charges will increase by £85,000 per annum as a result of purchasing the new machinery; however, other fixed costs are not expected to change.

In the report the assistant wrote:

> The figures shown above that relate to the proposed change are based on the current level of output and take account of a depreciation charge of £150,000 per annum in respect of the new equipment. The effect of purchasing the new equipment will be to increase the net profit to sales ratio from 18.3% to 26.6%. In addition, the purchase of the new equipment will enable us to reduce our stock level immediately by £130,000.
>
> In view of these facts, I recommend purchase of the new equipment.

The company has a cost of capital of 12 per cent.
Ignore taxation.

Required:
(a) Prepare a statement of the incremental cash flows arising from the purchase of the new equipment.
(b) Calculate the net present value of the proposed purchase of new equipment.
(c) State, with reasons, whether the company should purchase the new equipment.
(d) Explain why cash flow forecasts are used rather than profit forecasts to assess the viability of proposed capital expenditure projects.

10.3 The accountant of your company has recently been taken ill through overwork. In his absence his assistant has prepared some calculations of the profitability of a project, which are to be discussed soon at the board meeting of your company. His workings, which are set out below, include some errors of principle. You can assume that the statement below includes no arithmetical errors.

	2002 £000	2003 £000	2004 £000	2005 £000	2006 £000	2007 £000
Sales revenue		450	470	470	470	470
Less Costs						
Materials		126	132	132	132	132
Labour		90	94	94	94	94
Overheads		45	47	47	47	47
Depreciation		120	120	120	120	120
Working capital	180					
Interest on working capital		27	27	27	27	27
Write-off of development costs		30	30	30		
Total costs	180	438	450	450	420	420
Profit/(loss)	(180)	12	20	20	50	50

$$\frac{\text{Total profit/(loss)}}{\text{Cost of equipment}} = \frac{(£28,000)}{£600,000} = \text{Return on investment (4.7\%)}$$

You ascertain the following additional information:

- The cost of equipment contains £100,000, being the book value of an old machine. If it was not used for this project it would be scrapped with a zero net realisable value. New equipment costing £500,000 will be purchased on 31 December 2002. You should assume that all other cash flows occur at the end of the year to which they relate.
- The development costs of £90,000 have already been spent.
- Overheads have been costed at 50 per cent of direct labour, which is the company's normal practice. An independent assessment has suggested that incremental overheads are likely to amount to £30,000 per year.
- The company's cost of capital is 12 per cent.

Ignore taxation in your answer.

Required:

(a) Prepare a corrected statement of the incremental cash flows arising from the project. Where you have altered the assistant's figures you should attach a brief note explaining your alterations.

(b) Calculate:
  (i) The project's payback period.
  (ii) The project's net present value.

(c) Write a memo to the board advising on the acceptance or rejection of the project.

10.4 Arkwright Mills plc is considering expanding its production of a new yarn, code name X15. The plant is expected to cost £1 million and have a life of five years and a nil residual value. It will be ready for operation before 31 December 2002, and the initial period will be used to build up stocks; £500,000 has already been spent on development costs of the product, and this has been charged to revenue in the year it was incurred.

The following profit and loss statements for the new yarn are forecast:

	2003	2004	2005	2006	2007
	£m	£m	£m	£m	£m
Sales	1.2	1.4	1.4	1.4	1.4
Costs, including depreciation	1.0	1.1	1.1	1.1	1.1
Profit before tax	0.2	0.3	0.3	0.3	0.3

Tax is charged at 50 per cent on profits and paid one year in arrears. Depreciation has been calculated on a straight-line basis. Additional working capital of £0.6 million will be required at the beginning of the project. You should assume that all cash flows occur at the end of the year in which they arise.

Required:

(a) Prepare a statement showing the incremental cash flows of the project relevant to a decision concerning whether or not to proceed with the construction of the new plant.

(b) Compute the net present value of the project using a 10 per cent discount rate.

(c) Compute the payback period to the nearest year. Explain the meaning of this term.

10.5 Newton Electronics Ltd has incurred expenditure of £5 million over the past three years researching and developing a miniature hearing aid. The hearing aid is now fully developed, and the directors of the company are considering which of three mutually exclusive options should be taken to exploit the potential of the new product. The options are as follows:

1 The company could manufacture the hearing aid itself. This would be a new departure for the company, which has so far concentrated on research and development projects. However, the company has manufacturing space available, which it currently rents to another business for £100,000 per annum.

The company would have to purchase plant and equipment costing £9 million and invest £3 million in working capital immediately for production to begin.

A market research report, for which the company paid £50,000, indicates that the new product has an expected life of five years. Sales of the product during this period are predicted as follows:

	Predicted sales for the year ended 30 November				
	2002	2003	2004	2005	2006
Number of units (000s)	800	1,400	1,800	1,200	500

The selling price per unit will be £30 in the first year but will fall to £22 in the following three years. In the final year of the product's life, the selling price will fall to £20. Variable production costs are predicted to be £14 per unit, and fixed production costs (including depreciation) will be £2.4 million per annum. Marketing costs will be £2 million per annum.

The company intends to depreciate the plant and equipment using the straight-line method and based on an estimated residual value at the end of the five years of £1 million. The company has a cost of capital of 10 per cent.

2 Newton Electronics Ltd could agree to another company manufacturing and marketing the product under licence. A multinational company, Faraday Electricals plc, has offered to undertake the manufacture and marketing of the product, and in return will make a royalty payment to Newton Electronics Ltd of £5 per unit. It has been estimated that the annual number of sales of the hearing aid will be 10 per cent higher if the multinational company, rather than if Newton Electronics Ltd, manufactures and markets the product.

3 Newton Electronics Ltd could sell the patent rights to Faraday Electricals plc for £24 million, payable in two equal instalments. The first instalment would be payable immediately and the second instalment would be payable at the end of two years. This option would give Faraday Electricals the exclusive right to manufacture and market the new product.

Ignore taxation.
Assume it is now 30 November 2001.

Required:
(a) Calculate the net present value of each of the options available to Newton Electronics Ltd.
(b) Identify and discuss any other factors that Newton Electronics Ltd should consider before arriving at a decision.
(c) State what you consider to be the most suitable option, and why.

APPENDIX: PRESENT VALUE TABLE

Present value of 1, i.e. $(1 + r)^{-n}$

where r = discount rate

n = number of periods until payment

Periods (n)	\multicolumn{10}{c}{Discount rates (r)}	
	1%	2%	3%	4%	5%	6%	7%	8%	9%	10%	
1	0.990	0.980	0.971	0.962	0.952	0.943	0.935	0.926	0.917	0.909	1
2	0.980	0.961	0.943	0.925	0.907	0.890	0.873	0.857	0.842	0.826	2
3	0.971	0.942	0.915	0.889	0.864	0.840	0.816	0.794	0.772	0.751	3
4	0.961	0.924	0.888	0.855	0.823	0.792	0.763	0.735	0.708	0.683	4
5	0.951	0.906	0.863	0.822	0.784	0.747	0.713	0.681	0.650	0.621	5
6	0.942	0.888	0.837	0.790	0.746	0.705	0.666	0.630	0.596	0.564	6
7	0.933	0.871	0.813	0.760	0.711	0.665	0.623	0.583	0.547	0.513	7
8	0.923	0.853	0.789	0.731	0.677	0.627	0.582	0.540	0.502	0.467	8
9	0.914	0.837	0.766	0.703	0.645	0.592	0.544	0.500	0.460	0.424	9
10	0.905	0.820	0.744	0.676	0.614	0.558	0.508	0.463	0.422	0.386	10
11	0.896	0.804	0.722	0.650	0.585	0.527	0.475	0.429	0.388	0.350	11
12	0.887	0.788	0.701	0.625	0.557	0.497	0.444	0.397	0.356	0.319	12
13	0.879	0.773	0.681	0.601	0.530	0.469	0.415	0.368	0.326	0.290	13
14	0.870	0.758	0.661	0.577	0.505	0.442	0.388	0.340	0.299	0.263	14
15	0.861	0.743	0.642	0.555	0.481	0.417	0.362	0.315	0.275	0.239	15

	11%	12%	13%	14%	15%	16%	17%	18%	19%	20%	
1	0.901	0.893	0.885	0.877	0.870	0.862	0.855	0.847	0.840	0.833	1
2	0.812	0.797	0.783	0.769	0.756	0.743	0.731	0.718	0.706	0.694	2
3	0.731	0.712	0.693	0.675	0.658	0.641	0.624	0.609	0.593	0.579	3
4	0.659	0.636	0.613	0.592	0.572	0.552	0.534	0.516	0.499	0.482	4
5	0.593	0.567	0.543	0.519	0.497	0.476	0.456	0.437	0.419	0.402	5
6	0.535	0.507	0.480	0.456	0.432	0.410	0.390	0.370	0.352	0.335	6
7	0.482	0.452	0.425	0.400	0.376	0.354	0.333	0.314	0.296	0.279	7
8	0.434	0.404	0.376	0.351	0.327	0.305	0.285	0.266	0.249	0.233	8
9	0.391	0.361	0.333	0.308	0.284	0.263	0.243	0.225	0.209	0.194	9
10	0.352	0.322	0.295	0.270	0.247	0.227	0.208	0.191	0.176	0.162	10
11	0.317	0.287	0.261	0.237	0.215	0.195	0.178	0.162	0.148	0.135	11
12	0.286	0.257	0.231	0.208	0.187	0.168	0.152	0.137	0.124	0.112	12
13	0.258	0.229	0.204	0.182	0.163	0.145	0.130	0.116	0.104	0.093	13
14	0.232	0.205	0.181	0.160	0.141	0.125	0.111	0.099	0.088	0.078	14
15	0.209	0.183	0.160	0.140	0.123	0.108	0.095	0.084	0.074	0.065	15

The management of working capital

INTRODUCTION

In this chapter we consider the factors that must be taken into account when managing the working capital of a business. Each element of working capital will be identified, and the major issues surrounding them will be discussed.

> ### Objectives
>
> When you have completed this chapter you should be able to:
>
> * identify the main elements of working capital
> * discuss the purpose of working capital and the nature of the working capital cycle
> * explain the importance of establishing policies for the control of working capital
> * explain the factors that have to be taken into account when managing each element of working capital.

The nature and purpose of working capital

✻ **Working capital** is usually defined as current assets less current liabilities (creditors due within one year).

The major elements of current assets are:

* stocks
* trade debtors
* cash (in hand and at bank).

The major element of current liabilities is:

* trade creditors.

The size and composition of working capital can vary between industries. For some types of business, the investment in working capital can be sub-

Cash is used to pay trade creditors for raw materials, or raw materials are bought for immediate cash settlement; cash is spent on labour and other aspects that turn raw materials into work-in-progress and, finally, into finished goods. The finished goods are sold either for cash or for credit. In the case of credit customers, there will be a delay before the cash is received from the sales. Receipt of cash completes the cycle.

Figure 11.1 The working capital cycle

stantial. For example, a manufacturing company will invest heavily in raw material, work-in-progress and finished goods, and will often sell its goods on credit, thereby generating trade debtors. A retailer, on the other hand, will hold only one form of stock (finished goods), and will usually sell goods for cash.

Working capital represents a net investment in short-term assets. These assets are continually flowing into and out of the business, and are essential for day-to-day operations. The various elements of working capital are interrelated, and can be seen as part of a short-term cycle. For a manufacturing business, the working capital cycle can be depicted as shown in Figure 11.1.

The management of working capital is an essential part of the short-term planning process. It is necessary for management to decide how much of each element should be held. As we shall see later, there are costs associated with holding either too much or too little of each element. Management must be aware of these in order to manage effectively. Management must also be aware that there may be other, more profitable, uses for the funds of the business. Hence, the potential benefits must be weighed against the likely costs in order to achieve the optimum investment.

Working capital needs are likely to change over time as a result of changes in the business environment. This means that working capital decisions are rarely 'one-off' decisions. Managers must try to identify changes occurring so as to ensure that the level of investment in working capital is appropriate.

Activity 11.1

What kind of changes in the business environment might lead to a decision to change the level of investment in working capital? Try to identify four possible changes that could affect the working capital needs of a business.

In answering this activity, you may have thought of the following:

- changes in interest rates
- changes in market demand
- changes in the seasons
- changes in the state of the economy

You may have also thought of others.

In addition to changes in the external environment, changes arising within the business such as changes in production methods (resulting, perhaps, in a need to hold less stock) and changes in the level of risk managers are prepared to take, could alter the required level of investment in working capital.

In the sections that follow, we shall consider each element of working capital separately. We shall examine the factors that must be considered to ensure their proper management.

The scale of working capital

It is tempting to form the impression that, compared with the scale of investment in fixed assets by the typical business, the amounts involved with working capital are pretty trivial. This would be a false assessment of reality – the scale of working capital for most businesses is vast.

Exhibit 11.1 gives some impression of the working capital involvement for five UK businesses that are either very well known by name, or whose products are everyday commodities for most of us.

The totals for current assets are pretty large when compared with the total long-term investment. The amounts vary considerably from one type of business to the next. Pace is the only one of the five businesses that is a manufacturer. Somerfield is the only other one that holds a significant amount of stock. Stagecoach, Capital Radio and Railtrack all provide a service and therefore do not hold stock. Somerfield makes sales for immediate cash settlement, so it has no trade debtors; Stagecoach makes most of its sales for cash, so has relatively low trade debtors.

These types of variation in the amounts and types of working capital elements are typical of other businesses.

A summary of the balance sheets of five UK firms

Business	Pace Micro Technology plc	Stagecoach Holdings plc	Somerfield plc	Capital Radio plc	Railtrack Group plc
Balance sheet date	29.5.99	30.4.99	24.4.99	30.9.99	31.3.99
	%	%	%	%	%
Fixed assets	29	109	127	130	104
Current assets					
Stock	16	1	36	–	–
Trade debtors	78	4	–	32	5
Other debtors	9	6	13	19	3
Cash and near cash	34	17	11	6	6
	137	28	60	57	14
Current liabilities					
Trade creditors	31	8	59	12	5
Tax and dividends	17	5	11	49	1
Other short-term liabilities	18	13	17	17	12
Overdrafts and short-term loans	–	11	–	9	–
	66	37	87	87	18
Working capital	71	(9)	(27)	(30)	(4)
Total long-term investment	100	100	100	100	100

The fixed assets, current assets and current liabilities (creditors: amounts falling due within one year) are expressed as a percentage of the total net investment of the firm concerned. The firms were randomly selected, except that they were deliberately taken from different industries. Pace is the UK market leader in the manufacture and supply of receivers and decoders for digital, satellite and cable television. Stagecoach is a major passenger transport provider, principally through buses, coaches and trains. It owns South West Trains, and has a major stake in Virgin trains. Somerfield is one of the major UK supermarkets. Capital Radio is a commercial radio broadcaster, owning a number of local radio stations in the UK as well as the Capital Radio activity in London. Railtrack owns and manages the railway lines and stations used by the UK's train operating companies.

The management of stocks

A business may hold stocks for various reasons. The most common reason is, of course, to meet the immediate day-to-day requirements of customers and production. However, a business may hold more than is necessary for this purpose if it is believed that future supplies may be interrupted or scarce. Similarly, if the business believes that the cost of stocks will rise in the future, it may decide to stockpile.

For some types of business the stock held may represent a substantial proportion of the total assets held. For example, a car dealership that rents its premises may have nearly all of its total assets in the form of stock. In the case of manufacturing businesses, stock levels tend to be higher than in many other forms of business as it is necessary to hold three kinds of stock – raw materials, work-in-progress and finished goods. Each form of stock represents a particular stage in the production cycle. For some types of business, the level of stock held may vary substantially over the year owing to the seasonal nature of the industry, for example greetings card manufacturers, whereas for other businesses stock levels may remain fairly stable throughout the year.

Where a business holds stock simply to meet the day-to-day requirements of its customers and production, it will normally seek to minimise the amount of stock held. This is because there are significant costs associated with holding stocks. These include storage and handling costs, financing costs, the risks of pilferage and obsolescence, and the opportunities forgone in tying up funds in this form of asset. However, a business must also recognise that, if the level of stocks held is too low, there will also be associated costs.

Activity 11.2

What costs might a business incur as a result of holding too low a level of stocks? Try and jot down at least three types of cost.

In answering this activity you may have thought of the following costs:

- loss of sales, from being unable to provide the goods required immediately
- loss of goodwill from customers, for being unable to satisfy customer demand
- high transport costs incurred to ensure that stocks are replenished quickly
- lost production due to shortage of raw materials
- inefficient production scheduling due to shortages
- purchasing stocks at a higher price than might otherwise have been possible in order to replenish stocks quickly.

To try to ensure that the stocks are properly managed, a number of procedures and techniques may be used. These are reviewed below.

Forecasts of future demand

To try to ensure that there will be stock available to meet future sales a business must produce appropriate forecasts. These forecasts should deal with each product that the business makes. It is important that every attempt is made to ensure the accuracy of these forecasts, as they will determine future ordering and production levels. These forecasts may be derived in various ways. They may be developed using statistical techniques such as time series analysis, or they may be based on the judgement of the sales and marketing staff.

Financial ratios

One ratio that can be used to help monitor stock levels is the stock turnover period, which we examined in Chapter 6. You may recall that this ratio is calculated as follows:

$$\text{Stock turnover period} = \frac{\text{Average stock held}}{\text{Cost of sales}} \times 365$$

This will provide a picture of the average period for which stocks are held, and can be useful as a basis for comparison. It is possible to calculate the stock turnover period for individual product lines as well as for stocks as a whole.

Recording and reordering systems

The management of stocks in a business of any size requires a sound system of recording stock movements. There must be proper procedures for recording stock purchases and sales. Periodic stock checks may be required to ensure that the amount of physical stocks held is consistent with the stock records.

There should also be clear procedures for the reordering of stocks. Authorisation for both the purchase and the issue of stocks should be confined to a few senior staff if problems of duplication and lack of coordination are to be avoided. To determine the point at which stock should be reordered, information will be required concerning the lead time (that is, the time between the placing of an order and the receipt of the goods) and the likely level of demand.

Activity 11.3

An electrical retailer keeps a particular type of light-switch in stock. The annual demand for the light-switch is 10,400 units, and the lead time for orders is four weeks. Demand for the stock is steady throughout the year. At what level of stock should the company reorder, assuming that the company is confident of the figures mentioned above?

The average weekly demand for the stock item is 10,400/52 = 200 units. During the time between ordering the stock and receiving the goods the stock sold will be 4 × 200 units = 800 units. So the company should reorder no later than when the stock level reaches 800 units, in order to avoid a stockout.

In most businesses, there will be some uncertainty surrounding the above factors and so a buffer or safety stock level may be maintained in case problems occur. The amount of safety stock to be held is really a matter of judgement, and will depend on the degree of uncertainty concerning the above factors. However, the likely costs of running out of stock must also be taken into account.

Levels of control

Management must make a commitment to the management of stocks. However, the cost of controlling stocks must be weighed against the potential benefits. It may be possible to have different levels of control according to the nature of the stocks held. The **ABC system of stock control** (Figure 11.2) is based on the idea of selective levels of control.

A business may find that it is possible to divide its stock into three broad categories – A, B and C. Each category will be based on the value of stock held. Category A stocks will represent the high-value items. It may be the case, however, that although the items are high in *value* and represent a high proportion of the total value of stocks held, they are a relatively small proportion of the total *volume* of stocks held. For example, 10 per cent of the physical stocks held may account for 65 per cent of the total value. For these stocks, management may decide to implement sophisticated recording procedures, exert tight control over stock movements, and have a high level of security at the stock location.

Category B stocks will represent less valuable items held. Perhaps 30 per cent of the total volume of stocks may account for 25 per cent of the total value of stocks held. For these stocks, a lower level of recording and management control would be appropriate. Category C stocks will represent the least valuable items. Say 60 per cent of the volume of stocks may account for only 10

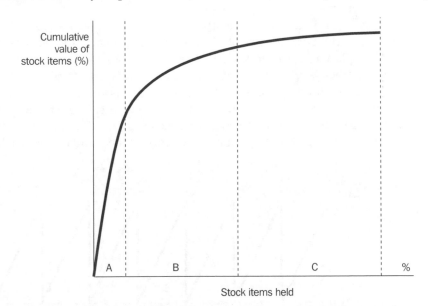

Category A contains stocks that, though relatively few in quantity, account for a large proportion of the total value of stocks. Category B stocks are those items that are less valuable, but more numerous. Category C comprises those stock items that are very numerous, but relatively low in value. Different stock control regimes would be applied to each category. For example, only category A stocks would attract the more expensive and sophisticated controls.

Figure 11.2 ABC method of analysing and controlling stock

per cent of the total value of stocks held. For these stocks the level of recording and management control would be lower still. Categorising stocks in this way can help to ensure that management effort is directed to the most important areas, and that the costs of controlling stocks are commensurate with their value.

Stock management models

✳ It is possible to use decision models to help manage stocks. The **economic order quantity (EOQ)** model is concerned with answering the question 'How much stock should be ordered?'. In its simplest form, the EOQ model assumes that demand is constant, so that stocks will be depleted evenly over time, and that stocks will be replenished just at the point the stock runs out. These assumptions would lead to a 'sawtooth' pattern to represent stock movements within a business, as shown in Figure 11.3.

The EOQ model recognises that the total cost of stocks is made up of the cost of holding stocks and the cost of ordering stocks. It calculates the optimum size of a purchase order by taking account of both of these cost elements. The cost of holding stocks can be substantial, and so management may try to reduce the average amount of stocks held to as low a level as possible. However, by reducing the level of stocks held, and therefore the holding costs, there will be a need to increase the number of orders during the period, and so ordering costs will rise.

Figure 11.4 shows how, as the level of stocks and the size of stock orders increase, the annual costs of placing orders will decrease because fewer orders will be placed. However, the cost of holding stock will increase, as there will be higher stock levels. The total costs curve, which is a function of the holding costs and ordering costs, will fall until the point E, which represents the minimum total cost. Thereafter, total costs begin to rise. The EOQ model seeks to identify the point E at which total costs are minimised. This will represent half of the optimum amount that should be ordered on each occasion.

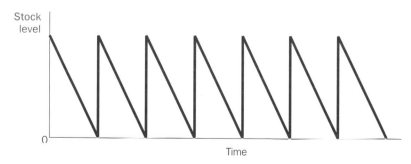

Here we assume that there is a constant rate of usage of the stock item, and that stocks are reduced to zero just as new stock arises. At time zero there is a full level of stock. This is steadily used as time passes; just as it falls to zero it is replaced. This pattern is then repeated.

Figure 11.3 Pattern of stock movements over time

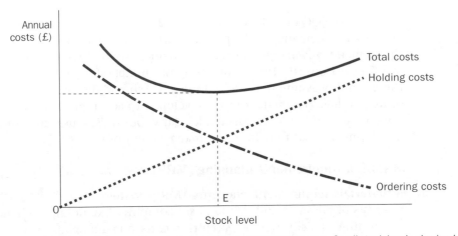

Annual costs (£)

Total costs

Holding costs

Ordering costs

E

Stock level

Small stock levels imply frequent reordering and high annual ordering costs. Small stock levels also imply relatively low stock-holding costs. High stock levels imply exactly the opposite. There is, in theory, an optimum order size that will lead to the sum of ordering and stock-holding costs (total costs) being at a minimum.

Figure 11.4 Stock-holding and stock order costs

Assuming, as we are doing, that stock is used evenly over time and that stock falls to zero before being replaced, the average stock level equals half of the order-size.

The economic order quantity can be calculated by using the following equation:

$$EOQ = \sqrt{\frac{2DC}{H}}$$

where:
D = the annual demand for the item of stock
C = the cost of placing an order
H = the cost of holding one unit of stock for one year.

Activity 11.4

HLA Ltd sells 2,000 units of Product X each year. It has been estimated that the cost of holding one unit of the product for a year is £4. The cost of placing an order for stock is estimated at £25.

Calculate the economic order quantity for the product.

Your answer to this activity should be as follows:

$$EOQ = \sqrt{\frac{2 \times 2,000 \times 25}{4}}$$

$$= 158 \text{ units (to the nearest whole number)}$$

This will mean that the business will have to order Product X about 13 times each year in order to meet sales demand.

The basic EOQ model has a number of limiting assumptions. In particular, it assumes that demand for the product can be predicted with accuracy, and that this demand is even over the period and does not fluctuate through seasonality or other reasons. It also assumes that no 'buffer' stock is required. However, these limiting assumptions do not mean we should dismiss the model as being of little value. The model can be developed to accommodate the problems of uncertainty and uneven demand. Many businesses use this model (or a development of it) to help in the management of stocks.

Materials requirements planning (MRP) systems

A **materials requirement planning (MRP) system** takes as its starting point forecasts of sales demand. It then uses computer technology to help schedule the timing of deliveries of bought-in parts and materials to coincide with production requirements to meet the demand. It is a co-ordinated approach that links material and parts deliveries to their scheduled input to the production process. By ordering only those items that are necessary to ensure the flow of production, stock levels may therefore be reduced. MRP is really a 'top-down' approach to stock management, which recognises that stock ordering decisions cannot be viewed as being independent from production decisions. In more recent years, this approach has been extended so as to provide a fully integrated approach to production planning, which also takes account of other manufacturing resources such as labour and machine capacity.

Just-in-time (JIT) stock management

In recent years, some manufacturing businesses have tried to eliminate the need to hold stocks by adopting **'just-in time' stock management**. This method was first used in the United States defence industry during the Second World War, but in more recent times has been widely used by Japanese businesses. The essence of this approach is, as the name suggests, to have supplies delivered to a business just in time for them to be used in the production process. By adopting this approach the stockholding problem rests with suppliers rather with than the business itself.

In order for this approach to be successful, it is important for the business to inform suppliers of their production plans and requirements in advance, and for suppliers to deliver materials of the right quality at the agreed times. Failure to do so could lead to a dislocation of production and could be very costly. Thus a close relationship is required between the business and its suppliers.

Although a business will not have to hold stocks there may be certain costs associated with this approach. As the suppliers will be required to hold stocks for the business they may try to recoup this additional cost through increased prices. The close relationship necessary between the business and its suppliers may also prevent the business from taking advantage of cheaper sources of supply if they become available.

Many people view JIT as more than simply a stock control system. The philosophy underpinning this method is concerned with eliminating waste and striving for excellence. There is an expectation that suppliers will always deliver parts on time and that there will be no defects in the parts supplied. There is also an expectation that the production process will operate at maximum efficiency. This means there will be no production breakdowns and the queuing and storage times of products manufactured will be eliminated, as only that time spent directly on processing the products is seen as adding value. While these expectations may be impossible to achieve, they do help to create a culture that is dedicated to the pursuit of excellence and quality.

Exhibit 11.2

Tesco plc is one of the leading supermarket chains in the UK. To gain an advantage in the intensely competitive market, the company has invested heavily in technology to support its JIT system and other stock management systems. Laser technology is used to improve its distribution flow and to replenish stocks quickly. As a result, Tesco plc now holds less than two weeks of stock and almost half of the goods received by suppliers are sent immediately to the stores rather than to the warehouse.

The improvement in distribution procedures has allowed stores to reduce the amount of each line of stock held which, in turn, has made it possible to increase the number of lines of stock held by each store. It has also made it possible to convert storage space at the supermarkets into selling space.

Reference: The Economist, 1995

The management of debtors

Selling goods or services on credit results in costs being incurred by a business. These costs include credit administration costs, bad debts, and opportunities forgone in using the funds for more profitable purposes. However, these costs must be weighed against the benefits of increased sales resulting from the opportunity for customers to delay payment.

Selling on credit is very widespread, and appears to be the norm outside the retail trade. When a business offers to sell its goods or services on credit, it must have clear policies concerning:

- which customers it is prepared to offer credit to
- what length of credit it is prepared to offer
- whether discounts will be offered for prompt payment
- what collection policies should be adopted.

In this section, we shall consider each of these issues.

Which customers should receive credit?

A business offering credit runs the risk of not receiving payment for goods or services supplied. Thus, care must be taken over the type of customer to whom credit facilities are offered. When considering a proposal from a customer for the supply of goods or services on credit, the business must take a number of factors into account. The following **five Cs of credit** provide a business with a useful checklist.

- *Capital.* The customer must appear to be financially sound before any credit is extended. Where the customer is a business, an examination of its accounts should be carried out. Particular regard should be given to the profitability and liquidity of the customer. In addition, any onerous financial commitments must be taken into account.
- *Capacity.* The customer must appear to have the capacity to pay amounts owing. Where possible, the payment record of the customer to date should be examined. If the customer is a business, the type of business operated and the physical resources of the business will be relevant. The value of goods that the customer wishes to buy on credit must be related to the total financial resources of the customer.
- *Collateral.* On occasions, it may be necessary to ask for some kind of security for goods supplied on credit. When this occurs, the business must be convinced that the customer is able to offer a satisfactory form of security.
- *Conditions.* The state of the industry in which the customer operates and the general economic conditions of the particular region or country may have an important influence on the ability of a customer to pay the amounts outstanding on the due date.
- *Character.* It is important for a business to make some assessment of the character of the customer. The willingness to pay will depend on the honesty and integrity of the individual with whom the business is dealing. Where the customer is a limited company this will mean assessing the characters of its directors. The business must feel satisfied that the customer will make every effort to pay any amounts owing.

Once a customer has been considered creditworthy, credit limits for the customer should be established, and procedures should be laid down to ensure that these are adhered to.

Activity 11.5

Assume you are the credit manager of a business and that a limited company approaches you with a view to buying goods on credit. What sources of information might you decide to use to help assess the financial health of the potential customer?

There are various sources of information available to a business to help assess the financial health of a customer. You may have thought of some of the following:

- *Trade references.* Some businesses ask potential customers to furnish them with references from other suppliers who have had dealings with them. This may be extremely useful, provided the references supplied are truly representative of the opinions of a customer's suppliers. There is a danger that a potential customer will attempt to be selective when furnishing details of other suppliers, in order to gain a more favourable impression than is deserved.

- *Bank references.* It is possible to ask the potential customer for a bank reference. Although banks are usually prepared to oblige, the contents of such a reference are not always very informative. If customers are in financial difficulties, the bank may be unwilling to add to their problems by supplying poor references.

- *Published accounts.* A limited company is obliged by law to file a copy of its annual accounts with the Registrar of Companies. The accounts are available for public inspection and provide a useful source of information.

- *The customer.* You may wish to interview the directors of the customer company and visit its premises in order to gain some impression about the way the customer conducts its business. Where a significant amount of credit is required, the business may ask the customer for access to internal budgets and other unpublished financial information to help assess the level of risk to be taken.

- *Credit agencies.* Specialist agencies exist to provide information that can be used to assess the creditworthiness of a potential customer. The information that a credit agency supplies may be gleaned from various sources including the accounts of the customer, court judgements, and news items relating to the customer from both published and unpublished sources.

Length of credit period

A business must determine what credit terms it is prepared to offer its customers. The length of credit offered to customers can vary significantly between businesses, and may be influenced by such factors as:

- the typical credit terms operating within the industry
- the degree of competition within the industry
- the bargaining power of particular customers
- the risk of non-payment
- the capacity of the business to offer credit
- the marketing strategy of the business.

The last point identified may require some explanation. The marketing strategy of a business may have an important influence on the length of credit allowed. For example, if a business wishes to increase its market share it may decide to liberalise its credit policy in an attempt to stimulate sales. Potential customers may be attracted by the offer of a longer period in which to pay. However, any such change in policy must take account of the likely costs and benefits arising.

To illustrate this point, consider Example 11.1.

Example 11.1

Torrance Ltd was formed in 2000 in order to produce a new type of golf putter. The company sells the putter to wholesalers and retailers and has an annual turnover of £600,000. The following data relate to each putter produced.

	£	£
Selling price		36
Variable costs	18	
Fixed cost apportionment	6	24
Net profit		12

The cost of capital (before tax) of Torrance Ltd is estimated at 15 per cent.

Torrance Ltd wishes to expand sales of this new putter, and believes this can be done by offering a longer period in which to pay. The average collection period of the company is currently 30 days. The company is considering three options in order to increase sales. These are as follows:

	Option		
	1	*2*	*3*
Increase in average collection period (days)	10	20	30
Increase in sales (£)	30,000	45,000	50,000

Prepare calculations to show which credit policy the company should offer its customers.

In order to decide on the best option to adopt, the company must weigh the benefits of each option against their respective costs. The benefits arising will be represented by the increase in profit from the sale of additional putters. From the cost data supplied we can see that the contribution (that is, sales less variable costs) is £18 per putter, 50 per cent of the selling price. The fixed costs can be ignored in our calculations as they will remain the same whichever option is chosen.

The increase in contribution under each option will therefore be:

	Option		
	1	*2*	*3*
50% of increase in sales (£)	15,000	22,500	25,000

The increase in debtors under each option will be as follows:

	Option		
	1	*2*	*3*
Planned level of debtors	£	£	£
630,000 × 40/365	69,041		
645,000 × 50/365		88,356	
650,000 × 60/365			106,849
Less: Current level of debtors			
600,000 × 30/365	49,315	49,315	49,315
	19,726	39,041	57,534

The increase in debtors that results from each option will mean an additional cost to the company, since the company has an estimated cost of capital of 15 per cent. Thus, the increase in the additional investment in debtors will be:

	Option		
	1	2	3
Cost of additional investment (15% of increase in debtors) (£)	(2,959)	(5,856)	(8,630)

The net increase in profits will be:

	Option		
	1	2	3
	£	£	£
Cost of additional investment (15% of increase in debtors)	(2,959)	(5,856)	(8,630)
Increase in contribution (see above)	15,000	22,500	25,000
Net increase in profits	12,041	16,644	16,370

The calculations show that Option 2 will be the most profitable one for the company, although there is little to choose between Options 2 and 3.

Example 9.1 illustrates the way in which a business should assess changes in credit terms. However, if there is a risk that, by extending the length of credit, there will be an increase in bad debts, this should also be taken into account in the calculations, as should any additional collection costs that will be incurred.

Cash discounts

✳ A business may decide to offer a **cash discount** in an attempt to encourage prompt payment from its credit customers. The size of any discount will be an important influence on whether a customer decides to pay promptly.

From the point of view of the business, the cost of offering discounts must be weighed against the likely benefits in the form of a reduction in the cost of financing debtors and any reduction in the amount of bad debts.

In practice, there is always the danger that a customer may be slow to pay and yet may still take the discount offered. Where the customer is important to the business it may be difficult for the business to insist on full payment.

Surveys indicate that small businesses have a much greater proportion of overdue debts than large businesses. The government has intervened to help deal with this problem and the law now permits small businesses to charge interest on overdue accounts. However, it is unlikely that legislation alone will make a significant improvement. Many small businesses are concerned that charging interest would be viewed by large customers as a provocative act. What is really needed to help small businesses is a change in the payment culture.

Self-assessment question 11.2

Williams Wholesalers Ltd at present requires payment from its customers by the month end after month of delivery. On average it takes them 70 days to pay. Sales amount to £4 million per year and bad debts to £20,000 per year.

It is planned to offer customers a cash discount of 2 per cent for payment within 30 days. Williams estimates that 50 per cent of customers will accept this facility but that the remaining customers, who tend to be slow payers, will not pay until 80 days after the sale. At present the company has a partly used overdraft facility costing 13 per cent per annum. If the plan goes ahead, bad debts will be reduced to £10,000 per annum and there will be savings in credit administration expenses of £6,000 per annum.

Should Williams Wholesalers Ltd offer the new credit terms to customers? You should support your answer with any calculations and explanations that you consider necessary.

Collection policies

A business offering credit must ensure that amounts owing are collected as quickly as possible. An efficient collection policy requires an efficient accounting system. Invoices must be sent out promptly along with regular monthly statements. Reminders must also be dispatched promptly where necessary.

When a business is faced with customers who do not pay, there should be agreed procedures for dealing with them. However, the cost of any action to be taken against delinquent debtors must be weighed against the likely returns. For example, there is little point in pursuing a customer through the courts and incurring large legal expenses if there is evidence that the customer does not have the necessary resources to pay. Where possible, the cost of bad debts should be taken into account when pricing products or services.

Management can monitor the effectiveness of collection policies in a number of ways. One method is to calculate the **average settlement period for debtors** ratio, which we dealt with in Chapter 6. This ratio, you may recall, is calculated as follows:

$$\text{Average settlement period for debtors} = \frac{\text{Trade debtors}}{\text{Credit sales}} \times 365$$

Although this ratio can be useful, it is important to remember that it produces an *average* figure for the number of days for which debts are outstanding. This average may be badly distorted by a few large customers who are also very slow payers.

A more detailed and informative approach to monitoring debtors is to produce an **ageing schedule of debtors**. Debts are divided into categories according to the length of time the debt has been outstanding. An ageing schedule can be produced for managers, on a regular basis, to help them see the pattern of outstanding debts. An example of an ageing schedule is set out in Example 11.2.

Example 11.2

Ageing schedule of debtors at 31 December 2001

Days outstanding

Customer	1 to 30 days	31 to 60 days	61 to 90 days	more than 90 days	Total
	£	£	£	£	£
A Ltd	20,000	10,000	–	–	30,000
B Ltd	–	24,000	–	–	24,000
C Ltd	12,000	13,000	14,000	18,000	57,000
Total	32,000	47,000	14,000	18,000	111,000

This shows a business trade debtor figure at 31 December 2001, which totals £111,000. Each customer's balance is analysed according to how long the debt has been outstanding.

Thus we can see from the schedule that A Ltd has £20,000 outstanding for 30 days or less (that is, arising from sales during December 2001) and £10,000 outstanding for between 31 and 60 days (arising from November 2001 sales). This information can be very useful for credit control purposes.

Many accounting software packages now include this ageing schedule as one of the routine reports available to managers. Such packages often have the facility to put customers on 'hold' when they reach their credit limits.

A slightly different approach to exercising control over debtors is to identify the pattern of receipts from credit sales that occur on a monthly basis. This involves monitoring the percentage of trade debtors that pay (and the percentage of debts that remain unpaid) in the month of sale and the percentage of debtors who pay in subsequent months. To do this, credit sales for each month must be examined separately. To illustrate how a pattern of credit sales receipts is produced, consider a business that has budgeted credit sales of £250,000 in June and plans to receive 30 per cent of the amount owing in the same month, 40 per cent in July, 20 per cent in August and 10 per cent in September. The budgeted pattern of credit sales receipts and amounts owing is shown as Example 11.3.

 Example 11.3

Pattern of credit sales receipts

Month	Receipts from June credit sales	% received	Amount outstanding from June sales at month end	% outstanding
	£		£	
June	75,000	30	175,000	70
July	100,000	40	75,000	30
August	50,000	20	25,000	10
September	25,000	10	–	–

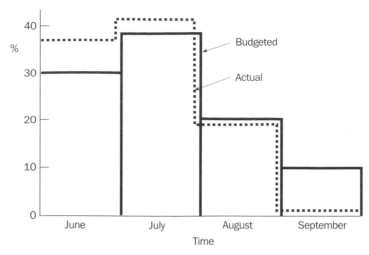

The areas bounded by the solid lines represent the planned percentages of the June sales proceeds that are received in each month. The areas bounded by broken lines represent what actually occurred regarding the cash receipts from the June sales.

Figure 11.5 Pattern of budgeted and actual cash receipts for June sales

The information shown in Example 11.3 can be used as a basis for control. The actual pattern of receipts can be compared with the expected (budgeted) pattern of receipts in order to see if there was any significant deviation (see Figure 11.5). If this comparison shows that debtors are paying more slowly than expected, management may decide to take corrective action.

Activity 11.6

What kind of corrective action might the managers of a business decide to take if they found that debtors were paying more slowly than anticipated?

Managers might decide to do one or more of the following:

- Offer cash discounts to encourage prompt payment.
- Change the collection period.
- Improve the accounting system to ensure that customers are billed more promptly, reminders are sent out promptly, and so on.
- Change the eligibility criteria for customers who receive credit.

The management of cash

Why hold cash?

Most businesses will hold a certain amount of cash as part of the total assets held. The amount of cash held, however, may vary considerably between businesses.

Activity 11.7

Why do you think a business may decide to hold at least some of its assets in the form of cash?

According to economic theory there are three motives for holding cash. These may be identified as follows:

- *Transactionary motive.* In order to meet day-to-day commitments, a business requires a certain amount of cash. Payments in respect of wages, overhead expenses, goods purchased and so on must be made at the due dates. Cash has been described as the 'life blood' of a business. Unless it 'circulates' through the business and is available for the payment of maturing obligations, the survival of the business will be put at risk. We saw earlier in the book, including in Chapter 5, that profitability alone is not enough. A business must have sufficient cash to pay its debts when they fall due.
- *Precautionary motive.* If future cash flows are uncertain for any reason it would be prudent to hold a balance of cash. For example, a major customer that owes a large sum to the business may be in financial difficulties. Given this situation, the business can retain its capacity to meet its obligations by holding a cash balance. Similarly, if there is some uncertainty concerning future outlays, a cash balance will be required.
- *Speculative motive.* A business may decide to hold cash in order to be in a position to exploit profitable opportunities as and when they arise. For example, by holding cash, a business may be able to acquire a competitor business that suddenly becomes available at an attractive price. Holding cash has an opportunity cost for the business, which must be taken into account. Thus, when evaluating the potential returns from holding cash for speculative purposes, the cost of forgone investment opportunities must also be considered.

How much cash should be held?

Although cash can be held for each of the reasons identified, it may not always be necessary to hold cash for these purposes. If a business is able to borrow quickly, the amount of cash it needs to hold can be reduced. Similarly, if the business holds assets that can easily be converted to cash (for example, marketable securities such as shares in Stock Exchange listed companies, government bonds) the amount of cash held can be reduced.

The decision as to how much cash a particular business should hold is a difficult one. Different businesses will have different views on the amount of cash that it is appropriate to hold.

Activity 11.8

What do you think are the major factors that influence how much cash a business will hold? See if you can think of five possible factors.

Factors that influence the decision as to how much cash will be held are varied, and may include:

- *The nature of the business.* Some businesses such as utilities (water companies, electricity companies, gas companies and so on) may have cash flows that are both predictable and reasonably certain. This will enable them to hold lower cash balances. For some businesses, cash balances may vary greatly according to the time of year. A seasonal business may accumulate cash during the high season to enable it to meet commitments during the low season.
- *The opportunity cost of holding cash.* Where there are profitable opportunities it may not be wise to hold a large cash balance.
- *The level of inflation.* The holding of cash during a period of rising prices will lead to a loss of purchasing power. The higher the level of inflation the greater will be this loss.
- *The availability of near-liquid assets.* If a business has marketable securities or stocks that may easily be liquidated the amount of cash held may be reduced.
- *The availability of borrowing.* If a business can borrow easily (and quickly) there is less need to hold cash.
- *The cost of borrowing.* When interest rates are high the option of borrowing becomes less attractive.
- *Economic conditions.* When the economy is in recession businesses may prefer to hold on to cash in order to be well placed to invest when the economy improves. In addition, during a recession, businesses may experience difficulties in collecting debts. They may therefore hold higher cash balances than usual in order to meet commitments.
- *Relationships with suppliers.* Too little cash may hinder the ability of the business to pay suppliers promptly. This can lead to a loss of goodwill. It may also lead to discounts being forgone.

Controlling the cash balance

A number of models have been proposed to help control the cash balance of the business. One model that has been developed proposes the use of upper and lower control limits for cash balances and the use of a target cash balance. The model assumes that the business will invest in marketable investments that can easily be liquidated. These investments will be purchased or sold, as necessary, in order to keep the cash balance within the control limits.

The model proposes two upper and two lower control limits (see Figure 11.6). If the business finds that it has exceeded an *outer* limit, the managers must decide whether or not the cash balance is likely to return to a point within the *inner* control limits set over the next few days. If this seems likely, then no action is required. If, on the other hand, it does not seem likely, management must change the cash position of the business by either buying or selling marketable securities.

In Figure 11.6 we can see that the lower outer control limit has been breached for four days. If a four-day period is unacceptable, managers must sell marketable securities in order to replenish the cash balance.

The model relies heavily on management judgement to determine where the control limits are set and the time period within which breaches of the

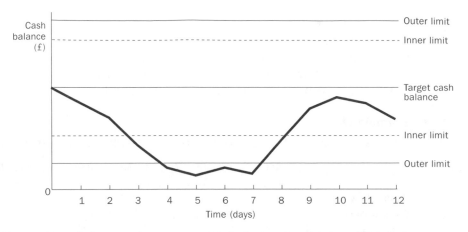

Upper and lower limits are set by management for the business's cash balance. When the balance goes beyond either the upper or lower limits, unless it is clear that the balance will return fairly quickly to within the upper or lower limit respectively, action will need to be taken. If the upper limit is breached, some cash will be used to buy some marketable securities. If the lower limit is breached, the business will need to sell some securities or borrow some cash.

Figure 11.6 Controlling the cash balance

control limits are acceptable. Past experience may be useful in helping managers decide on these issues. There are other models, however, that do not rely on management judgement and which, instead, use quantitative techniques to determine an optimal cash policy.

Cash budgets and the management of cash

To manage cash effectively, it is useful for a business to prepare a cash budget. This is a very important tool for both planning and control purposes. Cash budgets were considered in Chapter 9, and it is therefore not necessary to consider them again in detail. However, it is worth repeating the point that these statements enable the managers of a business to see the expected outcome of planned events on the cash balance. The cash budget will identify periods when there are expected to be cash surpluses and when there are cash deficits expected.

When a cash surplus is expected to arise, managers must decide on the best use of the surplus funds. When a cash deficit is expected to arise, managers must make adequate provision by borrowing, liquidating assets or rescheduling cash payments/receipts to deal with this. Cash budgets are also useful in helping to control the cash held. The actual cash flows can be compared with the budgeted cash flows for the period. If there is a significant divergence between the budgeted cash flows and the actual cash flows, explanations must be sought and corrective action taken where necessary.

To refresh your memory, an example of a cash budget is given below. Remember there is no set format for this statement. Managers can determine how best the information is presented to them. However, the format set out below appears to be in widespread use. Cash budgets covering the short term are usually broken down into monthly periods in order to allow a close monitoring of cash movements. In addition, cash inflows are usually shown above cash outflows, and the difference between these (that is, the net cash flow) for a month is separately identified along with the closing cash balance.

Example 11.4

The cash budget for the six months to 30 November 2002 is as follows:

	June £	July £	August £	September f.	October £	November £
Cash inflows						
Credit sales	–	–	4,000	5,500	7,000	8,500
Cash sales	4,000	5,500	7,000	8,500	11,000	11,000
	4,000	5,500	11,000	14,000	18,000	19,500
Cash outflows						
Motor vehicles	6,000					
Equipment	10,000					7,000
Freehold premises	40,000					
Purchases	–	29,000	9,250	11,500	13,750	17,700
Wages/salaries	900	900	900	900	900	900
Commission	–	320	440	560	680	680
Overheads	500	500	500	500	650	650
	57,400	30,720	11,090	13,460	15,980	26,930
Net cash flow	(53,400)	(25,220)	(90)	540	2,020	(7,430)
Opening balance	60,000	6,600	(18,620)	(18,710)	(18,170)	(16,150)
Closing balance	6,600	(18,620)	(18,710)	(18,170)	(16,150)	(23,580)

Although cash budgets are prepared primarily for internal management purposes, they are sometimes required by prospective lenders when a loan to a business is being considered.

Operating cash cycle

✳ When managing cash, it is important to be aware of the **operating cash cycle** of the business. This may be defined as the time period between the outlay of cash necessary for the purchase of stocks and the ultimate receipt of cash from the sale of the goods. In the case of a business that purchases goods on credit for subsequent resale on credit, the operating cash cycle can be shown in diagrammatic form, as shown in Figure 11.7.

Figure 11.7 shows that payment for goods acquired on credit occurs some time after the goods have been purchased, and therefore no immediate cash outflow arises from the purchase. Similarly, cash receipts from debtors will occur some time after the sale is made, and so there will be no immediate cash inflow as a result of the sale. The operating cash cycle is the time period between the payment made to the creditor for goods supplied and the cash received from the debtor.

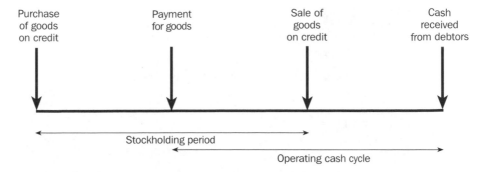

Purchase of goods on credit   Payment for goods   Sale of goods on credit   Cash received from debtors

Stockholding period

Operating cash cycle

The operating cash cycle is the time lapse between paying for goods and receiving the cash from the sale of those goods. The length of the operating cash cycle has a significant impact on the amount of funds that the business needs to apply to working capital.

Figure 11.7 The operating cash cycle

The operating cash cycle is important because it has a significant influence on the financing requirements of the business: the longer the cash cycle the greater the financing requirements of the business and the greater the financial risks. For this reason, a business is likely to want to reduce the operating cash cycle to the minimum possible.

For the type of business mentioned above, which buys and sells on credit, the operating cash cycle can be calculated from the financial statements by the use of certain ratios. The cash cycle is calculated as shown in Figure 11.8.

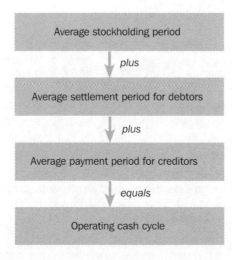

Average stockholding period

plus

Average settlement period for debtors

plus

Average payment period for creditors

equals

Operating cash cycle

Figure 11.8 Calculating the operating cash cycle

Activity 11.9

The accounts of Freezeqwik Ltd, a distributor of frozen foods, are set out below for the year ended 31 December 2000:

Profit and loss account for the year ended 31 December 2000

	£000	£000
Sales		820
Less Cost of sales		
Opening stock	142	
Purchases	568	
	710	
Less Closing stock	166	544
Gross profit		276
Administration expenses	120	
Selling and distribution expenses	95	
Financial expenses	32	247
Net profit		29
Corporation tax		7
Net profit after tax		22

Balance sheet as at 31 December 2000

	£000	£000	£000
Fixed assets			
Freehold premises at valuation			180
Fixture and fittings at written-down value			82
Motor vans at written-down value			102
			364
Current assets			
Stock		166	
Trade debtors		264	
Cash		24	
		454	
Less **Creditors: amounts falling due within one year**			
Trade creditors	159		
Corporation tax	7	166	288
			652
Capital and reserves			
Ordinary share capital			300
Preference share capital			200
Retained profit			152
			652

All purchases and sales are on credit.

Required:

(a) Calculate the operating cash cycle for the company.

(b) Suggest how the company may seek to reduce the cash cycle.

The operating cash cycle may be calculated as follows:

	No. of days

Average stockholding period:

$$\frac{(\text{Opening stock + Closing stock})/2}{\text{Cost of sales}} = \frac{(142 + 166)/2}{544} \times 365 \qquad \qquad 103$$

Average settlement period for debtors:

$$\frac{\text{Trade debtors}}{\text{Credit sales}} \times 365 = \frac{264}{820} \times 365 \qquad \qquad \frac{118}{221}$$

Less

Average settlement period for creditors:.

$$\frac{\text{Trade creditors}}{\text{Credit purchases}} \times 365 = \frac{159}{568} \times 365 \qquad \qquad \underline{102}$$

Operating cash cycle $\qquad \qquad \underline{119}$

The company can reduce the operating cash cycle in a number of ways. The average stockholding period seems quite long. At present, average stocks held represent more than three months' sales. This may be reduced by reducing the level of stocks held. Similarly, the average settlement period for debtors seems long, at nearly four months' sales. This may be reduced by imposing tighter credit control, offering discounts, charging interest on overdue accounts, and so on. However, any policy decisions concerning stocks and debtors must take account of current trading conditions.

The operating cash cycle could also be reduced by extending the period of credit taken to pay suppliers. However, for reasons mentioned below, this option must be given careful consideration.

Cash transmission

A business will normally wish to receive the benefits from providing goods or services at the earliest opportunity. The benefit received is immediate where payment is made in cash. However, when payment is made by cheque there is normally a delay of three to four working days before the cheque can be cleared through the banking system. The business must therefore wait for this period before it can benefit from the amount paid in. In the case of a business that receives large amounts in the form of cheques, the opportunity cost of this delay can be very significant.

To avoid this delay, a business could require payments to be made in cash. However, this is not usually very practical, for a number of reasons. Another option is to ask for payment to be made by standing order or by direct debit from the customer's bank account. This will ensure that the amount owing is transferred from the bank account of the customer to the bank account of the business on the day that has been agreed.

It is also possible now for funds to be transferred directly to a business bank account. As a result of developments in computer technology, a customer can pay for items by using a card (rather like a cheque card) that results in his/her/ its account being instantly debited and the business bank account being instantly credited with the required amount. This method of payment is now widely used by large retail businesses, and may well extend to other forms of business.

The management of trade creditors

Trade credit is regarded as an important source of finance by many businesses. It has been described as a 'spontaneous' source of finance, as it tends to increase in line with the increase in the level of sales achieved by a business. Trade credit is widely regarded as a 'free' source of finance and therefore a good thing for a business to use. However, there may be real costs associated with taking trade credit.

Customers who pay on credit may not be as well favoured as those who pay immediately. For example, when goods are in short supply, credit customers may receive lower priority when allocating the stock available. In addition, credit customers may be given lower priority in terms of delivery dates or the provision of technical support services. Sometimes, the goods or services provided may be more costly if credit is required. However, in most industries trade credit is the norm and, as a result, the above costs will not apply unless, perhaps, the credit facilities are abused by the customer. A business purchasing supplies on credit may also have to incur additional administration and accounting costs dealing with the scrutiny and payment of invoices, the maintaining and updating of creditors accounts, and so on.

Where a supplier offers a discount for prompt payment, a business should give careful consideration to the possibility of paying within the discount period. An example may be useful to illustrate the cost of forgoing possible discounts.

Example 11.3

Simat Ltd takes 70 days to pay for goods supplied by its supplier. To encourage prompt payment the supplier has offered the company a 2 per cent discount if payment for goods is made within 30 days.

Simat Ltd is not sure whether it is worth taking the discount offered. What is the annual percentage cost to Simat Ltd of forgoing the discount?

If the discount is taken, payment could be made on the last day of the discount period (that is, the 30th day). However, if the discount is not taken, payment will be made after 70 days. This means that by not taking the discount Simat Ltd will receive an extra 40 days' (that is, 70 − 30) credit. The cost of this extra credit to the company will be the 2 per cent discount forgone. If we annualise the cost of this discount forgone, we have:

$$365/40 \times 2\% = 18.3\%*$$

We can see that the annual cost of forgoing the discount is quite high, and it may be profitable for the company to pay the supplier within the discount period, even if it means that it will have to borrow to enable it to do so.

The above points are not meant to imply that taking credit is a burden to a business. There are of course real benefits that can accrue. Provided that trade credit is not abused by a business, it can represent a form of interest-free loan. It can be a much more convenient method of paying for goods and services than paying by cash, and during a period of inflation there will be an economic gain by paying later rather than sooner for goods and services purchased. For many businesses, these benefits will exceed the costs involved.

Controlling trade creditors

In order to monitor the level of trade credit taken, management can calculate the **average settlement period for creditors**. You may recall from Chapter 6 that this ratio was as follows:

$$\text{Average settlement period} = \frac{\text{Trade creditors}}{\text{Credit purchases}} \times 365$$

Once again this provides an average figure, which can be distorted. A more informative approach would be to produce an ageing schedule for creditors. This would look much the same as the ageing schedule for debtors described earlier.

SUMMARY

In this chapter we have identified and examined the main elements of working capital. We have seen that the management of working capital requires an evaluation of both the costs and benefits associated with each element. Some of these costs and benefits may be hard to quantify in practice. Nevertheless, some assessment must be made in order to try and optimise the use of funds within a business. We have examined various techniques for the management of working capital. These techniques vary in their level of sophistication: some rely heavily on management judgement, while others adopt a more objective, quantitative approach.

---

*This is an approximate annual rate. For the more mathematically minded, the precise rate is:

$$(((1 + 2/98)^{9.125}) - 1) \times 100\% = 20.2\%.$$

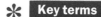

Key terms

working capital *p 299*
ABC system of stock control *p 305*
economic order quantity (EOQ)
  p 306
materials requirement planning
  (MRP) system *p 308*
just-in-time (JIT) stock
  management *p 308*

five Cs of credit *p 310*
cash discount *p 313*
average settlement period for
  debtors *p 314*
ageing schedule of debtors *p 314*
operating cash cycle *p 320*
average settlement period for
  creditors *p 325*

REVIEW QUESTIONS

11.1 Tariq is the credit manager of Heltex plc. He is concerned that the pattern of monthly sales receipts shows that credit collection is poor compared with budget. Heltex's sales director believes that Tariq is to blame for this situation, but Tariq insists that he is not. Why might Tariq not be to blame for the deterioration in the credit collection period?

11.2 How might each of the following affect the level of stocks held by a business?

- an increase in the number of production bottlenecks experienced by the business
- a rise in the level of interest rates
- a decision to offer customers a narrower range of products in the future
- a switch of suppliers from an overseas business to a local business
- a deterioration in the quality and reliability of bought-in components.

11.3 What are the reasons for holding stocks? Are these reasons different from the reasons for holding cash?

11.4 Identify the costs of holding:
(a) too little cash, and
(b) too much cash.

EXAMINATION-STYLE QUESTIONS

Questions 11.4 and 11.5 are more advanced than 11.1–11.3. Those with a coloured number have an answer at the back of the book.

11.1 Hercules Wholesalers Ltd has been particularly concerned with its liquidity position in recent months. The most recent profit and loss account and balance sheet of the company are as follows:

Profit and loss account for the year ended 31 May 2001

	£	£
Sales		452,000
Less Cost of sales		
Opening stock	125,000	
Add purchases	341,000	
	466,000	
Less Closing stock	143,000	323,000
Gross profit		129,000
Expenses		132,000
Net loss for the period		(3,000)

Balance sheet as at 31 May 2001

	£	£	£
Fixed assets			
Freehold premises at valuation			280,000
Fixtures and fittings at cost less depreciation			25,000
Motor vehicles at cost less depreciation			52,000
			357,000
Current assets			
Stock		143,000	
Debtors		163,000	
		306,000	
Less **Creditors due within one year**			
Trade creditors	145,000		
Bank overdraft	140,000	285,000	21,000
			378,000
Less **Creditors due after more than one year**			
Loans			120,000
			258,000
Capital and reserves			
Ordinary share capital			100,000
Retained profit			158,000
			258,000

The debtors and creditors were maintained at a constant level throughout the year.

Required:
(a) Explain why Hercules Wholesalers Ltd is concerned about its liquidity position.
(b) Explain the term *operating cash cycle* and state why this concept is important in the financial management of a business.
(c) Calculate the operating cash cycle for Hercules Wholesalers Ltd based on the information above. (Assume a 360-day year.)
(d) State what steps may be taken to improve the operating cash cycle of the company.

11.2 International Electric plc at present offers its customers 30 days' credit. Half the customers, by value, pay on time. The other half take an average of 70 days to pay. It is considering offering a cash discount of 2 per cent to its customers for payment within 30 days.

   It anticipates that half of the customers who now take an average of 70 days to pay will pay in 30 days. The other half will still take an average of 70 days to pay. The scheme will also reduce bad debts by £300,000 per year.

   Annual sales of £365 million are made evenly throughout the year. At present the company has a large overdraft (£60 million) with its bank at 12 per cent per annum.

Required:
(a) Calculate the approximate equivalent annual percentage cost of a discount of 2 per cent, which reduces the time taken by debtors to pay from 70 days to 30 days. (This part can be answered without reference to the narrative above.)
(b) Calculate debtors outstanding under both the old and new schemes.
(c) How much will the scheme cost the company in discounts?
(d) Should the company go ahead with the scheme? State what other factors, if any, should be taken into account.
(e) Outline the controls and procedures that a company should adopt to manage the level of its debtors.

11.3 The managing director of Sparkrite Ltd, a trading company, has just received summary sets of accounts for 1999 and 2000:

Sparkrite Ltd
Profit and loss statements for years ended 30 September 1999 and 2000

	1999 £000	1999 £000	2000 £000	2000 £000
Sales		1,800		1,920
Less Cost of sales				
Opening stock	160		200	
Purchases	1,120		1,175	
	1,280		1,375	
Less Closing stocks	200		250	
		1,080		1,125
Gross profit		720		795
Less Expenses		680		750
Net profit		40		45

Balance sheets as at 30 September 1999 and 2000

	1999		2000	
	£000	£000	£000	£000
Fixed assets		950		930
Current assets				
Stock	200		250	
Debtors	375		480	
Bank	4		2	
	579		732	
Less **Current liabilities**	195		225	
		384		507
		1,334		1,437
Financed by				
Fully paid £1 ordinary shares		825		883
Reserves		509		554
		1,334		1,437

The financial director has expressed concern at the deterioration in stock and debtors levels.

Required:
(a) Show, by using the data given, how you would calculate ratios that could be used to measure stock and debtor levels in 1999 and 2000.
(b) Discuss the ways in which the management of Sparkrite Ltd could exercise control over:
(i) stock levels
(ii) debtor levels.

11.4 Your superior, the general manager of Plastics Manufacturers Limited, has recently been talking to the chief buyer of Plastic Toys Limited, which manufactures a wide range of toys for young children. At present, it is considering changing its supplier of plastic granules and has offered to buy its entire requirement of 2,000 kg per month from you at the going market rate, provided that you will grant it 3 months' credit on its purchases. The following information is available:

1 Plastic granules sell for £10 per kg, variable costs are £7 per kg, and fixed costs £2 per kg.
2 Your own company is financially strong, and has sales of £15 million per year. For the foreseeable future it will have surplus capacity, and it is actively looking for new outlets.
3 Extracts from Plastic Toys accounts:

	1998	1999	2000
	£000	£000	£000
Sales	800	980	640
Profit before interest and tax	100	110	(150)
Capital employed	600	650	575

	1998	1999	2000
	£000	£000	£000
Current assets			
Stocks	200	220	320
Debtors	140	160	160
	340	380	480
Current liabilities			
Creditors	180	190	220
Overdraft	100	150	310
	280	340	530
Net current assets	60	40	(50)

Required:

(a) Write some short notes suggesting sources of information that you would use in order to assess the creditworthiness of potential customers who are unknown to you. You should critically evaluate each source of information.

(b) Describe the accounting controls that you would use to monitor the level of your company's trade debtors.

(c) Advise your general manager on the acceptability of the proposal. You should give your reasons and do any calculations you consider necessary.

11.5 Mayo Computers Ltd has an annual turnover of £20 million before taking into account bad debts of £0.1 million. All sales made by the company are on credit, and, at present, credit terms are negotiable by the customer. On average, the settlement period for trade debtors is 60 days. The company is currently reviewing its credit policies to see whether more efficient and profitable methods could be employed. Only one proposal has so far been put forward concerning the management of trade credit.

The credit control department has proposed that customers should be given a 2½ per cent discount if they pay within 30 days. For those who do not pay within this period, a maximum of 50 days' credit should be given. The credit department believes that 60 per cent of customers will take advantage of the discount by paying at the end of the discount period, and the remainder will pay at the end of 50 days. The credit department believes that bad debts can be effectively eliminated by adopting the above policies and by employing stricter credit investigation procedures, which will cost an additional £20,000 per annum. The credit department are confident that these new policies will not result in any reduction in sales.

Required:

Calculate the net annual cost (savings) to the company of abandoning its existing credit policies and adopting the proposals of the credit control department. (Hint: In order to answer this question you must weigh the costs of administration and cash discounts against the savings in bad debts and interest charges.)

Financing the business

INTRODUCTION

In this chapter we examine various aspects of financing the business. We begin by considering the various sources of finance available to a business and the factors to be considered in choosing an appropriate source of finance. We then go on to consider various aspects of the capital markets, including the role of the Stock Exchange, the role of venture capital organisations, and the ways in which share capital may be issued.

Objectives

On completion of this chapter you should be able to:

- identify the main forms of finance available to a business and explain the advantages and disadvantages of each form
- explain the role and nature of the Stock Exchange
- explain the role of venture capital organisations in financing businesses
- discuss the ways in which share capital may be issued.

Sources of finance

When considering the various sources of finance for a business, it is useful to distinguish between *external* sources and *internal* sources of finance and when considering the various external sources of finance, it is probably helpful to distinguish between *long-term* and *short-term* sources. In the sections that follow, we consider the various sources of external finance under each of the above headings. We then go on to consider the various sources of internal finance available.

Figure 12.1 summarises the main sources of long-term and short-term external finance. By external sources we mean sources that require the agreement of someone beyond the directors and managers of the business. Thus, finance from an issue of new shares is an external source because it

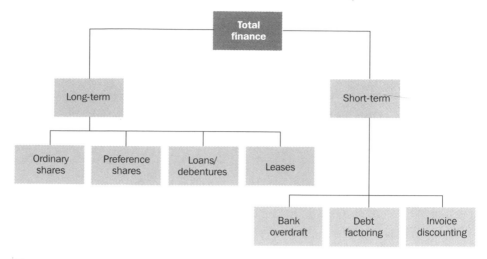

Figure 12.1 Major sources of external finance

requires the compliance of potential shareholders. Retained profit, on the other hand, is considered an internal source because the directors of the business have power to retain profits without the agreement of the shareholders whose profits they are.

Long-term sources of external finance

For the purpose of this chapter, long-term sources of finance are defined as sources of finance that are not due for repayment within one year. Figure 12.1 reveals that major forms of long-term external finance are:

- ordinary shares
- preference shares
- loans
- leases, that is, finance leases and sale-and-lease-back arrangements.

In order to decide on the most appropriate form of external finance, we must be clear about the advantages and disadvantages of each.

Ordinary shares

Ordinary shares form the backbone of the financial structure of a company. Ordinary share capital represents the risk capital of a company. There is no fixed rate of dividend, and ordinary shareholders will receive a dividend only if profits available for distribution still remain after other investors (preference shareholders and lenders) have received their interest or dividend payments. If the company is wound up, the ordinary shareholders will receive any proceeds from asset disposals only after lenders and creditors and, often, after preference shareholders have received their entitlements. Because of the high risks associated with this form of investment, ordinary shareholders will normally require a comparatively high rate of return from the company.

Although ordinary shareholders have limited loss liability, based on the amount that they have agreed to invest, the potential returns from their investment are unlimited. Ordinary shareholders will also have control over the company. They will be given voting rights, which will give them the power to elect the directors and to remove the directors from office.

From the company perspective, ordinary shares can be a valuable form of financing as, at times, it is useful to be able to avoid paying a dividend. In the case of a new expanding company, or a company in difficulties, the requirement to make a cash payment to investors can be a real burden. Where the company is financed by ordinary shares, this problem need not occur. However, the costs of financing ordinary shares may be high over the longer term, for the reasons mentioned earlier. Moreover, the company does not obtain any tax relief on dividends paid to shareholders, whereas interest on borrowings is tax deductible.

Preference shares

Preference shares offer investors a lower level of risk than ordinary shares. Provided there are sufficient profits available, preference shares will normally be given a fixed rate of dividend each year, and preference dividends will be paid before ordinary dividends are paid. Where the company is wound up, preference shareholders may be given priority over the claims of ordinary shareholders. (The documents of incorporation will determine the precise rights of preference shareholders in this respect.) Because of the lower level of risk associated with this form of investment, investors will be offered a lower level of return than that normally expected by ordinary shareholders.

There are various types of preference shares that may be issued by a company. *Cumulative* preference shares give investors the right to receive arrears of dividends that have arisen as a result of the company having insufficient profits in previous periods. The unpaid dividends will accumulate and will be paid when the company has generated sufficient profits. *Non-cumulative* preference shares do not give investors the right to receive arrears of dividends. Thus, if a company is not in a position to pay the preference dividend due for a particular period, the preference shareholder loses the right to receive the dividend. *Participating* preference shares give investors the right to a further share in the profits available for dividend after they have been paid the fixed rate due on the preference shares and after ordinary shareholders have been awarded a dividend. *Redeemable* preference shares allow the company to buy back the shares from shareholders at some agreed future date. Redeemable preference shares are seen as a lower-risk investment than non-redeemable shares, and so carry a lower dividend. A company can also issue redeemable ordinary shares, but these are rare, in practice.

Activity 12.1

Would you expect the market price of ordinary shares or preference shares to be the more volatile? Why?

The dividends of preference shares tend to be fairly stable over time, and there is usually an upper limit on the returns that can be received. As a result, the share price, which reflects the expected future returns from the share, will normally be less volatile than for ordinary shares.

Preference shares are no longer an important source of new finance for companies. A major reason why this particular form of fixed-return capital has declined in popularity is that dividends paid to preference shareholders are not allowable against taxable profits, whereas interest on loan capital is an allowable expense. From the company's point of view preference shares and loans are quite similar, so the tax deductibility of loan interest is an important issue.

Loan and debentures

Many companies rely on loan capital, as well as share capital, to finance operations. Lenders will enter into a contract with the company in which the rate of interest, dates of interest payments and capital repayments and security for the loan are clearly stated. In the event that the interest payments or capital repayments in respect of the loan are not made on the due dates, the lender will usually have the right, under the terms of the contract, to seize the assets on which the loan is secured and sell them in order to repay the amount outstanding. Security for a loan may take the form of a fixed charge on particular assets of the company (freehold land and premises is often favoured by lenders) or a floating charge on the whole of the company's assets. A floating charge will 'crystallise' and fix on particular assets in the event that the company defaults on its obligations.

Activity 12.2

What do you think is the advantage for the company of having a floating charge rather than a fixed charge on its assets?

A floating charge on assets will allow the managers of the company greater flexibility in their day-to-day operations than a fixed charge. Assets can be traded without reference to the lenders.

Investors will normally view loans as being less risky than preference shares or ordinary shares. Lenders have priority over any claims from shareholders, and will usually have security for their loans. As a result of the lower level of risk associated with this form of investment, investors are usually prepared to accept a lower rate of return.

One form of long-term loan associated with limited companies is the *debenture*. This is simply a loan that is evidenced by a trust deed. The debenture loan is frequently divided into units (rather like share capital), and investors are invited to purchase the number of units they require. The debenture loan may be redeemable or irredeemable. Debentures of public limited companies are often traded on the Stock Exchange, and their listed value will fluctuate according to the fortunes of the company, movements in interest rates, and so on.

Another form of long-term loan finance is the *eurobond*. Eurobonds are issued by listed companies (and other large organisations) in various countries, and the finance is raised on an international basis. They are bearer bonds, which are often issued in US dollars but which may also be issued in other major currencies. Interest is normally paid on an annual basis. Eurobonds are part of an emerging international capital market, and they are not subject to regulations imposed by authorities in particular countries. There is a secondary market for eurobonds that has been created by a number of financial institutions throughout the world. Here holders of eurobonds are able to sell them to would-be holders. The issue of eurobonds is usually made by placing them with large banks and other financial institutions, who may either retain them as an investment or sell them to their clients.

The extent of borrowing, by UK companies, in currencies other than sterling has expanded massively in recent years. In 1991 only 7 per cent of borrowings by UK Stock Exchange listed companies was in non-sterling currencies. This increased at a fairly steady rate, such that in both 1997 and 1998 the proportion was over 50 per cent.

Activity 12.3

Why might a company prefer to issue eurobonds in preference to more conventional forms of loan capital?

Companies are often attracted to eurobonds because of the size of the international capital market. Access to a large number of international investors is likely to increase the chances of a successful issue. In addition, the lack of regulation in the eurobond market means that national restrictions regarding loan issues may be overcome.

Interest rates on loan finance may be either floating or fixed. A floating rate means that the required rate of return from lenders will rise and fall with market rates of interest. However, the market value of the lender's investment in the business is likely to remain fairly stable over time. The converse will normally be true for fixed-interest loans and debentures. The interest payments will remain unchanged with rises and falls in market rates of interest, but the value of the loan investment will fall when interest rates rise and will rise when interest rates fall.

A company may issue redeemable loan capital that offers a rate of interest below the market rate. In some cases, the loan capital may have a zero rate of interest. Such loans are issued at a discount to their redeemable value and are referred to as *deep discount bonds*. Thus a company may issue loan capital at (say) £80 for every £100 of nominal value. Although lenders will receive little or no interest during the period of the loan, they will receive a gain when the loan is finally redeemed. The redemption yield, as it is referred to, is often quite high and, when calculated on an annual basis, may compare favourably with returns from other forms of loan capital with the same level of risk. Deep discount bonds may have particular appeal to companies with short-term cash flow problems. They receive an immediate injection of cash, and there are no significant cash outflows associated with the loan until the maturity date. Deep discount bonds are likely to appeal to investors who do not have short-term cash flow problems, as they must wait for the loan to mature before receiving a significant return.

Convertible loan stocks and debentures

Convertible loan stocks or debentures give investors the right to convert the loan into ordinary shares at a given future date and at a specified price. The investor remains a lender to the company, and will receive interest on the amount of the loan until such time as the conversion takes place. The investor is not obliged to convert the loan or debenture to ordinary shares. This will be done only if the market price of the shares at the conversion date exceeds the agreed conversion price.

An investor may find this form of investment a useful hedge against risk. This may be particularly useful when investment in a new company is being considered. Initially the investment is in the form of a loan, and regular interest payments will be made. If the company is successful the investor can then decide to convert the investment into ordinary shares.

The company may also find this form of financing useful. If the company is successful the loan becomes self-liquidating, as investors will exercise their option to convert. The company may also be able to offer a lower rate of interest to investors because investors expect future benefits arising from conversion. However, there will be some dilution of both control and earnings for existing shareholders if holders of convertible loans exercise their option to convert.

Figure 12.2 plots the issues of capital made by UK-listed companies in recent years. The chart reveals that loan capital and ordinary shares are the major sources of long-term external finance. Preference shares are a much less important source of new finance.

Warrants

Holders of **warrants** have the right, but not the obligation, to acquire ordinary shares in a company at a given price. In the case of both convertible loan capital and warrants, the price at which shares may be acquired is usually higher than the market price prevailing at the time of issue. The warrant will usually state the number of shares that the holder may purchase and the time limit within which the option to buy shares can be exercised. Occasionally, perpetual warrants are

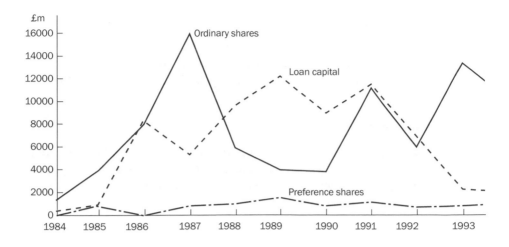

£m

The popularity of ordinary shares and that of loan capital seem broadly to move counter to one another. When ordinary shares are popular loan capital is unpopular, and vice versa. This tends to reflect the level of interest rates and business confidence. Preference shares have dwindled to virtually nothing, in terms of new issues.

Figure 12.2 Capital issues of UK-listed companies, 1984–93

Source: Constructed with data from Annual Abstract of Statistics 1999

issued that have no set time limits. Warrants do not confer voting rights or entitle the holders to make any claims on the assets of the company.

Share warrants are often provided as a 'sweetener' to accompany the issue of loan capital or debentures. The issue of warrants in this way may enable the company to offer lower rates of interest on the loan or to negotiate less restrictive loan conditions. The issue of warrants enables the lenders to benefit from future company success, provided the option to purchase is exercised. However, an investor will exercise this option only if the market price exceeds the option price within the time limit specified. Share warrants may be *detachable*, which means that they can be sold separately from the loan capital.

Activity 12.4

What will be the difference in status within a company between holders of convertible loan capital and holders of loans with share warrants attached if both groups decide to exercise their right to convert?

The main difference will be that when holders of convertible loan capital exercise their option to convert, they become ordinary shareholders and are no longer lenders of the company. However, when lenders with warrants exercise their option to convert, they become both ordinary shareholders and lenders of the company.

When convertible loan capital holders exercise their option to convert, they swap their loan for shares. When warrant holders exercise their right to buy shares, they pay cash for those shares.

Mortgages

✳ A **mortgage** is a form of loan that is secured on freehold property. Financial institutions such as banks, insurance companies and pension funds are often prepared to lend to businesses on this basis. The mortgage may be over a long period.

Loan covenants

✳ When drawing up a loan agreement, the lender may impose certain obligations and restrictions in order to protect the investment in the business. **Loan covenants** (as they are referred to) often form part of a loan agreement, and may deal with such matters as:

- *Accounts.* The lender may require access to the financial accounts of the business on a regular basis.
- *Other loans.* The lender may require the business to ask the lender's permission before taking on further loans from other sources.
- *Dividend payments.* The lender may require dividends to be limited during the period of the loan.
- *Liquidity.* The lender may require the business to maintain a certain level of liquidity during the period of the loan. This would typically be a requirement that the borrower business's current ratio was maintained at, or above, a specified level.

Any breach of these restrictive covenants can have serious consequences for the business. The lender may require immediate repayment of the loan in the event of a serious breach.

Activity 12.5

Both preference shares and loan capital are forms of finance that require the company to provide a particular rate of return to investors. What are the factors that may be taken into account by a company when deciding between these two sources of finance?

The main factors are as follows:

- Preference shares have a higher rate of return than loan capital. From the investor's point of view, preference shares are more risky. The amount invested cannot be secured, and the return is paid after the returns paid to lenders.
- A company has a legal obligation to pay interest and make capital repayments on loans at the agreed dates. A company will usually make every effort to meet its obligations, as failure to do so can have serious consequences. (These consequences have been mentioned earlier.) Failure to pay a preference dividend, on the other hand, is less important. There is no legal obligation to pay a preference dividend if profits are not available for distribution. Although failure to pay a preference dividend may prove an embarrassment for the company, and may make it difficult for the company to persuade investors to take up future preference share issues, the preference

A further point that has not been dealt with so far is that preference shares issued form part of the permanent capital base of the company. If they are redeemed at some future date, the law requires that they are replaced, either by a new issue of shares or by a transfer from reserves, in order to ensure that the capital base of the company stays intact. However, loan capital is not viewed, in law, as part of the permanent capital base of the company, and therefore there is no requirement to replace any loan capital that has been redeemed by the company.

Finance leases and sale and leaseback arrangements

When a business needs a particular asset (for example an item of plant), instead of buying it direct from a supplier, the business may decide to arrange for a financial institution, such as a bank, to buy the asset and then agree to lease the asset from the institution. A **finance lease** is, in essence, a form of lending. Although legal ownership of the asset rests with the financial institution (the lessor), a finance lease agreement transfers to the business (the lessee) virtually all the rewards and risks that are associated with the item being leased. The lease agreement covers a significant part of the life of the item being leased, and often cannot be cancelled.

In recent years, some important benefits associated with finance leasing have disappeared. Changes in tax law no longer make it such a tax-efficient form of financing, and changes in accounting disclosure requirements make it no longer possible to conceal this form of 'borrowing' from investors. Nevertheless, the popularity of finance leases has continued to increase. Other reasons must therefore exist for businesses to adopt this form of financing. These reasons are said to include the following:

- *Ease of borrowing*. Leasing may be obtained more easily than other forms of long-term finance. Lenders normally require some form of security and a profitable track record before making advances to a business. However, a lessor may be prepared to lease assets to a new business without a track record, and to use the leased assets as security for the amounts owing.

- *Cost.* Leasing agreements may be offered at reasonable cost. As the asset leased is used as security, standard lease arrangements can be applied and detailed credit checking of lessees may be unnecessary. This can reduce administration costs for the lessor, and thereby help in providing competitive lease rentals.
- *Flexibility.* Leasing can help provide flexibility where there are rapid changes in technology. If an option to cancel can be incorporated into the lease, the business may be able to exercise this option and invest in new technology as it becomes available. This will help the business avoid the risk of obsolescence.
- *Cash flows.* Leasing, rather than purchasing an asset outright, means that large cash outflows can be avoided. The leasing option allows cash outflows to be smoothed out over the asset's life. In some cases, it is possible to arrange for low lease payments to be made in the early years of the asset's life, when cash inflows may be low, and for these to increase over time as the asset generates positive cash flows.

✱ A **sale and leaseback** arrangement involves a business selling freehold property to a financial institution in order to raise finance. However, the sale is accompanied by an agreement to lease the freehold property back to the business to allow it to continue to operate from the premises. The rent payable under the lease arrangement is allowable against profits for taxation purposes. There are usually rent reviews at regular intervals throughout the period of the lease, and the amounts payable in future years may be difficult to predict. At the end of the lease agreement, the business must either try to renew the lease or find alternative premises. Although the sale of the premises will result in an immediate injection of cash for the business, it will lose benefits from any future capital appreciation on the property. Where a capital gain arises on the sale of the premises to the financial institution, a liability for taxation may also arise.

Gearing and the long-term financing decision

In Chapter 6 we saw that gearing occurs when a business is financed, at least in part, by contributions from fixed-charge capital such as loans, debentures and preference shares. We also saw that the level of gearing associated with a business is often an important factor in assessing the risk and returns to ordinary shareholders. In the example that follows, we consider the implications of making a choice between a geared and an ungeared form of raising long-term finance.

Example 12.1

The following is a shortened version of the accounts of Woodhall Engineers plc, a company that is not listed on a stock exchange:

Woodhall Engineers plc
Profit and loss account year ended 31 December 2000

	2000	1999
	£m	£m
Turnover	50	47
Operating costs	47	41
Operating profit	3	6
Interest payable	2	2
Profit on ordinary activities before tax	1	4
Taxation on profit on ordinary activities	—	—
Profit on ordinary activities after tax	1	4
Dividends	1	1
Profit retained for the financial year	—	3

Balance sheet at 31 December 2000

	2000	1999
	£m	£m
Fixed assets (less depreciation)	20	21
Current assets		
Stocks	18	10
Debtors	17	16
Cash at bank	1	3
	36	29
Creditors: amounts falling due within one year		
Short-term debt	11	5
Trade creditors	10	10
	21	15
Total assets less current liabilities	35	35
Less Long-term loans (secured)	15	15
	20	20
Capital and reserves		
Called-up share capital 25p ordinary shares	16	16
Profit and loss account	4	4
	20	20

The company is making plans to expand its factory. New plant will cost £8 million, and an expansion in output will increase working capital by £4 million. Over the 15 years' life of the project, incremental profits arising from the expansion will be £2 million per year before interest and tax. In addition, 2001's profits before interest and tax from its existing activities are expected to return to 1999 levels.

Two possible methods of financing the expansion have been discussed by Woodhall's directors. The first is the issue of £12 million 15 per cent debt repayable in year 2010. The second is a rights issue of 40 million 25p ordinary shares, which will give the company 30p per share after expenses.

The company has substantial tax losses, which can be offset against future profits, so you can ignore taxation in your calculations. The 2001 dividend per share is expected to be the same as that for 2000.

Prepare a forecast of Woodhall's profit and loss account (excluding turnover and operating costs) for the year ended 31 December 2001, and of its capital and reserves, long-term loans and number of shares outstanding at that date assuming:

1 the company issues debt;
2 the company issues ordinary shares.

The first part of the example requires the preparation of a forecast profit and loss account under each financing option. These profit and loss accounts will be as follows:

Forecast profit and loss account for the year ended 31 December 2001

	Debt issue	Equity issue
	£m	£m
Profit before interest and taxation (6.0+2.0)	8.0	8.0
Loan interest	3.8	2.0
Profit before tax	4.2	6.0
Taxation	—	—
Profit after tax	4.2	6.0
Dividends (net)	1.0	1.6
Retained profit for the year	3.2	4.4

The capital structure of the company under each option will be as follows:

	Debt issue	Equity issue
Capital and reserves		
Share capital 25p ordinary shares	16.0	26.0
Share premium account*	—	2.0
Retained profit	7.2	8.4
	23.2	36.4
No. of shares in issue (25p shares)	64 million	104 million

* This represents the amount received from the issue of shares that is above the nominal value of the shares. The amount is calculated as follows:

40m shares × (30p − 25p) = £2m.

Activity 12.6

Compute Woodhall's interest cover and earnings per share for the year ended 31 December 2001 and its gearing on that date, assuming:

(a) the company issues debt;
(b) the company issues ordinary shares.

Your answer should be as follows:

	Debt issue	Equity issue
Interest cover ratio		
$\dfrac{\text{Profit before interest and tax}}{\text{Interest payable}}$	$=\dfrac{(4.2+3.8)}{3.8}$	$\dfrac{(6.0+2.0)}{2.0}$
	$= 2.1$ times	4.0 times
Earning per share		
$\dfrac{\text{Earning available to equity}}{\text{Number of ordinary shares}}$	$=\dfrac{£4.2\text{m}}{64\text{m}}$	$\dfrac{£6.0\text{m}}{104\text{m}}$
	$= 6.6\text{p}$	5.8p
Gearing ratio		
$\dfrac{\text{Long-term liabilities}}{\text{Share capital} + \text{Reserves} + \text{Long-term liabilities}}$	$=\dfrac{£27\text{m}}{£23.2\text{m}+£27\text{m}}$	$\dfrac{£15\text{m}}{£36.4\text{m}+£15\text{m}}$
	$= 53.8\%$	29.2%

Activity 12.7

What would your views of the proposed schemes be in each of the following circumstances?

(a) if you were a banker and you were approached for a loan;
(b) if you were an equity investor in Woodhall and you were asked to subscribe to a rights issue.

A banker may be unenthusiastic about lending the company funds. The gearing ratio of 53.8 per cent is rather high, and would leave the bank in an exposed position. The existing loan is already secured on assets held by the company, and it is not clear whether the company is in a position to offer an attractive form of security for the new loan. The interest cover ratio of 2.1 is also rather low. If the company is unable to achieve the expected returns from the new project, or if it is unable to restore profits from the remainder of its operations to 1999 levels, this ratio would be even lower.

Equity investors may need some convincing that it would be worthwhile to make further investments in the company. The return to equity for shareholders in 1999 was 20 per cent. The incremental profit from the new project is £2 million and the investment required is £12 million, which represents a return of 16.7 per cent. Thus, the returns from the project are expected to be lower than for existing operations. In making their decision, investors should discover whether the new investment is of a similar level of risk to their existing investment and how the returns from the investment compare with those available from other opportunities with similar levels of risk.

Self-assessment question 12.1

Ashcroft plc, a family-controlled company, is considering raising additional funds to modernise its factory. The scheme is expected to cost £2.34 million and will increase annual profits before interest and tax from 1 January 2002 by £0.6 million. A summarised balance sheet and profit and loss account are shown below. Currently the share price is 200p.

Two schemes have been suggested. First, 1.3 million shares could be issued at 180p (net of issue costs). Second, a consortium of six City institutions have offered to buy debentures from the company totalling £2.34 million. Interest would be at the rate of 13 per cent per annum, and capital repayments of equal annual instalments of £234,000 starting on 1 January 2003 would be required.

Balance sheet at 31 December 2001

	£m	£m
Fixed assets (net)		1.4
Current assets		
Stock	2.4	
Debtors	2.2	
	4.6	
Creditors: amounts falling due within one year		
Creditors	3.0	
Corporation tax	0.3	
Proposed final dividend	0.2	
	3.5	
Net current assets		1.1
Total assets *less* Current liabilities		2.5
Capital and reserves:		
Called up share capital, 25p ordinary shares		1.0
Profit and loss account		1.5
		2.5

Profit and loss account year ended 31 December 2001

	£m
Turnover	11.2
Profit on ordinary activities before tax	1.2
Taxation on profit on ordinary activities	0.6
Profit on ordinary activities after tax	0.6
Dividends (net)	0.3
Retained profit for the financial year	0.3

Assume corporation tax is charged at the rate of 50 per cent.

(a) Compute the earnings per share for 2002 under the debt and the equity alternatives.

(b) Discuss the considerations that the directors should take into account before deciding upon debt or equity finance.

Short-term sources of finance

A short-term source of borrowing is one that is available for a short time period. Although there is no agreed definition of what 'short-term' means, we shall define it as being up to one year. The major sources of short-term borrowing are as follows.

Bank overdraft

✱ **Bank overdrafts** represent a very flexible form of borrowing. The size of the overdraft can (subject to bank approval) be increased or decreased according to the financing requirements of the business. It is relatively inexpensive to arrange, and interest rates are often very competitive. The rate of interest charged on an overdraft will vary, however, according to how creditworthy the customer is perceived to be by the bank. It is also fairly easy to arrange – sometimes an overdraft can be agreed by a telephone call to the bank. In view of these advantages, it is not surprising that this is an extremely popular form of short-term finance.

Banks prefer to grant overdrafts that are self-liquidating: that is, the funds applied will result in cash inflows that will extinguish the overdraft balance. The banks may ask for forecast cash flow statements from the business to see when the overdraft will be repaid and how much finance is required. The bank may also require some form of security on amounts advanced. One potential drawback with this form of finance is that it is repayable on demand. This may pose problems for a business that is illiquid. However, many businesses operate using an overdraft, and this form of borrowing, although in theory regarded as short term, can often become a long-term source of finance.

Debt factoring

✱ **Debt factoring** is a form of service that is offered by a financial institution (a factor). Many of the large factors are subsidiaries of commercial banks. Debt factoring involves the factor taking over the sales ledger of a company. In addition to operating normal credit control procedures, a factor may offer to undertake credit investigations and to provide protection for approved credit sales. The factor is usually prepared to make an advance to the company of up to 80–85 per cent of approved trade debtors. The charge made for the factoring service is based on total turnover, and is often around 2–3 per cent of turnover. Any advances made to the company by the factor will attract a rate of interest similar to the rate charged on bank overdrafts.

A company may find a factoring arrangement very convenient. It can result in savings in credit management and can create more certain cash flows. It can also release the time of key personnel for more profitable ends. This may be extremely important for smaller companies that rely on the talent and skills of a few key individuals. However, there is a possibility that some will see a factoring arrangement as an indication that the company is experiencing financial difficulties. This may have an adverse effect on confidence in the company. For this reason, some businesses try to conceal the factoring arrangement by collecting debts on behalf of the factor. When considering a factoring agreement, the costs and likely benefits arising must be identified and carefully weighed.

Invoice discounting

❋ **Invoice discounting** involves a business approaching a factor or other financial institution for a loan based on a proportion of the face value of credit sales outstanding. If the institution agrees, the amount advanced is usually 75–80 per cent of the value of the approved sales invoices outstanding. The business must agree to repay the advance within a relatively short period – perhaps 60 or 90 days. The responsibility for collection of the trade debts outstanding remains with the business, and repayment of the advance is not dependent on the trade debt being collected. Invoice discounting will not result in such a close relationship developing between the client and the financial institution as factoring. Invoice discounting may be a one-off arrangement whereas debt factoring usually involves a longer-term arrangement, between the customer and the financial institution.

Nowadays, invoice discounting is a much more important source of funds to companies than factoring. There are various reasons why invoice discounting is a more attractive source of raising finance. First, it is a confidential form of financing that the client's customers will know nothing about. Second, the service charge for invoice discounting is only about 0.2–0.3 per cent of turnover, compared with 2.0–3.0 per cent of turnover for factoring. Finally, many companies are unwilling to relinquish control over their sales ledger. Customers are an important resource of the business, and many companies wish to retain control over all aspects of their relationship with their customers.

Long-term versus short-term borrowing

Having decided that some form of borrowing is required to finance the business, the managers must then decide whether long-term borrowing or short-term borrowing is more appropriate. There are many issues that should be taken into account when deciding between long-term and short-term borrowing. These include the following:

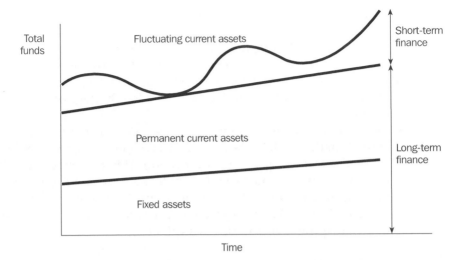

The broad consensus on financing seems to be that all of the permanent financial needs of the business should be financed from long-term sources. Only that part of current assets that fluctuates on a short-term, probably a seasonal, basis should be financed from short-term sources.

Figure 12.3 Short-term and long-term financing requirements

- *Matching.* The business may attempt to match the type of borrowing with the nature of the assets held. Thus assets that form part of the permanent operating base of the business, including fixed assets and a certain level of current assets, will be financed by long-term borrowing. Assets held for a short period, such as current assets held to meet seasonal increases in demand, will be financed by short-term borrowing. (See Figure 12.3.)

  A business may wish to match the asset life exactly with the period of the related loan; however, this may not be possible because of the difficulty of predicting the life of many assets.

Activity 12.8

Some companies may take up a less cautious financing position than shown in the diagram, and others may take up a more cautious financing position. How would the diagram differ under each of these options?

A less cautious position would mean relying on short-term finance to help fund part of the permanent capital base. A more cautious position would mean relying on long-term finance to help finance the fluctuating assets of the business.

- *Flexibility.* Short-term borrowing may be a useful means of postponing a commitment to taking on a long-term loan. This may be seen as desirable if interest rates are high and it is forecast that they will fall in the future. Short-term borrowing does not usually incur penalties if there is early repayment of the amount outstanding, whereas some form of financial penalty may have to be paid if long-term debt is repaid early.

- *Refunding risk.* Short-term borrowing has to be renewed more frequently than long-term borrowing. This may create problems for the business if it is already in financial difficulties, or if there is a shortage of funds available for lending.
- *Interest rates.* Interest payable on long-term debt is often higher than for short-term debt. (This is because lenders require a higher return where their funds are locked up for a long period.) This fact may make short-term borrowing a more attractive source of finance for a business. However, there may be other costs associated with borrowing (arrangement fees, for example) to be taken into account. The more frequently borrowings must be renewed the higher these costs will be.

Internal sources of financing

In addition to external sources of finance, there are certain internal sources of finance that a business may use to generate funds for particular activities. These sources usually have the advantage that they are flexible. They may also be obtained quickly – particularly from working capital sources – and need not require the permission of other parties. The main sources of internal funds are described below, and are summarised in Figure 12.4.

Retained profit

Retained profit is the major source of finance for most companies. By retaining profits within the company rather than distributing them to shareholders in the form of dividends, the funds of the company are increased.

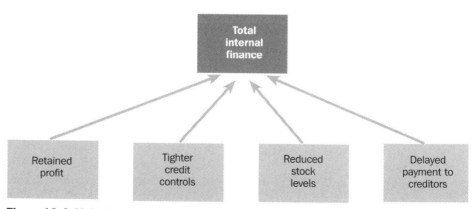

Figure 12.4 Major internal sources of finance

Activity 12.9

Are retained profits a free source of finance to the business?

It is tempting to think that retained profits are a 'cost-free' source of funds for a company. However, this is not the case. If profits are reinvested rather than distributed to shareholders, this means that the shareholders cannot reinvest the profits made in other forms of investment. They will therefore expect a rate of return from the profits reinvested that is equivalent to what they would have received had the funds been invested in another opportunity with the same level of risk.

The reinvestment of profit rather than the issue of new ordinary shares can be a useful way of raising equity capital. There are no issue costs associated with retaining profits, and the amount raised is certain, once the profit has been made. When issuing new shares, the issue costs may be substantial, and there may be uncertainty over the success of the issue. Retaining profits will have no effect on the control of the company by existing shareholders. However, where new shares are issued to outside investors, there will be some dilution of control for existing shareholders.

The retention of profits is something that is determined by the directors of the company. They may find it easier simply to retain profits rather than ask investors to subscribe to a new share issue. Retained profits are already held by the company, and so the company does not have to wait to receive the funds. Moreover, there is often less scrutiny when profits are being retained for reinvestment purposes than when new shares are being issued. Investors and their advisers will examine closely the reasons for any new share issue.

Some shareholders may prefer profits to be retained by the company, rather than be distributed in the form of dividends. By ploughing back profits, it may be expected that the company will expand, and share values will increase as a result. In the United Kingdom, not all capital gains are liable for taxation. (For the fiscal year 1999/2000, an individual with capital gains totalling less than £7,100 would not be taxed on those gains.) A further advantage of capital gains over dividends is that the shareholder has a choice as to when the gain is realised. Research indicates that investors are often attracted to particular companies according to the dividend/retention policies that they adopt.

Tighter credit control

By exerting tighter control over trade debtors it may be possible for a business to reduce the proportion of assets held in this form and to release funds for other purposes. It is important, however, to weigh the benefits of tighter credit control against the likely costs in the form of lost customer goodwill and lost sales. To remain competitive, a business must take account of the needs of its customers and the credit policies adopted by rival companies within the industry.

Activity 12.10

H. Rusli Ltd produces a single product, which is used in a variety of electronic products. Details of the product are as follows:

	per unit	
	£	£
Selling price		20
Less Variable costs	14	
Fixed costs	4	18
Net profit		2

Sales are £10 million a year and are all on credit. The average credit period taken by customers is 45 days, although the terms of credit require payment within 30 days. Bad debts are currently £100,000 a year. Debtors are financed by a bank overdraft costing 15 per cent a year.

The credit control department believes it can eliminate bad debts and can reduce the average credit period to 30 days if new credit control procedures are implemented.

These will cost £50,000 per year, and are likely to result in a reduction in sales of 5 per cent per year.

Should the company implement the new credit control procedures? (*Hint*: In order to answer this activity it is useful to compare the current cost of trade credit with the costs under the proposed approach.)

The current annual cost of trade credit is:

	£
Bad debts	100,000
Overdraft ((£10m × 45/365) × 15%)	184,931
	284,931

The annual cost of trade credit under the new policy will be:

	£
Overdraft (((95% × 10m) × (30/365)) × 15%)	117,123
Cost of control procedures	50,000
Net cost of lost sales (((£10m/£20) × 5%) × (20−14*))	150,000
	317,123

The above figures reveal that the business will be worse off if the new policies are adopted.

* The loss will be the contribution per unit, that is, the difference between the selling price and the variable costs.

Reducing stock levels

This is an internal source of funds that may prove attractive to a business. If a business has a proportion of its assets in the form of stock there is an opportunity cost, as the funds tied up cannot be used for more profitable opportunities. (This is also true, of course, for investment in trade debtors.) By liquidating stocks, funds become available for other purposes. However, a business must ensure that there are sufficient stocks available to meet likely future sales demand. Failure to do so will result in lost customer goodwill and lost sales.

The nature and condition of the stock held will determine whether it is possible to exploit this form of finance. A business may be overstocked as a result of poor buying decisions in the past. This may mean that a significant proportion of stocks held are slow moving or obsolete and cannot, therefore, be liquidated easily.

Delaying payment to creditors

By delaying payment to creditors, funds are retained within the business for other purposes. This may be a cheap form of finance for a business. However, as we saw in Chapter 11, there may be significant costs associated with this form of financing.

Self-assessment question 12.2

Helsim Ltd is a wholesaler and distributor of electrical components. The most recent financial statements of the company revealed the following:

Profit and loss account for the year ended 31 May 2000

	£m	£m
Sales		14.2
Opening stock	3.2	
Purchases	8.4	
	11.6	
Closing stock	3.8	7.8
Gross profit		6.4
Administration expenses	3.0	
Selling and distribution expenses	2.1	
Finance charges	0.8	5.9
Net profit before taxation		0.5
Corporation tax		0.2
Net profit after taxation		0.3

Balance sheet as at 31 May 2000

	£m	£m	£m
Fixed assets			
Land and buildings			3.8
Equipment			0.9
Motor vehicles			0.5
			5.2

	£m	£m	£m
Current assets			
Stock		3.8	
Trade debtors		3.6	
Cash at bank		0.1	
		7.5	
Less Creditors: amounts falling due within one year			
Trade creditors	1.8		
Bank overdraft	3.6	5.4	2.1
			7.3
Creditors: amounts falling due after one year			
Debentures (secured on freehold land)			3.5
			3.8
Capital and reserves			
Share capital			
Ordinary £1 shares			2.0
Profit and loss account			1.8
			3.8

Notes
1 Land and buildings are shown at their current market value. Equipment and motor vehicles are shown at their written-down values.
2 No dividends have been paid to ordinary shareholders for the past three years.

In recent months trade creditors have been pressing for payment. The managing director has therefore decided to reduce the level of trade creditors to an average of 40 days outstanding. In order to achieve this he has decided to approach the bank with a view to increasing the overdraft to finance the necessary payments. The company is currently paying 12 per cent interest on the overdraft.

Required:
(a) Comment on the liquidity position of the company.
(b) Calculate the amount of finance required in order to reduce trade creditors, as shown on the balance sheet, to an average of 40 days outstanding.
(c) State, with reasons, how you consider the bank would react to the proposal to grant an additional overdraft facility.
(d) Evaluate four sources of finance (internal or external, but excluding a bank overdraft) that may be used to finance the reduction in trade creditors, and state, with reasons, which of these you consider the most appropriate.

The role of the Stock Exchange

Earlier we considered the various forms of long-term capital that are available to a company. In this section, we examine the role that the **Stock Exchange** plays in the provision of finance for companies. The Stock Exchange acts as an important *primary* and *secondary* market in capital for companies. As a primary market, the function of the Stock Exchange is to enable companies to raise new capital. As a secondary market, its function is to enable investors to transfer their securities (that is, shares and loan capital) with ease. Thus, it provides a 'second-hand' market where shares and loan capital already in issue may be bought and sold.

In order to issue shares or loan capital through the Stock Exchange, a company must be listed. This means that it must meet fairly stringent Stock Exchange requirements concerning size, profit history, disclosure, and so on. Some share issues on the Stock Exchange arise from the initial listing of the company. Other share issues are undertaken by companies that are already listed on the Stock Exchange and which are seeking additional finance from investors.

The secondary market role of the Stock Exchange means that shares and other financial claims are easily transferable. This can bring real benefits to a company, as investors may be more prepared to invest if they know their investment can be easily liquidated whenever required. It is important to recognise, however, that investors are not obliged to use the Stock Exchange as the means of transferring shares in a listed company. Nevertheless, it is usually the most convenient way of buying or selling shares. Prices of shares and other financial claims are usually determined by the market in an efficient manner, and this should also give investors greater confidence to purchase shares. The company may benefit from this greater investor confidence by finding it easier to raise long-term finance and by obtaining this finance at a lower cost, as investors will view their investment as being less risky.

A Stock Exchange listing can, however, have certain disadvantages for a company. The Stock Exchange imposes strict rules on listed companies, including requiring additional levels of financial disclosure to that already imposed by law and by the accounting profession (for example, half-yearly financial reports must be published). The activities of listed companies are closely monitored by financial analysts, financial journalists and other companies, and such scrutiny may not be welcome, particularly if the company is dealing with sensitive issues or is experiencing operational problems. It is often suggested that listed companies are under pressure to perform well over the short term. This pressure may detract from undertaking projects that will only yield benefits in the longer term. If the market becomes disenchanted with the company, and the price of its shares falls, this may make it vulnerable to a takeover bid from another company.

Venture capital and long-term financing

✳ **Venture capital** is long-term capital provided by certain institutions to help businesses exploit profitable opportunities. The businesses of interest to the venture capitalist will have higher levels of risk than would normally be acceptable to traditional providers of finance, such as the major clearing banks. Venture capital providers may be interested in a variety of businesses, including:

- business start-ups
- acquisitions of existing businesses by a group of managers
- providing additional capital to a young, expanding businesses
- the buy-out of one of the owners from an existing business.

The risks associated with the business can vary in practice, but are often due to the nature of the products or the fact that it is a new business that either lacks a trading record or has new management. Although the risks are higher, the businesses also have potentially higher levels of return – hence their attraction to the venture capitalist. The types of business helped by venture capitalists are normally small or medium size, rather than large companies listed on the Stock Exchange.

The venture capitalist will often make a substantial investment in the business, and this will normally take the form of ordinary shares. In order to keep an eye on the sum invested, the venture capitalist will usually require a representative on the board of directors as a condition of the investment. The venture capitalist may not be looking for a quick return, and may well be prepared to invest in a business for five years or more. The return may take the form of a capital gain on the realisation of the investment.

Activity 12.11

When examining prospective investment opportunities, what kind of non-financial matters do you think a venture capitalist will be concerned with?

The venture capitalist will be concerned with such matters as the quality of management, the personal stake or commitment made by the owners to the business, the quality and nature of the product, and the plans made to exploit the business opportunities, as well as financial matters.

Share issues

A company may issue shares in a number of different ways. These may involve direct appeals by the company to investors, or may involve the use of financial intermediaries. The most common methods of share issues are as follows:

- rights issues
- bonus issues
- offers for sale
- public issue
- private placing.

Rights issues

The company may offer existing shareholders the right to acquire new shares in the company, in exchange for cash. The new shares will be allocated to shareholders in proportion to their existing shareholdings. To make the issue appear attractive to shareholders, the new shares are often offered at a price significantly below the current market value of the shares. **Rights issues** are now the most common form of share issue. For companies, it is a relatively cheap and straightforward way of issuing shares. Issue expenses are quite low, and issue procedures are simpler than for other forms of share issue. The fact that those offered new shares already have an investment in the company, which presumably suits their risk/return requirements, is likely to increase the chances of a successful issue.

The law now requires shares that are to be issued *for cash* to be offered first to existing shareholders. The advantage of this requirement is that control of the company by existing shareholders will not be diluted, provided they take up the rights offer. A rights offer allows existing shareholders to acquire shares in the company at a price below the current market price. This does not mean that entitlement to participate in a rights offer is a source of value to existing shareholders, however. Provided that shareholders either take up their rights and buy the new shares or sell the rights to someone else who will, they will be neither better nor worse off as a result of the rights issue. Calculating the value of the rights offer received by shareholders is quite straightforward. An example can be used to illustrate how this is done.

Example 12.2

Shaw Holdings plc has 20 million ordinary shares of 50p in issue. These shares are currently valued on the stock exchange at £1.60 per share. The directors of Shaw Holdings believe the company requires additional long-term capital, and have decided to make a one-for-four issue (that is, one new share for every four shares held) at £1.30 per share.

The first step in the valuation process is to calculate the price of a share following the rights issue. This is known as the *ex-rights price*, and is simply a weighted average of the price of shares before the issue of rights and the price of the rights shares. In the above example, we have a one-for-four rights issue. The theoretical ex-rights price is therefore calculated as follows:

	£
Price of four shares before the rights issue (4 × £1.60)	6.40
Price of taking up one rights share	1.30
	7.70
Theoretical ex-rights price	= 7.70
	5
	= £1.54

As the price of each share, in theory, should be £1.54 following the rights issue and the price of a rights share is £1.30, the value of the rights offer will be the difference between the two:

$$£1.54 - £1.30 = £0.24 \text{ per share}$$

Market forces will usually ensure that the actual price of rights and the theoretical price will be fairly close.

Activity 12.12

An investor with 2,000 shares in Shaw Holdings plc has contacted you for investment advice. She is undecided whether to take up the rights issue, sell the rights, or allow the rights offer to lapse.

Calculate the effect on the net wealth of the investor of each of the options being considered.

If the investor takes up the rights issue, she will be in the following position:

	£
Value of holding after rights issue ((2000 + 500) × £1.54)	3,850
Less: cost of buying the rights shares (500 × £1.30)	650
	3,200

If the investor sells the rights, she will be in the following position:

Value of holding after rights issue (2,000 × £1.54)	3,080
Sale of rights (500 × £0.24)	120
	3,200

If the investor lets the rights offer lapse, she will be in the following position:

Value of holding after rights issue (2,000 × £1.54)	3,080

As we can see, the first two options should leave her in the same position concerning net wealth as she was before the rights issue. Before the rights issue she had 2,000 shares worth £1.60 each or £3,200. However, she will be worse off if she allows the rights offer to lapse than under the other two options. In practice, however, the company may sell the rights offer on behalf of the investor and pass on the proceeds in order to ensure that she is not worse off as a result of the issue.

When considering a rights issue, the directors of a company must first consider the amount of funds that it needs to raise. This will depend on the future plans and commitments of the company. The directors must then decide on the issue price of the rights shares. Generally speaking, this decision is not of critical importance. In the example above, the company made a one-for-four issue with the price of the rights shares set at £1.30. However, it could have raised the same amount by making a one-for-two issue and setting the rights price at £0.65p, a one-for-one issue and setting the price at £0.325, and so on. The issue price that is finally decided upon will not affect the value of the underlying assets of the company or the proportion of the underlying assets and earnings of the company to which the shareholder is entitled. The directors of the company must, however, ensure that the issue price is not above the current market price of the shares, or the issue will be unsuccessful.

Bonus issues

A **bonus issue** should not be confused with a rights issue of shares. A bonus, or scrip, issue also involves the issue of new shares to existing shareholders in proportion to their existing shareholdings. However, shareholders do not have to pay for the new shares issued. The bonus issue is effected by transferring a sum from the reserves to the paid-up share capital of the business and then issuing shares, equivalent in value to the amount transferred, to existing shareholders. As the reserves are already owned by the shareholders they do not have to pay for the shares issued. In effect, a bonus issue will simply convert reserves into paid-up capital. In order to understand this conversion process, and its effect on the financial position of the company, let us consider the following example.

Example 12.3

Wickham plc has the following abbreviated balance sheet as at 31 March 2000.

	£m
Net assets	20
Financed by	
Share capital (£1 ordinary shares)	10
Reserves	10
	20

The directors decide to convert £5 million of the reserves to paid-up capital. As a result, it is decided that a one-for-two bonus issue should be made. Following the bonus issue, the balance sheet of Wickham plc will be as follows:

	£m
Net assets	20
Financed by	
Share capital (£1 ordinary shares)	15
Reserves	5
	20

Activity 12.13

Are the shareholders in Wickham plc better off as a result of receiving bonus shares?

We can see that the share capital of the company has increased, and there has been a corresponding decrease in the reserves of the company. The net assets of the company remain unchanged by the bonus issue.

Although each shareholder will own more shares following the bonus issue, the proportion held of the total number of shares in issue will remain unchanged and so the stake in the business and the net assets of the business will remain unchanged. Thus bonus issues do not, of themselves, result in an increase in shareholder wealth. They will simply switch part of the owners' claim from reserves to share capital.

Activity 12.14

Assume that the market price per share in Wickham plc before the bonus issue was £2.10. What will be the market price per share following the share issue?

The company has made a one-for-two issue. A holder of two shares would therefore be in the following position before the bonus issue:

Two shares held at £2.10 market price   £4.20

As the wealth of the shareholder has not increased as a result of the issue, the total value of the shareholding will remain the same. This means that, as the shareholder holds one more share following the issue, the market value per share will now be:

$$\frac{£4.20}{3} = £1.40$$

You may wonder, from the calculations above, why bonus issues are made by companies, particularly as the effect of a bonus issue may be to reduce the reserves available for dividend payments. Well, a number of reasons have been put forward to explain this type of share issue:

- *Share price.* The share price of a company may be very high, and, as a result, its share may become more difficult to trade on the Stock Exchange. It seems that shares that trade within a certain price range generate more interest and activity in the market. By increasing the number of shares in issue, the market value of each share will be reduced, which may have the effect of making the shares more marketable.
- *Lender confidence.* The effect of making a transfer from distributable reserves to paid-up share capital will be to increase the permanent capital base of the business. This move may increase confidence among lenders. In effect, a bonus issue will reduce the risk of the company reducing its equity capital through dividend distributions, thereby leaving lenders in an exposed position.
- *Market signals.* The directors may use a bonus issue as an opportunity to signal to investors their confidence in the future prospects of the business.

The issue may be accompanied by the announcement of good news concerning the company (for example, securing a large contract or achieving an increase in profits). Under these circumstances, the share price of the company may rise in the expectation that earnings/dividends per share will be maintained. Shareholders would therefore be better off following the issue. However, it is the *information content* of the bonus issue, rather than the issue itself, that will create this increase in wealth.

Offer for sale

This type of issue can involve a public limited company selling a new issue of shares to a financial institution known as an issuing house. However, shares that are already in issue may also be sold to an issuing house. In this case, existing shareholders agree to sell their shares to the issuing house. The issuing house will, in turn, sell the shares purchased from either the company or its shareholders to the public. The issuing house will publish a prospectus that sets out details of the company and the type of shares to be sold and investors will be invited to apply for shares. The advantage of this type of issue, from the company viewpoint, is that the sale proceeds of the shares are certain. The issuing house will take on the risk of selling the shares to investors. This type of issue is often used when a company seeks a listing on the Stock Exchange and wishes to raise a large amount of funds.

Public issue

This form of issue involves the company making a direct invitation to the public to purchase shares in the company. Typically, this is done through a newspaper advertisement. The shares may once again be a new issue or shares already in issue. An issuing house may be asked by the company to help administer the issue of the shares to the public and to offer advice concerning an appropriate selling price. However, the company rather than the issuing house will take on the risk of selling the shares. An offer for sale and a public issue will both result in a widening of share ownership in the company.

When making an issue of shares, the company or the issuing house will usually set a price for the shares. However, establishing a share price may not be an easy task, particularly where the market is volatile or where the company has unique characteristics. If the share price is set too high, the issue will be undersubscribed and the company (or issuing house) will not receive the amount expected. If the share price is set too low, the issue will be oversubscribed and the company (or issuing house) will receive less than could have been achieved.

One way of dealing with the problem is to make a *tender* issue of shares. This involves the investors' determining the price at which the shares are issued. Although the company (or issuing house) may publish a reserve price to help guide investors, it will be up to the individual investor to determine the number of shares to be purchased and the price the investor wishes to pay.

Once the offers from investors have been received, a price at which all the shares can be sold will be established (known as the *striking price*). Investors who have made offers at, or above, the striking price will be issued shares at the striking price; offers received below the striking price will be rejected. Although this form of issue is adopted occasionally, it is not popular with investors, and is therefore not in widespread use.

Private placing

This method does not involve an invitation to the public to subscribe to shares. Instead the shares are 'placed' with selected investors, such as large financial institutions. This can be a quick and relatively cheap form of raising funds, as savings can be made in advertising and legal costs. However, it can result in the ownership of the company being concentrated in a few hands. Usually, unlisted companies seeking relatively small amounts of cash will employ this form of issue.

SUMMARY

In this chapter we have identified and discussed the major sources of long-term and short-term finance available to businesses. We also discussed the factors to be considered in deciding between the various forms of finance available. We examined the role of the Stock Exchange, and saw that it performs two major roles: a primary role in raising finance for companies, and a secondary role in ensuring that investors can buy and sell securities with ease. Finally, we considered the main forms of share issue and the advantages and disadvantages of each.

Key terms

convertible loan stocks p 336
warrants p 336
mortgage p 338
loan covenants p 338
finance lease p 339
sale and leaseback p 340
bank overdrafts p 345

debt factoring p 345
invoice discounting p 346
Stock Exchange p 353
venture capital p 354
rights issues p 355
bonus issue p 357

REVIEW QUESTIONS

12.1 What are the benefits of issuing share warrants for a company?

12.2 Why might a public company that has a stock exchange listing revert to being an unlisted company?

12.3 Distinguish between an offer for sale and a public issue of shares.

12.4 Distinguish between invoice discounting and factoring.

EXAMINATION-STYLE QUESTIONS

Questions 12.4 and 12.5 are more advanced than 12.1–12.3. Those with a coloured number have an answer at the back of the book.

12.1 H. Brown (Portsmouth) Ltd produces a range of central heating systems for sale to builders' merchants. As a result of increasing demand for the company's products, the directors have decided to expand production. The cost of acquiring new plant and machinery and the increase in working capital requirements are planned to be financed by a mixture of long-term and short-term debt.

Required:
(a) Discuss the major factors that should be taken into account when deciding on the appropriate mix of long-term and short-term debt necessary to finance the expansion programme.
(b) Discuss the major factors that a lender should take into account when deciding whether to grant a long-term loan to the company.
(c) Identify three conditions that might be included in a long-term loan agreement, and state the purpose of each.

12.2 Answer all three questions below.

(a) Discuss the main factors that should be taken into account when choosing between long-term debt and equity finance.
(b) Explain the term *convertible loan stock*. Discuss the advantages and disadvantages of this form of finance from the viewpoint of both the company and investors.
(c) Explain the term *debt factoring*. Discuss the advantages and disadvantages of this form of finance.

12.3 Venture capital may represent an important source of finance for a business.

Required:
(a) What is meant by the term *venture capital*? What are the distinguishing features of this form of finance?
(b) What types of business venture may be of interest to a venture capitalist seeking to make an investment?
(c) Discuss the main factors a venture capitalist would take into account when considering a possible investment in a business.

12.4 Gainsborough Fashions Ltd operates a small chain of fashion shops in North Wales. In recent months the company has been under pressure from its trade creditors to reduce average credit period taken from three months to one month. As a result, the directors of the company have approached the bank to ask for an increase in the existing overdraft for one year to be able to comply with the creditors' demands. The most recent accounts of the company are as follows:

Balance sheet as at 31 May 2000

	£	£	£
Fixed assets			
Fixtures and fittings at cost		90,000	
Less Accumulated depreciation		23,000	67,000
Motor vehicles at cost		34,000	
Less Accumulated depreciation		27,000	7,000
			74,000
Current assets			
Stock at cost		198,000	
Trade debtors		3,000	
		201,000	
Creditors: amounts falling due within one year			
Trade creditors	167,000		
Accrued expenses	5,000		
Bank overdraft	7,000		
Taxation	5,000		
Dividends	10,000	194,000	7,000
			81,000
Creditors: amounts falling due after one year			
12% Debentures 1999/2000			40,000
			41,000
Capital and reserves			
£1 Ordinary shares			20,000
General reserve			4,000
Retained profit			17,000
			41,000

Abbreviated profit and loss account for the year ended 31 May 2000

	£
Sales	740,000
Net profit before interest and taxation	38,000
Interest charges	5,000
Net profit before taxation	33,000
Taxation	10,000
Net profit after taxation	23,000
Dividend proposed	10,000
Retained profit for the year	13,000

Notes

1 The debentures are secured by personal guarantees from the directors.
2 The current overdraft bears an interest rate of 12 per cent.

Required:

(a) Identify and discuss the major factors that a bank would take into account before deciding whether or not to grant an increase in the overdraft of a company.

(b) State whether, in your opinion, the bank should grant the required increase in the overdraft for Gainsborough Fashions Ltd. You should provide reasoned arguments and supporting calculations where necessary.

12.5 Telford Engineers plc, a medium-sized Midlands manufacturer of automobile components, has decided to modernise its factory by introducing a number of robots. These will cost £20 million and will reduce operating costs by £6 million per year for their estimated useful life of ten years. To finance this scheme, the company can either:

1 raise £20 million by the issue of 20 million ordinary shares at 100p; or
2 raise £20 million debt at 14 per cent interest per year, capital repayments of £3 million per year commencing at the end of 2005.

Extracts from Telford Engineers' accounts appear below:

Summary of balance sheet at 31 December

	1999	2000	2001	2002 (estimated)
	£m	£m	£m	£m
Fixed assets	48	51	65	64
Current assets	55	67	57	55
Less Amounts due in under one year				
Creditors	(20)	(27)	(25)	(18)
Overdraft	(5)	—	(6)	(8)
	78	91	91	93
Share capital and reserves	48	61	61	63
Loans	30	30	30	30
	78	91	91	93
Number of Issued 25p shares	80 million	80 million	80 million	80 million
Share price	150p	200p	100p	145p

Summary of profit and loss accounts for years ended 31 December

	1999	2000	2001	2002 (estimated)
	£m	£m	£m	£m
Sales	152	170	110	145
Profit before interest and taxation	28	40	7	15
Interest payable	4	3	4	5
Profit before taxation	24	37	3	10
Taxation	12	16	0	4
Profit after taxation	12	21	3	6
Dividends	6	8	3	4
Retained	6	13	0	2

For your answer you should assume that the corporate tax rate for 2003 is 40 per cent, that sales and operating profit will be unchanged except for the £6 million cost saving arising from the introduction of the robots, and that Telford Engineers will pay the same dividend per share in 2003 as in 2002.

Required:

(a) Prepare, for each scheme, Telford Engineers' profit and loss account for the year ended 31 December 2003 and a statement of its share capital, reserves and loans on that date.

(b) Calculate Telford's earnings per share for 2003 for both schemes.

(c) Calculate the level of earnings (profit) before interest and tax at which the earnings per share for each scheme is equal.

(d) Which scheme would you advise the company to adopt? You should give your reasons and state what additional information you would require.

Glossary of key terms

ABC system of stock control A method of applying different levels of stock control, based on the value of each category of stock. *p 305*

accounting The process of identifying, measuring and communicating information to permit informed judgements and decisions by users of the information. *p 1*

accounting conventions Accounting rules that have evolved over time in order to deal with practical problems rather than to reflect some theoretical ideal. *p 34*

accounting information system The system used within a business to identify, record, analyse and report accounting information. *p 4*

accounting rate of return (ARR) The average profit from an investment, expressed as a percentage of the average investment made. *p 269*

accounting (financial reporting) standards Rules established by the UK accounting profession, which should be followed by preparers of the annual accounts of companies. *p 103*

accrued expenses Expenses that are outstanding at the end of the accounting period. *p 56*

acid test ratio A liquidity ratio that relates the current assets (less stocks) to the current liabilities. *p 157*

activity-based costing (ABC) A technique for more accurately relating overheads to specific production or provision of a service. It is based on acceptance of the fact that overheads do not just occur but are caused by activities, such as holding products in stores, that 'drive' the costs. *p 223*

adverse variance A difference between planned and actual performance, usually where the difference will cause the actual profit to be lower than the budgeted one. *p 248*

ageing schedule of debtors A report dividing debtors into categories, depending on the length of time outstanding. *p 314*

asset A resource held by a business, that has certain characteristics. *p 20*

auditors Professionals whose main duty is to make a report as to whether, in their opinion, the accounting statements of a company do that which they are supposed to do; namely, to show a true and fair view and comply with statutory, and accounting standard, requirements. *p 104*

average settlement period for creditors The average time taken for a business to pay its creditors. *pp 152 and 325*

average settlement period for debtors The average time taken for debtors to pay the amounts owing. *pp 151 and 314*

average stock turnover period An efficiency ratio that measures the average period for which stocks are held by a business. *p 150*

bad debt   Amount owed to the business that is considered to be irrecoverable. *p 72*

balance sheet   A statement of financial position that shows the assets of a business and the claims on those assets. *p 16*

bank overdraft   A flexible form of borrowing that allows an individual or business to have a negative current account balance. *p 345*

batch costing   A technique for identifying full cost, where the production of many types of goods and services, particularly goods, involves producing in a batch of identical or nearly identical units of output, but where each batch is distinctly different from other batches. *p 220*

bonus issue   Reserves that are converted into shares and given 'free' to shareholders. *p 357*

bonus shares   see bonus issue. *p 90*

break-even analysis   The activity of deducing the break-even point of some activity through analysing costs and revenues. *p 186*

break-even chart   A graphical representation of the costs and revenues of some activity, at various levels, which enables the break-even point to be identified. *p 187*

break-even point   A level of activity where revenue will exactly equal total cost, so there is neither profit nor loss. *p 187*

budget   A financial plan for the short term, typically one year. *p 231*

budgetary control   Using the budget as a yardstick against which the effectiveness of actual performance may be asssessed. *p 258*

business entity convention   The convention that holds that, for accounting purposes, the business and its owner(s) are treated as quite separate and distinct. *p 34*

capital   The owner's claim on the assets of the business. *p 22*

capital expenditure   The outlay of funds on fixed assets. *p 118*

capital reserves   Reserve that arise from a 'capital' profit or gain rather than from normal trading activities. *p 89*

cash discount   A reduction in the amount due for goods or services sold on credit in return for prompt payment. *p 313*

cash flow   The movement of cash. *p 114*

cash flow statement   A statement that shows the sources and uses of cash for a period. *p 16*

claim   An obligation on the part of the business to provide cash or some other benefit to an outside party. *p 20*

common costs   Another name for indirect costs or overheads. These are costs that do not directly relate and are not measurable in respect of particular units of output, but relate to all output. *p 208*

comparability   The requirement that items that are basically the same should be treated in the same manner for measurement and reporting purposes. Lack of comparability will limit the usefulness of accounting information. *p 5*

compensating variances   The situation that exists when two variances, one adverse the other favourable, are of equal size and therefore cancel out. *p 258*

consistency convention   The accounting convention that holds that when a particular method of accounting is selected to deal with a transaction, this method should be applied consistently over time. *p 71*

contributions (per unit) Sales revenue per unit less variable costs per unit. *p 190*

control Compelling events to conform to plan. *p 236*

convertible loan stocks Loan capital that can be converted into equity share capital at the option of the holders. *p 336*

cost The amount of resources, usually measured in monetary terms, sacrificed to achieve a particular objective. *p 181*

cost behaviour The manner in which costs alter with changes in the level of activity. *p 210*

cost centre Some area, object, person or activity for which costs are separately collected. *p. 219*

cost driver An activity that causes costs. *p. 223*

cost of sales The cost of the goods sold during a period. Cost of sales can be derived by adding the opening stock held to the stock purchases for the period and then deducting the closing stocks held. *p 51*

cost unit The objective for which the cost is being deduced, usually a product or service. *p 211*

current asset An asset that is not held on a continuing basis. Current assets include cash itself and other assets that are expected to be converted to cash at some future point in the future. *p 29*

current liabilities Amounts due for repayment to outside parties within 12 months of the balance sheet date. *p 30*

current ratio A liquidity ratio that relates the current assets of the business to the current liabilities. *p 156*

debenture A long-term loan, usually made to a company, evidenced by a trust deed. *p 93*

debt factoring A service offered by a financial institution (a factor) that involves the factor taking over the management of the trade debtors of the business. The factor is often prepared to make an advance to the business based on the amount of trade debtors outstanding. *p 345*

depreciation A measure of that portion of the cost (less residual value) of a fixed asset that has been consumed during an accounting period. *p 58*

direct costs Costs that can be identified with specific cost units, to the extent that the effect of the cost can be measured in respect of each particular unit of output. *p 208*

direct method An approach to deducing the cash flows from trading operations, in a cash flow statement, by analysing the business's cash records. *p 122*

directors Individuals who are elected to act as the most senior level of management of a company. *p 85*

discount factor The rate applied to future cash flows to derive the present value of those cash flows. *p 281*

dividends Transfers of assets made by a company to its shareholders. *p 87*

dividend payout ratio An investment ratio that relates the dividends announced for the period to the earnings available for dividends that were generated in that period. *p 165*

dividend per share An investment ratio that relates the dividends announced for a period to the number of shares in issue. *p 164*

dividend yield ratio   An investment ratio that expresses a company's dividend per share as a percentage of its current share price. It provides users with some measure of the dividend returns that the share generates. *p 175*

dual aspect convention   The accounting convention that holds that each transaction has two aspects, and that each aspect must be recorded in the financial statements. *p 37*

earnings per share   An investment ratio that relates the earnings generated by the business during a period, and available to shareholders, to the number of shares in issue. *p 166*

economic order quantity (EOQ)   The quantity of stocks that should be purchased in order to minimise total stock costs. *p 306*

equity   Ordinary shares and reserves of a company. *p 88*

equity dividends paid   A section of the cash flow statement that deals with the cash flows arising from ordinary share dividends paid. *p 119*

expense   A measure of the outflow of assets (or increase in liabilities) that is incurred as a result of generating revenues. *p 48*

favourable variance   A difference between planned and actual performance, usually where the difference will cause the actual profit to be higher than the budgeted one. *p 248*

finance   The raising, investment and management of funds. *p 2*

finance lease   A financial arrangement whereby the asset title remains with the owner (the lessor) but the lease agreement transfers virtually all the rewards and risks to the business (the lessee). *p 339*

financial accounting   The measuring and reporting of accounting information for external users (those users other than the managers of the business). *p 11*

financing   A section of the cash flow statement that deals with the cash flows arising from raising and repaying long-term finance. *p 119*

first in, first out (FIFO)   A method of stock valuation that assumes that the earlier stocks are to be sold first. *p 68*

five Cs of credit   A checklist of factors to be taken into account when assessing the creditworthiness of a customer. *p 310*

fixed asset   An asset held with the intention of being used to generate wealth rather than being held for resale. Fixed assets can be seen as the tools of the business, and are normally held by the business on a continuing basis. *p 28*

fixed cost   A cost that stays the same when changes occur to the volume of activity. *p 181*

flexible budget   A budget that is adjusted to reflect the actual level of output achieved. *p 245*

flexing (the budget)   Revising the budget to what it would have been had the planned level of output been diffeerent. *p 247*

full costing   Deducing the total direct and indirect (overhead) costs of pursuing some activity or objective. *p 206*

gearing   The existence of fixed payment bearing securities (for example, loans) in the capital structure of a business. *p 159*

gearing ratio   A ratio that relates the contribution of long-term lenders to the total long-term capital of the business. *p 161*

going concern convention The accounting convention that holds that the business will continue operations for the foreseeable future. In other words, there is no intention or need to liquidate the business. *p 37*

gross profit The amount remaining (if positive) after trading expenses (for example, cost of sales) have been deducted from trading revenues (for example, sales). *p 51*

gross profit margin ratio A profitability ratio relating the gross profit for the period to the sales for the period. *p 149*

historic cost convention The accounting convention that holds that assets should be recorded at their historic (acquisition) cost. *p 36*

indirect costs (or overheads) All costs except direct costs: that is, those that cannot be directly measured in respect of each particular unit of output. *p 208*

indirect method An approach to deducing the cash flows from trading operations, in a cash flow statement, by analysing the business's final accounts. *p 123*

inflation A tendency for a currency to lose value over time owing to increasing prices of goods and services. *p 278*

intangible assets Assets that do not have a physical substance (for example, patents, goodwill and debtors). *p 22*

interest cover ratio A gearing ratio that divides the net profit before interest and taxation by the interest payable for a period. *p 162*

internal rate of return (IRR) The discount rate for a project that will have the effect of producing a zero NPV. *p 284*

investigating variances The act of looking into the practical causes of budget variances, once those variances have been identified. *p 256*

invoice discounting A loan provided by a financial institution based on a proportion of the face value of credit sales outstanding. *p 346*

job costing A technique for identifying the full cost per unit of output, where that output is not similar to other units of output. *p 209*

just-in-time (JIT) stock management A system of stock management that aims to have supplies delivered to production just in time for their required use. *p 308*

last in, first out (LIFO) A method of stock valuation that assumes that the latest stocks are the first to be sold. *p 68*

liabilities Claims of individuals and organisations, apart from the owner, that have arisen from past transactions or events such as supplying goods or lending money to the business. *p 23*

limited company An artificial legal person that has an identity separate from that of those who own and manage it. *p 83*

limited liability The restriction of the legal obligation of shareholders to meet all of the company's debts. *p 85*

limiting factor Some aspect of the business (for example, lack of sales demand) that will prevent it from achieving its objectives to the maximum extent. *p 232*

loan covenants Conditions contained within a loan agreement that are designed to protect the lenders. *p 338*

long-term liabilities Those amounts due to other parties that are not liable for repayment within the next 12 months after the balance sheet date. *p 30*

management accounting The measuring and reporting of accounting information for the managers of a business. *p 11*

management by exception A system of control, based on a comparison of planned and actual performance, that allows managers to focus on areas of poor performance rather than dealing with areas where performance is satisfactory. *p 236*

management of liquid resources A section of the cash flow statement that deals with the cash flows arising from movements in short-term liquid resources. *p 119*

margin of safety The extent to which the planned level of output or sales lies above the break-even point. *p 191*

marginal analysis The activity of decision making through analysing variable costs and revenues, ignoring fixed costs. *p 194*

marginal cost The additional cost of producing one more unit. This is often the same as the variable cost. *p 202*

master budgets A summary of the individual budgets, usually consisting of a budgeted profit and loss account, a budgeted balance sheet and a budgeted cash flow statement. *p 233*

matching convention The accounting convention that holds that, in measuring income, expenses should be matched to revenues that they helped generate, in the same accounting period as those revenues were realised. *p 55*

materials requirement planning (MRP) system A computer-based system of stock control that schedules the timing of deliveries of bought-in parts and materials to coincide with production requirements to meet demand. *p 308*

materiality convention The accounting convention that states that, where the amounts involved are immaterial, only what is expedient should be considered. *p 58*

money measurement convention The accounting convention that holds that accounting should deal only with those items that are capable of being expressed in monetary terms. *p 35*

mortgage A loan secured on property. *p 338*

net cash flow from operating activities A section of the cash flow statement that deals with the cash flows from trading operations. *p 117*

net present value (NPV) A method of investment appraisal based on the present value of all relevant cash flows associated with the project. *p 275*

net profit The amount remaining (if positive) after the total expenses for a period have been deducted from total revenues. *p 51*

net profit margin ratio A profitability ratio relating the net profit for the period to the sales for the period. *p 148*

nominal value The face value of a share in a company. *p 87*

objectivity convention The accounting convention that holds that, in so far as is possible, the financial statements prepared should be based on objective verifiable evidence rather than matters of opinion. *p 39*

operating cash cycle The period between the outlay of cash to purchase supplies and the ultimate receipt of cash from the sale of goods. *p 320*

operating cash flow per share An investment ratio that relates the operating cash flows available to ordinary shareholders to the number of ordinary shares. *p 167*

operating cash flows to maturing obligations ratio A liquidity ratio that compares the operating cash flows with the current liabilities of the business. *p 158*

operating gearing The relationship between the total fixed and the total variable costs for some activity. *p 192*

ordinary shares Shares of a company owned by those who are due the benefits of the company's activities after all other stakeholders have been satisfied. *p 87*

overhead (or indirect costs) Any cost except a direct cost; a cost that cannot be directly measured in respect of each particular unit of output. *p 208*

overhead absorption (recovery) rate The rate at which overheads are charged to cost units (jobs), usually in a job costing system. *p 212*

payback period (PP) The time taken for the initial investment in a project to be repaid from the net cash inflows of the project. *p 272*

preference shares Shares of a company owned by those who are entitled to the first part of any dividend that the company may pay. *p 88*

prepaid expenses Expenses that have been paid in advance at the end of the accounting period. *p 58*

price/earnings ratio An investment ratio that relates the market value of a share to the earnings per share. *p 168*

private company A limited company for which the directors can restrict the ownership of its shares. *p 86*

process costing A technique for deriving the full cost per unit of output, where the units of output are exactly similar or it is reasonable to treat them as being so. *p 208*

profit The increase in wealth attributable to the owners of a business that arises through business operations. *p 47*

profit and loss account A financial statement that measures and reports the profit (or loss) the business has generated during a period. It is derived by deducting from total revenues for a period, the total expenses associated with those revenues. *p 16*

profit–volume (PV) chart A graphical representation of the contributions (revenues less variable costs) of some activity, at various levels, which enables the break-even point, and the profit at various activity levels, to be identified. *p 190*

provision for doubtful debts An amount set aside out of profits to provide for anticipated losses arising from debts that may prove irrecoverable. *p 73*

prudence convention The accounting convention that holds that financial statements should err on the side of caution. The prudence convention represents a pessimistic rather than an optimistic view of financial position. *p 37*

public company A limited company for which the directors cannot restrict the ownership of its shares. *p 86*

realisation convention The accounting convention that holds that revenue should be recognised only when it has been realised. *p 55*

reducing balance method A method of calculating depreciation that applies a fixed percentage rate of depreciation to the written-down value of an asset in each period. *p 61*

relevance The ability of accounting information to influence decisions. Relevance is regarded as a key characteristic of useful accounting information. *p 5*

reliability The requirement that accounting should be free from material error or bias. Reliability is regarded as a key characteristic of useful accounting information. *p 5*

reserves Part of the owners' claim on a limited company that has arisen from profits and gains, to the extent that these have not been distributed to the shareholders. *p 86*

residual value The amount for which a fixed asset is sold when the business has no further use for it. *p 60*

return on capital employed (ROCE) A profitability ratio expressing the relationship between the net profit (before interest and taxation) and the long-term capital invested in the business. *p 147*

returns from investment and servicing of finance A section of the cash flow statement that deals with the cash flows arising from interest and dividends received and from interest paid. *p 117*

return on ordinary shareholders' funds (ROSF) A profitability ratio that compares the amount of profit for the period available to the ordinary shareholders with their stake in the business. *p 146*

revenue A measure of the inflow of assets (for example, cash or amounts owed to a business by debtors), or a reduction in liabilities, which arise as a result of trading operations. *p 48*

revenue reserve Part of the owners' claim of a company that arises from realised profits and gains, including after-tax trading profits and gains from disposals of fixed assets. *p 109*

rights issues Issues of shares for cash to existing shareholders on the basis of the number of shares already held. *pp 92 and 355*

risk The likelihood that what is estimated to occur will not actually occur. *p 277*

risk premium A rate of return in excess of that which would be expected from a risk-free investment, to compensate the investor for bearing risk. *p 292*

sale and leaseback An agreement to sell an asset (usually property) to another party and simultaneously to lease the asset back in order to continue using the asset. *p 340*

sales to capital employed ratio An efficiency ratio that relates the sales generated during a period to the capital employed. *p 153*

semi-fixed (semi-variable) cost A cost that has an element of both fixed and variable cost. *p 185*

share A portion of the ownership, or equity, of a company. *p 84*

share premium Any amount above the nominal value of shares that is paid for those shares. *p 90*

stable monetary unit convention The accounting convention holds that money, which is the unit of measurement in accounting, will not change in value over time. *p 38*

standards quantities and costs Planned quantities and costs (or revenues) for individual units of input or output. Standards are the building blocks used to produce the budget. *p 254*

stepped fixed cost A fixed cost that does not remain fixed over all levels of output but which changes in steps as a threshold level of output is reached. *p 184*

Stock Exchange   A market where 'secondhand' shares may be bought and sold and new capital raised. *p 353*

straight-line method   A method of accounting for depreciation that allocates the amount to be depreciated evenly over the useful life of the asset. *p 60*

tangible assets   Those assets that have a physical substance (for example, plant and machinery, motor vehicles). *p 22*

taxation   A section of the cash flow statement that deals with the cash flows arising from taxes paid and refunded. *p 117*

timeliness   A requirement that accounting information should be available at reasonably frequent intervals, and that the time that elapses between the end of the financial period and the production of accounting reports should not be too long. Lack of timeliness will limit the usefulness of accounting information. *p 5*

trading and profit and loss account   A type of profit and loss account prepared by merchandising businesses (for example, retailers and wholesalers) that measures and reports the gross profit (loss) from trading and then deducts overhead expenses to derive the net profit (loss) for the period. *p 51*

understandability   The requirement that accounting information should be capable of being understood by those for whom the information is primarily compiled. Lack of understandability will limit the usefulness of accounting information. *p 5*

variable cost   A cost that varies according to the volume of activity. *p 181*

variance   The financial effect, on the budgeted profit, of the particular factor under consideration being more or less than budgeted. *p 248*

venture capital   Long-term capital provided by certain institutions to small and medium-size businesses to exploit relatively high risk opportunities. *p 354*

warrants   A document giving the holder the right, but not the obligation, to acquire ordinary shares in a company at an agreed price. *p 336*

weighted average cost (AVCO)   A method of valuing stocks that assumes that stocks entering the business lose their separate identity and any issues of stock reflect the weighted average cost of the stocks held. *p 68*

working capital   Current assets less current liabilities (creditors due within one year). *p 299*

Solutions to self-assessment questions

Chapter 2

2.1 The balance sheet you prepare should be set out as follows:

Simonson Engineering Company
Balance sheet as at 30 September 2000

	£	£	£
Fixed assets			
Freehold premises			72,000
Plant and machinery			25,000
Motor vehicles			15,000
Fixtures and fittings			9,000
			121,000
Current assets			
Stock-in-trade		45,000	
Trade debtors		48,000	
Cash in hand		1,500	
		94,500	
Current liabilities			
Trade creditors	18,000		
Bank overdraft	26,000		
	44,000		
			50,500
Total assets less current liabilities			171,500
Long-term liabilities			
Loan			51,000
Net assets			120,500
Capital			
Opening balance			117,500
Add profit			18,000
			135,500
Less Drawings			15,000
			120,500

2.2 The balance sheet provides an insight into the 'mix' of assets held. Thus, it can be seen that, in percentage terms, approximately 60 per cent of assets held (in value) are in the form of fixed assets, and that freehold premises comprise more than half of the value of fixed assets held. Current assets held are largely in the form of stock (approximately 46 per cent of current assets) and trade debtors (approximately 42 per cent of current assets).

The balance sheet also provides an insight to the liquidity of the business. The current assets are £104,000 and can be viewed as representing cash or near cash assets held, compared with £42,000 in current liabilities. In this case, it appears that the business is fairly liquid, as the current assets exceed the current liabilities by a large amount. Liquidity is very important in order to maintain the capacity of the business to pay debts.

The balance sheet gives an indication of the financial structure of the business. In the balance sheet provided, it can be seen that the owner is providing £63,000 and long-term lenders are providing £160,000. This means that outsiders contribute, in percentage terms, more than 71 per cent of the total long-term finance required, and the business is therefore heavily reliant on outside sources of finance. The business is under pressure to make profits that are at least sufficient to pay interest, and to make capital repayments when they fall due.

Chapter 3

3.1

TT Limited

Balance sheet as at 31 December 2000

Assets	£	Claims	£
Delivery van (12,000 − 2,500)	9,500	Capital (50,000 + 26,900)	76,900
Stock-in-trade (143,000 +			
12,000 − 74,000 − 16,000)	65,000	Trade creditors (143,000 −	
		121,000)	22,000
Trade debtors (152,000 −			
132,000 − 400)	19,600	Accrued expenses (630 + 620)	1,250
Cash at bank (50,000 − 25,000 −			
500 − 900 − 300 − 12,000 −			
33,500 − 1,650 − 12,000 +			
35,000 − 9,400 + 132,000 −			
121,000)	750		
Prepaid expenses (5,000 + 300)	5,300		
	100,150		100,150

Profit and loss account for the year ended 31 December 2000

		£
Sales (152,000 + 35,000)		187,000
Less Cost of stock sold		
(74,000 + 16,000)		90,000
Gross profit		97,000
Less		
Rent	20,000	
Rates (500 + 900)	1,400	
Wages (33,500 + 630)	34,130	
Electricity (1,650 + 620)	2,270	
Bad debts	400	
Van depreciation	2,500	
Van expenses	9,400	
		70,100
Net profit for the year		26,900

The balance sheet could now be rewritten in a more stylish form as follows:

TT Limited
Balance sheet as at 31 December 2000

	£	£	£
Fixed assets			
Motor van			9,500
Current assets			
Stock-in-trade	65,000		
Trade debtors	19,600		
Prepaid expenses	5,300		
Cash	750		
		90,650	
*Less **Current liabilities***			
Trade creditors	22,000		
Accrued expenses	1,250		
		23,250	
			67,400
			£76,900
Capital			
Original			50,000
Retained profit			26,900
			£76,900

3.2 Sales increased by nearly 24 per cent over the previous year, but the 'bottom line' fell from a net profit of £37,000 to a loss of £58,000. The rapid expansion of the business has clearly brought problems in its trail. In the previous period, the business was making a gross profit of more than 31p for every £1 of sales made. This reduced in the year to 31 May 2001 to around 26p for every £1 of sales made. This seems to suggest that the rapid expansion was fuelled by a reduction in prices. The gross profit increased in absolute terms by £20,000; however, there was a drastic decline in net profits during the period. In the previous period, the business was making a net profit of nearly 6p for every £1 of sales, whereas for the year to 31 May 2001, this reduced to a loss of nearly 7p for every £1 of sales made. This means that overhead expenses have increased considerably. Some increase in overhead expenses may be expected in order to service the increased level of activity. However, the increase appears to be exceptional. If we look at the list of overhead expenses, we can see that the bad debts written off seem very high (more than 10 per cent of total sales). This may be a further effect of the rapid expansion that has taken place. In order to generate sales, insufficient regard may have been paid to the creditworthiness of customers. A comparison of overhead expenses with those of the previous period would be useful.

Chapter 4

4.1 1 The summarised balance sheet of Bonanza Ltd, immediately following the rights and bonus issue, is as follows:

Balance sheet as at 31 December 2000

Net assets (235 + 40 (cash from the rights issue))	£275,000
Capital and reserves	
Share capital	
100,000 shares of £1 each ((100 + 20 = 120) + 60)	180,000
Share premium account (30 + 20 – 50)	–
Revaluation reserve (37 – 10)	27,000
Profit and loss account balance	68,000
	£275,000

Note that the bonus issue of £60,000 is taken from capital reserves (that is, reserves unavailable for dividends) as follows:

	£
Share premium account	50,000
Revaluation reserve	10,000
	60,000

More could have been taken from the revaluation reserve and less from the share premium account without making any difference to dividend payment possibilities.

2 There may be pressure from a potential creditor for the company to limit its ability to pay dividends. This would place creditors in a more secure position because the maximum 'buffer' or safety margin, between the value of the assets and the amount owed by the company, is maintained. It is not unusual for potential creditors to insist on some measure to lock up shareholders' funds in this way, as a condition of granting the loan.

3 The summarised balance sheet of Bonanza Ltd, immediately following the rights and bonus issue (assuming a minimum dividend potential objective), is as follows:

Balance sheet as at 31 December 2000

	£
Net assets (235 + 40 (cash from the rights issue))	275,000
Capital and reserves	
Share capital	
100,000 shares of £1 each ((100 + 20 = 120) + 60)	180,000
Share premium account (30 + 20)	50,000
Revaluation reserve	37,000
Profit and loss account balance (68 – 60)	8,000
	275,000

4 Before the bonus issue, the maximum dividend was £68,000. Now it is £8,000. Thus the bonus issue has had the effect of locking up an additional £60,000 of the assets of the company in terms of the company's ability to pay dividends.

5 *Lee's position*
Before the issues Lee had 100 shares worth £2.35 (i.e. £235,000/100,000) each or £235 in total.

Lee would be offered 20 shares in the rights issue at £2 each, or £40 in total. After the rights issue Lee would have 120 shares worth £2.2917 (i.e. £275,000/120,000) each or £275 in total. The bonus issue would give 60 additional shares to Lee. After the bonus issue Lee would have 180 shares worth £1.5278 (i.e. £275,000/180,000) each or £275 in total.

None of this affects Lee's wealth. Before the issues Lee had £235 worth of shares and £40 more in cash. After the issues Lee has the same total, but all £275 is in the value of the shares.

6 The things that we know about the company are as follows:

(a) It is a private (as opposed to a public) limited company. (It has 'Ltd' (limited) as part of its name, rather than 'plc' (public limited company).)

(b) It has made an issue of shares at a premium, almost certainly after it had traded successfully for a period. (There is a share premium account. It would be very unlikely that the original shares, issued when the company was first formed, would have been issued at a premium.)

(c) Certain of the assets in the balance sheet have been upwardly revalued by at least £37,000. (There is a revaluation reserve of £37,000. This may just be what is left after a previous bonus issue had taken part of the balance.)

(d) The company has traded at an aggregate profit (though there could have been losses in some years), net of tax and any dividends paid. (There is a positive balance on the profit and loss account.)

4.2

Pear Limited
Balance sheet as at 30 September 2000

	£000	£000
Fixed assets		
Cost (1,570 + 30)	1,600	
Depreciation (690 + 12)	702	
		898
Current assets		
Stock	207	
Debtors (182 + 18)	200	
Cash at bank	21	
	428	
Less **Creditors: amounts due within one year**		
Trade creditors	88	
Other creditors (20 + 30 + 15 + 2)	67	
Taxation	19	
Dividend proposed	25	
Bank overdraft	105	
	304	
Net current assets		124
Less **Creditors: amount due after more than one year**		
10% debenture – repayable 2005		(300)
		722

	£000	£000
Capital and reserves		
Shares capital		300
Share premium account		300
Retained profit at beginning of year	104	
Profit for year	18	122
		722

Profit and loss account for the year ended 30 September 2000

	£000	£000
Turnover (1,456 + 18)		1,474
Cost of sales		768
Gross profit		706
Less Salaries	220	
Depreciation (249 + 12)	261	
Other operating costs (131 + 2)	133	
		614
Operating profit		92
Interest payable (15 + 15)		30
Profit before taxation		62
Taxation (62 × 30%)		19
Profit after taxation		43
Dividend proposed		25
		18

Chapter 5

5.1

Cash flow statement for the year ended 31 December 2000

	£m	£m
Net cash inflows from operating activities		66
(see analysis below)		
Returns from investment and servicing of finance		
Interest received	2	
Interest paid	(4)	
Net cash outflow from returns on investment and servicing of finance		(2)
Taxation		
Corporation tax paid (see note below)	(12)	
Net cash outflow for taxation		(12)
Capital expenditure		
Land and buildings	(22)	
Plant and machinery (see note below)	(19)	
Net cash outflow for capital expenditure		(41)
		11

	£m	£m
Equity dividends paid		
Dividends paid (see note below)	(16)	
Net cash outflow for equity dividends		(16)
		(5)
Management of liquid resources		
Investment in treasury bills	(15)	
Net cash outflow for management of liquid resources		(15)
Financing		
Issue of debenture stock	20	
Net cash inflow from financing		20
Net increase in cash		0

To see how this relates to the cash of the business at the beginning and end of the year it is useful to show a reconciliation as follows:

Analysis of cash during the year ended 31 December 2000

	£m	£m
Balance at 1 January 2000		4
Net cash inflow		—
Balance at 31 December 2000		4

Calculation of net cash inflow from operating activities

		£m
Net operating profit (from the profit and loss account)		62
Add Depreciation		
Land and buildings	6	
Plant and machinery	10	
		16
		78
Less Increase in debtors (26 − 16)	10	
Decrease in creditors (26 − 23)	3	13
		65
Add Decrease in stocks (25 − 24)		1
		66

Notes

Dividends

	1999	2000
	£m	£m
Total for the year (profit and loss account)	14	18
Still outstanding at the end of the year (balance sheet)	12	14
Paid during the year (interim dividend)	2	4

Thus the amount paid during 2000 was £12 million from 1999, plus £4 million for 2000, that is £16 million in total.

Fixed asset acquisitions	Land and buildings £m	Plant and machinery £m
Position at 31 December 1999	94	53
Less 2000 depreciation	6	10
	88	43
Position at 31 December 2000	110	62
Acquisitions	22	19

Taxation

	£m
Amount owing at 1.1.2000	4
Tax charge for 2000	16
	20
Amount owing at 31.12.2000	8
Amount paid during 2000	12

Chapter 6

6.1 In order to answer this question you may have used the following ratios:

A plc   B plc

$$\text{Current ratio} = \frac{853}{422.4} = 2.0 \qquad = \frac{816.5}{293.1} = 2.8$$

$$\text{Acid test ratio} = \frac{(853 - 592)}{422.4} = 0.6 \qquad = \frac{(816.5 - 403)}{293.1} = 1.4$$

$$\text{Gearing ratio} = \frac{190}{(687.6 + 190)} \times 100 = 21.6\% \quad = \frac{250}{(874.6 + 250)} \times 100 = 22.2\%$$

$$\text{Interest cover ratio} = \frac{(131.9 + 19.4)}{19.4} = 7.8 \text{ times} \quad = \frac{(139.4 + 27.5)}{27.5} = 6.1 \text{ times}$$

$$\text{Dividend payout ratio} = \frac{135.0}{99.9} \times 100 = 135\% \quad = \frac{95.0}{104.6} \times 100 = 91\%$$

$$\text{Price earnings ratio} = \frac{£6.50}{31.2p} = 20.8T \qquad = \frac{£8.20}{41.8p} = 19.6T$$

A plc has a much lower current ratio and acid test ratio than those of B plc. The reasons for this may be partly due to the fact that A plc has a lower average settlement period for debtors. The acid test ratio of A plc is substantially below 1.0, which may suggest a liquidity problem.

The gearing ratio of each company is quite similar. Neither company has excessive borrowing. The interest cover ratio for each company is also similar. The respective ratios indicate that both companies have good profit coverage for their interest charges.

The dividend payout ratio for each company seems very high indeed. In the case of A plc, the dividends announced for the year are considerably higher than the earnings generated during the year that are available for dividend. As a result, part of the dividend was paid out of retained profits from previous years. This is an unusual occurrence. Although it is quite legitimate to do this, such action may nevertheless suggest a lack of prudence on the part of the directors.

The P/E ratio for both companies is high, which indicates market confidence in their future prospects.

Chapter 7

7.1 (a) The break-even point if only product A were made would be:

Fixed costs/(Sales revenue per unit − Variable cost per unit)
= £40,000/(£30 − (15 + 6)) = 4,444 units (per annum)

(b)

Product	A	B	C
	(per unit)	(per unit)	(per unit)
	£	£	£
Selling price	30	39	20
Variable materials	(15)	(18)	(10)
Variable production costs	(6)	(10)	(5)
Contribution	9	11	5
Time on machine (hours)	2	3	1
Contribution per hour on machines	£4.50	£3.67	£5.00
Order of priority	2nd	3rd	1st

(c)

				Contributions
				£
Produce:	5,000 Product C using	5,000	hours generating	25,000
	2,500 Product A using	5,000	hours generating	22,500
		10,000	hours	47,500
			Less Fixed costs	40,000
			Profit	7,500

Leaving a demand for 500 units of product A and 2,000 units of product B unsatisfied.

Chapter 8

8.1 (a) The budget may be summarised as:

	£	
Sales revenue	196,000	
Direct materials	(38,000)	
Direct labour	(32,000)	
Total overheads	(77,000)	(that is, £2,400 + 3,000 + 27,600 + 36,000 + 8,000)
Profit	49,000	

This job may be priced on the basis that both overheads and profit should be apportioned to it on the basis of direct labour cost, as follows:

	£	
Direct materials	4,000	
Direct labour	3,600	
Overheads	8,663	(that is, £77,000 × 3,600/32,000)
Profit	5,513	(that is, £49,000 × 3,600/32,000)
	21,776	

This answer assumes that variable overheads vary in proportion to direct labour cost.
Various other bases of charging overheads and profit loading the job could have been adopted. For example, material cost could have been included (with direct labour) as the basis for profit loading, or even apportioning overheads.

(b) This part of the question is, in effect, asking for comments on the validity of 'full cost plus' pricing. This approach can be useful as an indicator of the effective long-run cost of doing the job. On the other hand, it fails to take account of such factors as the state of the market and other external factors.

Chapter 9

9.1 Raw materials stock budget for the six months ending 31 December (in units):

	July units	Aug. units	Sept. units	Oct. units	Nov. units	Dec. units
Opening stock	500	600	600	700	750	750
Purchases	600	600	700	750	750	750
	1,100	1,200	1,300	1,450	1,500	1,500
Less Issued to production	500	600	600	700	750	750
Closing stock	600	600	700	750	750	750

Raw materials stock budget for the six months ending 31 December (in financial terms):

	July £	Aug. £	Sept. £	Oct. £	Nov. £	Dec. £
Opening stock	4,000	4,800	4,800	5,600	6,000	6,000
Purchases	4,800	4,800	5,600	6,000	6,000	6,000
	8,800	9,600	10,400	11,600	12,000	12,000
Less Issued to production	4,000	4,800	4,800	5,600	6,000	6,000
Closing stock	4,800	4,800	5,600	6,000	6,000	6,000

Creditors budget for the six months ending 31 December:

	July £	Aug. £	Sept. £	Oct. £	Nov. £	Dec. £
Opening balance	4,000	4,800	4,800	5,600	6,000	6,000
Purchases	4,800	4,800	5,600	6,000	6,000	6,000
	8,800	9,600	10,400	11,600	12,000	12,000
Less Payments	4,000	4,800	4,800	5,600	6,000	6,000
Closing balance	4,800	4,800	5,600	6,000	6,000	6,000

Cash budget for the six months ending 31 December:

	July £	Aug. £	Sept. £	Oct. £	Nov. £	Dec. £
Inflows						
Receipts: debtors	2,800	3,200	3,200	4,000	4,800	5,200
cash sales	4,800	6,000	7,200	7,800	8,400	9,600
Total inflows	7,600	9,200	10,400	11,800	13,200	14,800
Outflows						
Payments to creditors	4,000	4,800	4,800	5,600	6,000	6,000
Direct costs	3,000	3,600	3,600	4,200	4,500	4,500
Advertising	1,000	–	–	1,500	–	–
Overheads:						
80%	1,280	1,280	1,280	1,280	1,600	1,600
20%	280	320	320	320	320	400
New plant			2,200	2,200	2,200	
Total outflows	9,560	10,000	12,200	15,100	14,620	12,500
Net inflows/(outflows)	(1,960)	(800)	(1,800)	(3,300)	(1,420)	2,300
Balance carried forward	5,540	4,740	2,940	(360)	(1,780)	520

Note how budgets are linked: in this case, the stock budget to the creditors budget and the creditors budget to the cash budget.

The following are possible means of relieving the cash shortages revealed by the budget:

- Make a higher proportion of sales on a cash basis.
- Collect the money from debtors more promptly, for example during the month following the sale.
- Hold lower stocks, both of raw materials and of finished stock.
- Increase the creditor payment period.
- Delay the payments for advertising.
- Obtain more credit for the overhead costs – at present, only 20 per cent is on credit.
- Delay the payments for the new plant.

9.2 (a) and (b)

Toscanini Ltd
Budget

	Original	Flexed		Actual	
Output (units)	4,000	3,500		3,500	
(production and sales)					
	£	£		£	
Sales	16,000	14,000		13,820	
Raw materials	(3,840)	(3,360)	(1,400 kg)	(3,420)	(1,425 kg)
Labour	(3,200)	(2,800)	(700 hrs)	(2,690)	(690 hrs)
Fixed overheads	(4,800)	(4,800)		(4,900)	
Operating profit	4,160	3,040		2,810	

	£	Manager accountable
Sales volume variance		
(4,160 − 3,040)	1,120 (A)	Sales
Sales price variance		
(14,000 − 13,820)	180 (A)	Sales
Materials price variance		
(1,425 × 2.40) − 3,420	zero	−
Materials usage variance		
[(3,500 × 0.4) − 1,425] × £2.40	60 (A)	Production
Labour rate variance		
(690 × £4) − 2,690	70 (F)	Personnel
Labour efficiency variance		
[(3,500 × 0.20) − 690] × £4	40 (F)	Production
Fixed overhead spending		
4,800 − 4,900	100 (A)	Various, depending on the nature of the overheads
Total net variances	1,350 (A)	
Budgeted profit	4,160	
Less: Total net variance	1,350	
Actual profit	2,810	

(c) Feasible explanations include the following:

Sales volume	Unanticipated fall in world demand would account for 400 × £2.24 = £496 of this variance. The remainder is probably caused by ineffective marketing, though a lack of availability of stock to sell may be a reason.
Sales price	Ineffective selling seems the only logical reason.
Materials usage	Inefficient usage of material, perhaps because of poor performance by labour or substandard materials.
Labour rate	Less overtime worked or lower production bonuses paid as a result of lower volume of activity.
Labour efficiency	More effective working, perhaps because less hours were worked than planned.
Overheads	Ineffective control of overheads.

(d) Clearly not all of the sales volume variance can be attributed to poor marketing, given a 10 per cent reduction in demand.

It will probably be useful to distinguish between that part of the variance that arose from the shortfall in general demand (a planning variance) and a volume variance that is more fairly attributable to the manager concerned. Thus accountability will be more fairly imposed.

	£
Planning variance (10% × 4,000) × £2.24	896
'New' sales volume variance	
(4,000 − (10% × 4,000) − 3,500) × £2.24	224
Original sales volume variance	1,120

Chapter 10

10.1 (a) Relevant cash flows

	2002 £000	2003 £000	2004 £000	2005 £000	2006 £000	2007 £000
Sales revenue	–	80	120	144	100	64
Loss of contribution		(15)	(15)	(15)	(15)	(15)
Variable costs		(40)	(50)	(48)	(30)	(32)
Fixed costs		(8)	(8)	(8)	(8)	(8)
Operating cash flows		17	47	73	47	9
Working capital	(30)					30
Capital cost	(100)					
Net relevant cash flows	(130)	17	47	73	47	39

(b) Payback period

	2002	2003	2004	2005
Cumulative cash flows	(130)	(113)	(66)	7

Thus, the plant will have repaid the initial investment by the end of the third year of operations.

(c) Net present value

	2002	2003	2004	2005	2006	2007
Discount factor	1.00	0.926	0.857	0.794	0.735	0.681
Present value	(130)	15.74	40.28	57.96	34.55	26.56
Net present value	45.09					

Chapter 11

11.1

	£	£
Existing level of debtors (£4m × 70/365)		767,000
New level of debtors		
£2m × 80/365	438,000	
£2m × 30/365	164,000	602,000
Reduction in debtors		165,000
Costs and benefits of policy		
Cost of discount (£2m × 2%)		40,000
Less Savings		
Interest payable (£165,000 × 13%)	21,450	
Administration costs	6,000	
Bad debts	10,000	37,450
Net cost of policy		2,550

The above calculations reveal that the company will be worse off by offering the discounts.

Chapter 12

12.1 (a)

	Debt £m	Equity £m
Profit before interest and tax	1.80	1.80
Interest payable	0.30	–
Profit before tax	1.50	1.80
Less Corporation tax	0.75	0.90
Profit available to equity	0.75	0.90
Shares issued	4.0m	5.3m
EPS	18.75p	17.0p

(b) The following factors should be taken into account:

- stability of sales and profits
- stability of cash flows
- interest cover and gearing levels
- equity investors' attitude towards risk
- dilution of control caused by new share issue
- security available to offer lenders
- effect on earnings per share and future cash flows.

12.2 (a) The liquidity position may be assessed by using the liquidity ratios discussed in an earlier chapter:

$$\text{Current ratio} = \frac{\text{Current assets}}{\text{Current liabilities}}$$

(creditors due within one year)

$$= \frac{£7.5 \text{ m}}{£5.4 \text{ m}}$$

$$= 1.4$$

$$\text{Acid-test ratio} = \frac{\text{Current assets (less stock)}}{\text{Current liabilities}}$$

(creditors due within one year)

$$= \frac{£3.7 \text{ m}}{£5.4 \text{ m}}$$

$$= 0.7$$

The ratios calculated above reveal a fairly weak liquidity position. The current ratio seems quite low, and the acid test ratio seems very low. This latter ratio suggests that the company does not have sufficient liquid assets to meet its maturing obligations. It would, however, be useful to have details of the liquidity ratios of similar companies in the same industry in order to make a more informed judgement. The bank overdraft represents 67 per cent of the short-term liabilities and 40 per cent of the total liabilities of the company. The continuing support of the bank is therefore important to the ability of the company to meet its commitments.

(b) The finance required to reduce trade creditors to an average of 40 days outstanding is calculated as follows:

	£m
Trade creditors at balance sheet date	1.80
Trade creditors outstanding based on 40 days' credit	
40/365 × £8.4 (i.e. credit purchases)	0.92
Finance required	0.88

(c) The bank may not wish to provide further finance to the company. The increase in overdraft will reduce the level of trade creditors but will increase the exposure of the bank. The additional finance invested by the bank will not generate further funds, and will not therefore be self-liquidating. The question does not make it clear whether the company has sufficient security to offer the bank for the increase in overdraft facility. The profits of the company will be reduced, and the interest cover ratio, based on the profits generated to the year ended 31 May 2000, would reduce to 1.5 times if the additional overdraft was granted (based on interest charged at 12 per cent per annum). This is very low, and means that a relatively small decline in profits would mean that interest charges would not be covered.

(d) A number of possible sources of finance might be considered. Four possible sources are as follows:

- *Issue of equity shares.* This option may be unattractive to investors. The return on equity is fairly low at 7.9 per cent, and there is no evidence that the profitability of the business will improve. If profits remain at their current level, the effect of issuing more equity will be to further reduce the returns to equity.
- *Issue of loans.* This option may also prove unattractive to investors. The effect of issuing further loans will have an effect similar to that of increasing the overdraft. The profits of the business will be reduced, and the interest cover ratio will decrease to a low level. The gearing ratio of the company is already quite high at 48 per cent, and it is not clear what security would be available for the loan.
- *Chase debtors.* It may be possible to improve cash flows by reducing the level of credit outstanding from debtors. At present the average settlement period is 93 days, which seems quite high. A reduction in the average settlement period by approximately one-third would generate the funds required. However, it is not clear what effect this would have on sales.
- *Reduce stock.* This appears to be the most attractive of the four options discussed. At present the average stockholding period is 178 days (based on year end stock levels), which seems to be very high. A reduction in this stockholding period by less than one-third would generate the funds required. However, if the company holds a large amount of slow-moving and obsolete stock, it may be difficult to reduce stock levels easily.

Solutions to selected examination-style questions

Chapter 2

2.1

Profit and loss account for Day 1

	£
Sales (70 × £0.80)	56
Cost of sales (70 × £0.50)	35
Profit	21

Cash flow statement for Day 1

	£
Opening balance	40
Add cash from sales	56
	96
Less cash for purchases (80 × £0.50)	40
Closing balance	56

Balance sheet as at end of Day 1

	£
Cash balance	56
Stock of unsold goods (10 × £0.50)	5
Helen's business wealth	61

Profit and loss account for Day 2

	£
Sales (65 × £0.80)	52.0
Cost of sales (65 × £0.50)	32.5
Profit	19.5

Cash flow statement for Day 2

	£
Opening balance	56.0
Add cash from sales	52.0
	108.0
Less cash for purchases (60 × £0.50)	30.0
Closing balance	78.0

Balance sheet as at end of Day 2

	£
Cash balance	78.0
Stock of unsold goods (5 × £0.50)	2.5
Helen's business wealth	80.5

Profit and loss account for Day 3

	£
Sales (20 × £0.80 + 45 × £0.40)	34.0
Cost of sales (65 × £0.50)	32.5
Profit	1.5

Cash flow statement for Day 3

	£
Opening balance	78.0
Add cash from sales	34.0
	112.0
Less cash for purchases (60 × £0.50)	30.0
Closing balance	82.0

Balance sheet as at end of Day 3

	£
Cash balance	82.0
Stock of unsold goods	—
Helen's business wealth	82.0

2.4 (a)

Balance sheet as at 30 June 2000

	£000	£000	£000
Fixed assets			
Freehold premises			320
Machinery and tools			207
Motor vehicles			38
			565
Current assets			
Stock-in-trade		153	
Debtors		185	
		338	
Less **Current liabilities**			
Creditors	86		
Bank overdraft	116	202	
			136
			701
Less **Long-term liabilities**			
Loan from Industrial Finance Co.			260
			441
Capital			441

(b) The balance sheet reveals a high level of investment in fixed assets. In percentage terms, we can say that more than 60 per cent of the total investment in assets has been in fixed assets. The nature of the business may require a heavy investment in fixed assets. The investment in current assets exceeds the current liabilities by a large amount (approximately 1.7 times). As a result, there are no obvious signs of a liquidity problem. However, the balance sheet reveals that the company has no cash balance and is therefore dependent on the continuing support of the bank (in the form of a bank overdraft) in order to meet obligations when they fall due. When considering the long-term financing of the business, we can see that about 37 per cent of the total long-term finance for the business has been supplied by loan capital and about 63 per cent by the owners. This level of borrowing seems quite high, but not excessive. However, we would need to know more about the ability of the company to service the loan capital (that is, make interest payments and loan repayments) before a full assessment could be made.

Chapter 3

3.1 (a) Capital does increase as a result of the owners introducing more cash into the business, but it will also increase as a result of introducing other assets (a motor car, for example) and by the business generating revenues by trading. Similarly, capital decreases not only as a result of withdrawals of cash by owners, but by withdrawals of other assets (for example, stock for the owners' personal use) and through trading expenses being incurred. In practice, for the typical business in a typical accounting period, capital will alter much more as a result of trading activities than for any other reason.

(b) An accrued expense is not one that relates to next year. It is one that needs to be matched with the revenues of the accounting period under review, but which has yet to be met in terms of cash payment. As such, it will appear on the balance sheet as a current liability.

(c) The purpose of depreciation is not to provide for asset replacement. Rather, it is an attempt to allocate the cost of the asset (less any residual value) over its useful life. Depreciation is an attempt to provide a measure of the amount of the fixed asset that has been consumed during the period. This amount will then be charged as an expense for the period in order to derive the profit figure. Depreciation is a book entry (the outlay of cash occurs when the asset is purchased) and does not normally entail setting aside a separate amount of cash for asset replacement. Even if this were done, there would be no guarantee that sufficient funds would be available at the end of the asset's life for its replacement. Factors such as inflation and technological change may mean that the replacement cost is higher than the original cost of the asset.

(d) In the short term, it is possible for the current value of a fixed asset to exceed its original cost. However, nearly all fixed assets will wear out over time as a result of being used to generate wealth for the business. This will be the case for factory buildings. As a result, some measure of depreciation should be calculated to take account of the fact that the asset is being consumed. Some businesses revalue their freehold buildings where the current value is significantly different from the original cost. Where this occurs, the depreciation charged should be based on the revalued amount. This will normally result in higher depreciation charges than if the asset remained at its historic cost.

3.3 The upward movement in profit and downward movement in cash may be due to various reasons, which include the following:

- the purchase of assets for cash during the period (for example, motor cars and stock), which were not all consumed during the period, and therefore are not having an effect on expenses to the same extent as the effect on cash
- the payment of an outstanding liability (for example a loan), which will have an effect on cash but not on expenses in the profit and loss account
- the withdrawal of cash by the owners from the capital invested, which will not have an effect on the expenses in the profit and loss account
- the generation of revenues on credit where the cash has yet to be received. This will increase the sales for the period but will not have a beneficial effect on the cash balance until a later period.

Chapter 4

4.1 (a) A reserve is part of the owners' claim of a company. The other part is share capital. Reserves arise from gains or profits accruing to the shareholders, to the extent that these have not been distributed to the shareholders or converted into share capital through a bonus issue.

(b) The nominal value of a share is its 'face' and balance sheet value. To a great extent this is a meaningless figure, since it will only by coincidence represent the worth of a share at any point in time. It is normally the value at which the original share issue was made when the company was first formed.

(c) A rights issue is an issue of new shares to existing shareholders, at a discount (typically about 20 per cent) on the current market value of the existing shares. Existing shareholders are given the 'right' to buy new shares in proportion to the number of shares which they already own. Thus, in a one-for-five rights issue, a holder of 1,000 shares would be given the right to buy 200 new shares.

4.4 Limited companies can no more set a limit on the amount of debts they will meet than can human persons. They must meet their debts up to the limit of their assets, just as we must. In the context of owners' claim, 'reserves' mean part of the owners' claim against the assets of the company. These assets may or may not include cash. The legal ability of the company to pay dividends is not related to the amount of cash which it has.

Preference shares do not carry a guaranteed dividend. They simply guarantee that the preference shareholders have a right to the first slice of any dividend that is paid. Shares of many companies can, in effect, be bought by one investor from another through the Stock Exchange. Such a transaction has no direct effect on the company, however. These are not new shares being offered by the company, but existing shares that are being sold 'second-hand'.

The auditors are not appointed by the directors, but normally by the shareholders, to whom they report. The responsibility for preparing the annual accounts falls on the directors, not the auditors. The auditors' responsibility is to review those accounts and express an opinion on them, principally on whether they show a true and fair view of the company's position and performance.

Company law sets out the basic framework of company reporting; this is augmented and clarified by accounting standards, which are produced by a committee independent of the government. According to company law, company accounts are intended to show a true and fair view.

Chapter 5

5.1 (a) An increase in the level of stock in trade would ultimately have an adverse effect on cash.

(b) A rights issue of ordinary shares will give rise to a positive cash flow, which will be included in the 'financing' section of the cash flow statement.

(c) A bonus issue of ordinary shares has no cash flow effect.

(d) Writing off some of the value of the stock has no cash flow effect.

(e) A disposal for cash of a large number of shares by a major shareholder has no cash flow effect, as far as the business is concerned.

(f) Depreciation does not involve cash at all. Using the indirect method of deducing cash flow from operations involves the depreciation expense in the calculation, but this is simply because we are trying to find out from the profit (after depreciation) figure what the profit before depreciation must have been.

5.3

Torrent plc
Cash flow statement for the year ended 31 December 2000

	£m	£m
Net cash inflows from operating activities		247
(see calculation below)		
Returns from investment and servicing of finance		
Interest received	14	
Interest paid	(26)	
Net cash outflow from returns on investment and servicing		
of finance		(12)
Taxation		
Corporation tax paid (see note below)	(41)	
Net cash outflow for taxation		(41)
Capital expenditure		
Payments to acquire tangible fixed assets	(67)	
Net cash outflow for capital expenditure		(67)
		127
Equity dividends paid		
Dividends paid (see note below)	(50)	
Net cash flow for equity dividends paid		(50)
		77
Management of liquid resources		—
Financing		
Repayments of debenture stock	(100)	
Net cash outflow from financing		(100)
Net increase (decrease) in cash		(23)

Analysis of cash during the year ended 31 December 2000

	£m
Balance at 1 January 2000	(6)
Net cash outflow	23
Balance at 31 December 2000	(29)

Analysis of balances of cash as shown in the balance sheet

	2000	1999	Change in year
	£m	£m	£m
Cash in hand and at bank	5	2	
Bank overdrafts	(34)	(8)	
	(29)	(6)	23

Notes

1 *Dividend* Since all of the dividend for 2000 was unpaid at the end of 2000, it seems that the business pays just one final dividend each year, some time after the year end. Thus it is the 1999 dividend that will have led to a cash outflow in 2000.

2 *Taxation*

	£m
Amount owing at 1.1.2000	23
Tax charge for 2000	36
	59
Amount owing at 31.12.2000	18
Amount paid during 2000	41

3 *Debentures* It has been assumed that the debentures were redeemed for their balance sheet value. This is not always the case, however.

4 *Shares* The share issue was effected by converting the share premium account balance and £60 million of the revaluation reserve balance to ordinary share capital. This involved no flow of cash.

Calculation of net cash inflow from operating activities

	£m	£m
Net operating profit (from the profit and loss account)		182
Add Depreciation		
Patents and trademarks (37 − 32)*	5	
Plant etc. (125 − 102)*	23	
Fixtures etc. (163 + 67 − 180)*	50	78
		260
Less Increase in debtors (132 − 123)	9	
Decrease in creditors (39 − 30)	9	
Decrease in accruals (15 − 11)	4	22
		238
Add Decrease in stocks (41 − 35)	6	
Decrease in prepayments (16 − 13)	3	9
		247

* Since there were no disposals the depreciation charges must be the difference between the start and end of the year fixed asset values, adjusted by the cost of any additions.

The following comments can be made about Torrent plc's cash flow as shown by the cash flow statement for the year ended 31 December 2000:

- There was a positive cash flow from operating activities.
- There was a net cash outflow in respect of financing.
- The outflow of cash to acquire additional tangible fixed assets was very comfortably covered by cash generated by operating activities, even after allowing for the net cash outflows for financing and tax. This is usually interpreted as a 'strong' cash flow situation.
- There was a fairly major repayment of debenture loan.
- Overall there was a fairly significant reduction in cash over the year, leading to a negative cash balance at the year-end.

Chapter 6

6.1 The effect of each of the changes on ROCE is not always easy to predict.

(i) An increase in the gross profit margin *may* lead to a decrease in ROCE in particular circumstances. If the increase in the margin resulted from an increase in price, which in turn led to a decrease in sales, a fall in ROCE can occur. A fall in sales can reduce the net profit (the numerator in ROCE) if the overheads of the business did not decrease correspondingly.

(ii) A reduction in sales can reduce ROCE for the reasons mentioned above.

(iii) An increase in overhead expenses will reduce the net profit, and this in turn will result in a reduction in ROCE.

(iv) An increase in stocks held will increase the amount of capital employed by the business (the denominator in ROCE) where long-term funds are employed to finance the stocks. This will, in turn, reduce ROCE.

(v) Repayment of the loan at the year end will reduce the capital employed, and this will increase the ROCE.

(vi) An increase in the time taken for debtors to pay will result in an increase in capital employed if long-term funds are employed to finance the debtors. This increase in long-term funds will in turn reduce ROCE.

6.2 (a) This part of the question has been dealt with in the chapter.

(b) The ratios reveal that the debtors turnover ratio for Business A is 63 days, whereas for Business B the ratio is only 21 days. Business B is therefore much quicker in collecting amounts outstanding from customers. Nevertheless, there is not much difference between the two businesses in the time taken to pay trade creditors. Business A takes 50 days to pay its creditors, whereas Business B takes 45 days. It is interesting to compare the difference in the debtor and creditor collection periods for each business. As Business A allows an average of 63 days' credit to its customers, yet pays creditors within 50 days, it will require greater investment in working capital than Business B, which allows an average of only 21 days to its debtors but takes 45 days to pay its creditors.

Business A has a much higher gross profit percentage than Business B. However, the net profit percentage for the two businesses is identical. This suggests that Business A has much higher overheads than Business B. The stock turnover period for Business A is more than twice that of Business B. This may be due to the fact that Business A maintains a wider range of goods in stock in order to meet customer requirements. The evidence suggests that Business A is the business that prides itself on personal service. The higher average settlement period is consistent with a more relaxed attitude to credit collection (thereby maintaining customer goodwill), and the high overheads are consistent with the incurring of additional costs in order to satisfy customer requirements. The high stock levels of Business A are consistent with maintaining a wide range of stock in order to satisfy a range of customer needs.

Business B has the characteristics of a more price-competitive business. The gross profit percentage is much lower than that of Business A, indicating a much lower gross profit per £1 of sales. However, overheads are kept low in order to ensure that the net profit percentage is the same as that of Business A. The low stock turnover period and average collection period for debtors are consistent with a business that wishes to reduce investment in current assets to a minimum, thereby reducing costs.

Chapter 7

7.4 (a) Total time required on cutting machines = $(2{,}500 \times 1.0) + (3{,}400 \times 1.0) + (5{,}100 \times 0.5) = 8{,}450$ hours.

Total time available on cutting machines = 5,000 hours, i.e. a limiting factor.

Total time required on assembling machines = $(2{,}500 \times 0.5) + (3{,}400 \times 1.0) + (5{,}100 \times 0.5) = 7{,}200$ hours.

Total time available on assembling machines = 8,000 hours, i.e. not a limiting factor.

Product	A (per unit) £	B (per unit) £	C (per unit) £
Selling price	25	30	18
Direct materials	(12)	(13)	(10)
Variable production costs	(7)	(4)	(3)
Contribution	6	13	5
Time on cutting machines (hours)	1.0	1.0	0.5
Contribution per hour on cutting machines	£6	£13	£10
Order of priority	3	1	2

Therefore, produce: 3,400 Product B using 3,400 hours
3,200 Product C using 1,600 hours
5,000 hours

(b) Assuming that the company would make no savings in variable production costs by subcontracting, it would be worth paying up to the contribution per unit (£5) for Product C: that is, £5 × (5,100 − 3,200) = £9,500 in total.

Similarly, it would be worth paying up to £6 per unit for Product A or £6 × 2,500 = £15,000 in total.

7.5 (a) Contribution per hour of unskilled labour of Product A is:

$$(£30 − £6 − £2 − £12 − £3)/(6/6) = £7$$

Given the scarcity of skilled labour, for the management to be indifferent between the products, the contribution per skilled labour hour must be the same. Thus:

For product B the selling price must be [£7 × (9/6)] + £9 + £4 + £25 + £7 = £55.50
For product C the selling price must be [£7 × (3/6)] + £3 + £10 + £14 + £7 = £37.50

(b) The company could pay up to £13 an hour (that is, £6 + £7) for additional hours of skilled labour.

Chapter 8

8.1 All three of these costing techniques are means of deducing the full cost of some activity. The distinction between them lies essentially with the difference in the style of the production of the goods or services involved.

- *Job costing* is used where each unit of output or 'job' differs from others produced by the same business. Because the jobs are not identical, it is not normally acceptable to those who are likely to use the cost information to treat the jobs as if they are identical. This means that costs need to be identified, job by job. For this purpose, costs fall into two categories: direct costs and indirect costs (or overheads).

  Direct costs are those that can be measured directly in respect of the specific job, such as the amount of labour that was directly applied to the job or the amount of material that has been incorporated in it. To this must be added a share of the indirect costs. This is usually done by taking the total overheads for the period concerned and charging part of them to the job. This, in turn, is usually done according to some measure of the job's size and importance, relative to the other jobs done during the period. The number of direct labour hours worked on the job is the most commonly used measure of size and/or importance.

  The main problem with job costing tends to be the method of charging indirect costs to jobs. Indirect costs, by definition, cannot be related directly to jobs, and must, if full cost is to be deduced, be charged on a basis that is more or less arbitrary. If indirect costs accounted for a small proportion of the total, the arbitrariness of charging them would probably not matter. Indirect costs, in many cases, however, form the majority of total costs, so arbitrariness is a problem.

- *Process costing* is the approach taken where all output is of identical units. These can be treated, therefore, as having identical cost. Sometimes a process costing approach is taken even where the units of output are not strictly identical. This is because process costing is much simpler and cheaper to apply than the only other option, job costing. Provided that users of the cost information are satisfied that treating units as identical when they are not strictly so is acceptable, the additional cost and effort of job costing is not justified.

  In process costing, the cost per unit of output is found by dividing total costs for the period by the total number of units produced in the period.

  The main problem with process costing tends to be that at the end of any period/beginning of the next period, there will probably be partly completed units of output. An adjustment needs to be made for this work in progress if the resulting figures for cost per unit are not to be distorted.

- *Batch costing* is really an extension of job costing. Batch costing tends to be used where production is in batches. A batch consists of more than one, perhaps many, identical units of output. The units of output differ from one batch to the next. For example, a clothing manufacturing business may produce 500 identical jackets in one batch. This is followed by a batch of 300 identical skirts.

  Each batch is costed, as one job, using a job costing approach. The full cost of each garment is then found by dividing the cost of the batch by the number of garments in the batch.

  The main problem of batch costing is exactly that of job costing, of which it is an extension. This is the problem of dealing with overheads.

8.4

Offending phrase	*Explanation*
'Necessary to divide the business up into departments'	This can be done, but it will not always be of much benefit to do so. Only in quite restricted circumstances will it give significantly different job costs.
'Fixed costs (or overheads)'	This implies that fixed costs and overheads are the same thing. They are not really connected with one another. 'Fixed' is to do with how costs behave as the level of output is raised or lowered; 'overheads' is to do with the extent to which costs can be directly measured in respect of a particular unit of output. Though it is true that many overheads are fixed, not all are. Also, direct labour is usually a fixed cost.
	All of the other references to fixed and variable costs are wrong. The person should have referred to indirect and direct costs.
'Usually this is done on the basis of area'	Where overheads are apportioned to departments, they will be apportioned on some logical basis. For certain costs, for example, rent, floor area may be the most logical. For others, for

example, machine maintenance costs, floor area would be totally inappropriate.

'When the total fixed costs for each department have been identified, this will be divided by the number of hours that were worked'

Where overheads are dealt with on a departmental basis, they may be divided by the number of direct labour hours to deduce a recovery rate. However, this is only one basis of applying overheads to jobs. For example, machine hours or some other basis may be more appropriate to the particular circumstances involved.

'It is essential that this approach is taken in order to deduce a selling price'

In practice, it is relatively unusual for the 'job cost' to be able to dictate the price at which the manufacturer can price its output. Job costing may have its uses, but setting prices is not usually one of them.

Chapter 9

9.3

	Budget			Actual
	Original	Flexed		
Output (units)	1,000	1,100		1,100
(production and sales)				
	£	£		£
Sales	25,000	27,500		28,200
Labour	(5,000)	(5,500)	(2,200 hrs)	(5,550) (2,150 hrs)
Raw materials	(10,000)	(11,000)	(1,100 kg)	(11,630) (1,170 kg)
Fixed overheads	(3,000)	(3,000)		(3,200)
Operating profit	7,000	8,000		7,820

Sales variances
Volume
£(7,000 − 8,000)   = £1,000 (F)
Price
£(27,500 − 28,200)   = £700 (F)

Direct labour variances
Efficiency
((1,100 × 2) − 2,150) × £2.50   = £125 (F)
Rate
(2,150 × £2.50) − £5,550   = £175 (A)

Direct materials variances
Usage
((1,100 × 1) − 1,170) × £10   = £700 (A)
Price
(1,170 × £10) − £11,630   = £70 (F)

Fixed overhead variances
Spending
£3,000 − £3,200   = £200 (A)

Budgeted profit = (1,000 × £7)   = £7,000

	£	£
Budgeted profit		7,000
Sales: Volume	1,000 (F)	
Price	700 (F)	1,700
Direct materials: Usage	700 (A)	
Price	70 (F)	(630)
Direct labour: Efficiency	125 (F)	
Rate	175 (A)	(50)
Fixed overheads: Expenditure		(200)
		7,820

9.4 (a) Finished goods stock budget for the three months ending 30 September (in units of production):

	July	Aug.	Sept.
	000 units	000 units	000 units
Opening stock (note 1)	40	48	40
Production (note 2)	188	232	196
	228	280	236
Less Sales (note 3)	180	240	200
Closing stock	48	40	36

(b) Raw materials stock budget for the two months ending 31 August (in kg):

	July	Aug.
	000 kg	000 kg
Opening stock (note 1)	40	58
Purchases (note 2)	112	107
	152	165
Less Production (note 4)	94	116
Closing stock	58	49

(c) Cash budget for the two months ending 30 September:

	Aug.	Sept.
	£	£
Inflows		
Debtors: Current month (note 5)	493,920	411,600
Preceding month (note 6)	151,200	201,600
Total inflows	645,120	613,200

	Aug.	Sept.
	£	£
Outflows		
Payments to creditors (note 7)	168,000	160,500
Labour and overheads (note 4)	185,600	156,800
Fixed overheads	22,000	22,000
Total outflows	375,600	339,300
Net inflows/(outflows)	269,520	273,900
Balance c/fwd	289,520	563,420

Notes

1 The opening balance is the same as the closing balance from the previous month.
2 This is a balancing figure.
3 This figure is given in the question.
4 This figure derives from the finished stock budget.
5 This is 98 per cent of 70 per cent of the current month's sales revenue.
6 This is 28 per cent of the previous month's sales revenue.
7 This figure derives from the raw materials stock budget.

Chapter 10

10.1 (a) Annual depreciation

Project 1 (£100,000 − £7,000)/3 = £31,000
Project 2 (£60,000 − £6,000)/3 = £18,000

Analysis of the projects

Project 1	Year 0	Year 1	Year 2	Year 3
	£000	£000	£000	£000
Net profit (loss)		29	(1)	2
Depreciation		31	31	31
Capital cost	(100)			
Residual value				7
Net cash flows	(100)	60	30	40
10% discount factor	1.000	0.909	0.826	0.751
Present value	(100.00)	54.54	24.78	30.04
Net present value	9.36			

Clearly, the IRR lies above 10 per cent. Try 15 per cent:

15% discount factor	1.000	0.870	0.756	0.658
Present value	(100.000)	52.20	22.68	26.32
Net present value	1.20			

Thus, the IRR lies a little above 15 per cent, around 16 per cent.

Cumulative cash flows	(100)	(40)	(10)	30

Thus, the payback will occur after about 2 years, 3 months (assuming that the cash flows accrue evenly over the year).

Project 2	Year 0	Year 1	Year 2	Year 3
	£000	£000	£000	£000
Net profit (loss)		18	(2)	4
Depreciation		18	18	18
Capital cost	(60)			
Residual value				6
Net cash flows	(60)	36	16	28
10% discount factor	1.000	0.909	0.826	0.751
Present value	(60.00)	32.72	13.22	21.03
Net present value	6.97			

Clearly, the IRR lies above 10 per cent. Try 15 per cent:

15% discount factor	1.000	0.870	0.756	0.658
Present value	(60.00)	31.32	12.10	18.42
Net present value	1.84			

Thus, the IRR lies a little above 15 per cent, around 17 per cent.

Cumulative cash flows	(60)	(24)	(8)	20

Thus, the payback will occur after about 2 years, 3 months (assuming that the cash flows accrue evenly over the year).

(b) Presuming that Mylo Ltd is pursuing a wealth maximisation objective, Project 1 is preferable since it has the higher NPV. The difference between the two NPVs is not very large, however. The decision may therefore be susceptible to forecast error.

(c) NPV is the preferred method of assessing investment opportunities because it fully addresses each of the following:

- *The timing of the cash flows.* By discounting the various cash flows associated with each project according to when they are expected to arise, the fact that cash flows do not all occur simultaneously is accommodated. Associated with this is the fact that by discounting, using the opportunity cost of finance (that is, the return that the next-best alternative opportunity would generate), the net benefit after financing costs have been met is identified (as the NPV).
- *The whole of the relevant cash flows.* NPV includes all of the relevant cash flows, irrespective of when they are expected to occur. It treats them differently according to their date of occurrence, but they are all taken account of in the NPV, and they all have, or can have, an influence on the decision.
- *The objectives of the business.* NPV is the only method of appraisal in which the output of the analysis has a direct bearing on the wealth of the business. (Positive NPVs enhance wealth, negative ones reduce it.) Since most private sector businesses seek to increase their value and wealth, NPV clearly is the best approach to use, at least out of the methods we have considered so far.

10.5 (a)

Option 1	2001 £m	2002 £m	2003 £m	2004 £m	2005 £m	2006 £m
Plant and equipment	(9.0)					1.0
Sales		24.0	30.8	39.6	26.4	10.0
Variable costs		(11.2)	(19.6)	(25.2)	(16.8)	(7.0)
Fixed costs (ex. depr'n)		(0.8)	(0.8)	(0.8)	(0.8)	(0.8)
Working capital	(3.0)					3.0
Marketing costs		(2.0)	(2.0)	(2.0)	(2.0)	(2.0)
Opportunity costs		(0.1)	(0.1)	(0.1)	(0.1)	(0.1)
	(12.0)	9.9	8.3	11.5	6.7	4.1
Discount factor	1.0	0.91	0.83	0.75	0.68	0.62
Present value	(12.0)	9.0	6.9	8.6	4.6	2.5
NPV	19.6					

Option 2	2001 £m	2002 £m	2003 £m	2004 £m	2005 £m	2006 £m
Royalties	–	4.4	7.7	9.9	6.6	2.8
Discount factor	1.0	0.91	0.83	0.75	0.68	0.62
Present value	–	4.0	6.4	7.4	4.5	1.7
NPV	24.0					

Option 3	2001	2003
Instalments	12.0	12.0
Discount	1.0	0.83
Present value	12.0	10.0
NPV	22.0	

(b) Before making a final decision, the following factors should be considered:

- The long-term competitiveness of the business may be affected by the sale of the patents.
- At present the company is not involved in manufacturing and marketing products. Is this change in direction desirable?
- The company will probably have to buy in the skills necessary to produce the product itself. This will involve costs, and problems will be incurred. Has this been taken into account?
- How accurate are the forecasts made, and how valid are the assumptions on which they are based?

(c) Option 2 has the highest NPV and is, therefore, the more attractive to shareholders. However, the accuracy of the forecasts should be checked before a final decision is made.

Chapter 11

11.1 (a) The liquidity ratios of the company seem low. The current ratio is only 1.1 and the acid test ratio is 0.6. This latter ratio suggests that the company has insufficient liquid assets to pay its short-term obligations. A cash flow projection for the next period would provide a better insight to the liquidity position of the business. The bank overdraft seems high, and it would be useful to know whether the bank is pressing for a reduction and what overdraft limit has been established for the company.

(b) This term is described in the chapter.

(c) The operating cash cycle may be calculated as follows:

No. of days

Average stockholding period
$$\frac{\text{(Opening stock + closing stock)/2}}{\text{Cost of sales}} = \frac{((125 + 143)/2)}{323} \times 360 \qquad 149$$

Average settlement period for debtors
$$\frac{\text{Trade debtors}}{\text{Credit sales}} \times 365 = \frac{163}{452} \times 360 \qquad \frac{130}{279}$$

Less

Average settlement period for creditors
$$\frac{\text{Trade creditors}}{\text{Credit purchases}} \times 365 = \frac{145}{341} \times 360 \qquad \underline{153}$$

Operating cash cycle $\qquad \underline{126}$

(d) The company can reduce the operating cash cycle in a number of ways. The average stockholding period seems quite long. At present, average stocks held represent almost five months' sales. This may be reduced by reducing the level of stocks held. Similarly, the average settlement period for debtors seems long, at more than four months' sales. This may be reduced by imposing tighter credit control, offering discounts, charging interest on overdue accounts, etc. However, any policy decisions concerning stocks and debtors must take account of current trading conditions.

The operating cash cycle could also be reduced by extending the period of credit taken to pay suppliers. However, for reasons mentioned in the chapter, this option must be given careful consideration.

11.5   New proposals from credit department

	£000	£000
Current level of investment in debtors		
(£20m × (60/365))		3,288
Proposed level of investment in debtors		
((£20m × 60%) × (30/365))	986	
((£20m × 40%) × (50/365))	1,096	2,082
Reduction in level of investment		1,206

The reduction in overdraft interest as a result of the reduction in the level of investment will be £1,206,000 × 14% = £169,000

	£000	£000
Cost of cash discounts offered (£12m × 2½%)		300
Additional cost of credit administration		20
		320
Bad debt savings	100	
Interest charge savings (see above)	169	269
Net cost of policy each year		51

These calculations show that the company would incur additional annual costs in order to implement this proposal. It would therefore be cheaper to stay with the existing credit policy.

Chapter 12

12.1 (a) The main factors to take into account are:

- *Risk.* If a business borrows there is a risk that, at the maturity date of the loan, the business will not have the funds to repay the amount owing and will be unable to find a suitable form of replacement borrowing. With short-term loans, the maturity dates will arrive more quickly, and the type of risk outlined will occur at more frequent intervals.
- *Matching.* A company may wish to match the life of an asset with the maturity date of the borrowing. In other words, long-term assets will be purchased with long-term loan funds. A certain level of current assets that form part of the long-term asset base of the business may also be funded by long-term borrowing. Those current assets that fluctuate because of seasonality and so on will be funded by short-term borrowing. This approach to funding assets will help reduce risks for the company.
- *Cost.* Interest rates for long-term loans may be higher than for short-term loans, as investors may seek extra compensation for having their funds locked up for a long period. However, issue costs may be higher for short-term loans as there will be a need to refund at more frequent intervals.
- *Flexibility.* Short-term loans may be more flexible. It may be difficult to repay long-term loans before the maturity period.

(b) When deciding to grant a loan, the following factors should be considered:

- security
- purpose of the loan
- the ability of the borrower to repay
- the loan period
- the availability of funds
- the character and integrity of the senior managers.

(c) Loan conditions may include:

- the need to obtain permission before issuing further loans
- the need to maintain a certain level of liquidity during the loan period
- a restriction on the level of dividends and directors' pay.

12.2 (a) When deciding between long-term debt and equity finance, the following factors should be considered:

- *Cost.* The cost of equity is higher over the longer term than the cost of loans. This is because equity is a riskier form of investment. Moreover, loan interest is tax deductible, whereas dividend payments are not. However, when profits are poor, there is no obligation to pay equity shareholders, whereas the obligation to pay lenders will continue.
- *Gearing.* The company may wish to take on additional gearing in order to increase the returns to equity. This can be achieved provided the returns from the loans invested exceed the cost of servicing the loans.
- *Risk.* Loan capital increases the level of risk to equity shareholders, who will in turn require higher rates of return. If the level of gearing is high in relation to industry norms, the credit standing of the business may be affected. Managers, although strictly concerned with the interests of shareholders, may feel their own positions are at risk if a high level of gearing is obtained. However, they may be more inclined to take on additional risk if their remuneration is linked to the potential benefits that may flow from higher gearing.

(b) Convertible loan stock provides the investor with the right, but not the obligation, to convert the loan stock into ordinary shares at a specified future date and a specified price. The investor will exercise this option only if the market value of the shares is above the 'exercise price' at the specified date. The investor will change status from that of lender to that of owner when the option to convert is exercised.

Index

Note: Page numbers in **bold** indicate highlighted **key terms** and their **glossary** definitions

net cash flow from 117–18, **117,** 120– 1, 122–30, **370**
single-product 207–8
see also multi–product
opportunity costs 276, 282, 287, 318
ordering/reordering systems 304
ordinary shares **87,** 332–3, 336–7, **371**
return on *see* ROSF
overdraft, bank **345, 366**
overheads (indirect costs) 208–10, **208, 369, 371**
absorption (recovery) rate **212,** 222, **371**
budget 233, 234–5
collection and behaviour 211–16
cost drivers 223–4, **223, 367**
on departmental basis 218–19
levels of 221–2
recovery rates 222
segmenting 216–18
spending variance 252, 256
owners 84
equity *see* capital
responsibilities 105, 107
as users of information 2, 3, 7–10
see also directors; management

par value *see* nominal value
participating preference shares 333
partners 84
past transaction/events 21, 142
payback period *see* PP
payout ratio, dividend **165, 367**
P/E (price/earnings ratio) 168–72, **168, 371**
performance
compared with budgets 244, 246–54
planned 142–3, 236
see also financial performance
perpetual life of company 84
perpetual warrants 336–7
physical life of asset 60
planning
and control 7–9
long-term 9, 230–2, 244
materials requirements (MRP) **308, 370**
planned performance 142–3, 236
short–term *see* budgets
see also budgets
position *see* financial position

position statement *see* balance sheet
PP (payback period) 272–5, **272,** 283, 287, 290–1, **371**
precautionary motive for holding cash 317
predictions and financial ratios 172–3
preference shares **88,** 332, 333–4, 337, 338–9, **371**
premises *see* property
premium
risk **277**
shares **90, 372**
prepaid expenses 57–8, **58, 371**
present value *see* NPV; PV
price
break-even 220
changing 67
cost plus 225
/earnings ratio (P/E) 168–72, **168, 371**
variances 250–1, 255, 256
primary market, Stock Exchange as 353
private limited companies **86, 371**
private placing 360
process costing **208, 371**
production budget 233, 234
profit 9, 47, **371**
and budgets 248
gross *see* gross profit
net *see* net profit
as percentage of investment *see* ARR
retained 95, 348–9
-volume (PV) chart 190–1, **190, 371**
see also cost–volume–profit; reserves
profit and loss account **16,** 47–79, **371**
audit fee 101
and balance sheet 49–50
and budgets 233, 246
and cash flow 55–8, 116–17, 126, 131
cost of sales 51–2, **51**
dividend 101
examples 16–17, 18, 19, 50, 77–8, 145
expenses, classification of 52–4
and financial ratios 145
format/layout 50–1, 101
interpreting 77–9
limited companies 85, 99–102
reporting period 54
tax 101